ISLAND STORY

ISLAND STORY

Journeying Through
Unfamiliar Britain

BY J.D. TAYLOR

Published by Repeater Books
An imprint of Watkins Media Ltd

19–21 Cecil Court
London
WC2N 4EZ
UK

www.repeaterbooks.com
A Repeater Books paperback original 2016
1

Distributed in the United States by Random House, Inc., New York.

Cover design: Johnny Bull
Typography and typesetting: Jan Middendorp
Typefaces: Chaparral Pro, P22 Underground Pro

ISBN: 978-1-910924-20-4
Ebook ISBN: 978-1-910924-21-1

To my old man

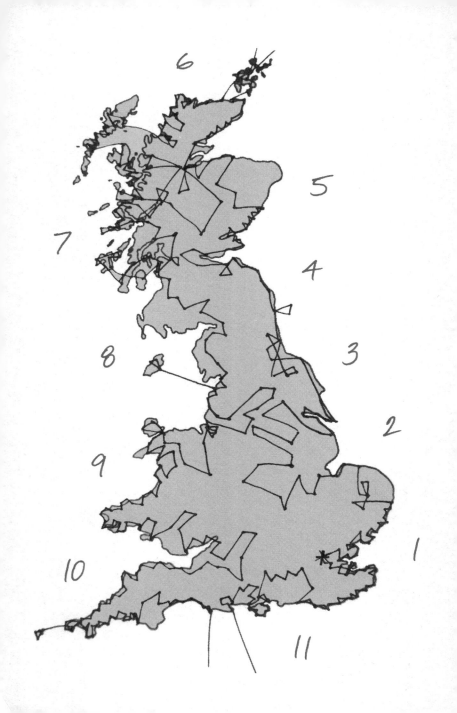

CONTENTS

Introduction

Picture the mind as a terrain. Highways, byways, laybys and traps, laid over an expanse as vast as the sun and as predictable as laughter. These roads of the mind ebb and flow like electric charge. Nothing is still, though tranquillity remains a prevailing illusion. Each route is circular, beginning and ending with where you are now.

I have pottered down such paths, searching for some elusive satisfaction that the sages call peace. Others stalk the same terrain with alacrity and obsession, letting grey streets or green horizons imprint themselves with genetic certainty. They commend the well-trodden path, less likely to lose one's footing or track. Habits groove into stubborn repetition: keep off the grass. Others take shortcuts, *desire paths*, where grass is gored by impatient feet, the soil bald and smooth, leaving behind a perpendicular line from A to C without the romance of B.

Each mind contains its entire universe, for each senses everything it can know at any given time. And yet if each contains a near-infinite range of imaginary possibility, it's remarkable how each senses and acts alike. Neurones and algorithms reinforce similar behaviours for simplicity's sake. Some enjoy telling others to keep off their grass. They talk of territory, not terrain, and navigate by map, not meander. The distinction is significant. For this terrain expands as far as one's ability to sense it, the view from where one stands, sits or crawls.

It may be strange to begin an account of an unlikely cyclo-safari across Britain with a thought experiment. Confusion is at the root of any journey through the unrecognised, assailed by fears of becoming lost, the legality of peeing (or sleeping) in bushes, or not returning home on time. Disliking disorientation, one habitually returns to the familiar. But what is down that way?

Over four months I went cycling across Britain, gathering stories, seeking out something I couldn't yet name. Serendipity and a smartphone chartered my course, and a compass when either failed. I camped in parks and playing fields, forests and castles, and I slept in the houses of an improbable number of strangers. Some I met in pubs, others had heard word of my journey. Along the way I met farmers and fishermen, miners, nurses and teachers, civil servants and millionaires, professors and probation officers, artists and students, a film actor, homeless people for whom a sleeping bag was no stunt, and many men and women working in the service sector or unemployed, poverty blurring the boundaries. I asked them about their lives. The method was like that of William Cobbett, "reasoning with some, laughing with others, and observing all that passes". I transcribed their stories and wrote my impressions, reading widely, pursuing clues, seeking coherency.

The idea to just *go out there* had embedded itself long ago, resurfacing during emotional dislocation, like stress at work, or an irresolvable falling-out with a close friend. I desired the not-known path, to boot through the brickwork barricading this well-worn way from the splendour of the strange. Serene forest scenes, air zinging with juniper, whatever that smelled like. Intimacy with sun, not screen. But my skint status and a depressed acquiescence tethered me down. I made the common error of confusing disappointment with adulthood. Then something unusual happened.

Good time to rehearse my alibi. For the next many months I'd be asked to account for myself. I am twenty-seven years old, a native son of South London. My twenties have disappeared in its bars and its bar work, and working in a brain-injury service and a men's suicide-prevention initiative. I'd written benefits applications for carers and then appeals when they were turned down, issued food vouchers and platitudes on how things would improve. I'd seen first-hand the cruelty and stupidity of a war against the poor, and a prevailing helplessness that calloused into indifference. I felt unsatisfied by the answers to the left and right of me. In doubting them, I doubted myself too. What did I know? My friends were people like me, I'd barely seen much of Britain at all. So I resolved to hear and observe what life was like for others, and from that, make up my own mind.

South London's lesser state schools strive to blunt the intellectual curiosity of all those who enter them. In my case, they were only partly successful. I've no Oxbridge credentials or well-connected kin, and live in social housing with my partner. Mine's a common story. But hear me speak and I am middle class, unprepossessing, softly spoken. Education's had that impact. Being shy by nature I've often felt an outsider, blending in with conversational camouflage. My city's a haven for outsiders. Now cranes dominate the horizon, communities being replaced with commercial opportunities, familial homes converted into aspirational housing. Their cause is not endogenous. A paper trail into the tax havens or an anti-capitalist tract could only give half their story. What else could it indicate?

So I sought to make a destination of the horizon, and find out other stories. But the sluggish waters of pubs provide safe harbour for almost every peccadillo. One needs more than discontent and wanderlust. A bung, for instance. Like a PhD scholarship from a small university I'd won the year before. That's the clincher. It gives a modest income to rummage through a dead philosopher's treatises on desire. It gives immodest free time.

I'd never 'travelled' before, in the gap-year backpacker sense. But I couldn't afford endless train tickets or cosy cottage B&Bs. Means made the method. With no more than a score spent on the tent I'd call home, I borrowed or was gifted the rest. And then there was the bike.

"Not stolen is it?" I asked Bob at his second-hand shop off the Walworth Road. £70 seemed too good, churlish to haggle. "Oh no", he chuckled, earnestly. I'd learn the truth of this. With ten gears and a rusty chain, the Raleigh Pioneer felt like it'd never gone beyond the Elephant & Castle. We had that in common. Its dramatics come later, alongside the eccentrics, sad and hopeful stories, heady encounters, lost histories and bizarre adventures. Between those, the story of an island.

This is no quest to unearth the *real* Britain or other things of fable. Much of modern national identity is rooted in what people believe about the present and past, rather than what's actually the case. Myths have more operative power. Ossian, Arthur, St George and the Barddas are all fabrications. What will future historians make as their modern counterparts?

In attempting to incorporate many aspects of an island, I cannot satisfy all. The most accurate map has the scale 1:1, like the "map of the Empire whose size was that of an Empire" depicted by Borges. Such a map serves no one. The last who tried this was John Leland, who "fell beside his wits" some years into undertaking his "Laboriouse Journey and Serche" across 16th century Britain, mapping each inch of the island with words. There is no *completing* any journey; the mind lingeringly retraces its wanderings. This is a work about the pleasure and commitment of journeying. Perspective is one with its location. When one's sense of perspective changes, a new terrain comes into being.

CHAPTER I

Prehistories

"You been chucked out or summat mate?" – Tucker.

It's a fair question. Clearly I'd fallen on hard times. Sun long-set, I'd re-surfaced on Canvey Island, Essex, from a day's forays in blind wilderness. Slimy salty chips from the esplanade, pebble-dash squaring off against the cool teal-grey sea. Behind me was "Fantasy Island", the sarcastic moniker of a deserted amusement arcade, spangling golds a-glimmer, jingle jungle. The lights of a nearby boozer had compelled me.

I'm bedraggled and weary, and struggling with the weight of two large sacks and a sleeping bag. A tough-looking geezer with a skinhead sharp enough to spark a match holds the door open for me, sympathetically. The barmaid ahead beckons me, her bright peroxide bob bringing colour to the otherwise dark brickwork of the pub. "You alwight lav?" Give me a second...

Stowing my worldly belongings beneath a barstool, I request the therapeutic intervention of a pint. A pool table stands alone, forlorn, and a fruitie rattles and sings like a bored child. The barmaid's eyebrow arches mischievously as she takes my change, and, after a spell of silence so pregnant not even Bon Jovi's soaring choruses can dispel it, bald-headed Tucker asks what everyone else is thinking. It takes some moments to summon an answer.

What was my alibi again?

I'd left home that afternoon with no fixed trajectory. East, broadly. How far would I get? Southend, possibly. The suggestion of cycling there seemed a joke to many. "Today?" "On that?" "You are joking..." I felt like Don Quixote but was compared to Del Boy. But I wanted to understand Romford, Billericay and Basildon, Essex towns as quotidian and obscure as the production of cheddar, the conservatism of electorates, or the consistent disappointment of the island's national sports teams. It wasn't a linear route, nor a particularly obvious one. I'd once cycled fifty miles on a circular ride before, and couldn't walk the next day. My rusty bike might be fine for a trip down the shops, but for cycling seventy miles all day, every day, on a circumnavigatory journey around the British Isles?

As my partner Sarah waved me off, her wry scepticism was obvious. I'd be home in a few days surely, tail between legs. "How long will it take you?", she asked. "No idea sweetie", I replied, and it was true. I'd not undertaken any training or even determined a route. I didn't even have a map.

Objectively speaking, this was a *bad idea*. But there's method in this madness, for without prior plans or preconceptions, I'd be at the mercy of people's testimonies, goodwill and my own impressions. None could be called reliable either, but at least they were unfamiliar. I sought revelation in the new.

So without fanfare, I set off, leaving behind the estate I called home in South London. It's familiar country so far, the Georgian townhouses of Kennington, through to the town-planning mess of the Elephant & Castle, where sun-baked bus fumes burn my throat. South London's social housing is being demolished and replaced with luxury apartments, its communities priced out to the suburbs. The craft beer bars, organic bakeries and galleries are garrisons along a front-line. Only a matter of time before my estate is also bulldozed, replaced with luxury 'affordable housing' five times my neighbours' salaries, pre-purchased by investors seeking a secure return. Two ways of understanding a property-owning democracy.

But mentioning ideology would have an Oxbridge journalist spit out their latte. Like the island's infrastructure, power shapes the scene, whilst remaining out of sight. Meritocracy, the rule of private enterprise. People used to call it hegemony, but even that connoted mutton chops and donkey jackets. *Don't take it seriously*, the mantra of our more cool and asinine era. But being skint makes one serious, if a little morose! Now Borough High Street, the conspicuous consumption of its luxury street market, the Shard, which, more than anything, impales South London into prone submission. Over London Bridge and the muggy Thames, into the old City, a place where corporations live and money votes. Everyone knows of London, and London knows of nothing else. *London!* I can't bear it any longer, stewing in its stresses, disappointments and ineffectual raging. I have to find the exit.

East along Whitechapel High Street, the composition changing. Even the city's new wealth hasn't altered the profile of this poor migrant quarter, its street market and takeaways still owning the scene, salty boozers and supermarkets giving way to the university complex at Mile End and, ahead, Stratford. Again it's all familiar but contested, like children disputing the estate of an absent father whose death hasn't yet been ascertained.

Haribo-coloured phalli and luxury apartment blocks, a vast mall beside an even vaster mall, an eye-watering traffic system. "Regenerated" by the Olympics, the area's parkland and allotments have been concreted over and its poor tenants evicted, for the sake of a sports show the city couldn't afford. Toshing through contemporary ruins like these, seeking ways to release repressed desires for freedom, Laura Oldfield Ford has described Stratford as "colonized, submerged beneath dull expanses of corporate landscaping". Iain Sinclair, another familiar traveller, called the Olympics the "scam of scams", a slurry of heritage phantasmagoria or "ghost milk".

But neither soothsayer approached the quotidian features of this landscape. Discount chain supermarkets and pubs are heaving, people enjoying the modern activity called bargain-hunting.

But that isn't insightful either. The answer's indicated by the high streets of Forest Gate, Manor Park and Ilford, the peeling poundshops, internet cafés and non-European foodstores of the parades, and the cramped terraces veering off behind them, the sheer poverty of the surrounding area and its marked ethnic composition, mostly Bangladeshi and Pakistani. Obscene displays of corporate riches and private wealth are only possible through the systematic defeat and acquiescence of a large body of low-paid workers. East London's situation seems indicative of something much wider. The question is less *how*, more *why?*

Chadwell Heath and into Romford, and another change. A frontier is crossed, separating a largely poor Bangladeshi and Pakistani area from a largely poor white-British area. Each community deploys its tribal markers to assert a common identity, one whose high-contrast burn in the multicultural city leads at times to self-parody. The United Kingdom Independence Party seems popular, as I pass through, purple pound signs posted on the sides of houses and roads. The largely white working class with its markers of modern 'Englishness' remains despised by its middle class uppers, but snobbery has taken a moral tone of late. *Chavs* is well known. It extends further, into *bad* junk food and *bad* obese bodies, bad sports clothes and bad tattoos, badly behaved children and their bad language, and their bad attitudes to migrants, made to compete for the lowest wage. The Spanish au pair who doesn't ask for holiday pay, the unthreatening Polish plumber who doesn't answer back. A vast swathe of the population had been made to feel inferior, tacky, vulgar, violent, stupid, ugly, chavvy. Despite the obvious contradictions, these pound signs raised two fingers up to the middle classes and their political establishment. It will be the first of many subterranean signs of revolt.

Harold Wood and into Noak Hill, endless early 20th century council estates of the red-brick, low-rise, Tudor Walters standard, spacious and with neat gardens. They forgot to build amenities of any kind, and there's no obvious place of communal interaction, few pubs for the feckless drinking classes, few leisure centres, nary even a church. Housing by numbers. Though they're a profound improvement on the inner-city slums they relieved, sociality and communality were not incorporated into the design regulations. I'd lived on a similarly vast council estate on the other side of London in St Pauls Cray, Kent, in my late teens. There are countless others surrounding London. Built approximately nowhere with no transport connections, mine was a fertile seedbed for casual aggression and depression.

But this relates to the déclassé Victorian terraces east of Stratford too. The lack of colour and variety to these structures stunts the imagination. Social status is zoned into these suburbs. Net curtains, statins, anti-depressants, property speculation or the pillorying of the poor as TV entertainment. The city's cleaners, carers, delivery-drivers and shop-workers hail from places like these. By a small wood near Noak Hill, intimating Essex country, a friendly woman points me the way to Billericay, and I asked about the area. "Not so bad", she thought.

There's a danger in reading the landscape through a looking-glass, of reproducing "Brixton in Ullapool and Tunbridge Wells in Scourie", as Edwin Muir said of English travellers in Scotland. When confronted with the unfamiliar, many travellers bloviate about sore feet and bike repairs, hotel room service, dinner-party conversations and other tiresome auto-memoirs. I resolve not to do this. Better to assess the terrain as it is, through those who live it. The "landscape itself, to those who know how to read it aright, is the richest historical record we possess", wrote historian W.G. Hoskins. Into apt country: Essex.

Through Billericay, among over-preened rose bushes and privet hedges, paved driveways, four by fours, empty birdfeeders, evidence of continual DIY. Signs of a suburban structure of feeling that has internalised the messy complexity of social life and relations into four solid CCTV-monitored walls. "Don't

you find shopping boring though Ange? I do hate it... I grab anything I can see, bung it in my wheelie, he writes me a cheque,
we bung it in the car and we bring it home", boasts Beverly.
But *Abigail's Party* is nearly forty years old. *Peep Show* is more
apt, the dislocation of modern adult life into isolated suburban
lounges, eyes lit by screens, negative solidarity. "I feel like my
soul is being chipped away bit by bit", says Jez; "Welcome to
the world of work", replies Mark, stiffly. Two polar reactions to
disappointed desire, the pressure on romantic monogamy and
career success to bear the burden of disappointed fantasies of
the good life. Unlike socialism, the suburbs made few promises.
Discount supermarket alcohol and widescreen TVs with infinite
shows have had more political impact in this terrain than any
political-party speech or pamphlet.

Occasional fields appear, interrupting a scape that then
becomes dominated by an expanse of light industrial warehouses. The buildings are all grubby, the area unflinchingly tart
and suspicious of reforming impulses. "Basildon? It's MILES
away!" says one man, a little out of town. The accent's sourer than
East London, vowels more elongated and flattened, more mono-
tone. Ten minutes later, I'm among its deserted street market,
in a commuter new town surrounded by boarded-up shops and
a bawdy boozer. Into the latter I turn. Conversation's rough and
ready, quick to dispense with formalities, suspicious of abstract
thinking. "We're all different, but once you start bullshitting and
lying, I don't want to know", says one young man on an adjacent
table, on the question of identity. "I don't give a monkey's, let's
hope I don't get breathalysed", says another, as tequila chasers
are passed round. "Fair play", I reply, already disorientated. Darkness is falling, fatigue riddles my bones. The prospect of finding
some secluded spot to sleep fills me with dread and uncertainty.
It won't be in Basildon.

Pitsea, London's influence ebbing. Concrete flyovers, industrial estates and the stenches of sewage treatment and a nearby

landfill site. Buzzing pylons and distant port lights, a grey zone, stone becoming marsh becoming Thames becoming sky. There's an unlikely natural haven at Wat Tyler County Park, a pleasant strip of nature tamed, the air humming with evening birdsong and the icky-sweet smell of decomposing rubbish. I rove around the deserted terrain, ex-industrial land reclaimed, resistant to abstract interpretation. The nearby Tesco was, until recently, the largest supermarket in Europe. Nothing else here. Yet beneath the man-made nature-scape is a history riper than the rotting waste, one that merits digression.

It's unclear why the park's named after the leader of the Peasants' Revolt of 1381, who led the rebels of Kent, whilst Jack Straw headed those of Essex. The revolt did begin in nearby Fobbing, on the other side of Vange Creek, when villagers chased out a tax-collector, killed his servants, and began to attack the manors of the gentry. They were ostensibly up in arms against paying a flat-rate Poll Tax, but many also wanted to end the unfair feudal system, wherein the majority of the population were forced, as serfs, to work the local lord's lands, forests and mines without payment, or face imprisonment. The Black Death had wiped out much of the working population in 1349, yet a statute two years later set a maximum wage at a prohibitively low level. A corrupt Church continued to extract money from the poor through tithes whilst siding with the powerful. The implicit parallels with the contemporary moment are striking, yet the story is little understood. What had led the people of Essex, Kent and the surrounding regions to rise up, and demand popular government and the equal rights of the commons?

They gathered at Mile End and Blackheath, awaiting a response from the teenage king and his retinue. When none came, sympathisers in London opened the city gates. The peasants surged inside, burning down prisons, palaces and legal archives, attacking lawyers, merchants and tax collectors. The Archbishop of Canterbury was beheaded, and rebels elsewhere ransacked Cambridge University. It was a popular revolt against elites. Agitators spread the revolt. Many were rebellious members of the clergy, Lollards, a term with a thick connotation of laziness, lying around, workshy habits. They followed John Wycliffe, who was translating the Bible into English, so that the majority could understand it. They were sceptical of the Eucharist and contemptuous of church wealth. John Ball was one of the most radical of them, preaching the equality of all human beings under God.

Some rebels wrote to each other, spreading the revolt, others moved from town to town, like John Wrawe, who went from Essex into Suffolk, leading people to rise up and attack the property of those who'd exploited them. The dispossessed and poor had long been aggrieved, but once they saw the force and the reality of the uprising, they joined in. For a time there was a popular collective desire for equality and justice.

Tyler eventually forced a meeting with King Richard II at Smithfield. He demanded that the Church's wealth be given to the poor, that justice be fairer, that "all men should be free and of one condition", as one chronicler paraphrases, thereby dissolving feudal society's class distinctions between knights, clergy, lords and serfs. Tens of thousands had massed, including skilled yeomen, priests and knights. They called themselves "the commons", the common people in whom power was intrinsically held. Democracy, another era would call it. According to that same chronicle, "the said commons had a watch-word in English among themselves, "With whom haldes yow?", to which the reply was "Wyth kynge Richard and wyth the trew commons".

The King promised to grant all the demands of the true commons, but had Tyler murdered there and then on sly pretences. The peasants were assured they'd be given their charter of rights, and were dispatched out of the city, only to be hunted down and murdered at their camp in Billericay in the following weeks. Their mistake was to trust in the goodwill of the powerful. The

Poll Tax would return again in 1989 under Margaret Thatcher. Silent scene.

And so a short spin to nearby Canvey Island, nightfall now. A sour array of drab terraces slink into the sea. Chips from Nigel's, sitting out on the Eastern Esplanade, surveying the lit chimneys of the distant power station on the Isle of Grain, the oil storage tankers on Canvey's edge. The atmosphere is distilled in the no-nonsense beer and amphetamine rock of Wilko Johnson and Dr Feelgood, down by the jetty. Irreverent and unpretentious, there is a peculiar energy to Canvey. Unvarnished, plain-speaking, tough-headed. My body is broken. A strong drink is needed...

"Wos appened mate?"

Four sets of eyes glare in mute incomprehension. Words find their way out the wilds, as much an instruction to myself as to Tucker, the barmaid and the gaping boozer.

"I'm gonna cycle round Britain mate. Find out about the island."

He and his mate laugh, and I laugh too, words so obviously naïve, especially from the weedy guy uttering them. They buy me a pint. "Why would ya wanna see Canvey?" It's a question I'd often be asked in many parts. "Tell me about life in this place." This question, asked without much thought at the time, would become my opening line thereafter. And so they did: they rubbished nearby pubs, spoke of the flood of 1953, and Dr Feelgood, and the island's cult football team. Canvey revels in its exceptions, unexceptional though they are. In its antipathy to outsiders it promised a microcosmic glimpse of its parent Fantasy Island. Tucker's about to quit tattooing, sick of tribal tattoos, burnout on the coalface of mass individualism.

"Good luck san, you'll need it." Indeed. Approaching midnight, I drunkenly head out into a torrential downpour.

Hadleigh Park Colony. The Salvation Army established a farm, factory and brickworks here in 1891, on the northern banks of the Thames estuary. It would "supply a place where broken men of bad habits... can be reformed, and ultimately sent out to situations, or as emigrants to Canada", as one backer put it. They made bricks, toys and pottery, bred cattle, chicken and horses, and grew crops in fields, orchards and greenhouses. Four hundred men of the East End poor would be sent to live here at any one time in corrugated barracks. Then as now, their poverty was attributed to a moral failing, their immorally workshy attitudes required reprogramming. The hard work and clean air was considered improving.

The farm still exists, but not to the same extent. Fittingly perhaps, I'd been too drunk last night to locate the old colony where I'd been tipped to wild-camp, and in the desperation of the midnight deluge, I'd put up my tent in what looked like secluded parkland. Morning's cruel light reveals an all-too-public dog-walkers' domain. Pooches sniff the tent, owners wait awkwardly from a distance. The owner of the nearby Benfleet boating club tells me to hop it. A Bermondsey man, he's amused by my story and I buy myself some time. He talks of the East Londoners who've moved out here, many buying caravans, chalets, some even boats. Politely, he declines an offer of cooked beans from my camping stove. Gruelling hangover. These bad habits will not be reformed just yet.

But everything hurts. I can hardly walk, let alone think, and would sooner have a healthy tooth yanked out than spend another day in the saddle. I survey my belongings. Surely there's a way of lightening the load?

I've the shirt on my back and a pair of jeans, and another spare, and shorts too. Another shirt and two t-shirts are essential, and four days' undergarments. How long will I be gone? No idea, a month, six months, perhaps. I'll soon become comfortable with the laxer hygiene regime of the long-distance traveller, but that toothbrush, deodorant, razor, shower gel, nail-clippers, pomade and comb are indispensable. The towel doubles up as a pillow. The helmet and high-vis belt will improve survival odds on country roads. Jumper, Harrington jacket and trapper hat for the cold nights. A small laptop and camera for documenting the journey, but there's already a large speck in its lens. A Swiss Army knife and a compass. It'll help to know broadly which direction to cycle towards.

A garden trowel? Its use is suggested by the accompanying bog-roll. I'll be digging my toilet. Sleeping bag and mat? A matter of economy, to make sleeping in fields, beaches, parks and wasteland less unbearable. Repair kit and spare inner tube? I can hardly fix a puncture, but needs must. Scotch? A tried-and-tested sleeping remedy and salve for tired nerves. What else?

Two waterproof Carradice panniers, not especially large. Ilford's potholes broke the hooks of one, now fastened to the bike with ropes. Three books, unnecessary. Notebooks, headphones, ditto. A gram of MDMA and some acid? I'll keep these divination devices for the longer nights. This large stove and gas cans? More practical, but too bulky. They go, along with my food and bowl. "Do you want it?" I ask the postmistress of Shoeburyness later, as I parcel up my gear to send home. "Umm, the dog might like it." "It's yours!"

Feeling lighter but no less in pain, I head on. A lorry gives me a friendly toot. Inside, one of the fellas I'd drunk with last night commandeers the dashboard and grins. Reaffirmed and ready, bring on the road!

Shoeburyness was not far from where I'd awoken. A tough path cut from the farm through scrubby parkland, flanked on my right by estuarine saltings. The briny air trilled with parleying gulls and jingling sailboats. Then leafy detached tudorbethan suburbia, Chalkwell, Leigh and Westcliff-on-Sea, a London air still, a commuter zone. Southend comes next, the classic cockney daytrip-destination of choice. The esplanade is in good shape, fresh cream paint and the distant fronds of palm trees tickle the horizon. It is still loved, Southend, its improbable theme park, pier and crazy golf doing a good trade, as are the chippies and boozers behind them. Sat in deck-chairs or lying fully dressed on the modest, pebbly beach, most look content if somewhat disappointed, and some have umbrellas even though no rain is forecast. It's evidence of a specific kind of native wisdom, at peace with the inevitability of suffering. In the unlikely event that it doesn't rain by the seaside, the brolly can be used to fend off seagulls whilst eating an ice cream.

At Shoeburyness, the beach is cordoned-off due to the discovery of unexploded WW2 bombs. I ask a preoccupied-looking old gent about the area, who guffaws, kneads the pale skin of his mush where a phantom moustache resides, begins a sortie on Jerry artillery then loses his thread, and glares into the sea in silence. "Terrible thing, war", drifting out again. He points to a large boom built during that war to prevent German ships and submarines sailing up the Thames. A nearby Ministry of Defence sign warns that gun practice continues today. Further east is Foulness, an island belonging to the MOD but with a small population. It has been sub-contracted to a private military research firm to experiment with munitions. One is not allowed to visit except with special permission, and cameras are not permitted. It is the first of many signs of the widespread yet oddly unacknowledged activities of the military around the island.

North, past Southend's airport, among a familiar oneiric scene of retail parks and dual carriageways, fast-food drive-thrus, the banal Britain we spend all our time in and rarely think about. I wonder what its effects are at the basic level of the imagination, if somehow this similar-looking, predictable world inhibits the speculative possibility of difference and change. Pedalling on, the suburbia starting to thin, until short bursts of farmland begin to slice the scene, adding much-needed green between the villages of Sutton-with-Shopland and Stambridge.

A little after five I reach the edge of Wallasea Island, where a small ferry takes foot passengers over the River Crouch to Burnham. The last one's just departed. It's a three-hour cycle round otherwise, and I decide to call it a day. There's a small bar improbably open at the marina with views over the bay. The landlady tells me of a campsite nearby. A family is having farewell drinks, a teenage daughter about to head off to work in the nightclubs of Kavos. They warn her not to drink too much and chase after the boys, and she says she'll miss them all so terribly, words insincere but with generous feeling. And me on my lonesome, this vast island ahead, muscles and mind all mangled. Here is the threshold between home and the unknown, folly and pilgrimage. It takes a third bottle of beer to screw my courage back into the sticking place.

"Love is vital, love is worth it all", says John the ferryman, married forty-two years, as our small vessel chugs over the Crouch. Ahead is a cheery old village, its beer gardens spilling onto the shore, and all around us marsh, skirted in reeds.

Daniel Defoe passed here three hundred years ago on his island journey, and remarked on the "strange decay of the [female] sex" caused by these malarial marshes. Women particularly suffered poor health and died young, and Defoe heard of one farmer who was on his twenty-fifth wife. Not all travellers recognise the glee of locals in pulling their legs with grotesques. But much of the eastern coastline was marshy like this, inhospitable to dwellings and farming, until Dutch engineers began to oversee its drainage around the time of Defoe. But these dark mudflats still retain something of the not-quite-right about them. Local musicians, These New Puritans, have produced an esoteric poetics for this scene, making secret recordings in the marsh. Here's a distinctive border-zone between earth, sea and sky, with different modes of existence above and below the waterline.

H.G. Wells once gazed out at this scene and envisioned the smoking heat-rays of three-legged Martian fighting-machines wading through the waters from Foulness in *War of the Worlds*, as Londoners attempt to escape on steamboats. The invaders are "vital, intense, inhuman, crippled and monstrous", which is peculiarly apt for the surrounding salt wetland, a haven for all manner of life. The Martians are eventually annihilated not by military manoeuvre, but by lack of immunity to terrestrial bacteria.

John drops me at Burnham and sails off again. After flitting round the cheery village and yachting marina I continue north, across the Dengie Peninsula. After Southminster the scape is flat, spears of wheat drooping over the reclaimed marshland. There's an extraordinary array of local and migrating birds, adding colour, motion and song to the scene. The recent spike of anti-European political views along the eastern coast jars with its natural history. For invaders landed on the Essex coastline for millennia, their small craft navigating its inlets and creeks, beaching onto an unknown island.

And Essex was made a haven for all of them, for they were us. Prehistoric peoples came from across Europe, who later stride onto the historical record as Celts, Belgae, Romans, Angles, Jutes and Saxons, Vikings, Normans, each settling on the island, farming and working it, leaving traces behind in names and buildings. Some fled religious persecution in the Netherlands and France, others fled poverty and hunger in Ireland, and there have been more recent economic migrations, from the Caribbean, India, Pakistan, Bangladesh and Kenya, and other parts of the former empire, which continue today. And just as they've made this island home, so islanders have sailed out again, settling in other parts of the world, like Canada, North America, New Zealand, Australia, South Africa. These too can be traced back through history, like 'Brittany', settled by Britons fleeing the Saxons and, later, Saxons fleeing the Normans in Byzantium, employed in its Varangian Guard.

These are uneasy, contested histories. But to insist on the virtues of migration against those bad English xenophobes who seek to quit the EU is lazy and inaccurate. These communities are tolerant, and often knowledgeable of their own recent histories.

Their anger is not directed toward any migrant worker or European visitor, and racist violence is uncommon. There is a subtle element of class discrimination here. For they rage against their own political establishment, the narrow Westminster consensus that has allowed wages, infrastructure and local industries to collapse for the holy cause of private profit. Somehow the EU has been conflated with this, but the anger rarely sticks with that, the precise nature of its malevolence unclear.

There is also an antipathy toward the smug and sanctimonious middle classes, who condescend from their TV shows, lifestyle magazines and tabloid columns to correct the poor on their social priorities. Much of the mainstream Left finds itself in this policing role, sometimes unwittingly. The trade unions are bound and gagged by a thousand silken legal strings, and the remainder of the Left has drifted into the obsolescence of academia or futile party causes. There are these great swathes of anger without outlet, except the occasional anti-European candidate, until some gaffe reveals them as yet another cretinous establishment toady. They've kissed enough frogs round here. Migration is premised on dispersal. A vast group of the island's working class is migrating beyond the old political territories. There is no sign yet of where it will land. And that intrigues me.

Reaching the edge of the deserted rural peninsula, I follow a long trackway that terminates at a lofty stone barn overlooking the sea, site of St Peter on the Wall. Its interior is sober and grey, but its quiet ambience and sense of spatial and temporal remoteness are well-suited for reflective meditation. St Cedd established it in 654 CE, using the bricks from the nearby ruins of Othona, an abandoned Roman fort that once repelled Saxon pirates. Three centuries later, the king of the East Saxons summoned Cedd from Lindisfarne to convert the local heathens to the Roman religion. He would die of some mysterious plague ten years after his mission, and according to Bede, paganism quickly returned to the marshes.

The one other structure impinging itself on the sparsely-populated Dengie Peninsula is Bradwell-on-Sea nuclear power station, its vast grey cuboids hulking over the flat scape more like a modern university than some Chernobyl-in-waiting, cutting an incongruous mark on the landscape. Inside the chapel, two local volunteers preparing flowers debate its ethics, one arguing that wind farms are too ugly, the other that they can be improved, and merit investment. Are national grid pylons and concrete cooling chimneys any better? They agree to disagree, in another ritual of island life, that of reaching consensus on dissensus, abandoning reason for the sake of social accord, a scepticism for pursuing intellectual causes. Such liberalism is as charming as it is maddening.

At work is an allusive ideal of Nature and the most natural. And even Dengie can trip one up, this nature actually intensively farmed, like most of England, its telegraph poles and tarmac roads over artificially reclaimed land. Being so flat, it is susceptible to flooding in places, and coastal erosion in others, its *landness* no matter of fact but a conditional truce. A sea-wall protects it, but the effects of inevitable climate change caused by human activity and consumption have, over this century, caused glaciers and polar ice-caps to melt, swelling the tides and submerging the eastern coast. "Elemental change is accelerated here", says Jonathan Meades of the Essex littoral. Its fragility makes it exemplary, an "emblem of human powerlessness". Yet humans are things of nature too, the whole landscape human-shaped.

West, through the villages of St Lawrence, Steeple, Mayland and Mundon, and into Maldon, an old Saxon port-town still poised with graces over the Blackwater marshes. The rain is keeping up its armistice, and the early afternoon sun's delightful. A lone figure stands over the River Blackwater with a sword raised. Earl Byrhtnoth cuts a somewhat melancholic figure. The *Battle of Maldon* recounts the vain but heroic resistance of his English Saxons against a band of Viking raiders in 991 CE. It is one of the earliest English epic poems, and one of its finest. "Courage shall grow keener, clearer the will, the heart fiercer, as our force faileth", has one translation. The Vikings sought a large tribute, *danegeld*, protection money, but Byrhtnoth refused. One could place him in a counter-history with Straw and Tyler, of rebels who fought for freedom against tremendous military power. But that wouldn't be quite right either. A large supermarket has beached beyond the banks.

This new level of exertion is fiendish, and some appetite has built up. My usual monastic fare of pitta bread and bananas is insufficient, and I order a large three-course meal in a Mexican restaurant to assuage the hunger. Like worn muscles, it's something else I'll get used to, usually through great bags of nuts and raisins and, later, muesli mixed with water. Some distance lies ahead.

Wickham Bishops and Great Totham, Tiptree and Layer de la Haye – the North Essex countryside is far prettier than its London-blurred southern parts. The moderate-sized city of Colchester likewise wears an age and affluence of another order to its southern neighbours. Its centre is less distinct however. A cluster of generic malls linked by pedestrianised lanes, each offering a similar diet of chain stores. It is a British Town Centre, like any other. Though it gifts a university, I wonder if Essex's capital should be elsewhere. Perhaps it reflects the county's confused self-images. Fake tans and flat vowels of the outer London suburbs, kiss-me-kwik seaside shenanigans, the Real Nature along the marshes. Like all clichés, they are not untrue. But Essex is richer and stranger, and actively resists interpretation.

I lope around the gardens of its Norman castle, another totem of the island's contested histories. I wonder whether to ask the teenage lovers if they know all its histories, but lack that thick-skinned front also associated with Essex people and check Google. The castle's situated over the vast Roman temple to Claudius, the emperor who'd led the conquest of Britain in 43 CE, and was subsequently deified. The Romans made here, Camulo-dunum, their first capital, building a fortress and walls, theatres and a forum, and granted its citizens the same rights as Romans. But Claudius' imperial glory was founded on the military and economic subjugation of the Britannic tribes. Many had been forced into debts to their Roman lords to keep up with living costs, loans they couldn't repay. Few empires are conquered on the battlefield. Continual military campaigning had resulted in a number of atrocities, like the massacre of the druids at Anglesey in 60 CE, wiping out the cultural and spiritual elite of the Britons. Things were fermenting, ready to reach a head.

That same year, Boudica, chief of the Iceni tribe of modern-day Norfolk, had been dispossessed of her wealth by the Romans following the death of her indebted husband. Her daughters were raped by their soldiers. Allying with the Trinovantes of Suffolk, they marched to Camulodunum, left undefended, and burnt it down, before marching on London and St Albans, doing the same, in the process slaughtering around seventy- to eighty-thousand Romans and Britons. The rebels were finally routed by the smaller but better-armed legions at Watling Street.

Families picnic and teenagers dreamily gad about the castle. Who might the Iceni and Romans be substituted for now? Some stories are old, others remain hidden, unknown. The area has known other demotic, demagogic spasms. Witchfinder general Matthew Hopkins stirred up sufficient panic to oversee the exe-cution of three hundred 'witches' over a short period between 1644–6 in Essex and nearby counties. Nothing's known of Boud-ica beyond the Roman chronicles. Then Normans, subjugating the rebellious populace. Walls and castles that brought order, a false pleasure in the fixity of history, the myth of a one-island nation story. The castle has been used as a prison for heretics, and is now a tourist attraction. I pedal out of Essex, exhausted and tantalised.

"Just let nature get on with it", says Darren, the following morning, as we drink tea in his kitchen. Essex is behind me, and after Cattawade and Strutton, I reached Holbrook, Suffolk, a pretty village dominated by the naval Royal Hospital School. Bedsheets and a warm shower had never felt more pleasurable.

I stayed with Darren and Sue, two strangers who kindly offered a bed via a friend. Sue's a teacher, and Darren a musician and ecologist, whose enlightening conversation indicates further inconsistencies about the island. For here is no fixed entity. The coastline is continually eroding in places and flooding in others. Why not work with nature, instead of fighting it? Epimethean pragmatism over Promethean ambitions. Darren and his colleagues are re-establishing salt marshes that will naturally inhibit floods. They are locating badger sets and, over the course of some years, vaccinating populations against bovine TB. Their approach is stewardship, not mastery.

But appealing for responsibility itself contains a kernel of moral optimism. Just as rising tides are beyond the control of humankind, so too is the restraint of our own natural behaviour. The industry and activity needed to feed and occupy an ever-growing population will continue to deplete and damage our environments. If nature means untouched by humankind, then it's hard to know where one might find it. Outside the towns, the terrain is drained and farmed, cut through with underground pipes, and webbed in roads and wires, from telephones to electricity pylons.

Hard to find is not proof of non-existence, however.

"[M]ost of England is 1,000 years old", wrote Hoskins in 1955. In a "walk of a few miles one can touch nearly every century in that long stretch of time". This is an old island, and with the exception of a few northern industrial towns, most settlements can trace such a lineage, often to villages established by Anglo-Saxon settlers, some settled by earlier Britons, others abandoned like the old Roman forts. The island was thinly populated when they arrived, much covered in oak and ash forests. This woodland has been burned since Neolithic times for fuel and for establishing new farmland. Being closest to the Continent, Norfolk and Suffolk became some of the most populous parts of the island, and the significance of migration is stored in the name "Anglia". These villages grew, and with them parish churches, castles, monasteries and towns.

But seeking this ancient England can be delusory. Over the River Orwell, I pedal into Ipswich, a large and neglected town. Schools and dilapidated community centres stand beside half-built luxury high-rises, clad in gaudy colours. Disused churches jut against a repetition of offies and mean suburban terraces, and a traffic-planning system confusingly weaves into a bland, predictable town centre. The streets reverberate with curses and discarded cans. Like Basildon, here is average British life, and its obvious ugliness functions to obfuscate easy interpretation. It is not an unhappy place.

Out along a busy A-road, next approaching Woodbridge, a twee market town. There is an obvious class difference with nearby Ipswich, for here is an organic farmers' market with unpasteurised cheese, artisan jams and craft beers, aspirational baby-clothing outlets, a haven for second home owners and wealthy professionals working in the nearby towns. The town makes a more blatant claim for a thousand-year lineage. And yet the market square, boutiques and restored townhouses are as similarly contrived as Ipswich's urban incoherence, and therefore all the more authentic.

Most of these scapes bear the imprint of the last three centuries, in their Victorian terraces, their enclosed, hedgerowed farms established by private landowners and parliamentary enclosure over the 17th and 18th centuries, far larger in scale than the medieval smallholdings they replaced. "Half a century ago, Norfolk might be termed a rabbit and rye country", wrote Arthur Young in 1804, without the wheat and barley since farmed on a massive scale. There is a danger in feeling nostalgia for a 'hand-made world', slow and wholesome, like that which was longingly fantasised about by Eric Gill, and intimated in the works of William Morris. Human beings are industrial creatures, putting the land to work to service our basic needs well beyond that thousand-year timeframe. It extends far back into pre-history.

Even reading the landscape isn't always instructive. Through Melton and Rendlesham Forest, signs warn of crossing frogs, and cyclists wave with a polite amiability unknown in London. It feels peaceful, old. Looking out from Orford over the gentle sea, the scenery gives the lie of permanence and fixity. But under those waters is a country that became an island that became sea, Doggerland.

Britain was a European peninsula until around 125-thousand years ago, when global warming caused glaciers to melt and seas to rise, creating an island. The fertile strip between East Anglia and the Continent was partially submerged, but remained the island of Doggerland until 5000 BCE, following the end of the most recent Ice Age. It was a place of human habitation, as well as a resting point through which migrating humans travelled on their way west to Britain. Antlers and bones are still being discovered from that drowned world, dredged by trawlers, but unlike Gilgamesh, Noah and Lyonesse, no myths survive of its peoples and cultures.

The rising tides continue to nip away at this coastline. Erosion at Pakefield, Happisburgh and Lynford on the East Anglian coast has revealed caves and ancient bones. The 2001–13 Ancient Human Occupation of Britain Project analysed these findings, estimating that humans have lived here for at least a million years. Among the oldest are stone tools and footprints matched to *homo antecessoris* at Happisburgh, indicating an ancient, natural ingenuity for working with our hands. Successive waves of humans have settled here since, but the island's climate has fluctuated from balmy Mediterranean-type conditions (the remains of hippo have been found in the Yorkshire Dales) to freezing tundra and desert permafrost, fit only for mammoth and deer. Climactic swings prevented lasting human settlement, wiping out the earlier *homo heidelbergensis* and *neanderthalis* and forcing migration again. The most recent occupation of the island by *homo sapiens* began 11,500 years ago, with the start of the Holocene era. Neolithic humans only started to settle and farm the land six thousand years ago.

So much for our thousand-year lineage. All this is merely a nano-second in the Earth's long history, and one that looks increasingly precarious. Geologists now term this the Anthropocene era. Ingenuity with our hands and a versatile adaptability has caused the disappearance of forests, the loss of flood-regulating marshes, and the unleashing of chemicals that bored holes in the atmosphere. Ice caps melt faster than scientific predictions, and by the end of the century it is probable that, save another feat of human ingenuity, much of Norfolk, Suffolk, Essex and the Thames estuary will be underwater. It will be the latest event in a millennia-deep history of natural struggle.

One can imagine future humans navigating the wetlands of Ipswich and Basildon, wading through floating plastics, wires and polystyrene takeaway boxes, upended yachts and roof tiles, discovering a coin with a woman's face. An ancient nature goddess, they might think, as they fondly invent an image of the wholesome ways of the past.

Sea becomes one with the sky. We're beyond the zones of memory and forgetting now, caught between time-zones and their contradictory flows. A small vessel chugs over the drowned world towards a narrow spit, Orford Ness. Before Foulness, this flat expanse was used by the MOD for ballistic experiments with nuclear missiles, between 1949 and 1971. It's now a National Trust site, and one can peek around the cluster of huts from which the scientists worked, or drift down to the detonation points on the beach, a lonesome lighthouse to one's left, and

two peculiar concrete huts in the distance that resemble pago-
das, or possibly Neolithic cromlechs, covered tombs. There's a
thrill in ignoring the *Do Not Touch* signs to cheekily prod two
unexploded warheads. Then over the bone-like shingle where
campion grows between metallic fragments, into the bomb-
control centres that now home barn owls and butterflies. Time
ceased around 1969.

This was the "other island" for a long time, a place locals were
afraid to name. I speak to a retired school teacher from South
London who volunteers here. She shows me how to read a sea
map (upside down) and with another old boy, helps me identify
the principality of Sealand in the distance, an offshore military
rig that now claims to be an independent state, with a population of one. Like Darren, she describes the bizarre and hidden
military experiments conducted on the coastline, like at Shingle
Street, where apocryphal stories of "burning seas" and rebuffed
German invasions during WW2 were likely produced as black
propaganda to bolster morale. She talks of her late husband, lost
at sea whilst sailing. The tranquillity of that sea is deceptive, with
countless sunken ships lurking beneath cruel rocks.

Late afternoon, the rain returns in another vicious deluge.
Turns out neither my jacket nor panniers are waterproof, and the
ride is punishing. Another cyclist shoots a pained grimace and
I give a thumbs up. His laughter keeps me pedalling. Soaked to
the skin, I eventually reach Aldeburgh, a fetchingly fusty seaside
town. There's an old moot hall by the sea, and the town was the
first nationally to appoint a female mayor in 1908. A third of its
properties are now second homes, largely owned by wealthy Londoners, who make up much of the well-heeled clientele of the
Mill Inn, where I stop to dry out. Yet three hours on, the rain's
beating down and I'm still drenched. I put it to the public vote.

The barman suggests cycling up the road a few miles and camping ("It'll be an adventure!"). An old boy chuckles and disagrees
("Stay here!"). I text Sarah for a deciding vote. There's a youth

hostel in nearby Blaxhall. It's most tempting and I'm shattered, still no more adept at long days in the saddle. Out into the rain.

Four days since leaving home, and fatigue's not yet abated. I appease it with excessive calorie consumption: packs of biscuits, chocolate milk where I can get it, gallons of beer. Yet for all the strain, I feel lighter and less burdened than ever before. It will take a few more days of rough going to articulate why.

Late morning, and I wind down narrow hedgerow-lanes that weave through fields and open country, among poppies and dozy cattle. It's a Constable scene, sweet and serene, dotted with the odd village pub, even a picturesque ruined abbey at Leighton. I plunge through the knotty Dunwich forest, where a quagmire claims my balance and splats me down, then reconnect with the coast.

The ruins of a medieval friary overlooking a wide bay hint at Dunwich's fate. One can handle the stones, all that remains of what was once East Anglia's most bustling sea-port and town, claimed by storms over the 13th and 14th centuries. Crooked medieval towers still poked through the sand until the late 19th century, and Dunwich was a notorious rotten borough, fielding two MPs to represent thirty-two voters. Now there are merely pebbles, and the tide, and a car-park and a large number of tourists. Brian Eno's 'Dunwich Beach, Autumn 1960' hints at the brooding menace and sense of loss that one can read into the bay, where even the graves are washed away.

"Memories lie slumbering within us for months and years", reflects W.G. Sebald in *Rings of Saturn*, a book as much about the East Anglian coastline as about the difficulties of remembering. These memories remain dormant, "quietly proliferating, until they are woken by some trifle and in some strange way blind us to life". Perhaps it's apt that since his move to the Suffolk coast, the cultural theorist Mark Fisher has written of "the disappearance of the future" in British politics, "eroded" in the defeat of a progressive working class modernism, overturned by Thatcher. Genteel Suffolk is a place of haunting, like these drowned worlds here, or the devilish black dog myths of local folklore in woods like Dunwich and Minsmere, or the ghost stories of M.R. James. Its age and placidity lends itself to horror.

Slumbering memories raise the question of agency: in what ways are our experiences buried, blinded from our sight? To what extent do we elect certain memories and stories to tell ourselves, and what values are employed in the selection process? These "abandoned" zones like Dunwich and Orford Ness bustle with tourists. The wealthy second home towns of Woodbridge, Aldeburgh and Southwold ahead stake a claim to a wholesome tradition, "unspoilt", offering food and drink that claims to be "real", "home-made", "organic" and "local". There's a subtle eugenics in its folky striving for authenticity and creativity, but then again the rich have always invented rituals to elevate their conspicuous consumption. This is the normative idyll to follow, "Real Britain", this wealthy zone of South East England. Nowhere shows football. Yet many of their residents had their first homes in the capital, and were pricing out locals, whilst places like Ipswich, Basildon and Yarmouth further along escape view, working class towns blighted with witless shopping centres, all alike, and numbers-driven mass housing. Beyond the sideshow about European integration, there was a far more expansive immigration of the moneyed middle classes with their need for second homes. But at this point I'd read nothing about this, nor was there any immediately obvious explanation. In Ipswich and Basildon it was just struggles with rent, to buy a place, the struggle to get by. Like in Billericay, the household and the family remained the constrained locus of collective imaginings.

But cheery Lowestoft is a delight. Its old pier rusts precipitously over a sweeping bay. There's deck chairs and fish and chips, a funfair and a sign claiming to be the most easterly point of the island, and families lolloping about on the beach, bickering and laughing, enjoying themselves. I hear a local accent for the first time in Argos where I buy a poncho, its vowels clipped and light ("thang' you suh"). I'll hear more of it north, as I pedal through Gorleston and across a bridge into Great Yarmouth, an old fishing town with dusty quays at its rear, and a cheery seaside resort on the other side.

Yarmouth's the first lively town I've encountered since Southend, demotic and diverse. Past B&Bs depending on the housing benefit trade, there's the wistful glamour of faded ballrooms and boarding houses, and far more amusements than one's inner child could wish for. I potter along the promenade, chatting to people on the beach. One group of sunburnt lads take a break from digging a huge hole with cool cans of lager. "We're building the Alan Partridge hotel", says one, laughing.

This is now Norfolk, and the county difference is imperceptible. I head west over the Norfolk Broads, a flat expanse out of a Dutch postcard, all cattle, windmills and wee rills threading blues through the green. It's a hot afternoon and the road is choked with fast-moving traffic. An hour later, I reach Blofield, where I pause in one of the most common features of the terrain, a McDonald's drive-thru. They sell sameness: they look the same everywhere, serve the same range and quality of meals, are universally popular, and employ local people. With an ice cream and milkshake, I find a place to charge my phone and rest a while.

When was the last time you were in a unique-looking pub or shopping centre? There is pleasure, indeed refuge, in being in a familiar, anonymising locale. The reality's constructed, it being so unlikely that one place could be exactly like another, but McDonald's, like the Tesco supermarket or Wetherspoon's pub, has achieved it. It appeals to a modesty in popular culture, a reluctance to indulge in unscripted self-expression and flamboyance. It reflects a desire for reassuring simplicity and convenience. One could not even dream of these places, they occupy no conscious space. Instead they are spaces for dreaming in, for being invisible and unconscious in. The golden arches offer a semblance of tradition and normality that seems homely, relaxing, even though such American cuisine was unknown here even fifty years ago. Queuing for another milkshake, I find optimism in the place. If we can adapt to this consumer modernism and indeed be lovin' it, without self-reproach, then what else is possible for an egalitarian, democratic politics, hidden in the depressed contemporary moment? What else might we desire?

It's a tenuous point, but the proximity of alternate timezones, like Orford Ness, Doggerland and Dunwich, facilitates speculative dreaming. I continue west, bypassing Norwich and cutting through the dusky forests at Swardeston. It's now nightfall. The forests are thick, the thin trees and foliage casting a wall of black over which the zaffre-blue of the night sky looms like a cathedral vault. A black dog appears in front of me on the unlit road. Local legend has it that on quiet roads like this, such a dog is the devil in disguise. Its bark is unnerving.

I ride around it, increasing speed, but one narrow road follows another, each threading nowhere, the woodland scene interrupted by derelict barns and abandoned-looking cottages. Mice skitter over the path. For a time I cannot make out the road ahead. The wind picks up, and I hear a woman's voice singing, as if just behind my shoulder. I turn round, but there's no one there, the scene deserted, save for the black trees and moths, and mice, and that devil dog somewhere on my tail. Feeling a little terrified, I pedal with everything I've got until the woods are behind me, and I find myself in the old market town of Wymondham.

Happy drunks gallivant over the market lanes, and pubs blare out reassuringly bland indie-rock. Relief. But it's late, and I've nowhere to sleep. After skirting around the town, I spot signs for a playing field, and pitch up behind some play-centre.

It's my second attempt at wild camping in England, an illegal practice, and this attempt is no more successful than the first. I hear a gaggle of teenagers marauding in the distance. Nervous of my vulnerability, I chance on barbed psychology, and venture out to greet them.

"Don't worry, I'm not a ghost!"

They scarper past shrieking, terrified by a moonlit, lunatic spectre.

"There is no antidote against the Opium of time, which temporally considereth all things", writes Thomas Browne, doctor and dilettantish genius of Norwich. "Our Fathers finde their graves in our short memories... Generations passe while some trees stand, and old Families last not three Oaks."

His *Urne-Buriall* is a beautiful meditation on the brevity of life's "pure flame" and his hopes for the Christian afterlife, written in 1658 as a study of urns recently discovered in Walsingham. His melancholy words also pass verdict on another local story, Kett's Rebellion, which began at an oak tree on Mousehold Heath back in 1549.

Wealthy gentry had begun building fences and digging ditches around common land, enclosing public spaces for their own private profit. They were increasing rents and cutting wages. The aggrieved commons gathered, and decided to tear down the fences that local landlord, Robert Kett, had placed over the common land at Wymondham. After pleading with them, Kett took the unlikely decision to lead the rebels. They tore down his neighbour's fences, then marched towards Norwich, where they established a peaceful protest camp at Mousehold Heath, just as rebellious peasants had done previously in 1381.

Thousands gathered there by the day, and at other camps across East Anglia. One can only speculate on the energy of their discussions and optimism. After six weeks, the rebels sent 29 grievances to the Lord Protector Edward Seymour, acting effectively as monarch in lieu of the boy-king Edward VI. They demanded a return to fairer prices and rents, for fair and equitable local government, that the common land should not be privatised by landowners. "[N]o lord of no manor shall common upon the common."

There was something of the Peasants' Revolt's naïve association of the interest of the "trew commons" with that of the monarch. Kett and the rebels saw themselves as loyal subjects of the King, and demanded only the removal of a few corrupt members of the gentry.

The protest camp was declared a rebellion, and warrants made for the leaders' arrest. Needing food and sensing the need for escalation, the rebels seized the city, but lacked a lasting strategy. They managed to defeat a better-armed royal army inside Norwich several times, but were later outgunned outside it by a second force of European mercenaries. Kett was captured and hung from Norwich castle. A plaque on its walls remembers him as a "noble and courageous leader in the long struggle of the common people of England to escape from a servile life into the freedom of just conditions". The plaque was raised by the citizens of Norwich in 1949, not long after the victory against fascism. They were like seeds, these struggles, alive beneath one's feet.

Norwich is a small, old city, marked out by its affluent suburbia and, after rings of confusing traffic systems, the imposing cube form and battlements of a Norman castle and cathedral, each cut from piercing white limestone. Unlike much of England, the traditional bastions of power still dominate the horizon. The town is more modern though residually quaint and compact. Hitler planned to give his first post-invasion speech from here. One wonders how Norwich, with its long rebellious history, would've tolerated such rule.

North, along the Marriot's Way cycle track. It's a cheery morning, and the old train line's flanked by bluebells and cowparsley, butterflies and swallows, hikers and cyclists out for the day. I feel much lighter along the path, and after a few hours I pass Reepham, and cycle into Foxley Wood, Norfolk's largest remaining ancient forest. I wander in and chart a path between thick grasses, immersing in lush springy trees. I go to celebrate with a KitKat, when I notice something quite disturbing.

At the back of the bicycle is one pannier, not two. This one contains smelly clothes and a washbag, whilst the other contained my laptop and valuables.

Where has it gone? I've cycled around thirty miles since leaving Wymondham, and the bag could've fallen anywhere along that route. But what route? I can hardly remember what way I came. The bag has no nametag or obvious marker. Whoever finds it will look inside and be tempted by its contents. What if it's back in Norwich, the police probing it as a suspect package, ready to detonate? The possibilities are terrifying. I race back towards Norwich, asking everyone I pass if they've spotted a bag.

A family of cyclists at Reepham saw one of the plastic hooks on a path nearby, but no bag. My heartbeat doubles, and desperation surges as blank expressions and replies in the negative keep coming. After another mile, an old cyclist thinks he saw it seven miles ago at a car-park in Norwich. For the next hour and a half I ride back towards Norwich, asking everyone I pass, popping into local cafes and calling up others. A walker remembers spotting it on the bicycle somewhere along the path. It has to be here somewhere along the shrubby verge, but there's no sign of it.

At the edge of Norwich, I pause in a car-park. A man hails me from his car. "Something's trailing off your bike", he says, pointing to the sleeping bag hanging off. I explain my situation. He beckons me over to his boot, where lo it is there! Russell has waited around two hours after picking it up, whilst out for a walk. He was about to leave when I'd appeared. He insists on not taking any reward for his goodwill and patience. Thank you, Russell!

From despair to dizziness. The sun is baking hot and I feel faint and exhausted, as if on the rotating plate of a microwave. I cut my fingers badly whilst trying to fix the bag back on, and have difficulty focusing on the road ahead. It's another fifteen miles back to Reepham, and it's late afternoon. Every thirty seconds I turn round to check the bag's still attached.

After an exhausting couple of hours I reach the shrine of Our Lady of Walsingham. A small grey chapel sits surrounded by undulating country fields and flooded groves where children lark. It was once "England's Nazareth", a popular destination for medieval pilgrims who were too ill or poor to afford the dangerous journey to Jerusalem, its location inspired by the appearance of Mary in the vision of an 11th century noblewoman. During the English Reformation her statue was taken to London and burnt. Catholicism would remain illegal and suppressed until its "emancipation" in 1829. The church was built in 1897, but its cramped dark interior, with countless glowing candles, still possesses something of the mysterious and unworldly, the flickering flames emitting a sound and heat like the interior of a cramped train clattering through a tunnel.

In the deserted chapel, I kneel down and make a prayer, appealing to whichever deities have the unlikely property of existence. I thank the generosity of strangers, and pray for the wellbeing of loved ones at home. Hope wells up inside me as I clamber up and shuffle out of the chapel. I feel unburdened of that exhaustion, ready to submit to the arbitrary chance of the road.

Out, along bright burnished fields of wheat, and into the town of Little Walsingham, marked by its number of hospices and gaggles of cardinals and bishops, waving pints of beer and laughing outside the Bull Inn. This old religion, Catholicism, was once the glue of disparate communities of Britons and Romans, Angles, Saxons and Jutes, Danes and Normans, providing a shared worldview and system of beliefs. Monasteries preserved and transmitted a literary and artistic culture, and few modern architects have matched the majesty and awe of a gothic cathedral like Norwich's. It may be illusory, but so what? The veracity of the material world isn't what's at stake, but the ability to find inner resources to summon courage and hope within suffering,

43

to remain resilient. I wonder if modern times have matched the ancient promise of baptism, rebirth and redemption. Norfolk is a curiously apt place for it. There are more medieval churches concentrated here than anywhere else in Europe.

Wells, a sedate harbour town on the North Norfolk coastline. Families pick crabs with buckets and nets. I ask one dad and his daughter what they'll do with the creatures, wrestling at the bottom of a plastic container. "They're not for eating", he chuckles. In the distance, sailboats jut and jangle in the breeze, and I stand beside a fisherman awhile, both of us idly contemplating the seas.

My body feels exhausted and weighty, like a heavy ill-fitting outer garment. Inside, my mind feels elated, live-wired into the terrain. Outer layers, hardened, cynical and jaded, are being peeled away like the skin of an onion, revealing a fresher way of seeing and feeling, ready for the new.

Kleep kleep! Oystercatchers glide west over the horizon, across marram dunes, to Scolt Head Island. With the last of my strength, I follow their guide.

Once upon a time, a boy went down to the beach and began to dig a hole. He began early in the morning with just a plastic spade, but his energy was indefatigable, for his goal was to tunnel through to the other side of the world. Australia, China, Zimbabwe, somewhere like that. By early afternoon he was several metres deep under the sands. His mother called him, but there was no reply. The sands shifted, the sea sighed, and the tunnel collapsed. The boy was eventually found, suffocated. It was not known whether he'd caught a glimpse of the other side shortly before his death.

It happened not long before I'd first come to Hunstanton, as a small child on a family holiday. I remember the boys who'd dig pits and throw crabs in for entertainment, their pincers manically clawing at one another. The difference between life and death seemed casual and indiscriminate. But I can find no sign of the boy now, nor can anyone recall him, and I wonder if it was a figment of my imagination.

Morning, and I am pushing the bicycle along a deserted promenade, assailed by great white sheets of rain. The funfair is closed up. Macabre clown faces leer from a ghost-house, beside a helter-skelter and a lonesome waltzer, signs warning of CCTV cameras and the dangers of leaving out hands. The scene is unattended and abandoned. A small tattooist kiosk is the one thing open, the walls offering an array of flash and tribal artwork. I think of Tucker's lament, and press on.

I reached this purpose-built Victorian seaside resort late last night. It is uniquely situated on an east-coast promontory that faces west, thereby exposed to beautiful sunrises *and* sunsets, like the one me and another man, standing beside his car, marvelled at last night. "Truly extraordinary", he'd agreed. Rains were forecast, and I'd checked into a youth hostel run by a gregarious young family. This morning I awoke exhausted, unable to move my legs without pain. The rain was already lashing down. A day of rest was called for.

Fierce gales buffet the seafront. I join another couple of hikers hunkering behind a closed cockle stall, shielded from the barrage. Then past deserted grease tea caffs, where Morrissey's 'Everyday is Like a Sunday' plays to no one. Among the shingle beneath the cliffs one can find shark teeth, I've been told, but I forage ineffectually and move back into the town, past various tatty chippies, charity shops, anglers' grottos and "Britain's biggest joke shop". The unsavoury weather's having the greater laugh. Even the local sea-life centre had been knocked out by recent floods. "English weather!" a lady chuckles.

After a good lunch and conversation in a misplaced Wells Deli, I post my broken pannier home. At Fatbirds bikes I acquire another by Altura at a good price, and my mudguard, broken by yesterday's rigmarole, is repaired without charge. Defeated by the rain, I return to the hostel, where the news relays a predictable series of terrifying and misleading headlines. I root through the books.

Three years after the outbreak of the French Revolution, Admiral Nelson wrote to the Duke of Clarence about the conditions of labourers in this part of rural Norfolk. "They are really in want of everything to make life comfortable", he writes, and "[drink] nothing but water".

Between 1780 and 1830 the local population doubled. The enclosure of common land by profiteers, a series of bad harvests, rising rents, inflated Corn Law prices and growing unemployment finally led to the Swing Riots across Norfolk and the South East in 1830. Wealthy farmers employed labourers on insecure short-term contracts, often paying poverty wages. Poor Law payments, whose modern equivalent is the dole, were being cut, and many unemployed labourers were being shunted into punitive workhouses. Destitute, desperate, and with no other political outlet, the labourers started rioting over wages, wrote threatening letters to landowners and magistrates under the pseudonym Captain Swing, burnt down tithe barns (a tenth of a farm's produce was still given to the Church), attacked workhouses, and destroyed threshing machines, usually on Saturday nights after the pubs closed.

Nelson's unheeded warning is worded in ways reminiscent of John Ball, during the Peasants' Revolt. He complained that the gentry had "wines, spices, and fine bread, when we have only rye and the refuse of straw; and if we drink, it must be water". Like the assembled commons, and the labourers around Kett, their demands were not especially modern or new. They harked back to the old; they demanded a restitution of lost rights. Some, like Ball, used religion to hark back to a natural equality before God, Eden-like, which called into being a mythic prehistory.

In contesting the present, they restaged the past, resourcefully drawing out myths and stories to recommon the commons, to present a counter common sense. This had also been the case for the Magna Carta, whose constitutional importance primarily stemmed from its early 17th century repurposing by English parliamentarians. The rights of the commons had begun as a declarative demand and imposition, and were then secured through common law. The riots eventually died down, with hundreds of labourers either being executed or transported overseas, later followed by the East End drunks of Hadleigh Colony. Once populous, the Norfolk countryside depopulated as families migrated to the new industries of the Midlands, or overseas.

The sleepy villages and hedgerows of the Burnhams along the coastline are now wealthy second home terrain, respite of bankers, advertisers and property speculators, offering the ruse of unopposed traditional gentility. Profiting from the privatisation of public goods or preaching, like medieval clergy, the godliness of free markets, they are part of a modern enclosure of the commons. For more than two centuries now, the island remains a "family with the wrong members in control", as George Orwell put it, dominated by a parasitic rich "less useful to society than his fleas are to a dog".

But nothing suggests that the other family members would do anything constructive about it. The Swing rioters, like Kett or the trew commons, rose up without an alternative political and economic model. They believed that the king would side with them in rooting out a few bad apples and offering a few piecemeal reforms. They invested too much confidence in their leaders and not enough in themselves, and against every popular instinct, were led to believe that in politics, reason prevails. A peculiar fatalism now chokes the island, steeped in centuries-deep disappointment. It requires a deeper reading.

Early evening now. A plastic fork is insufficient to pierce these rubbery chips, but at least Mat's conversation is more consoling, as I dine in a kebab shop. The Q in QFC stands for Questionable. Eight years since leaving Turkey, he mulls returning. Into the

Golden Lion, Hunstanton's not-so-old oldest pub. The bartender talks of the difficulty of affording to live in the area. Round here, the Burnhams are nicknamed 'Chelsea-on-Sea'. "What can you do?" he asks rhetorically. I suggest a major social house-building programme, along conventional Keynesian lines. "Who would pay?" I suggest closing tax loopholes and increasing taxes on wealthy corporations and individuals, and he laughs, and gives me a knowing look.

I drift back down along the quiet promenade and into a deserted amusement arcade, still improbably open at this hour. A platoon of bow-tied youth polish screens of penny machines with looks of glum dejection. The Sex Pistols' 'Pretty Vacant' blares from all corners of the chamber, and combines with the flashing fruit machines into an overwhelming sensory attack. The scene contains in miniature all the contradictions of the island.

The pubs are deserted, and the only drinkers seem to be off-duty staff, evidence of a peculiar kind of unproductive, reciprocal local economy straight out of a Magnus Mills' novel. In another empty seaside boozer, staff curse as they play video games on phones, and the Rolling Stones filter over a scene of solitary tipplers. Meandering back to the hostel, I stop for one last nightcap in the Old Marine Bar, which is neither old nor has any obvious relation to the sea, being some distance from it.

Inside I talk with Sean, a Londoner whose life has taken him everywhere. He's roadied for The Prodigy ("good people") and Richard Ashcroft, and later Coldplay and McFly. Sound-checks for the latter were ear-splittingly painful. He travelled the world between tours, spending the money he made. After caring for his ill father he came here, to the sea, seeking escape. We laugh a lot and talk until late, trading stories. "The fish change with the months", he says, bass, mackerel and sharks migrating here in the summer, replacing cod and rays. Migration's natural, he adds. But "Nature" has little bearing on the imagination and desires of humankind. Little adds up.

CHAPTER 2

Made in England

*"Go see broken Britain, ha ha" – send-off in Corby, after
the offer of cocaine and stolen bicycles.*

Wheels growl under granulating grit. An elderly lady attempts
to navigate her oversized estate car into the car-park without
success. She perches over the wheel with hawk-like keenness, as
if trying to identify an unusual smell on the dashboard. After a
few attempts, she manages to take up just a space and a third.
"Morning Jill!" cries one of a group of men in the distance, as
she clambers out, sheepishly. They gad around in high-vis bibs
branded in supermarket heraldry, in the shadow of a distant
portico. "Morning Bob!"

Late morning, that time of day when the elderly and unemployed have the towns to themselves, the teenagers still in bed,
kids at school, and the not-so-young and middle-aged yawning
through work. The men are unusually aged, too wizened for this
kind of thing. One in the same baronial garb stamps out of the
store and approaches them. A half-smoked rollie is reunited with
a bearded lower lip. "Jus' quit, tha's it. I'm sicka been picked on."
The others look at him blankly. "Wha' about...?"

Some kind of local workfare scheme is in operation, coercing
men who'd be more familiar with the helms of a harvester or
haddock trawler into checkouts and shelving. One training
scheme after another, evading arbitrary DWP admin errors and
ill-excused sanctions. Under current rules he'll receive no benefits for three months for the impertinence of voluntarily leaving
a job. The cost of bringing a tribunal against the manager who

has hounded him out now costs around a month and a half's wages. How he'll feed himself now or pay his rent isn't clear, but no mystery. The local foodbank, the payday lender, the generosity of a sibling, or, if he's lucky to find one, another stupefying low-paid job. Before they can issue any consolations, he flicks his cigarette under Mrs Biddie's car, and stomps out.

In the hostel that morning, Mischa, a young architecture student, described a vision to me. He'd pedestrianise Parliament Square and build a vast structure at its centre, towering over Churchill and Jan Smuts, dedicated to representing freedom. It'd be a vast thing, three or four storeys high. Kids would climb around it, tourists would queue up, climb for a pose, survey the Westminster panorama. It would be an international symbol of the country's commitment to freedom, to liberalism in home affairs and the dismantling of totalitarianism overseas.

It was a gloriously naïve, wonderful proposition. In the public library, aisles of the unemployed browse Facebook or Reed, icons clicked and noses picked. Freedom. But many confuse the opportunity to choose between soap powder A or soap powder B with the ability to live one's life without coercive intrusion, or with equal access to the resources and opportunities of a wealthy, developed economy, from midwife to mortuary.

But what use is a history lesson? Another kind of darkness shrouds the scene. I pedal out towards Kings Lynn, the thickety Norfolk country zinging with scents of hawthorn and bergenia that grow about here. Grouse potter confusedly along the verges like inebriated farmhands. Lanes wind through one hamlet then another, each crowned with its own medieval church the colour and character of forest deer, regarding the passer slowly and benignly. Then Sandringham, one of the royal family's many holiday homes, tours crowd the manicured grounds, Americans ogling this fiction of dear old England. South, past stud farms close to the abandoned village of Babingley, the rural terrain eventually greys into the sluggish suburbs of Kings Lynn.

Cool clouds hang low, snagging the Sky dishes and TV aerials that crown these suburb streets. Red brick or yellow, all of one style, early 20th century, bay window if yer lucky, backyard conservatory, detached from the selfish fucking bastards next door with their noisy kids/dog/parties/washing machine (delete as appropriate). Security's a priority. Timber palisades, domestic CCTV, the street-side conversation robustly unfriendly. Mood: stalemate. Cutting along the cycle route, the empty parks and disused playgrounds give way to a town centre with every chain shop you might've missed in every other British town.

I rove around, following the shoppers in the pedestrianised precinct, stopping in various shops for supplies. Exchanges begin testy but give way to laughter. "On that? You are joking." Seeking out what's got this area biting its upper lip. "To neither condemn, complain nor lament these things, but first understand them." Spinoza's dictum. The disorganised mishmash of chain stores, the poorly organised traffic systems and overpriced, mediocre housing. Like Ipswich, Basildon or Yarmouth, British Town Centres, places more realistic of contemporary life than these rural idylls and holiday hamlets before. Real, but without any sense of being reality. Places without any cultural representation. Places where people go to do or experience things that have little relation to their locations. The reassurance of a Big Mac in a McDonald's that looks and tastes the same as everywhere else. Pawnshop or phoneshop, six bars of chocolate for 99p, treats to anticipate.

Psychologically escape life on rainy island. "English summer!" says another lady again, the clouds looking constipated. Meteorological pessimism remains the most common supernatural belief-system. "They've got it in for us!" she says, packing bananas and tomatoes into a brown paper bag, flicked over her wrists and neatly knotted. It's hard to ascertain who, or what, she means.

Lynn has a history of great wealth, trading overseas in the

pre-capitalist Hanseatic League, but there's no record of it, and by the old Ouse, one of the few wharf-side buildings of any real age belongs to a company operating the local probation service. I pedal on.

More confusing traffic systems follow. Grit teeth and chin down to the monotony of the hard shoulder, westward into Lincolnshire, riding towards Sleaford. The landscape changes rapidly. No longer the wistful Broads, untamed, untouched, nor the piny forests around Lynn. The horizon's been bulldozed and blasted out, replaced with toughened expanses growing rapeseed, wheat, peas, all on an epic scale. Everything put to work. Greenhouses span the scape, whilst factories churn out Scottish salmon, Danish lager and Irish butter. Freight trucks rattle past, to and from the out-of-sight depots and distribution complexes that feed and clothe the island.

I know nothing of this kind of country. One small town then another, each gruffly alike: Sutton Bridge, Holbeach, and into Spalding. Places where King John once lost the crown jewels in a flash-flood, now a plethora of chippies and kebabberies, hairdressers, boozers and, compared to Norfolk, very few churches. The same pent-up, pissed-off air as the London-Essex sprawl. Most of these same boozers look closed up and there's few people round on entry into Spalding. I'm in a part of England that's never been listened to before.

Take Spalding. On arrival it seems like another depressed market town, akin to Lynn. A paunch of poundshops and timbered-up pubs are belted in by rings of warehouses, trade stores and bungalowlalia. Bookies and takeaways cater some wants. But it's also got a fair number of *Polski sklep*s, and the employment agencies list their ads in Polish on fluorescent neon cards. The few people I pass, mostly men, don't speak English. But nor do they all speak Polish either. There are Latvians and Lithuanians here, and Slovaks, and from other Baltic, Central and Eastern European states most English people couldn't locate. Here they are, picking the nation's fruit and veg or processing it in vast hangars. They seem frozen out of the twee image of "Buying British", yet essential to the low price of spinach, strawberries and much else beside. Local elections across eastern England return increasingly anti-European candidates.

There's an issue of low pay here, of overseas workers taking too low a liveable wage for local-born workers to bother competing. But there's a cultural one too, a fear that places are being "overrun", as another migrant will (paradoxically) put it tomorrow. A worry that a set of modern English working class cultures is disappearing, the indirect effect of major growers and factories being free to maximise their profits at great social expense. Then there are cuts to organisations that help migrants integrate, cuts to community and adult education, and a reactionary press that is convincingly blaming free market capitalism's effects on poor migrants themselves. And those hectoring middle classes that conflate English national identification with racism, whose hostility to the 'lumpen proletariat' they no longer bother veiling. No, this is a commons on the political move, and it includes those migrant workers within it, who are also without mainstream political and cultural representation. The area's banality cloaks it with invisibility.

I want to talk to them, but there's no Polish boozer I can locate. I cycle past exhausted-looking, skinny labourers shuffling out of the centre, beer bottles clanking inside stuffed plastic bags. Back to the home they make for themselves, that safe living-room space. Later in the journey, when I've acquired the brass-neck to interview all and sundry, I'd've pulled over, asked him *what* and *why*. But everything's still new, unfamiliar. There's a large Romany population in Spalding too, out of easy reach. Systematically discriminated against by local government officials and routinely subjected to racist attitudes in the popular press, I can understand their reticence. Not every community's an open-door.

Through Bourne, another similar-looking town. Nothing is being said, everywhere silent. This is the first bit of England that feels entirely detached from London and its wealth-orbit. Even the experiences of Poles or Traveller descendants I've known in London seem divorced from this hard-working, unskilled way of life out here. No bars, restaurants or universities in these parts.

Nighttime, Thurlby. These vast flat expanses are ill-suited for the discretion required for wild camping. Fortunately there's a youth hostel in the small village. Showered and fed, I stroll out to the village's one pub, as deserted as all else. Two local women enter and find a table. Sugar-sweet fruit ciders, white-wine spritzers, complaints about "pikies and their pushchairs". Dark as things can be, the road draws closer to the contradictions of the island.

Let's play a game. If at home, this'll require a little imagination, but is possible for bus or car passengers, be they in Peterborough or Penge, Perth or Port Talbot. It's called British Suburb Bingo. Heads down! Now, with the next house, can you see...

- A paved-over front garden, vacant?
- A rose-bush in that garden, all leaves removed?
- A four by four or other oversized car, unaccustomed to marsh or mire?
- A rustic-looking mass-produced house-name, e.g. Ivy Cottage or Riverdene?
- A bird-feeder, without seed and unattended?
- Pseudo-municipal or cod-cheery signs, e.g. "Beware the dog wife", "Smile you're on CCTV"?
- Aggressive handwritten or large Times New Roman warnings about parking, dog-fouling?
- Mock-Tudor gabling, windows or window-frames on a 20th century house, detached?
- National flag, upstairs window?

- Chintzy ornaments on downstairs window-sill, e.g. china frogs, gnomes, teddies, ceramic plates?
- To get a full house, does this building look so similar to every other you've passed that, were you blindfolded, driven in a car for many hours and then dropped off again by the very same house, you'd swear it was an entirely different house, in a different county...?

Bingo!

There's a particular code of Britishness that's reappearing in town and country. It's in a common style of housing, just as it's in a common style of clothing, with prescriptive gender hair lengths and variants of shoe, but it exceeds both. It expresses a basic social need to fit in and look like others, avoid being ostracised. But it also reflects the limits of the choices and freedoms supposedly offered. The out-of-town retail parks and supermarkets sell a similar kind of existence to the high street chains. Objects from China express personal identities in a narrow range of style, limited by economies of scale.

Yet England at least still dreams of these rural idylls. Despite being a predominantly urbanised country, there's a desire to bring as much of the country into one's suburban semi, surrounded by gardens and pets.

Listening to cool wind whistling through the trees, there's something comforting about that rural imagery. Snaking out to Peterborough, through the villages of Baston, Market Deeping and Helpston, home of John Clare, much suggests no trespass of the last hundred years.

And at the blacksmith's shop his hour will stand
To talk of 'Lunun' as a foreign land,
For from his cottage door in peace or strife
He ne'er went fifty miles in all his life.

Clare's verse still applies to these gentle scenes, the gloomy churches around Langtoft, of "croodling" across flooded fords and fields of "mire and sludge", past "fluskering" songbirds and gypsy camps. It's still in the accent, one of compressed vowels and elongation, like the Tata Steel driver I pass near Peterborough: "'w't m't?'"

But these rustic enclaves muddy the prevailing confusion. Ivy Cottage and Riverdene... Clare's cottager might today have a job in a food-processing factory, his blacksmith a truck mechanic, annual holidays to the same resort in Lanzarote. Both would live in Peterborough, which I now approach, a town with contradictions built into its infrastructure. Conservative-voting but overwhelmingly working class, most of its population live in a featureless suburban sprawl outside its centre, like Werrington, where I pass, despite being surrounded by open country. A postwar New Town built up through European and Asian migration, there are no signals of flag-tribalism.

It's quite nice actually, once one gets past the endless underpasses, overpasses and model roundabouts of the 60s townplanners, and beyond the retail parks produced by their 80s and 90s successors. The surfeit of concrete surfaces has snuffed out attempts at graffiti, the task of tagging it all too exhausting to contemplate. Built on the back of the brick trade, the older centre's defined by a luminescent sandstone, and appears wellheeled, on the make. Wandering round an animated square with a fountain at its centre, a Norman cathedral with impressively high gables and arches nearby, a preacher shouts down hell and sin to bemused indifference.

All of it, these suburbs, shops and houses, the rural and the urban, these food-industries and industrial-food, this conflation of rustic and domestic, privacy with personal expression, cultural liberalism with migrant-phobia, what does it amount to? A riddle.

The holding of two or more contrary beliefs has a more precise psychological term: cognitive dissonance. In 1957, Festinger and Carlsmith came up with a boring experiment. Its political implications remain tantalisingly unexplored. Participants had to spend an hour turning spools on pegs, and removing spools from pegs then putting them back. They were then asked to convince another subject to participate in the study, by pretending it was really interesting. Some were paid $20 for this, others $1, and a control group was asked not to lie. The scientists then measured the participants' enjoyment of the overall exercise.

All found it very boring, except those paid a dollar, who said it was very interesting and enjoyable. The $20 group were able to justify lying (the "dissonance") by the high monetary reward, from which they could detach their internal attitudes. But the lack of meaningful reward for the $1 group forced them to change their internal attitudes in order to relieve the stress caused by the conflict between bored attitude and persuasive behaviour. They left with their attitudes transformed; they genuinely enjoyed the experiment.

Induced compliance. Wherever someone is coerced with little reward into a determined behaviour or mindset they cannot reasonably avoid, they will persuade themselves of its necessity and utility in order to relieve stress, and may even come to champion it. Is it fair that the $1 group didn't get $20, or that they had to lie? No, but if one must take aboard a falsehood and make it one's own so that one's mind is at peace, that will happen, and reason will not interrupt it. British liberals and the Left find themselves goggle-eyed each election by the desertion of working class support, but a swing of 'shy Tories' may not be so mysterious. Wealth inequality's no university experiment. Something of that $1 experience is coded into the physical and mental programming.

I push out of Peterborough, still confused. Past one of the island's twenty thousand steam-train museums, the rains of the previous night reveal their mischief. Roads are flooded. I decide to follow a cycle route, but it leads into a cul-de-sac. Worse is to come. I push along a half-constructed road as another deluge begins. Soon the rain washes with the exposed clay to create a quagmire. My wheels become trapped in the sludge, and it takes some effort to clear out the chain.

There are many words for mud in English. If it's watery like brown ale, then it's *blash*; if sticky and stinky, *gawm*; when wet, *cludgy*; and what of *loam, smirch, stabble, gumbo, adobe, swill, slake, sleech, slop, slosh, slime, slurry, slush, clod, clag*, or *parafango*? Some capture the onomatopoeia of wellies in mud, others are just delightfully odd. This particular mud would be called *clart* in the North East (or just *shite*). These inane thoughts occupy the mind for the next two hours as I pedal into the pisswind.

Somewhere along the way I've crossed the border but, blinded by the rain, I didn't spot it. I reach Corby, an independent Scottish county-town located in the East Midlands. Defined by its huge steelworks and Scots community, it's a grubby and tough town. I drift around 60s shopping parades and retail parks, before homing in on a chippie selling haggis, black pudding and copious Irn Bru. Outside, listen to the accent here, a uniquely Corby conflation of Midlands consonantal drawl with Glaswegian vowels and inflections, distinguished at the end of a phrase or when pronouncing O(ch).

Inside the Corby Candle, old fellas sit around the bar in silent vigil of the barmaid's figure, with the rapt attention of Modigliani. Others lark around the pool table, some ex-steel workers, many unemployed. Gruff, friendly. Rounds of mild move round the bar, feet navigating the *gawm* emanating from the flooded bogs. The barmaid and landlady complain that the area's "overrun" with Eastern Europeans, but there's little malice. "Let them get on with it", says the older lady. "I just don't like the ones claiming", the younger replies.

I'm confused by the contradictions here, being among Scottish immigrants or their second-generation descendants in a town now marked by unemployment. But they are "us", this is "ours", not the "Polish" who don't drink here, and few know, but who are still said to be "taking over". This has been said of almost every migrant community, be they Irish, Jewish, Jamaican or Pakistani. But somehow the talk against European workers is much freer than I'd expected, but with less hostility and violence than one might also imagine. I'm welcomed here, also an outsider, in on the banter. I suspect that once the ice is broken via weather or football talk, a Polish farmhand, carer or machine-operator would also be warmly embraced here. But the communities live separately, and myths fill the void of familiarity.

I get talking to a young local man with the same Corby Caledonian accent. Born locally, his family moved up to Stranraer ("full of junkies') after a relative was murdered. It's hard to gather why he's back here. We talk about familiar Irish towns we trace descent from, where everyone's related and the "priest's yer granddad". I'm offered more drinks, help carrying my gear, a place to stay, even a free line of coke to see me off. It's my lasting regret that I didn't take him up on the latter two. "Everyone knows each other here, it's a community." As I'm leaving the empty car-park of a mattress store, he whispers that he can help me get a better bike. How? Paying a tramp to nick one. "You can ge' anythin' here for twenty poun'."

I've also been given directions to a big estate on the edge of town, where there's a very special chippie. I pass through shabby housing estates, people all-too-polite in their directions, til under a semi-derelict 60s shopping parade I find it. It's off the menu at the Viking fish bar, but after a cheeky smile I'm given what looks like a battered saveloy. It tastes like warm chocolate ice cream in a crispy cocoon. Who'd've guessed a deep-fried Mars Bar would be so delicious? Washed down with another can of Irn Bru, arteries straining under the pressure, I'm ready for the rains.

Ten miles pass in a calorific jiffy, hills disappearing into the horizon. Cattle and sheep blur with the hedgerows that blur with the A6 that blurs with Kibworth that blurs into Leicester.

Into the "Cultural Quarter", its rich industrial and architectural heritage scrubbed up and rebranded for Leicester's bright young things. My friend Laura lives in a converted hosiery factory with her partner Ben and friend Caitlin. Over dinner and more beers we continue the discussion set out in Corby, of this cognitive dissonance called Britain.

What's life like in this place? If you want to make a person laugh, ask them. It's my opening gambit. Each conversation begins with a series of jokes. Life seems like a series of accidents and coincidences, with most interlocutors unsure why they're here or what exactly they're supposed to be doing. "I don't know what I'll be when I grow up", jokes Ben the next morning. But few subscribe to morbid fate. Twenty, thirty, fifty, eighty: we will grow up, eventually.

My friends depart to their respective academic jobs, and I follow, plenty of leads to pursue. The first being this Cultural Quarter, a regenerated hub for Leicester's creative class. Roaming around the aspirational apartments and office blocks, it's hard to gather what exactly's being created here. Wealth no doubt, but not the kind that'll warm your toes or impress your lover. Property is the island's new gold standard, and its ownership and improvement the new form of religious observation. But what else to Leicester?

There's another kind of quartering nearby. I wander through St Matthew's Estate, England's most income-deprived area until the last decade. It's a strange place, isolated from the rest of the city by thick arterial roads where trucks and transits roar past. Its location is akin to a leper-colony, and the crude concrete of 60s planners faces inward, flats piled high above each other. It seems to imprison the energies of tenants as much as to identify to the rest of the city where the other half live. Yet there's a friendliness in the air here, wafts of nag champa and boiled rice, bubbles of chatter in Somali and Tigrinya by a launderette and community centre, signs in neat Arabic.

Down Belgrave Road is the "Golden Mile", site of Leicester's bustling Indian community. The city has the largest Diwali celebrations outside of India. Sari stores nudge next to opulent jewellery stores, sweetshops and bakeries, curried aromas travelling out from the restaurants. But there's also Portuguese grocers, English chippies, Chinese takeaways and angling shops. Non-league English hip hop blares out from white vans driven by young Asians. A statue of Mahatma Gandhi surveys the scene, an open-air exhibition of the island's diversity.

This clash of quirks and scenes is a continual surprise. On the side of a budget supermarket is a plaque commemorating the birth of the tragic John Merrick, the "Elephant Man" exhibited in Victorian freakshows. A local exhibition recounts the life of Daniel Lambert, who at fifty stone was for some time the fattest recorded man in history. A jail-keeper and dog-breeder, like Merrick, he ended up surviving by selling himself as entertainment. A pre-welfare parable for our post-welfare TV freakshows.

I head over to the Attenborough Tower in the city's university, nicknamed the "cheese grater" for its stature and slanting windows. Inside I just about navigate its bizarre Paternoster lift, a continually-running step-on-step-off thing that precedes the days of health and safety. There are awesome views from the top. I tootle out, back around through its pedestrianised shopping precincts and huge market. This is not a British Town Centre, but something far more commendable.

We have Lambert and Gandhi, but what of Simon de Montfort, the 13th century Earl of Leicester who nearly overthrew the king? A small statue, hidden above a church. He established the first elected parliament, including the "commons" for the first time – male merchants and knights, giving political representation to the towns. Betrayed by other ambitious barons, he and his followers were ambushed and put to the sword six months later. There's little of Richard III either, though the local rags scrutinise his ongoing excavation. I sneak into the car-park of the local social services, where diggers are pulling out his body. No passing stranger could satisfactorily answer me. "Where? Dunno." Google had the answer. The confusion's suggestive of a deeper void of power in the landscape, skeletons turning over in their graves, ghosts abroad the land, turds in the water-closet.

A sweet malty fug drifts out of Everard's brewery on the edge of town. Like the British Sugar complex in Peterborough, and the industrial farming and manufacturing all around me, I recognise something else that doesn't fit with my prejudices. I'd expected everything north of Colchester to be a rusting, deindustrialised mess. "We used to make things", the common lament of a faded ex-imperial island now dispatched to the dogs. Something's being made here. But it's not clear who's making it, or who profits from it. Steel palisades round the complex, CCTV posts leering out.

Riding into Warwickshire, the country becomes increasingly hilly. Villages cheerfully gallivant past like children chasing bunny rabbits. Glen Parva, Slang Spinney – could one feel hateful in a place called Slang Spinney? For no more than a few seconds, surely. Wheat stalks burdened by the weight of their ears. I scutter along the ancient Fosse Way, a Roman road that once linked Exeter to Lincoln, the western boundary of their empire.

These rustic reveries are interrupted again at the edge of the vast Rolls Royce factory outside Coventry, surrounded by an equally empty and overdeveloped technology park. The inventor of the jet engine, Frank Whittle, hails from nearby Earlsdon. The first modern bicycles, Triumph motorbikes, Peugeot and Rover cars, London Taxis, Coventry's past is interwoven with its high-tech manufacturing history. But I'll hear later that most of the automobile and aerospace industries have cut down their workforces and disappeared altogether, the profit now in luxury Aston Martins, Jaguar racers and space-age weaponry. Much is being made here, but beyond the needs or reach of the surrounding towns.

Familiar rings of suburbia: light industrial warehouses, retail parks, red-brick semis with vast driveways. Into Coventry, I pass a lady on horseback, an atavistic echo of Lady Godiva, riding through the streets naked in protest against tax injustices, pre-Pussy Riot. Approaching the centre, the scape's a little more bruised than Leicester, but seems to reassert itself against its own ugliness. Think of Two-Tone records, Jamaican ska meets British rock, the Ghost Town where all the clubs are closing down. That moment in the early 80s, when Cov's motor industries were already collapsing, seems on loop in Ansty, its run-down pubs and closed shops suggesting slow recovery. "You could see the frustration and anger in the audience", Jerry Dammers remembers. Men rant from their transit vans at me, in a place where there's nothing to eat except kebabs and supermarket sandwiches. Or the chain pub carvery, the same everywhere. Indigestion and heavy drinking.

But there are working men's clubs still open. Dave, who I'll meet in the centre later, will tell me about his dad's involvement in one. They're democratically run by a council, and in exchange for a small membership fee you can get some of the cheapest beer in town. Profits are put back into the club, making the drinks even cheaper. Once the refuge of working men, the decline of factories has shut down many, and made the rest seem parochial or unfriendly. Neither's justified. Ansty's club survives but has been rebranded, offering dining, business conference facilities and jazz nights, indicating shifting tastes, even cultures of class.

Through Walgrave and Stoke, more pinched working class suburbs, and through the city's confusing traffic system into a smart, confident metropolis. Coventry was largely erased by the Luftwaffe, its renowned medieval town centre and cathedral all casualties in the fire. Some of the cathedral's walls remain and its ruins can be surveyed. At its altar is a wooden cross that fell intact from the flames, an unlikely myth that the town clutches to. Its spirit is peace, recovery without seeking revenge. The modern cathedral adjacent is equally wonderful, vast tapestries and ethereal lights, and a sculpture by Epstein, two patina-green figures attached to its external wall, the winged muscular figure of archangel Michael, spear in hand, over the shackled, subdued Satan, confident without being aggressive.

Skateboards skid and clatter across the vast plaza around it. Dave waves in the distance. It's a pleasure to see him, one of my closest friends, the first familiar face on the road. After drifting round awhile, we settle into the Whitefriars where, with his partner Helen, we compare observations.

The university has undertaken a silent coup in the city. Seemingly all the major buildings near the cathedral belong to this expanding empire of higher education. Heavy industry replaced with knowledge-production, perhaps? Pubs sell food and drinks for eye-wateringly cheap prices. Both work in the university in different kinds of teaching. The university attracts a large number of non-EU overseas students, often charged far greater tuition fees than home students. University departments are being crudely merged together, with less experienced staff taking on greater teaching roles as senior staff apply for one lucrative commercial grant after another. Universities make increasingly bombastic sales promotions about careers, skills and global prospects that cannot be reasonably fulfilled. Dave and Helen talk of a tightrope walk over vastly different cultural barriers often in the same classroom, from the oral culture of Omani engineers to the deferential, text-based learning of young Chinese scholars.

What's changing? Something. This knowledge-production is becoming increasingly marketised, as universities compete to sell dream careers and experiences. International students tend to be from the wealthier classes of their home states. Students show off selfies eating dinner with the Prime Minister. Teachers are offered bribes, they tell me. Corruption could easily seep in, as staff pay is effectively cut through hourly-paid lecturing and short-term contracts. The aggressive impulses of business management are uprooting whatever cultures of learning-for-its-own sake still remain, with the imperative to win grants and publish quantity over quality. Higher education is becoming a more cerebral extension of the UK's bloated service sector, fixated with efficiency outputs and consumer choice.

Though the problem's nationwide, it seems apt that this arises in the Midlands, where so much making and manufacture has disappeared, the fortunes of many towns now pegged onto students. But an hour's drive south from England's motor city is Oxford, with its dreamy spires, High Table, Bullingdon Club and a far older, pervasive and discreet culture of elite patronage, privilege and power. A world apart from Cov. Few seem happy with this new settlement. But it's unclear where the fences of enclosure actually are, and there has not yet been articulated a persuasive alternative for a publicly-owned and protected higher education system. Hope is in short supply, pessimism the mood.

We drink up. It's not been our usual kind of conversation. No setting the world to rights tonight. Things are murkier and less clear. Something remains unaccounted for.

There's an oft-quoted line by Edmund Burke that makes me want to gouge my left eye out. "It is more easy to change an administration than to reform a people." The so-called "temper of a people" is the true basis of a given political constitution. Raze every church, castle and alehouse to the ground, and the English would regroup in their Range Rovers at some country pile, and over much hawdah-hawdahs, frothing flagons and tweedy panjandrums, naturally restore their hereditary monarchy and noble houses of parliament, in the same way that, were you to leave stumps, bats and a ball by some scrubby green, they'd unconsciously form a perennially disappointing cricket team.

A question lingers. What's in a *people*? Dave has warned me against reading too much into buildings and walls, in the unlikely projections of passing strangers. Yet the sheer pessimism commonly expressed is remarkable. "It's got a lovely history... Shame it's a shithole now", Ian will tell me, later, in Wolverhampton. It stands for every comment of the last few days.

Wander into a pub, ask the person adjacent at the bar about life in this place. At first, jokes: "Why would you want to come here?" Subject this pessimism to further questioning, and two tendencies emerge: a sincere belief that the area's fallen on hard times, usually due to recent European migrants; or that actually the area's not so bad, but just has a bad reputation. A kind of negative pride within this pessimism. "A shithole, but it's mine."

This pessimistic temperament suggests an outlook trained to see the worst in others. The outlook that positive political and social change is impossible, or, in the current framework, unattainable, and so therefore undesirable. That in any given situation, the worst of two outcomes will occur. Hence the utility of remaining with what currently works (badly) rather than trying out anything new, which would no doubt be catastrophically worse.

What's the root of this pessimism? "Look around you", a typical reply. Images: decaying ex-industrial town filled with benefits-scrounging Europeans; TV news of latest child molestation; foreign natural disaster or story indicating that elsewhere things are *even worse*; historical narrative of decline due to military inaction leading to loss of empire; health service in crisis; politicians of every stripe fiddling their expenses; online social world of insecure pride – latest achievement, pouty selfies, outraged opinions. Incorrect but convincing, even reassuring, images.

In that suggestive reply, *look around you*, there's a premise that this pessimism is encoded into these ways of living and the landscape itself. Perhaps one could archaeologically excavate this temper to discover if and whether there was some earlier event, hidden or repressed from memory. Perhaps a moment of defeat, of being left with a dollar instead of twenty, finding yourself telling lies to your children.

Perhaps it's something else entirely. *A cyclist walks into a bar…*

Reading some political parable out of all this may be the start of an equally bad joke. There are more straightforward possibilities: a common disavowal for enthusiasm and bragging, or a fair reflection on the island's erratic and impulsive weather, applied to other affairs. I set out to test this.

Sky is steely grey and sore, the air as damp as flannels. I push the bike out through the red-brick back-to-backs of Earlsdon and back onto the road. The terrain's bumpy from the outset, the flatness of Essex and East Anglia deceiving me into overestimating my stamina. Past mock-Tudor villas and the aspirational complexes of Warwick University, one sees petty class conflicts again zoned into the scapes. Then sheer countryside, back along the Fosse Way, an obsessively straight road seemingly etched into the earth by an orbital laser-beam. Pissing behind a hedge, I notice a sign pointing one way to a wedding, another to a crematorium, life's existential majesty captured on a country byway.

Nursing homes and Christadelphian chapels give way to a Georgian spa town. Throngs of tourists cleave the lanes and boulevards of Leamington, selfie sticks and empty backpacks drifting aimlessly by the Roman Pump Rooms and the old bathing complexes. For centuries people came for the healing powers of the water, giving the lie to the novelty of New Age cures. Now, the desire for a mere day's distraction. "Back to the coach by 3!" It's a sweet if somewhat quiet and slow-seeming place, with more buzz in the south towards Heathcote, the barbers, street drinkers and Polski skleps adding some edge.

Undulating fields of corn and wheat. Back on the road, south this time, to the quiet market town of Kineton. More ghost-hunting. Somewhere among those fields, the battle of Edgehill took place. It was so inconsequential and ill-coordinated that it reflects the wider course of the English Civil War, an island-wide conflict barely known by the public beyond the names Cromwell, Cavalier and Roundhead. Over three-and-a-half centuries ago, it presented the opportunity for the commons to establish a genuinely democratic republic with a written constitution, under which all would be equal. The term "Leveller" – previously used for those who levelled fences enclosing common land – was repurposed to describe the politics of a large movement of soldiers and citizenry, whose demands were articulated by figures like Thomas Rainsborough and John Lilburne. Their "Agreement of the People" demanded equality before the law, democracy, fair taxation and an end to "the exercise of an unlimited or arbitrary power". Many believed that the world was about to end. It enables a peculiar combination of puritanical iconoclasm and political radicalism to occur with intense religious zealotry, as much Red Army as modern-day jihadi.

At Edgehill in 1642, the opposing sides of King and Parliament more or less stumbled across each other, and began to brawl. Many were unequipped to fight and so fled the scene, looting from the other side's baggage as they ran. Cromwell died seven years after his outright victory in 1651, having become no more than a military dictator over a disunited country, the Levellers either shot dead or dispersed. Aside from massacring the Irish, warring with the Dutch and invading Jamaica, his Protectorate had undertaken little. Mitigating a power vacuum, one part of the army recalls the King's son to retake the throne. The island's experiment in republicanism was over, now shrouded in the romance of roundheads and cavaliers and historical re-enactment societies, and pub quiz questions on who banned dancing and Christmas. It concealed the common nature of those beliefs in a collective equality and freedom that remain here, dormant, in these $1 communities.

Ye olde sweete shoppes, Tudorbethan on crystal meth, the next-level Shakespearian dross of Stratford-upon-Avon is another bold contrast with the preceding towns. Cars and coaches have swamped the centre with the inertia of an occupying army. Fish, chips and ice cream are on sale by the bustling canal, a lively atmosphere. The Royal Shakespeare Company's modern-day temple by the Avon captures the contradictions of the bard's birthplace. It combines a Victorian workhouse with a baroque cathedral, its high-vaulted apse and imposing red-bricks exuding the weight of his standard over centuries of English-learning and the uncritical awe given to his reputation. Along with Spitfires and the speeches of Churchill, Shakespeare's served up on the island's citizenship-catechism with some dedication. "Foolery, sir, does walk around the orb like the sun; it shines everywhere."

Escape the tourists! Cycling out past the train station, Stratford's other side is revealed, down-at-heel and with familiar retail-park brands. Through upmarket Henley, retired colonels and range cooker territory, then threading through the Arden forest and its minty airs. Terrain and tongues shift by the mile. Eastwood, and now the West Midlands accent is discernible. Fishing lakes, two lads lackadaisically disregarding the rod to tug on a spliff. Cannabinoid lazy haze, bucolic. In Hollywood, dense suburbia, an Indian shopkeeper compares pools results with a local man. I'm noticing a subtle shift in manners too, a greater ease in conversation. It is no less friendly than anywhere else, but more gentle and patient, and conducive to conversation.

So this is the West Midlands, not so much a region as a continuous urban area composed of deindustrialised towns and cities, from Coventry in the east to Wolverhampton in the west, and Birmingham in its centre. But do not call it Greater Birmingham. If anything it is uncentred, sharing only a common code of suburban semis, satellite dishes, bird-feeders and passive aggressive warnings. But with continual surprises.

For one, accents transform in a matter of miles. Brummies lilt, singsong-like; Wolves folk by contrast are nicknamed "yam yams" for their elongated, birdy elocution. The Black Country extends only as far as Tipton and Dudley, itself with its own codes. *Ah bist ya*? The vast industries that boomed from the early 19th century drew in workers from the surrounding country, blighted by land enclosure and poverty, this accent fusing elements of East Anglia, Yorkshire and Wales, producing a wacky and distinctive hybrid.

Past Selly Oak there's Bourneville, a model workers' village built in the late 19th century by George Cadbury for his chocolate workers. The houses are all of Arts and Crafts style, delighting in their own prettiness, and the village was supplied with public baths, a museum, schools and chapels and, of course, no pubs. This lager lacuna should well be chided, but Bourneville achieves something that its neighbours do not: the construction of a community, not merely a set of neighbouring houses.

But avoid sugary sentimentality, which Bourneville also flogs inexpensively. Through Harborne and into the integrated traffic systems of Dudley. Capital of the Black Country, it's now marked by the absence of industry. The town centre's dead, much boarded up and empty, trade terminated by the opening of an out-of-town mall, one man tells me. He talks about Sir Lenny Henry, an oddly apt symbol for Dudley. He grew up in a multicultural yet racially divided town, starting out (regretfully) in the Black and White Minstrel Show, becoming popular for his stand-up comedy, putting racial difference on stage, enabling many to confront it, laugh about it, and in the process understand it. He now does Shakespeare and has raised millions for charitable causes, helping establish Comic Relief. People passively watch television specials whilst donating money to distant issues, their causes or economic reasons for persistence never explained, be it Redcar or Rwanda. Charities like those I've worked in are often dependent on grants from Comic Relief or the Lottery, as successive governments cut taxes for the wealthy and cover the shortfall with slashed social spending. Lenny Henry is also the face of a ubiquitous budget hotel chain that is *everywhere*, usually beside a chain pub or indistinct retail park, places that eliminate their own placeness. There's a Premier Inn a short drive from Merry Hill, the distant mall blamed for Dudley centre's sorry state. All accounts suggest it makes a good trade.

Industrial warehouses, suburban semis, retail parks and thoughtfully designed but quartered council estates. Sun setting, I reach Wolverhampton, its suburban periphery more straitened than its neighbours. The scrap timber merchant and the bailiff enjoy a good trade. The town centre is impressive, with some beautiful civic architecture, from the city gallery and vast civic hall to a large library and a web of still-beautiful streets. The 19th century was its heyday, a manufacturing hub patronised by the Mander family, but unlike Dudley there's still some buzz to its centre.

Students parade down the lanes in tiger and panda onesies, near-empty bottles of spirits twisting and twirling with the dexterity of marching batons. I pedal past plastic-bat goth bars, Afro-Caribbean takeaways, Polish men carrying sleeping bags and cans of beer, bored kids arsing around outside McDonald's, and the mental revelry of karaoke in McGhee's, drunks brawling and caterwauling, right by where I find Kerry, my friend and host for the night. We drink with her mates, who brief me on the Black Country, and these histories of making things and not-making things. With its overlapping histories and time-zones, I wonder where it fits into this temper of pessimism. The next day proves instructive.

Bicycles, locks and furniture. Barstool obituaries of each passing town usually list its manufactured products in the same tones as a person's religious views or romantic life. Regardless of whether their profits were ever fairly distributed among workers, it's clear that people collectively participate in the cultural identity industry affords. We used to make things... Deindustrialisation isn't experienced simply as a kind of ugliness to the landscape, but more like a trauma in its collective mindset, like a death or messy estrangement.

I have breakfast with Emma, Kerry's flatmate. She's a part-time pub manager, part-time teacher, educating young mums and the unemployed in budgeting and childcare in nearby Tipton. "People complain about scrounging, about workshy lazy bastards. Most people I meet, they're just trying to get by."

It's a contemporary Catch-22: many lack basic qualifications, and there are very few new jobs in the area. Beyond a certain age, adult education isn't free, and few can afford to up sticks and leave the area. Those jobs that appear pay so little that even remaining on the dole with housing benefit makes more sense. "I see exactly why they do it. They play the system in the nicest possible way." Working tax credits supplement poverty wages, though this comes with the added shame of being a benefits claimant. For single parents, there's little work that fits around school times. Emma works with young mums, teaches them long multiplication and compound interest using examples from hire purchase stores like Bright House. Gifted with freedom, I head out.

"Ya lock yer car doors go'n through", Ian had said of Heath Town last night. A no-go area, a poverty zone. Like St Matthews in Leicester, it is a large planned estate from the 1960s, annexed from the rest of the city and any useful amenities by a snaking arterial road. Dark blocks and pedestrian overpasses block out the horizon on approach. Kids kick balls about and hip hop blares out from different corners. The local council has sent virtually all its asylum-seeking refugees to the estate, thereby concentrating poverty and unemployment in one location.

What do these estates tell us about life today? Lynsey Hanley wrote of growing up on nearby Chelmsley Wood, describing the isolation of living on a dislocated and soulless complex of featureless housing, a "proletarian hell" and prison of the poor. Cheaply built at the time and badly designed, prone to damp and antisocially high, there's substance to her grievance. These estates fail where Bourneville succeeds, treating its tenants as equal members of a given community, with a natural right to pleasant surrounds and places of leisure as well as central heating and indoor toilets. But the second-generation tenants of these estates have no memory of the overcrowded, insanitary slums these modern blocks replaced, and no access to the initial affections of their first tenants. As James Meek rightly observes, council housing "went from something that was much better than tenants expected to something much worse than they hoped". Like England's early republic, the era of publicly-owned quality housing was smothered before it could be realised.

Most of the shops are boarded-up and there's fuck all to do. A young man with a slashed-up face points me to the one open shop. Inside, I get talking with a young man from Helmand, Afghanistan. His father, uncle and grandfather have been killed by the Taliban, and he's a refugee. He's worried about being identified, and says that many Afghani refugees have brought over their internecine allegiances: "some are army, some are militia, some American".

The country has not been welcoming. "Lithuanians are good", polite, but there's more aggression here than he expected. "Very bad!" he starts, his pessimism at one with the island. But he struggles to explain why and, like others, amends his view to one of negative pride: "Very bad here, and very good here. You get good and bad everywhere." He introduces me to a couple of other locals. One gestures at my camera and warns that I'll be beaten up and robbed if I "wave it round". I can't discern if it's sensible advice or a threat against an outsider making cultural capital out of the poor. Some mix of the two.

Out of Heath Town, I follow the main-line canal along a rough and at times treacherous towpath some fifteen miles to Birmingham. A number of Travellers are out fishing in the early afternoon sun. One man tells me he's hoping to catch perch, "maybe even carp", in these grey canals. Edible? He laughs and shakes his head, as if I'd suggested swallowing the can containing his beer. It's a fine pretext to meditate by a body of water, one of humanity's oldest pleasures.

The canal is also an opportunity to survey what remains of the industries of the West Midlands. The world's first industrial revolution of the 18th and 19th centuries began here at the same time as Manchester. Water was ideal for transporting heavy goods over England's uneven terrain. Factories were first built beside rivers, but the boom in steam-power led to the construction of three thousand miles of canals by the 1820s to meet demand. Mills, factories and ironworks built up in rapid numbers, aided by new industrial techniques and the supply of nearby coal. This Black Country continued as a thriving, dirty landscape of large-scale manufacture until the 1960s and '70s.

The factories are mostly derelict now, and the light industrial and trade warehouses that replaced some look in similar disuse. Friendly locals greet and cheer me on as I huff along the broken-up paths. It's a spectacularly ugly scape, but perhaps the friendliest too. Busy locals' boozers and little streets, more clues about the place. "City of a thousand trades" was once Birmingham's nickname. Turning the metals and minerals of the surrounding terrains into workable things. But no one can think of what's made here now. Everything once put to work, everything a little dirty. Even the tap water leaves a calciferous coating on the back of your teeth.

Then the end of the line, and a final playful surprise: the National Sea Life Centre, surrounded by a filthy canal and yuppie apartment complexes. Birmingham.

No towering cathedrals or palaces, royal residences or venerable heritage. Across an impressive town square, a security guard chases a surly lad on a race-bike. There's something democratic and public-spirited about it, even if the centre's been too easily surrendered to the motor dreams of the 60s. The town hall and city museum still cherish visions of collective flourishing through technological progress, the rare but real philanthropic edge of one or two urban industrial capitalists. The far vaster result is this pockmarked landscape of dirty canals, collieries, damp slums and "satanic mills", its droning bass and spine-shaking percussion expressed, atavistically, in the hard rock and metal bands produced in abundance by Brum since: Black Sabbath, Judas Priest, Lemmy, Napalm Death.

Epstein's second attempt at a satanic figure in the city museum accounts for this ambiguity. Whereas in Coventry he was subdued by St Michael, reconciled with defeat, here the other aspect of Lucifer is presented: fallen angel, accursed harbinger of light, a symbol of humanity's Promethean ambitions to attain a level of mastery over nature akin to the gods, its rapid industrialisation inevitably leading to its own self-destruction. The cars and trades of the West Midlands have for the most part disappeared, though money is still being made in property, transport, finance, industrial research and its many large universities. And of course the service sector, one which, with its poverty wages, is imbued with more state subsidies via tax credits than any 'lame duck' nationalised industry.

Birmingham feels immaculately planned in places. Huge 60s office blocks and hotel chains dominate the horizon, vast malls at their heels. Unlike Coventry, Birmingham's relaxed about its ugliness. It is urbane and irreverent, with other priorities. It doesn't obstruct the making of money. I drift through Digbeth, where a community of punks complain about gentrification outside pubs that haven't been caressed with paint for decades. Past vegan co-ops and hydroponics shops, down Inge Street, close to China Town, where the National Trust has preserved a few cramped back-to-backs, dwellings of the dirt-poor, for historical interest. Will Heath Town or Chelmsley Wood get the same treatment? Through the Gay Village, then out to the large Indian communities of Sparkhill and Moseley. I grab a Balti curry in one restaurant, Birmingham's own contribution to British cuisine, invented in the late 1970s, a bland curry cooked in a wash-bowl served up for drunk British diners. It makes use of local materials: potatoes, spinach, mushrooms and peas, at home in any hotpot or stew, nicely washed down with a pint of mild lager. The

Indian waiter addresses me as "mate" and asks if I'd prefer chips instead of rice.

Marvel at this city, the most often derided of any in England. It has produced a litany of upstarts: W.H. Auden, the first authorised English-language Bible, Benjamin Zephaniah, and The Streets. Even its sarcastic curry is worthy of academic appreciation, and the city gives us this, with the discipline of Cultural Studies founded here in 1964. After exploring the Bullring mall, a more recent effort of the city's crude commercialism, I pedal through Lozells and into Handsworth, where on one street corner I'm light-heartedly chided by stoned old Jamaicans and, a block later, stocious Poles. Sari shops neighbour Vietnamese supermarkets, Irish shebeens and Caribbean bakeries.

Then back out into the uncentred republic of the West Midlands. West Bromwich, Moxley, and Walsall, enclaves of white Englishness. In this vast infra-urban sprawl, which is the "real England"? Pessimists would say the Bullring, optimists the Gay Village or China Town. To attach its identity to something historic or multicultural seems too reductive. If there's one lasting impression that's instructive, it's its lack of *here*ness. Back in Wolves, having passed another set of retail parks, semi-detacheds and deindustrialised wastelands, I ruminate on all I've seen in the local McDonald's, over a burger and milkshake that'd taste identical in Watford or Whitby.

From standing stones to Roman temples, Anglo-Saxon market towns to gothic cathedrals, the early modern enclosure of common land, the spa towns and market towns, to the canals, factories and the apogee of Victorian Britain, the railways, terraced houses, hospitals and schools that still function as the island's infrastructure. Hail our own era's efforts, the concrete quarters for the poor, the motorways and retail parks, the out-of-town Tescopolis, the modern university complex and its indebted consumers and casualised labourers, the palisaded distribution centres and rusting warehouses, the peeling pubs and stewing resentment, the bloody Premier Inns, a truly boring dystopia. What kind of *people* are made by all this? Who's behind its manufacture? Does anyone actually want this end product?

I need a drink.

"There is nothing which has yet been contrived by man, by which so much happiness is produced as by a good tavern or inn." So says Samuel Johnson, native of Lichfield, the beautiful Staffordshire market town I accidentally stumble across the next afternoon. The quote's familiar, repeated on pub chalkboards across the English-speaking world, and found again outside the King's Head, a lovely old boozer built in 1408. I venture inside for a cheeky pint.

Inside, Julie serves up regimental ales and tells me about the big soldiers' reunions that take place here, of the nearby army bases and the town's long association with ale production. Lichfield still appoints two testers each year to ensure the local sauce is of "satisfactory standard", a job opportunity with more competition than the opening of a local supermarket. I can vouch for its quality.

I'd come in to seek refuge from my mind's terrain. A bit of banter, maybe some local history, that's fine. Nah. A local fella pops in with an acoustic guitar and interrupts us. Without prompt, he rapidly describes the continuing expansion of our universe within a multiverse of infinite possibilities. "Everything is expanding, our brains, this room!" The speed of light, twelve million miles a minute – even in Lichfield. Nothing is fixed, all things are possible. "Our attachment to paper and gold, so stupid."

Let's pin down this trickster. What does it help to know this? "You can't jus' change brain chemistry. We've been like this for hundreds e' thousands e' years, millions e' years." His reply seems to indict my scepticism as much as any latent hope in the reform of the human character. Can we shift with time when even time outstrips us? The dying thoughts of the last dodo. He chuckles, and issues a warning before leaping out. "If you ever meet your anti-self – whatever you do, don't shake hands with him. Otherwise the entire universe will explode."

Timely advice, next time one's travelling in the vortex between two universes.

I venture out round the old little city. There's a quaint cobbled marketplace where the last public burning at the stake for heresy took place. Edward Wightman's crimes in 1612 included believing that Jesus was a mortal man. The three spires of the gothic cathedral still tower over the town, its interior a worthy transmitter of reverence and awe. I pedal off, oriented broadly northeast, towards the town of a stranger who's kindly offered me a bed. The road skirts by the National Forest, cuts through Branston like a hot knife through cheese, and eventually touches Burton-upon-Trent.

Accents are flattening in their range and intonation, the off-key melodies of the West Midlands left behind. Burton looks to have been constructed with the gusto of a hungover apology to appease its brewing industry. Much of the island's beer is made here, some through massive British conglomerates like Marston's, others through companies with American ownership like Coors. IPA and pale ale were invented in Burton. Bovril and Marmite stew in vast vats on the outskirts, other beloved staples of the bland and heavy English palate. I pop into the rowdy Anchor to taste the local tipple.

"A'ight duck?" The beer's alarmingly cheap. A taciturn gentleman in a three-piece suit flogs cigs by the bar, and the scene's lively. Pint glasses shatter through inebriated misoperation. Only early afternoon! Jokes are loud and bawdy. "What d'ya call a..." Silvers clatter into the jukey. Baritone notes beside me as Tina Turner hollers 'Rolling On a River'. What's all this about ducks? A drunk cockney staggers in beside me and presses the question to the others. "Ya call ea chova dack instead ov cant." Can't fathom it. Still, the beer's damn good. Tina Turner's proving popular. Chorus in unison, "If I lost you, would I cry?" Pints later, I retake the road.

The A-roads are hairy. I'd never drive under such beery conditions, but dumb bravado brings pleasure to the risky ride beside the white vans of the Midlands. Into Derby, a larger and more affluent-looking city compared to its neighbours. Cathedrals and medieval alleyways butt against the trappings of the modern town, chain stores housed inside Victorian parades and arcades. I'm surveying the motorway traffic from a footbridge when I get talking to Steve, a local with more answers to my questions that I'd anticipated. He accounts for the place.

"This is a place that makes things!" He runs through factories at dizzying speed: Tutbury, Nestle factory, most of Europe's instant coffee; Burnaston, Toyota, cars; Osmaston, Bombardier trains, "just got the Crossrail contract". He talks with some pride. John and Thomas Lombe built the first modern factory in the world here in 1722, a six-storey silk mill with three hundred staff. Men, women and children worked together. Now it's high-skilled plastics, metals, textiles. "Even power!" A third of the country's electricity is made along the Trent, he says, as if it's a son who's just won the Derbyshire Under-12s golden boot. Drax, Cottam, Ferrybridge, West Burton. It chimes with some sentiments heard in the last few days, but jars with others. Why is he proud of it? Don't these factories just exploit their workers, as they always have?

"Courtaulds, you 'eard of 'em?" He points out the London gallery. Ah. "Textiles, huge. Big employer round 'ere. Thousands." Steve left school with few O-levels and immediately got a job at their factory. He started in 1971 and worked his way up, working acetate, raylon, acrylics, among those thousands. He wasn't rich, but it paid well. But higher local energy costs and cheaper access to non-unionised labour overseas led to many factories moving to Asia. Courtaulds were, like Rolls Royce, assisted with government money in the 1970s to continue their operations, thereby keeping them afloat for a time. But by the 1990s the business had been broken up by international buyers, seeking out new forms of profit. Around five hundred still have jobs locally, "for now".

As he describes his worries for young people today, trapped in unskilled jobs with lowering wages, something starts to click. *We used to make things...* This pride in making and doing, contributing and "paying yer way", belongs to a forgotten, abandoned political constituency, that of the English working class. A prevailing historical narrative has erased them from contemporary existence. "We're all middle class now", words so often misattributed to ex-trade unionist John Prescott that they've indelibly stuck. That they could be believed, and so propagated, indicates the desolation of the English working class who had supported Labour, and who now has no other collective identity to unite behind. Somehow being able to afford an annual trip to Spain or buying a council flat at some low government-subsidised rate is a game-changer, that degree at a "post-1992" university somehow puts you on the same par as the journalists, politicians and business figures who come out with this slush. The working class has been deserted, then told it was never there.

Some Home Counties hack will write in the *Guardian* about the problem of the "white working class". But black and Asian workers are part of this socioeconomic category too. The real issue is simply class and work. *We used to make things.* Steve's pessimistic about the future of manufacturing and energy, whilst remaining, dissonantly, upbeat about the economy. "We're still in the top ten of economies, it's astonishing for a country this size." His thoughts take a new tangent, now imaginatively participating in the sharing of 'The Economy's' success. Tackling the "deficit" and kickstarting "growth" for small businesses are matters of personal concern. Society's needs, like social care, education or caring for the disabled are unimportant or, at best, a natural consequence of the correct balance of the free market. "No such thing as a free lunch."

Steve contains within his chest all the contradictions of the contemporary English working class. Committed to making things, but convinced that everything that once made such making possible – education, apprenticeships, a living wage, re-nationalising industries and banks and placing them into transparent, accountable public ownership, protection from overseas trade, quality housing, adult education and the rest – are unrealistic. Pessimism has ruled it out. But look around you. We agree that the present state isn't working. Those power plants, factories and utilities are now owned by hedge fund groups and the governments of Spain, France, Singapore, Canada, China and elsewhere, like Iberdrola, E.ON, RWE and EDF, to name a handful. Virtually every publicly owned body, our commons, has been enclosed and sold by our elected government to distant, unaccountable bodies, granting them the right to tax the islanders for necessary services at vastly inflated rates, far into the future. It seems that no one can do anything about it.

We agree in our critique. But Steve's committed to the moral belief that people should work, even when automated factories could render such work unnecessary, enabling most people to be able to work part-time, or even less, supported by a universal basic income. Conservatives have co-opted pride in "hard work" within their aspirational rhetoric. Steve owns his own property and is now mulling over his pension options. He's bought in. But maybe it's not just about money, leisure and time. Even a universal basic income, as remote a prospect as it currently is, still will not satisfy the common need to work in some constructive and useful fashion.

I need another drink.

Something has become clearer, but its realisation depresses me. I feel older and heavier now, as I pedal down Brian Clough Way, towards the flat rustscapes of Long Eaton. It's like spotting a grey hair and, through closer inspection, discovering half a dozen more. Chimneys of discarded industries, retail parks, a territory of pubs, chippies and St George's flags of Draycott, Beeston, and into my final destination.

David meets me in the centre of Nottingham. A friend of a friend, he's kindly offered me a place to stay and help repairing my bike. He smiles, is gracious and issues wise observations as I tail him up to Canning Circus. A local man, bike enthusiast and university researcher, his insights are as consoling as the porters we clink in the beer-garden.

In the Midlands, these working class communities where things were once made now seem abandoned of political importance. Poverty creeps. There's a danger of seeking out some master to put it right, David warns. "We've found a problem, do something about it." He remembers the riots of August 2011, the local police station getting firebombed. "For one small moment", something important happened. Young people were out in the streets, talking politics and the future. They felt like they had power, that for a moment they might be heard, at last, by resorting to violence. Since then, unrest's receded. Power is nowhere and everywhere, like underground oil lines and multinational coal plants, as opaque and ill-understood as the wider global economy. Many rioters were given jail sentences for stealing things like bottled water, and a false narrative of consumer nihilism and hedonism was placed over the protests.

David's mate Steve talks of a "fear operation" stalling all thought of tackling political and social injustice. They're angry here, these young people, but pessimistic too. The universe is constantly expanding, said that Litchfield Loki. But in the present moment it feels instead like it's contracting, receding, looking within. David rejects an off-the-rail answer. "Think about things slowly, carefully."

Baby's going home. West of Lenten, Nottingham, I rest my orphan Raleigh Pioneer outside its birthplace.

But there's fuck all here, no sign of that Raleigh factory. I cycle up the appropriately named Triumph Road into a derelict factory, now populated by a blue portakabin, a guard in high-vis engaged in a crossword. "This is John Player's." Cigarettes. "Yer wanna go back up Faraday Road." Passers-by don't know either. Just like the corpse of Richard III. Try Google. And so I find myself at the foot of a complex of student apartments, besides the flying saucers and Lego-brick blocks of Nottingham University's futuristic Jubilee Campus. For the sake of profit, Raleigh took its factory to the Far East. The only memento of that tribute is in the engineering and business colleges here today, disproportionately attended by students from that region, a curious cultural and economic exchange.

Lenten, and little more succour. The jawbone-white high-rise blocks are already recognisable from the *This is England* films and TV series of Shane Meadows, produced over the last ten years, about young people trying to keep their minds in the wounded landscape of Thatcher's England. Small town unemployment and frustrations play out violently among decayed 60s concretopia and deindustrialisation. I think of Combo, the traumatised skinhead and bully who is later revealed to be one of its most tragic, brutalised anti-heroes. He gets all the best lines, just like Shakespeare's fools. "Two fucking world wars! Men have laid down their lives for this. For this, and for what? So people can stick their fucking flag in the ground and say 'yeah this is England, and this is England, and this is England'."

The austere blocks glare, caught in a snarl like a Staffie dog's teeth against the patchy grass wasteland around them. The council is pulling them down, their white façades promising "homes that people want to live in". It's unclear whether locals were consulted, or if they'll be able to afford whatever the blocks are replaced with. As I'm wandering around, a police car stops outside a school and, a moment later, a distressed woman is bundled into the back.

The Raleigh factory had been caught on film. Albert Finney

played Arthur Seaton in *Saturday Night and Sunday Morning* (1960), capturing a young working class man's aimless frustration with a life trapped in dead-end factory work. The work is as mind-numbingly dull as turning spools round on pegs, but piecework repays repetitive conformity. The people around him are "like sheep", the price of acquiescence being "television sets, enough to live on, council houses, beer and pools – some have even got cars". Ultimately Arthur too becomes ensnared through his own choices of escapism, sex, heavy drinking and arrogance. Marriage, parenthood and drudgerous employment: the walls of the working class prison momentarily revealed. But around the low-rise red-brick estates of Sneinton and St Ann's, caught in Meadows' camera in more recent times, nothing suggests a sea-change. Supermarkets, call centres, the distribution centres around the nearby motorways perhaps, and a lot of unemployment. An elderly Jamaican lady tells me to visit the castle. She's never been.

Nottingham's steeped across a number of perilous hills, but the bicycle's sufficient for exploration. Through the tennis lawns and gentrified luxury of The Park, a stone's throw from Lenten, wealth and want in characteristically English proximity. Back into town. There are some superb public spaces here, from the old market square to the pedestrianised centre. The old lace quarter's been partially reanimated through a number of local bars and venues, and the town's many students bring vibrancy. Chinese hipsters pose moodily in front of graffiti, a nearby junkie slunk over his knees by a gated block of luxury apartments.

Then to the vast castle that hulks over the town, much of it built into cavernous rock. It's long been a symbol of despotic power since the myths of Robin Hood, a local hero whose name lives on in folklore across the English-speaking world. Curious that we should find the most famous militant for social justice and wealth equality from this rebellious city. Sherwood Forest once stretched across Nottingham and Leicester, but something sticks with Notts. The castle's been burned down twice by local rebels, first after the English Civil War to prevent Cromwell declaring himself king, and a second time in 1831 by men and women demanding the right to vote. The machine-smashing Luddites led their rebellion against poverty wages from here during the 1810s, destroying factories and assassinating mill owners. More British Army soldiers were sent out to crush them than against Napoleon. They took their name from the semi-mythic King Ludd, from whom comes the name *London*, but who has long been associated with Sherwood Forest.

Two hundred years later, look around at the low-paid, low-skilled work and its demoralising effects. Yesterday's Arthur Seaton or Combo is today heard in the music of Sleaford Mods, in songs about *fuck all*, venting out a nihilistic rage against the poverty, boredom and hypocrisy of the current moment, about job-centres, boozing, about being sick of it all. Like Arthur Seaton, there's never any obvious way out of it.

So this is England? Nottingham circled, I've threaded out west, towards the garden city suburbs of Aspley, Broxtowe and Cinderhill, built for the workers of nearby collieries that closed after the Miner's Strike of 1984–5. Like St Matthews and Heath Town they are quartered, ghettoised and built facing inwards. The Notts miners broke from the National Union of Miners under Arthur Scargill, believing government claims that their jobs would be safe. Their defection from the miners' nation-wide struggle imperilled the legitimacy of the strike and fatally wounded the sense of collective solidarity at its heart. *I'm alright Jack*, the ethos. The claims were knowingly false. Now this garden city is paying some kind of price, its roads in disrepair, drives broken up, St George's territory, and every amenity except an offie and kebbabery closed down. Not everywhere's got a story like Peterborough or Derby, fit and working again.

Darkness is setting in, a familiar shadow hugging the super-market scene by Hunstanton. I pedal out but don't get far before my front brake callipers snap. Twenty-five miles separate me from Matlock, where more friends of friends have offered a place to stay. I don't fancy wild camping in Aspley. I think of something David told me. When all else fails, don't cease. Keep advancing towards the edge of the horizon.

Kimberley, Eastwood, Codnor and Ripley: small Notts towns that thread together sullenly. Places where the only thing open is the pub or offie. Steve knew Eastwood well. "Skag town", he called it. A young woman staggers across the road, strung-out. D.H. Lawrence hailed from here, exiled by his learning and obstreperous personality, a "savage enough pilgrimage". Much here might still enrage him.

Ambergate, the scenery changing. The road's no longer flanked by barely pulsing townscapes but steep rock-cliffs and viridian forests. Becks rill behind dense foliage. Whatstandwell then Matlock Bath, the towns changing temper, now giddy and light-hearted. Bikers overtake me. A cable car snakes over a parade of ice cream stores and chip shops. And, at last, Matlock, its old sandstone townhouses gently shimmering like dusty pearls. There is a new kind of air out here, fresh, clean and at peace. Knackered, I push my bike up the final hill to Jamie's, snuggled into the steep mountainside.

"Everyone can be happy, if they're free to express themselves as they want." Jamie hands me a slice of cake, for it's his birthday tonight, and one over to Paul, his partner. It seems a little too whimsical after days in the beat-up towns of the Midlands, but there's no part of his statement that I can object to. "Power is within each one of us", he says. Change begins in our very gestures and words, in the ways we react and cooperate with others, and in the ways we understand and express our ideas and feelings. To counteract the "fear operation" that has closed down dissent and dreaming in the Midlands, Jamie calls on us to discover our inner power capable of realising a better world for all, not just our disappointed selves. Our actions, our very *making*, or lack of, impact those around us now, and those who will come after us. "[I]t's time the whole thing was changed, absolutely", D.H. Lawrence wrote, issuing words in 1928 better re-purposed for today. "[Y]ou've got to smash money and this beastly *possessive* spirit. I get more revolutionary every minute, but for *life*'s sake."

I can't sleep tonight. All these encounters and stories suggest no easy way of remaking these communities and ways of life. One of the roots of political idealism is a moral demand to do more, think more, be a better person. Its demands take the form of *this is what we need to do* to get from A (now) to B (a better world), be it through consciousness-raising, grassroots democratic participation, multitudinal insurrection, counter-hegemonic strategic optimism... whatever. A more frank way of posing the problem is to consider what stops people getting from A to B. What features of the terrain block passage, inhibit desire, forbid trespass? That proposition asks for an account of what *is*, rather than what one might like there to be. At last I realise why I set out in the first place. It wasn't only for the smell of juniper or for a jolly away from the library. It was to understand a problem. Why, despite the economic downturn, worsening living standards and welfare and wages cuts, are so many voting conservatively, thinking pessimistically, working harder, acquiescing in all this? The answer lies somewhere between Merry Hill and the mines.

CHAPTER 3

The People's Republic

"It's a shit town, but it's our town" – Lloyd.

The me I was is disappearing. Everything I knew before feels as relevant to this terrain as a medieval metallurgy technique. I now depend on strangers for directions, information, even places to stay. The extent of people's generosity has been surprising and inspiring. I've kept a blog along the way, cheating myself of sleep in the process, but through that offers of assistance, accommodation and unusual stories have kept coming, from Orkney to Devon, Horsham to Preston. Something of the ethos is striking a chord, this amateurish attempt to understand something of that unknown island written out of popular representation. First, I've got to get there.

That could be tricky. Yesterday evening, having dragged against the front wheel for some days, the brake finally broke off on the steep road to Matlock. The bike's a state, its budget parts revealing their limitations. At Stanley Fearn's this morning, Rob issues a bleak prognosis. The chain is the most worn he's ever seen, and he's amazed the bicycle even rides. It takes them some hours to repair the front brake and fork, but by early afternoon the call comes through. Bring on the Peak District!

The terrain ahead appears menacing and beautiful. Gazing out at the distant peaks, one feels so far removed from the transient concerns of the world and one's life. I moseyed round Matlock earlier, collecting dog-ends of clues. An older woman in a café spoke of the hypnotic attraction of that view, said that one could easily "lose hours" in the contemplation of the distant fells and sheep. Unspoiled, one can roam freely into this vast mountainous expanse at the heart of England, venture among Neolithic sacred stones and caves with inexplicable etchings, ancient attempts to connect with the infinite. One cave goes by the name of Blue John Cavern, another the Devil's Arse. Curiosity electrifies.

Rain's falling heavily. The plastic poncho flaps about in the wind, little more than a bin-liner with a face cutout. I pedal up through Darley Dale and Rowsley, among charmed farmers' cottages built of bulky sandstone. Steepening still, joints are already aching as I graze by Chatsworth House, a juggernaut pile of aristocratic excess. Cheviot sheep spangle the rocky heathland, otherwise little changed since the "waste and howling wilderness" Daniel Defoe encountered three centuries ago. The real charmer is the toy-town village of Edensor, with its mock-Alpine Victorian chalets and solemn gothic revival church by George Gilbert Scott. Peek inside the life-size skeleton statues, owl of Minerva and head of Medusa, glaring goggle-eyed right back at you.

Yet Edensor's bathos is outdone a few miles further inland at Bakewell, an ornate little town on the Wye. Its deserted church contains stacks of empty coffins, Neolithic stones, creepy gargoyles and a uniquely Anglo-Viking imagery of keys and swirls on the old headstones. It neatly presents the Norse cosmology. Nine worlds centre on the Tree of Knowledge, Yggdrasil, meeting-place of the gods. The tree is plagued by various creatures, from a dragon gnawing at its roots, to four stags ever-eating its foliage, to a wise eagle at its top, whose flapping wings cause winds in the human world, with a mischievous squirrel carrying insults between base and apex. Odin hung himself from "that tree of which no man knows from where its root runs", as the Poetic Edda puts it, and hung for nine days, til on the cusp of death he was finally able to understand the magic power of the runes. The stones connect Yggdrasil to the redemptive lore of Jesus Christ, that Roman import as lasting as their roads and towns, who hung not from a tree but a cross, and returned from death with the Word, the promise of eternal life. The imagery attempts to persuade local Danes that Christianity is not only compliant with Viking ideas, but superior to them.

Perhaps it is only in England, this cold rainy island on the edge of the world, that such an unlikely conflagration of global cultures could occur. Whilst Danes settled in the mountains east, Welsh migrants followed the River Derwent up, creating an unlikely fusion of cultures. It has led to a distinctive friendliness that never dissipates, an openness among strangers to talk with me, to tell me of their weather and their lives.

From Bakewell I pedal to Hassop, then follow the Monsal Trail. This old railway line cuts through spooky tunnels and viaducts with sweeping views of the rolling green dales. Some of these ancient limestone walls were formed 33 million years ago, when the island was as hot as the Bahamas. Flat and deserted, it is pure cycling heaven.

The route rejoins the A6, snaking and steepening up to Buxton. It's at first an underwhelming industrial intrusion into the delights of the Derbyshire Dales. A local man rants at his ex-wife and children outside a discount supermarket. I ask a couple strolling by about life here. Andy is a mine of information. He chuckles nervously between issuing each perceptive observation. "Nowt round 'ere 'cept quarrying and eel farming!"

Buxton was once an attractive Georgian spa town but, unlike Leamington, has fallen on hard times of late. The old baths are boarded up and a heritage project to renovate them seemingly abandoned. The pedestrianised high street looks unloved in parts, and beguiling in others, particularly the poky antique stores filled with magic lamps and forgeries of the Renaissance Masters. Its famous mineral water is totally radioactive, and was even marketed as "the radioactive water" until the 1920s. "It's in the rocks", everywhere, he says. Radon bursts from crevices in winter. I join a long queue to fill up my flasks at the public tap. The water's uncannily hot.

Accents alter, like the geology. Fusion of Lancashire and York-shire, combining a polyphonic lilt that lacks the Manc drone, yet gentle in its elocution, without the clumsy bee-bah of Yorkshire. There's a charming self-deprecation in people's humour that makes me happy. It's a new feeling after the flattened emotions of the Midlands and East Anglia. I'm ready to be seduced.

Ten gears and a knackered chain aren't the best assistance in scaling the spiked sierra that gives this district its name. I'm nearly broken by Chapel-en-le-Frith, an unlikely Norman incur-sion into this contested terrain. A kebabra serves up every con-ceivable kind of drunk takeaway grub one could imagine. I sit with a young dad and his daughter beneath a TV screen, the Eng-lish football team putting in a characteristically disorganised, navel-gazing performance. "Fat Rooney!" shouts the proprietor in a back-room, the same game relayed with a three second delay by a Turkish channel. "He's got loads of good lads but they need to gel together as a team", the young man reckons, his comment accounting for the country as a whole, its council estates and country estates. Whistle blows, a mediocre two-all draw.

The arc up over to Hayfield is brutal. Every limb has an ache of its own, and I can't get beyond a few metres before needing to pull over and rest again. Finally at the crest of the cruel hill, I plunge back down into Hayfield, another picturesque old village. An old boy tips me to check out a car park on the edge of town. Curious, I eventually track down the plaque he referred to, mark-ing the start of the Kinder Trespass of 1932.

Until the early 19th century, these infertile lands had been farmed in common, but then parliamentary acts had them forci-bly enclosed and put in private hands. Some of the most beautiful parts of the island were no longer accessible. Some workers got together to challenge this, to demand the public's right of way. Members of the British Workers' Sports Federation massed here and went out for a stroll. Gamekeepers and police brawled with them once they trespassed into private property, and many were bludgeoned down then thrown in prison. But their demands were popular. How can one man possess what is nature's alone, and not his to take? By 1951 the Peak District had become the first national park. What had been deemed violent and illegal two decades earlier was now the common right of all. Would it be just to be punched by a policeman for simply following an ancient trackway? So much else currently protected by the law may appear similarly outdated, cruel and absurd in future decades.

Intriguing, but night's falling and serious rain's forecast. I'm too cold and wet to wild-camp, and cannot afford to stay in the pricey B&Bs of Hayfield. There's a youth hostel, I'm told, but it's all the way in Edale, back over the steep hill to Chapel and then up another gruelling climb. It closes in half an hour, but the ride's over an hour away. "You'll never make it!" a local woman commiserates in the village shop.

They've said that to a lot of people. Crazed with desperation, I pedal manically back over the mountain to Chapel. It's now too dark to make out the road ahead, cloaked in the shadow of the forests and hills. It's too risky to cycle, so I try hitching for a few minutes, but the cars ignore me. Cursing the moon, rage redoubles the final climb to the peak of Mam Tor.

Face-to-face with the clouds, a nocturnal mist lurks nefariously on the unlit road. Occasionally thick cones of light appear ahead as a Land Rover narrowly overtakes. The rain returns in gobby drops, and the mist soaks to the bone. Badgers dash across the lane towards Edale, and bird-like moths scare me witless, appearing momentarily in the front light's range. Black forests whoop and whir around me, as I pursue this broken road, eddying this direction and that in ways one cannot anticipate.

Suddenly the road begins to plunge back down, snaking round treacherous cliffs. Collapse or carry on? Soaked as I am, I'll likely fall ill if I camp in the rain, but there's nowhere to stop. From fear, an inner strength is forced into being. I whizz through Edale and out, and eventually work out which narrow track pulls up to the isolated hostel. I sprain every muscle in my body pedalling up that final bastard hill.

This life! I arrive just as the door's being locked, but the philanthropist on the other side lets me in. Refuge. The ecstasies and agonies of the day have done me in. Broken brakes and such desperation are things I hope never to experience again. But to have survived it feels wonderful. "Like a borderline religious experience", an American birdwatcher called Nat says, describing his own feelings about the landscape, as I finish the last of the food in my pannier. But he does not know of the revelatory nature of cycling. It is a profoundly philosophical activity. Just as it disciplines the body, so it exercises the mind in its inner resilience. "Life is like riding a bicycle", Einstein said. "To keep your balance, you must keep moving."

After yesterday's ordeal up Mam Tor, a death pact has now been made with this knackered bicycle. In the words of Flann O'Brien, I've become "more than half a bicycle", my personality and atoms interchanged with my transport. Riding out of the quaint little town of Hope, I feel it moving with me, responding instinctively to my designs with an autonomy and personality of its own. It has replaced my body as my prime means of movement. I could sense that it had been reluctant earlier, unsure if this transinsular trip was just a cocky dare. Now we both had some proof of commitment. I promised to reward its pluck with a new chain in the next town. I could feel the ride becoming easier as we veered by the gorgeous dams of Bamford, and down the Rivelin Valley. Cirrus snogs the roof of the horizon, the air balmy and breezy. "Thank you", I whisper to it.

It has proven surprisingly resilient so far. Yes, the brakes have broken and gears only shift with a kick or bump in the road, and the chain's likely to snap at any second, but apart from that... it's holding together. No cycling sores either, and I can feel my stamina growing by the day. I no longer need beer to null the aches!

The drama and adventure of these new experiences rarely has me harking back to my vitamin D deprived life of teaching and study, though at night I miss my partner, and call or text her each evening. We agree to meet in Edinburgh. Reaching there on this thing no longer seems as insane as it did a few days ago. Perhaps I might even make it there in one piece.

Loxley, Sheffield. Time to return to the company of the human race. A chatty young mum ends our natter with an "a'ight luv?", and I want to throw my arms around her. At last, the North, a place I love like no other.

But what is the North? So many clichés obscure it: ferrets, flat-caps and frank sincerity. Uniformly grim, a greyscape of sooty mills, heavy drinking and domestic violence, or roman-ticised as a unique region of working class solidarity, pints of mild and Betty's hot-pots. These representations are most often produced in the wealthier South, where every regional accent indicates working class, whilst the middle class South stands for England itself.

No doubt it's a place, possibly even a state of mind. Too irrev-erent for a head of state, the republic expands from Grimsby in the east to Liverpool in the west, from Buxton in the south to Newcastle in the north. But this over-simplistic term The North occludes the distinct rivalries of its regions. Yorkshire's a differ-ent beast to Lancashire, and the towns of Tyne and Wear some-thing else entirely. Proceed carefully.

I weave past dusty Victorian terraces into Hillsborough, a bustling expanse of bakeries and caffs, ringed by a motley assort-ment of industrial estates, funfairs and even a casino. The foot-ball stadium crowns the scene. I've been told to check out the Hillsborough Disaster memorial, though the first man I encoun-ter doesn't know where it is, and the second gives me directions to two, a small unofficial plaque on a roundabout, and a larger memorial stone recently erected by the grounds, surrounded by scarves and tributes. You'll never walk alone.

On April 15th 1989, 96 Liverpool fans were crushed to death and 766 injured at the overcrowded Leppings Lane Terrace. Though standing terraces, crowd penning and a lack of emergency medical treatment at the scene were all factors, it was a failure of police management that resulted in so many deaths. Eager to conceal their culpability, the South Yorkshire Police then conducted an abysmal smear campaign, leaking hostile stories to the press like those published in *The Sun*, blaming drunken fans for fighting or thieving from the dead. It would not be the first instance of local police misconduct.

Tram tracks trail into the impressive town centre. Sheffield has some ambitious and grandiose civic buildings, like the alabaster neo-classical columns of the City Hall, or the stern Art Deco of the Central Library. Its many pedestrianised streets, parks and open spaces give it a metropolitan, European flavour. Though it has its fair share of crap malls and British Town Centre chain stores, there's also a number of independent shops and bars, and the large covered market rewards the browser with plenty of sumptuous tastes and smells.

Exiting the Moor Market scene, I drift east, assessing Sheffield's modernist edge. Consider the turquoise jagged ridgeback of the Information Commons building, perching over the university complex like a nest of swarming cyberinsects. The concrete cuboid of the Arts Tower looms over the scene like a 1970s computer unit, consumed by its own intellectual arithmetic. Its windows chequer as they reflect the sunlight like lit buttons, and the structure's a fitting monument to art's progressive nature in a city based on industrial innovation. Another structure above the town looks more maligned. I drop the cycle off at Bike Rehab for a well-deserved new chain whilst I venture up the hill behind the station.

The Park Hill estate was built between 1957 and 61 as a future-facing city in the sky. Families previously overcrowded in back-to-back slums were given access to electricity, indoor bathrooms and clean, airy apartments for the very first time. In recent years it had been effectively condemned, a cipher for an unrealised future of British socialist modernism. But be wary of Yentob-like laudations that have nothing to say about actual living conditions. Architecture cannot reform human nature. I venture up to see if there's anyone left I can talk to.

The estate is vast, zigzagging over a steep ridge above the city's railway station, yet feels totally cut off from anywhere. There are no amenities or useful shops and, like most post-war council estates, the area feels cordoned off, the contagious poor quartered away from contaminating the city. Thick blocks barricade upon each other, focusing attention inwards onto public spaces that feel insular and under surveillance.

This was once a very nice community – countless old TV interviews with residents attest to that. Milkfloats down the walkways. Today almost every flat is boarded up with timber or steel. Pigeons circle the higher balconies, shrinking inside broken windows. Most of the walkways are barricaded up too, but one is not, and as I prowl along to check the view, I encounter a group of men and women, some of the last people still living on the estate.

A young family, a local lad with a Canadian girlfriend and three kiddies skidding nearby. His mum still has a flat and is waiting for the council to rehouse them. "It's rubbish!" she says, popping out for a second, then disappearing inside. One of the kids disagrees, pounding on the door. "It's not rubbish!" The man gazes down at the playground beneath the walkway, hands pursed over the railing. "I dun't know what's goin' on." He grew up here, and remembers all the drugs, a huge problem. A "violent place". Why? He shrugs.

He might be in his mid-20s but it's hard to ascertain as, like the buildings around us, he's prematurely aged and unwell. He points to the derelict wings, their prison-like features increasingly apparent. "Look. They're crumbling already." They neither scoff nor bemoan that the structure's now listed. He points out some Victorian terraces in the distance. "There's nothing here. All the people have gone, it's all gone."

Enjoying the novelty of Park Hill still, his partner disagrees on its merits. "It's like no place else." Perhaps. Nan rejoins us. They're refurbishing one wing of flats on Park Hill's furthest edge, she says. Will the old residents be moved back in? "No." For the first time, the young man laughs. "They just get moved t't other estates where they'll cause trouble!" Why did the estate fail, I ask them. He shrugs. Uncertainty, then sadness. I leave the family, still gazing down at me from the walkway as I stalk the remainder. The atmosphere's like a murder scene, but no one's come to bury the cadaver.

Past cracked slabs, lank grass and buddleia spears, I pick up the not-so-old pathway that leads back to the road. Ahead is Park Hill's regenerated future. Bought up by property speculators Urban Splash, the drab concrete's been reclad with funky primary colours and its windows enlarged.

Another young mum pushes a pram up the hill. "It's nice, they're doing it up for 'em." Who, I ask. She doesn't know. An ex-resident of Park Hill, she takes as given the common opinion that Park Hill's problems were self-inflicted. Drugs, crime, a few bad apples. The moral over the political. Ex-neighbours have been decanted out to the Manor or to satellite towns, Rotherham, Doncaster, estates near nowhere.

Sheffield's winded me in a way I'd not expected. Feeling blue, I stagger back into the centre. There's a particularly high number of homeless people. One with swollen hands and learning difficulties is flumped outside a supermarket. "Just want somewhere warm to sleep." Inside, the young cashier's training to be a dentist. Why? "For the money, private like, so I can retire at 30!" Without really thinking about it, I hand the pack of cookies I just bought to the fella outside.

Refuge in Wetherspoon's. The elongation's clipped and gummy. "Pin' tut abbutt, ta luv." But the city's disarmingly friendly. Yusuf's from the Channel Islands. He loves the city feel, the friendliness. I venture round the streets again, quietly absorbing. A rough sleeper accosts me. His name is Wayne and, like Odin, he says he has no place in the ground, no place in the world, and starts to incant his poems. He talks of drug addiction and of a near-death experience following a suicide attempt. For a moment he was on the other side. It was an ethereal and opaque blue, with inexplicable currents of energy pulling him this way and that. "When we die, we either go up or we go down. That's it." He invites me round to his flat, "Hendon chickens" he calls it, and manages to keep up a conversation on human mortality whilst soliciting a ciggie from a passing teenager. "It's a good place, a lovely place." He's not wrong.

Allie spots me drifting by the university complex, completely lost. An artist and proud citizen of Sheffield, she's a friend of my partner's and my host for the night. We met up earlier for some lunch where she told me a little of Sheffield's story, but we agreed to reconvene later in the Rutland Arms to compare observations. Joining us is Nick, a tattooist and disability worker who's hosting me in Wakefield.

They talk of class and Northernness as two misunderstood quantities. Like Dave, she warns against reading a place on face value, or falling for the same romance-or-ruin motifs of the North. "The history of the middle class Northerner is a story not often told." She talks of Michael Palin, Victor Burgin, and the experimentalism of the old art college. "Art cannot be accountable", she argues. They warn against seeing the landscape in black-and-white, but I can't help feeling that something has gone wrong. Sheffield throbs and pulses through its thriving university and still-impressive centre, but places like Park Hill, the Manor, Meadowhall or Orgreave will attest to a kind of silent war, subjugation and, for now, defeat. Like the young mum outside Park Hill, perhaps I'm also in danger of seeking a moral explanation. Things are greyer, less clear.

Like all the major industrial cities on this island, Sheffield's rapid expansion over the 19th century was an ill-coordinated jamboree of profit and production. Workers were pitilessly exploited, and there was no education or welfare system to speak of. Towns like Derby and Sheffield started to return the first Labour MPs and councils by the 1920s. It was through the state that new housing and schools were built, and later the clean-air suburbs of the Manor, the concretopia of Park Hill. After the war, steel production gradually came under public ownership, with British Steel forming in 1967. Private companies were not interested in investing profits in new technology or fair wages, and so, more for the sake of international competitiveness than any socialist commitment, the state kept the steel industry functioning.

By the end of the 70s, rising energy prices and international competition from newly industrialising countries hit Steel City hard. The plants needed new investment. Whilst some European states invested money into their flagging factories and utilities, in the UK Thatcher came to power, declaring open war on trade unions and nationalised industries. Between 1979 and 83 over a thousand jobs were lost each month in the city. Steel collapsed. Unemployment was up to fifty percent in some parts, and fifteen percent across the city by 1984, and heroin made inroads into Sheffield's broken economy.

Thatcher had been popular in the English shires but never the cities. Like London and Liverpool, Sheffield was in open rebellion. Its city government was nicknamed "The People's Republic of South Yorkshire", and it subsidised bus fares ("tuppence", Allie remembers) and declared itself a nuclear-free, demilitarised zone. The red flag was flown over City Hall on May Day. But its government had a huge housing stock that was already collapsing. No plans were made nationally, or locally, to establish new industries in place of steel. Nor were chain stores allowed to set up in the centre, Allie recalls, and few attractions were built. Sheffield felt like the underdog, but few I'd met were nostalgic for those depressed days. The pessimism of that time was captured more than anything else in the nuclear apocalypse of *Threads* (1984), a docudrama by the BBC, daring to contemplate the post-Anthropocene world.

British Steel was privatised in 1988, but by that stage had largely collapsed. Chancellor Nigel Lawson believed in the social good of privatisation. His personal memoirs reassert an "ideological belief in free markets and a wider distribution of private ownership of property". In 2007 the rump of the island's steel industry was bought up by Indian firm Tata. David Blunkett, once leader of the People's Republic, was now an ambitious minister in the New Labour project. The socialist principles of the Labour movement had been openly abandoned, even ridiculed, and the remainder of the island's utilities, law enforcement, local government departments, health and social care were restructured for privatisation. More than a third of former council homes are now owned by private landlords, I discover on my phone, as I charge it up in the old Waterworks Corporation building, now a Wetherspoon's pub.

Next door is a derelict 80s office block that I earlier tried, unsuccessfully, to find a way into. It was once the base of the National Union of Miners, whose president Arthur Scargill oversaw perhaps the most dangerous campaign of domestic opposition to a sitting government since TUC's 1926 UK General Strike. This war has marked the political and social landscape of the North like no other – everyone mentions it– and yet this banal, derelict corporate schlock is one of its few surviving physical signs. I go out hunting.

From Handsworth, I pedal down Orgreave Lane. The plodding brown semis haven't changed since 18th June 1984, when mounted police charged down here, whacking down pickets and anyone else foolish enough not to be running away. But aside from those terraces, there's nothing here. I pass a couple and ask them about it. They're unsure, "so long ago". They point me down the hill towards a luxury housing development in the midst of green fields.

Over 1979–81, two million manufacturing jobs had disappeared. In March 1984 the miners decided to go on strike, after Thatcher announced the closure of twenty mines and twenty thousand jobs, with a further seventy-five secretly earmarked for closure. The miners had brought down Heath's government in 1974 during a previous dispute, and entered the strike confident. But coal had been stockpiled this time, and riot police prepared for a likely strike. Changes to laws on solidarity strikes and secondary picketing prevented action by other trade unions, like the dockers and steel workers. Others were persuaded not to act at a crucial time, like the smaller mining union NACODS, and the Nottinghamshire miners who split from the NUM. There was no way Maggie and MacGregor would close pits with years of reserves, surely? That'd be madness, or possibly war. Like with the General Strike seven decades before, the TUC and Neil Kinnock's Labour Party were conspicuously inactive.

Miners began by picketing mines, but decided to escalate things by targeting the British Steel coking plant at Orgreave, where coal was transformed into coke, used for making steel. They hoped to bring down the steel industry and move the strike onto a new front. But as they arrived, the police had already got wind of their plans, and local South Yorkshire Police were bolstered by a huge force of Metropolitan Police officers. People still remember the police roadblocks, turning round cars trying to leave Yorkshire. On that hot afternoon, already vastly outnumbering the pickets, the police charged, chased and beat down the miners, later arresting 95 for rioting and unlawful assembly. As with Hillsborough, false statements were concocted and misinformation fed to the press.

Thatcher called the miners "the enemy within", and indeed they were. The miners were the last part of the labour movement to take a sustained stand against poverty wages, privatisation, deindustrialisation and low-skilled underemployment, the very things that now define life in the North. Unable to claim welfare payments, miners were starved back into work. By March the strike was called off; the following year, mines started closing in great number.

Thirty years since the strike, the final three deep coalmines have been scheduled to shut. A parliamentary bill will be debated that will effectively render strikes illegal, requiring a minimum support ballot that is infeasible. Yet this is no good versus evil fable. The NUM should've held a national ballot early on. It remains a wealthy union, despite its lack of membership or obvious welfare activity. Scargill siphoned off miners' subs to pay for his Barbican council flat up until 2011, which he secretly tried to buy in 1993, a recent court case revealed. The aggressive pickets of the Doncaster NUM did as much to persuade the defection of the Notts miners as any false promise about jobs for life.

Whatever way one looks at it, communities were split in a manner not known since the English Civil War, with feelings of mistrust and betrayal that linger. I consider Orgreave a turning point in a modern civil war for control of the island's resources. On one side, Thatcher's government and its right-wing allies; on the other, the working class of England, south Wales, Northern Ireland and the Scottish Lowlands, organised through their trade unions. The latter believed that all people are equal, and should be entitled to the same education and care from cradle to grave. The former believed that wealth is a natural reflection of individual superiority, and that public ownership stymies wealth creation. Indeed it does, for power is, in thermodynamic terms, a closed system, and public ownership prevented the majority from sinking into poverty. But this has now occurred. The miners were roundly defeated at Orgreave, and the working class has never recovered. The North would be punished for its refusal to cooperate in the new order.

Today there is no Orgreave, no monument. The luxury housing complex where the plant once stood has been rebranded as Waverley. I pull over at a bus-stop, and ask those waiting the same question as Park Hill. What happened here? And no one can tell me, not even where the coking plant used to be, except a young Senegalese man, who hazards a guess. I thank him.

I ride through Tinsley, before locating Meadowhall, a vast glass mall built over an old steelworks and opened in 1990. If there's any monument to the shifting fortunes of the North, it would be here; crowning a landscape where things are no longer made but sold. Local myth has it that its investors were nervous of commercial failure, and so commissioned a design that could be easily converted into a prison if retail therapy failed. Are they so incompatible? It's the first remotely busy place I've passed since Moor Market, a somnambulant, easy-thinking zone, a toy-shop for grown-ups. Tug at jewellery, grope smartphones, rub and sniff new clothes, then queue for McDonalds. Three generations of families out on a leisurely trip among the familiar, reassuring brands.

Like the pleasures of the London-Essex suburbs, Meadowhall proves good on a number of counts. For if economic emancipation means a life of cosy domesticity surrounded by entertaining gadgets, then capitalism has liberated the masses. Solidarity and collective feeling were based on a necessary mutual interdependence beyond the immediate family, to extended kin, workmates, neighbours, friends, union members or parishioners. But that's no longer necessary, or possible. Families are smaller, making childcare less of an onerous but communal activity. For many, both parents must now work to provide a liveable income, and hours are often precarious and inconsistent, involving far more travel to and from home and work. In this way roots cannot burrow, and in the absence of a community, the living room becomes the centre of personal and social enjoyment.

But in another sense, the dream of emancipation didn't disappear after 1985. If mass desire for collective freedom now seems of a bygone era, then individual desires burn bright. Racial tolerance, gender equality and sexual liberation have made immense progress over that same period, also reflecting protest struggles, hard-working and innovative campaigns, and changes to education and media coverage. Thatcher would've baulked at legalising gay marriage, and many remember Section 28. Desire for individual expression and freedom has absorbed some of the energy motivating those earlier solidarity struggles. Though by no means perfect, there are few places in the world more accepting and open-minded or, to speak more precisely of its spirit, indifferent to difference, than the big urban centres of England. The problem is that this isn't enough, and the deflated air in Meadowhall also makes that clear. As I drink a McDonald's milkshake and survey the scene, I see stressed couples, harsh looks, "we can't afford that, luv" to their kids. But one shouldn't have to pay so hard for every desire.

It'd be more accurate to stake Meadowhall's location as Rotherham, not Sheffield, but the faded reputation of this old steel town has seemingly scotched that. The town council's office is being converted into a Tesco, and like Dudley and Merry Hill, the remainder of its small, endearing Victorian centre has been devastated by Meadowhall's proximity, with just a handful of bookies, pubs and discount foodstores trading. Ashgar's lived here since 1966, and smokes a pipe. He worked with steel. "You could get jobs like nothing." From the 80s they began to go. He lost his job and has never worked since. What happened? "Greed. People wanted money." Who? "Factory owners." He blames Thatcher and my hometown. "London... they only care about money down there."

It annoys me hearing this, knowing first-hand the poverty in London that *is* worse than what I've encountered on the bike. But what can I tell him? That side of London also has no representation. He talks of Westminster politicians, Canary Wharf bankers, the house prices in Mayfair and Kensington. He hates my city, but for reasons most Londoners would agree with.

Wentworth, Hoyland and Birdwell. The architecture and accents are shifting, the red bricks of Rotherham replaced with a sootier yellow sandstone. The accent fuzzes in Barnsley, becoming clipped and foggy, all *thees* and *thas* without the *dee-dah* bounce of Sheffield. Like Rotherham the town's deprived-looking, with no major chains having outlets here, just a few depopulated pubs and closed-up caffs. Locals are reticent to talk about it. I catch one young man, Rory, who's just finished work at a bookies.

"The mines were 't big thing, now they're gone. People't just go round't different towns trying t't get jobs." What jobs? "There's nowt round 'ere't cept call centres." Online clothes retailer Asos has a large warehouse outside Wakefield, and Burberry has a clothes factory in Leeds, but it mainly employs Polish people, he says. Many of his mates still live at home, their wages being insufficient to pay local rents, however meagre. "Ain't much round 'ere" he says, as we survey the suffocated Victoriana. Just like in deindustrialised Wolverhampton, I'm warned to look after myself.

A cheerier couple point me to Dodworth, and tell me of something worth checking out. Further up the road, an inebriated pa tugged about by his three sons like an Inuit by his huskies points me towards the old colliery, the only place in Yorkshire with a mining memorial. "It's near the library!" they shout in unison, and easy to locate, beside a miner's welfare office, the replica of a pit wheel and a memorial plaque.

The collieries are now call centres or malls, the terrain wounded. I head out into the quiet country, evening now. Darton, West Bretton, the sun setting against black figurines in the sculpture park, shadows elongating, and into Horbury. "They might find a kind of loving to carry us through", wrote local Stan Barstow, a misguided faith in the domestic paradise. *A Kind of*

Loving (1960) can be read against Nottingham's *Saturday Night and Sunday Morning*. Playing by the rules unlike Arthur Seaton, Barstow's young marriage becomes another kind of prison. "The secret of it all is there is no secret", he concludes, wanly.

Ashgar had said "There's good and bad everywhere". There was something profoundly fatalistic in that epithet, but hopeful, too. Disabused of his delusions, Barstow was now able to reckon with the present whilst remaining deeply sceptical. It's a hard-headed, stoical, good-humoured attitude. There's great resilience in this part of the island.

Late morning at Nick's, Wakefield. Peel up the blind to reveal a mithered horizon, mardy clouds that'll be siling down later that afternoon. Gazing out at the English summer scene, my mind erases names of West Yorkshire towns I'd initially planned on exploring. I've discovered enough of its bitter recent history now. The future's more compelling.

Allie said something intriguing back in Sheffield, as we lunched in a backstreet canteen. She'd been describing her new-found love of mountain biking, but the comment now seemed to reckon with the prevailing mood. "The fear was really transform-ative", she'd said, of the terror of tumbling down some rocky dene. "I felt fear, and it made me want to live."

Fear, she'd known a long time. Fear of failure, fear of not meeting deadlines, of work being judged inferior, of being completely skint. Precarious living. But there was nothing she could directly do about the fear. It happened, regardless. Sink or swim. But out in the wilds with her partner Greg, she was forced to confront her own internal attitudes and responses to that fear. Beyond the threshold of terror was pure exhilaration. She was discovering an inner resilience that now served her in new situations.

The pain of depression and defeat leaves behind a psychological scar tissue that resists repetition. Allie's pleasure in being alive had come from a lateral direction, in the discovery of her own reserves of power, in the sheer adrenaline of mastering danger. In the mardy, mithered morning, that reckoning is instructive.

Among the ex-industrial surrounds of the River Calder, the newly-built Hepworth gallery hulks over the scene. A series of lazily voguish trapezoid blocks, granite-grey, its construction was not initially popular, but it's no uglier than anything else around, and a rare event of public art that isn't in London. I schlep around the Hepworth sculptures, cold yet curiously sensual, intimate.

Lloyd works at the gallery, though has the air of an ambitious journalist sniffing out municipal conspiracies, consigned by his editor to compiling traffic stats. "There's a new confidence back in Wakefield." Unity Hall has just reopened, and galleries are appearing showcasing local work. There's been some local opposition to the Hepworth. Angry letters to local rags, he says with a smirk. Its concrete appearance reminds many of 1960s system-built housing, cheap and shoddy. Lloyd's dad remembered the informal competitions amongst building firms over who could build blocks quickest. Whatever corners could be cut, were. Local politicians were wined and dined, and commissioned the cheap and ugly blocks in double digits. "It can take fifty years for a building to fit into a place." The Hepworth has that time, at least.

Leeds. Arterial roads and suburban neighbourhoods tumble down into it like the chasm of an earthquake. The city's jumbled on approach. Rings of early 20th century housing estates like Robin Hood give way to hulking hangars and warehouses that one must navigate carefully through the city's fiendish road traffic. Few cycle, and those who do should know better. But hold onto what wits you still have and pierce the ugly ring-road, as here is a large and in places magnificent city centre.

Look up, as one always should when encountering a new location. Survey the onion domes and ornate spires of Kirkgate Market, the largest indoor market in Europe, and venture inside to saunter by stalls of sweets, meats and knock-off garments.

Peruse the poundshops and bakeries of King Edward Street and Albion Place. Banal 60s blocks and ugly 80s projections butt besides gorgeous Victorian arcades. Manufacturing and commerce are built into this bustling city. A new mall has opened just down the road, replacing the affections of the one opened ten years earlier. Rifle through the tomes of the city library collecting clues, then out across City Square with its light-bearing maidens and bearded worthies, surveying a vast deserted plaza, a little piece of Paris or Barcelona in the aspirational North. Into the city gallery to inspect the emotionally suggestive, moonlit scenes of Atkinson Grimshaw. A nice place, I conclude, as I stop for a pint in Whitelock's. But the city's particular spirit is not amongst all that.

Back through the dirty ring-roads, coarse words exchanged with local drivers. Council blocks worthy of Lloyd's dad mark the terrain north, Lovell Park and the mischievously titled Little London estate. Navigating the highways at Sheepscar, I pedal on, past increasingly familiar sights, the vacant car-park of the New Roscoe pub, the rustic sooty sandstone of the High Street ahead. I pause by Sheepscar Park, familiar territory, and park up on Savile Drive. Red-brick back-to-backs, derelict shops, independent supermarkets, the peoples of Bangladesh and Barbados, Poland and Pakistan, the cultures of the world sharing in the mean poverty and disarming friendliness of the area. Chapeltown's hardly changed at all in twenty years.

My granddad came to Leeds from county Mayo, Ireland, aged 13. He found work shovelling snow, but then trained to become a bricklayer, which he did for the rest of his life. My gran's trajectory was not dissimilar, leaving a huge family in rural Donegal behind to work in England as a child-minder and cleaner. For a long time she cleaned Don Revie's house, Leeds United's much-loved manager, and a nice employer. They grew up in absolute poverty, and worked skin-and-bone to give a better quality of life to their six children.

Mum's memory of Leeds is ambivalent. She remembers a violent and poor city, hit hard by the decline of its manufacturing in the 70s. Fail the Eleven-Plus like almost all working class kids were supposed to, and you were streamed into unskilled work. Leave school at fifteen, few even bothering taking their O-levels. Saturday job in the market, membership at the Wigan Casino Club, sweet soul music, heavy-drinking nowhere town. Eighteen, she took the first opportunity to work overseas as an au pair.

Their first family home was slum-cleared. They had been fond of it, but there was no bathroom and neighbours shared a toilet. They moved into Chapeltown about a decade before the first of a series of major urban riots took place there. It was a markedly multicultural area, but not without sectarian tensions. My granddad died in the late 80s, apparently, she recalls, after the shock of his car being vandalised by Orange Order marchers, which he'd parked in the local Catholic Church. The Bangladeshi boys next door who'd kick the ball round Sheepscar Park with me and my brother were quietly afraid of the "black lads", who'd never play with us. This was less a multicultural utopia, more a confluence of different cultures.

Leeds came a long way in the first decade of the 21st century, booming on financial services and insurance. Gran's five surviving children now own their own homes across England and Ireland, with indoor bathrooms, have Mediterranean holidays and comfortable pensions. Some have university degrees. In two generations living standards for the working class transformed from absolute poverty to relative prosperity. The conditions that had established that transformation, like liveable wages negotiated by trade unions and a left-wing Labour Party, and programmes of affordable house-building, free healthcare, welfare benefits and adult education are now coming to an end.

Curiously, many working class voters have supported this. "We're all middle class now" – it doesn't matter if Prezza hasn't said it, or if it's true – most feel they have to believe it. It's encoded into the new retail parks and Barratt cul-de-sacs, into the vast car-parks of Tesco and Homebase, into the wings of Meadowhall, into Lord Prescott's entitlement to "Two Jags" and the "modernising" of the New Labour project. If something's going to reanimate these places, bring together these discordant, dissenting energies, it'll require a new kind of collectivity, a reimagining of the *people* of this republic, a recommoning of the commons. But how likely is that?

No one familiar round here now, no one in the street to ask my too vaguely-formulated question. Gran died a few years ago after a long convalescence in the nursing homes of Tong Road and Colton. Her house still looks the same, and the working men's club at the end of the road's still there.

Up Potternewton Lane, towards the university district of Headingley. It's a Saturday night. Throngs of young people in fancy dress parade for the Otley Run, a formalised piss-up that animates the evening ambience. I track down Woodies. Ben comes out to greet me. He's looking well, my older cousin. A talented musician and goalkeeper, he now works in insurance sales, like most of the men in our clan. He's circumspect about his work and spends most time talking about his daughter. We catch up in the beer garden, pints disappearing like the hours, then head back to his, where guitars are summoned and songs sung.

"The past is a point of reference, not a place of residence", he says, quoting the renowned sage Kriss Akabusi approvingly. Football droning in the background, I pass out, dead to the world. Later, Ben shoves a kebab into me. Caught in these overlapping time-zones and experiences, it's easy to lose yer head.

Boots and braces social clubs, sari shops and Polski skleps of Harehills gradually merge into the 60s slums in the sky of Seacroft. Down York Road, the landscape is increasingly inglorious: chain hotels and carvery pubs, fast-food drive-thrus, retail parks, transit zones, the public gardens of 21st century England.

The bicycle remains the prime way to absorb the changing scenery, even when it appals the aesthete's tastes. One is continually exposed to the landscape, and can therefore detect the subtle shifts in its topology and flora, in its forms of work and leisure, and relish the zest of its scents and sights. Trains may provide a selective montage, but they take passengers away from the human habitation that makes place. Walking provides more in-depth stills, but in fixating on the details it cannot reveal patterns or rhythms. Cycling, one sees the landscape as a rolling movie, at times dramatic, comic, tragic, and plain mysterious. It is just as Nan Shepherd writes, reflecting of her journeys around the Cairngorms. "This changing of focus in the eye, moving the eye itself when looking at things that do not move, deepens one's sense of outer reality."

Even somewhere like the suburbscapes, rustscapes and dirts-capes east of Leeds. This is working England, dole England, one that exists almost everywhere, and so constitutes nowhere, in contrast to the prevailing phantasmagoria of cricket lawns and village greens. With a new chain and five extra gears since its repair in Sheffield, the bike feels more confident over the undu-lating A-roads. The repairs have cost the same as the bike itself, but it feels like a brand new ride. There's great pleasure in shar-ing the road with another ill-prepared underdog. The absurd proposition bugs round my head that *maybe* we might just make it back home.

York strikes a different note to its neighbours. A small, well-scrubbed and ancient city, its centre is a pleasant if meticulously preserved image of the past. Unlike Leeds or Wakefield, its build-ings are unusually aged yet well-attended, as if the Industrial Revolution had never happened. I pedal through the villas of Dringhouses, then beneath its medieval battlements, into a web of cobbled lanes, independent shops and gastropubs. Generic indie busks from every street corner.

"It's like't maze round 'ere", a man says, as we sup at the bar of the Old Starre Inn, as chintzy as the name suggests. Neither of us are succeeding in navigating its confused temporal and spatial zones. It's a wealthy town, fattened on wool, railways and chocolate, now booming from its prestigious university and ye olde associations. But it's also an unlikely site of religious strife. One of the few sectarian massacres in the island's history took place here in 1190 against the town's Jewish population. Roman Catholicism was well established here, the surrounding country marked by its wealthy monasteries, profiting from the wool trade. Guy Fawkes grew up in York, later known for his attempt to explode parliament in the Gunpowder plot in an attempt to reinstall Catholicism in England. More recently, four men from West Yorkshire were involved in the Islamist bomb attacks against London of 7th July 2005. They were young fathers, carpet-fitters and fast-food workers.

Fortunately there's a historic distaste for religious violence in this country. York too had its role. The Roman emperor Constantine was crowned here in 306 CE, and his reign would see the construction of Byzantium and the spread of Christianity across the Mediterranean and over the Channel, made possible by his introduction of a new political principle, religious toleration. Romans, Saxons then Vikings would contribute their own culture. *Eboracum, Eoforwic, Jorvik, York* – no magic to changing names, just the mispronunciation of a succeeding migration.

Long empty lanes, the scapes emptying out into the first proper country since the Peaks. Rain and hail force me off the road by a Deighton pub, where a young woman bemoans small town life, and plots lines of escape. By eight the deluge ceases, and I crack on, making the most of the summer evening's extra hours.

Sleepy Selby, through Carlton and Snaith, by the toasty wheat smell of the Hovis bakery. There's a pleasure in just being absorbed by the open road and the meditative concentration of long-distant cycling. I've nowhere in mind to stop. In the darkening horizon, the chimneys of the distant Drax power plants begin to light, an unlikely sci-fi flourish to the otherwise flat farmscapes. I continue south, aimlessly, the bruise-blue twilight now brushed jet. Approximately nowhere, surrounded by rhubarb fields, the cycle breaks down again. I hop a hedge and call it a night. Camped in some farmer's field, among frisky foxes, gossiping geese and ruffling rabbits, the distant swoosh of a motorway becomes indistinct from the breeze. I'm among a new kind of peace.

Why do accents change every six miles?

It's not just subtle intonation. The fundamental operations of speaking shift with each particular territory. Glottal stops, nasal reflexes, rhotic rerrs, lilting lark-like in one town then plunging into monotonous drawl in another. Would da ave't breadcake, or wouldst tha prefer't breadcayek? The fifteen miles between Sheffield and Barnsley slip up the question. On the other side of the Peak District, they'd ask feret barmcake luv; in Notts they'd tek aht a cob duck; in Newcastle they'd av a stottie pet. Haddaway ya wazzak, or fak orf aht it? Even pronouns appear, disappear, or change use altogether, and no grammar is alike. Ah were in Selby, they wuz in Sunderland, e ain't in Stepney. There are already a number of languages spoken on the island, like Polish, Punjabi, Arabic and Urdu, beyond the older tongues of Scots Gaelic, Cornish and Welsh. But even English has no homogeneous features. It isn't just the terrain that continually transforms, but the accents and dialects within it. One could easily trace the tribes, their menfolk still doing battle on the football field, their supporters in the car-parks and boozers outside.

But this drift through the North's indicating a common picture, not just a preponderance of pie shops and back-to-backs. Wrong-footed by the preventable collapse of its industries, there's a prevailing bitterness in the air. People speak of their low-paid jobs in the service sector for the most part, subsidised for now by in-work benefits, with a few aspirational positions available in banking, insurance or the universities. The latter professions are being hailed as the future of the North, but even those within them speak of insecure conditions.

Take Moorends, a small ex-industrial town close to where I camped. One local man beside its newsagent told me that the colliery here had at least fifty years' reserves of coal. Millions were spent refurbishing it from the 80s until 2002, when the project was inexplicably abandoned. He shrugged. Nearby Hatfield has one of the last open coalmines, but even that's scheduled to close. Then Thorne, another small ex-working town, its population largely old and white British. There are two TV repair shops, reflecting a mature preference for fixing broken objects rather than replacing them altogether. In the square, a retired local government official named Bob tells me about the town. "They used to make ships, believe it or not." He chuckles. It seems unreal.

These small towns always have at least one scarcely profitable e-cigarette shop. In Thorne's, Claire tells me that the only work now is in a nearby food factory, unless you have a car and can get down to Doncaster. "Everyone knows each other", though. People are helping each other out, and it can be seen, in the bakeries and post office, in the friendly banter and gentle inquisitiveness I encounter. An old boy on a mobility scooter tells how he and his wife cashed in their pensions and travelled the world. "Now we've got nowt!" he laughs, but his batwing smile and content glow confirm he hasn't regretted it.

East, and the scape continues to flatten, as Yorkshire becomes Lincolnshire. Like Canvey Island and much of Eastern England, it had largely been marshland or even underwater until Dutch engineers like Cornelius Vermuyden drained it over the 16th century. But the towns are like those I've just passed. On Scunthorpe's outskirts, Jim laughs at meeting another Londoner. He ran away with a married woman some decades ago and got a job up here in steel. The scars around his eyes show the damage of the blast furnace. "Good job, though not many people liked it." Since the loss of the steel jobs, the town hasn't been the same.

Hardship isn't always obvious. Clothing is relatively cheap, and there's rarely an obvious feature of a house or person's appearance that suggests the destitution of depending on food vouchers or payday lenders. But Scunny's seen better days. Across the town, in backstreets, car-parks, or even the main thoroughfare, I see men slumped against walls, shoulders over knees, strung-out. They sell pints at the Blue Bell for £1.45, the cheapest I encounter. An act of philanthropy by local landlords?

Along the main drag, a doddering array of poundshops, charity stores and an unusually large number of pawnbrokers, people peering in. One man studies me as I amble. Andy laughs, baring his diseased gums, and takes another pull of his pipe. The town's "rough", he says. There is a big drug problem, and few jobs. He's a recovered addict. What could be done? He's unsure, but talks of educating the young and putting money into libraries, and quotes Shakespeare liberally. He points me east.

Out of town, I pass the vast steelworks now owned by Tata. Today's steel-lines are automated here, Rotherham, Corby and Teesside, and far less is produced by a fraction of the old workforce. The industry remains profitable, but clearly nothing's been reinvested into the area since privatisation. Towns like Scunny, Selby or the old market town of Brigg, next, just skitter about without direction, at the mercy of the economic winds.

I pedal on, veering off the road and into the surrounding country. Birdsong trills from the hedgerows, and as I approach the secluded woodland round Somerby Top, I trace the progress of a sparrowhawk over the rolling dingles. Great claps of thunder boom from darkened clouds ahead. White light pulses momentarily, and ten seconds later, another bone-chilling rumble, like the rapid progress of a military invasion. Desperate not to get caught in the storm, I press on, backtracking down by the thickets and fields, retaking the busy highway that soon washes me into Grimsby.

The English town is a peculiar beast. Aside from the Peaks,

I've never travelled more than five miles before encountering another. But some differentiation needs to be made between a bloated village, heritage market town (R. Charter 1066) or the toughened townscape so characteristically modern, and crap. Humour, then, a second game of bingo for small English towns. As you approach an urban area, confirm:

– Totally unnecessary traffic warnings and speed-reduction signs?
– Road suddenly riddled with potholes, having previously been smooth?
– Signs advertising a Park-and-Ride scheme, long defunct?
– Retail parks to your left *and* right, with familiar electronics and clothing outlets, flanked by fast-food drive-thrus?
– A vast out-of-town Tescopolis or Asda, nearby?
– Oversized detached houses with paved front-gardens?
– A solitary church steeple, marking the town centre ahead?
– And are the first shops visible retailing things no one could possibly desire?

Grimsby gets a full house. I pedal towards the town centre, whose previous features and amenities seem to have been replaced with a large mall, with a small monument paying lip-service to Grimsby's fishing history. I pop into a discount supermarket to buy some gaffer tape to seal the holes that have appeared across my fragile tent, then get talking to a local man outside.

"It's very bad, turn around!"

Why? "Too many people eatin' too much and drinkin' too much round 'ere." His face burns scarlet with frustration. Three women are no more cheery. One talks of the fishing that used to employ many. For a time in the mid-20th century there were six hundred trawlers, and much of the quayside remains intact, including an old warehouse that was once the largest ice factory in the world, in the largest fishing port in the world. But by the early 70s, Iceland began closing up its fishing fields to British trawlers, even sending gunboats out to cut the nets of any vessel that breached its territory during the Cod Wars. The UK joined the European Economic Community in 1973, and European quotas soon vastly restricted what they could catch.

The women blame the EU, as many do, but it's likely that over-fishing, competition and technological innovations would've curtailed trade anyhow. But fish remains key. Icelandic trawl-ers unload their catch here, where it is prepared and packed in vast hangars. "Lots of food-packing factories, fish", the older of them says. "But there's a lot of unemployment", the younger adds. "Not much culture!" laughs the third. She'll be soon proven wrong, with a peculiar twist.

The promise of £1.50 beer seduces me into the Parity, an other-wise large and charmless pint-dispenser. Rain starts to bucket down. "It's horrible! Nothing good round 'ere", says the young barman, with a wicked smile. There's a certain pleasure in hating – ask William Hazlitt. "There in't much." He gets me talking to the other young barman by the deserted counter. "I like it round 'ere", he insists. "I'm from Macclesfield... There, it's like a ghost town. At least round 'ere there's jobs."

Though it's only late afternoon, a group of heavily inebriated men shout and clatter about on the other side of the bar. Glasses crack against the floor. A third barman attempts to contain them. "Tommy, yer a film star", appeals one of the more boisterous of their number. Their mockery has them hooting with laughter, containing the aggression. But who are they referring to?

This is how I meet Tom Turgoose, the talented young actor who stars in many of Shane Meadows' films and television pro-grammes, set across Nottingham and South Yorkshire. In *This is England*, Turgoose plays Shaun, an angry, impressionable kid who falls under the sway of a group of skinheads. He's hardly aged, but the compliment's repaid. "You're probably the young-est person I've ever served John Smith's to!" In London he might be a barista, fashion model or coordinator of an aspirational drama school. Here he serves up pints of mild in a rough and tumble boozer. He's warm, friendly, inquisitive and sharp, like his characters. "It's all different", he says, struggling to account for England's identity.

Clouds declare ceasefire. Exiting north by shabby terraces and allotments, the scape is unrepentantly industrial. The refineries of Immingham appear in the distance, their pillars, vats and flaming chimneys as titanic and unworldly as a Martian moonbase. The town itself is sullen and subdued, like a precocious child's dull and gangly sibling. There's an inordinate number of takeaways.

I queue in one for tea, resisting the temptation of a baked bean pizza for something a little less nutritious. A heavily tattooed man queues beside me. He supports Scunny, and works as a security guard at one of the nearby power stations. He tells me about scabbing as a fireman during their last set of strikes in London, driving the antiquated trucks. Did he feel guilty? He looks on, unsure of the terms of the question. "They should be station managers", he says, after a time, of the ageing strikers. A workers' cooperative? Possibly, he thinks. On that, we agree.

After Immingham's man-made majesty, Goxhill's a gentle rustic expanse that fades into the Humber. The roads are empty and dusky. I'm seeking out a place to sleep now. There's an illicit thrill in reading the terrain with an illegal intent. Eye scans each passing field and narrow byway. Is it flat? Is the ground dry? Sufficient shelter from the road? Farmhouse nearby? Any livestock that could cause problems at three in the morning?

It's not for everyone, wild camping. There are no showers or running water, and one must dig the toilet. Still, I'm enjoying the novelty of it. Behind a building site in Barton, I chance upon a waste populated only by national grid pylons. A sike swishes beneath a hedgerow. As the moon changes guard with the sun, I lie back and listen. The breeze, the ducks, that nearby stream.

For this rare moment, my life is my own. The patter of the drops against my crudely repaired tent, the new ways my legs ache, and my mind, cracked open like a fruit, becoming aware of an unfamiliar world.

When did you last have an experience like this?

Gazing out over to the northern banks of the Humber estuary, a local man concisely summarises what exactly I've been falling in love with over the last few days.

"The bridge? There's a toll. It's £1 over, £10 back!"

Blunt, irreverent and wickedly funny. In not taking themselves seriously, the Northerners rarely take anyone else seriously either. It has been a potent bulwark against jingoism and prophets. But its barbed humour enables a reckoning with life's fundamental preoccupations, sex and death, that more infantilised or tyrannised cultures couldn't hack. It indicates a certain maturity, if not ease, with its own obsolescence in history's infinite arc. "A few years ago the BBC did *Down Your Way,* remember it?" I shake my head. "Well, then they came t' Barton the old boys said 'ey up, it's a good place to die'." He laughs for some time, then becomes gravely silent.

Samaritans signs festoon the long suspension bridge, traversing the wide Humber estuary where the Trent and Ouse end their days. Behind a basalt lighthouse spreads a dense and lush forest, extending into the horizon. On the other side, the road threads through suburban and light-industrial blandscapes, eventually becoming one with the brown bricolage of Hull.

Cheap suits, red kitchen-ware, sharp shoes, iced lollies
Electric mixers, toasters, washers, driers

Shopping parades are worthy of poetry, and Philip Larkin's 'Here' pays homage to Hull's suburban scapes, like those of Hessle. Its motley array of independent shops bustles, from local foods to caffs and mobility shops, something on sale for every foible. With Hull, I'd expected some shabby town of stenches and smoke. Instead the centre reveals a large and lovely place freckled with intrigue, from its bombastic Victorian civic architecture and winsome Queen Victoria Square to the old fishing harbour, the grotty chemical-works of Salt End and distant guns of Fort Paull. Drift down the tree-lit boulevards to the red-brick university to goose with the ghost of Larkin, its maudlin librarian. Hull even has its own telephone system, marked by cream-coloured phone booths. Locate Larkin's house along leafy Newland Park, then dally round the free Ferens Gallery, before shifting back into its old town. Looking out at the sea, one has the impression of gazing at Hull's other half, its identity founded in fishing, whaling and trading.

"Built out of fishing", a local man tells me. We're stood beside a statue of Gandhi, in the garden of the Wilberforce Museum. "These days", he comments mournfully, "they just pull out everything. Most of it gets flushed out dead, not alive. There used to be herring boats. Now trawlers from Iceland pull out everything." Similar stories to Grimsby. Hull's ports have heaved since the pre-capitalist Hanseatic League, a trading network linked to Germany, the Low Countries and Scandinavia. But it's the trade in people that Hull's more troublingly associated with.

It was the mid-18th century. Britain's growing mercantile might through the trade of sugar, cotton, tobacco, tea, coffee, opium and rum had transformed the tastes of the local population, and created a new middle class. The island had acquired a sweet tooth. Ten thousand tons of sugar were imported in 1700; a century later, this had increased eighty times. William Wilberforce's family had grown rich from Hull's merchant trade but, not unlike today, he was among a small privileged number who protested against the immoral conditions of their production. Sugar and tobacco came direct from the slave plantations of the West Indies, whilst the cotton that was feeding Britain's industrialisation was picked by the African slaves in America's southern plantations. Wilberforce campaigned tirelessly for the abolition of the transatlantic trade, which finally occurred in 1807.

Between 1500 and 1900, twelve million Africans were imprisoned, transported and sold across the Atlantic, the largest forced migration in history. The English were active slavers, profiting from transport, trading and plantation ownership – the latter were not abolished until 1838. In today's terms, the country made £2.5 trillion from slavery, helping finance the Bank of England, the expansion of the British Empire, and the neoclassical reconstruction of its cities, towns and ports. It enabled the British aristocracy and middle classes to enjoy a quality of life unknown since the Romans. Wilberforce and the abolitionists fought a tireless campaign against an extremely wealthy and powerful lobby, but succeeded through the moral populism of their campaign. "Am I not a man and a brother?", Wedgewood's slogan, often repeated on his popular ceramics.

Slavery should rightly invite us to feel shame at the island's history, but there is cause for pride. The British were the first to nationally seek the end of slavery, through a moral and political recognition that all people are natural equals, the very same premise evoked by the Levellers, Kett and the Peasants' Revolt. Wilberforce also sought to make trade unions illegal, and was contemptuous of the industrial working class. But his campaign sparked a desire for equality and freedom that would flash again across the 19th century and into the present, through the right to vote, the right to be educated, and the right to live in basic decency.

Hornsea. These Yorkshire sea resorts are at ease with disappointment. Milky-sweet tea, chips in polystyrene, erroneous crossword, letters doubled then erased, inked liked a Rorschach test. Gaze out the caravan window as storms harass the bay. Sullivan's serves up a vast pyramid of chips with dollops of sweet mushy peas, nutty and oily, neon-green, the best on earth. The service is cantankerous and miserable, compounding the bipolar nature of the resort.

Benches day-dream out at the ocean. Mike calls East Yorkshire his home, though still carries a bit of the King's Road in his accent. "When I used to come back into London for business, the best thing was getting out." No traveller can be prepared for just how universally despised London is beyond the M25, even among those raised there. He insists on the discreet beauty of the terrain. Indeed the coastline up to and out of Bridlington is wondrous. Bring binoculars up to Bempton Cliffs to peek at the swooping puffins and gannets. Soft sapphire seas glide easy into bays burred gold, and chalky cliffs, with none of the drama of shipwrecks, skerries or sea-cliff subsidence of East Anglia.

Bridlington might seem a rude interruption, but one must take care to consider these scenes all apiece. A shabby-looking town whose holiday resort days are behind it, boarding-houses are boarded up, its centre a warren of poundstores and charity shops. Boat trips for a quid. Cheap ice cream and pints, dodgy amusements, racist graffiti on the waltzer. Melancholia of a young woman on the wrong side of the till, among pallets of bargainville bacchanalia. One last form of gainful employment. We talk a while, but the intel's familiar. "A very small town, everybody knows each other." Would you want to escape, I ask. She's silent, then shakes her head, not at the question, but at the implication that it was a question. The patronising, erroneous suggestion of a choice. Fate will make fools of us all yet.

Filey's mood is not dissimilar, with a subtle class shift. The little seaside town is older than its neighbours and retains the charisma of a faded fishing village. Popular with slightly more affluent Northerners for their summer hols, it never found itself soliciting quid-schlock for diminishing returns. I'm staying with Ian, a local historian and photographer who heard of my trip online. He used to work the factory lines of Raleigh and Rowntree, and remembers the multicultural workforce, the grossly different pay for men and women. We meet by his home and take a stroll around Filey.

Ian hails from Hull, and has lived in different parts of the country before settling here. Compelled by the combination of factual obsession and a pleasure in storytelling that marks out the historian's craft, he's begun a vast historical survey of the town, undertaking and transcribing countless interviews. Many of the old fishermen and residents said the same thing. "Filey is paradise."

We follow a footpath around the bay, the sun's terracotta disk electrifying the magenta and damson horizon. Ian extends the equation. "People call East Yorkshire 'the edge of heaven'." Ian talks of Shelagh Delaney's love of Filey, of Margaret Drabble and Richard Hoggart holidaying as children, of amoral fishermen flinging shards of dried skate at "Prim" preachers, of the Roman signal stations along the coast, the drowned fishermen and German U-boats.

What draws us to stay with the past? Perhaps it's in the opportunity to speak of hope again, to speak of love. The fishermen of Filey had a profound connection with the seas around them, a vocation aeons-old. Now long-gone, like the trawlers of Grimsby, the steelworkers of Scunny, the deep-miners of Dodworth or the slavers of Hull, we cannot hear them speak uncertainties. The evidence of history leads Ian to feel markedly pessimistic about the future, of imminent ecological collapse. But they imagined Armageddon in Sheffield's *Threads*, and fantasies of population catastrophe are as old as Malthus's breeches. Some irreverent scepticism's also due.

But history's proven instructive in one regard. There's been a common pride in making things. In producing fish, or coal, or steel, or jumpers and jackets and whatever you care to mention, the working people of the North also produced the communities that clustered around these industries. Accents and dialects shifted, but there was a common class power. The country simply couldn't do without these things. Workers and their families organised through their unions, and for a long time secured themselves fairer wages and rights. But Thatcher's government had exploited a period of economic decline to maim those industries and undo the power of that working class. By the mid-90s they were disarmed. Coal, steel and fish were now imported, whilst dreams of domestic aspiration captured the desires of a new generation who'd never known rickets, slums or rag-and-bone men.

It isn't true that today nothing's made. Sheffield has its universities, Leeds its middling financial and insurance districts. Call centres and the service sector have filled the unemployment void, whilst property ownership and speculation are now the other pole of the economy, more secure than any pension. They're producing services, consumption, economic growth. But compared to what they replace, such products are hard to see, if they exist at all, and it is a perilous dependence. Any serious crash in the housing market or wider economy will destroy the lifetime earnings of millions. And many feel that vulnerability, and so clutch onto the nearest political party that rattles most persuasively about strong economies.

The North could become a place of production once again. It'd require increased taxation for investment, and protectionist tariffs against slave-wage produced imports. It'd require publicly repossessing, and not merely buying-out, the energy utilities and production facilities that've been sold off for peanuts during the scorched-earth phase of Thatcher's civil war. High-skilled automated production by nationalised industries would only require employing a few people, and so a universal basic income would be necessary to ensure proceeds were shared out fairly, whilst eradicating superfluous jobs in the service sector. The cult of hard work empowered the children of the 19th century, but shackles those of the 21st. But all this would require a sea-change in imagination and feeling, and the emergence of a *people* that were not yet on the cusp of becoming.

Politics has never been a matter of reason, but of feeling. The pessimism encountered in the Midlands has a discernible origin, in the willing demise of the industries and the defeat of striking workers. For these were never just jobs, but ways of life.

Between paradise and purgatory, we sit at the edge of heaven, Ian and I, til dusk interrupts our wanderings.

CHAPTER 4

Seek Bewilderment

"It's an unholy mess that's developing" – farmer Eden.

Yes, I think I've found it. Having sat by the edge of heaven the previous evening, this steep and narrow track gestures toward the final ascent. "Paradise" marks the spot, lettered black on white, scarfed in dog-rose over the slumbering stones of a chapel wall. Too steep to continue by pedal, I leap off and push the remainder. At the hill's summit, a cruelly aged keep leers down at a sweeping brown bay, where day-trippers creep like ants over the back of a washed-up seal. I hop the grey, decaying wall, refurbished by the dog-rose, and ivy, and lichen, and moss, and the manifold needs of life. I find a grave that belongs to Anne Bronte. "There is always a but in this imperfect world."

But imperfections must be cherished above all, for without these all we have are myths and gods, and the tall tales our species still revels in. Cherish the imperfections of Scarborough, exiled queen of Victoriana. Hers is a particularly sad majesty, for much is still intact, her boarding houses and grand hotels on clifftop promenades, her clattering tramways and Italian gardens, her dusty cabinets of curiosities at the Rotunda museum, and the Grand Hall of the old spa complex, with its chequered tiles and onion domes, designed by Paxton, architect of the Crystal Palace, with a similar ambitious vision of modernity. Thousands came to take the therapeutic waters, but the well's been off-limits since the 60s.

Some blame Health and Safety, but a cultural shift has also consigned her to irrelevance. Mediterranean package holidays are cheaper and more cheerful, and promise sun, unlike England's mercurial clouds. The town centre is now a muddle of cash-for-clothes dumps and poundshops, its gallant and wistful station unaware of its obsolescence in a meaner age, like the sadness of the final VHS cassette.

A fitting place to walk in the company of the island's ghosts, perhaps. Back up Queen's Parade I pass countless timber benches, each alike, each with its own plaque remembering the island's innumerable dead souls. For around five months, Wilfred Owen convalesced at the Clifton Hotel, haunted by memories of the Western Front, memories he'd attempt to exorcise, pen down, in the process producing what is now the cultural memory of the Great War.

But hauntings and flowers are the predictable quarry of the passing poet, and inedible at that. For Scarborough's loved in a way that accounts for neither, a love that cherishes its imperfections. It's easy to say *I love you* once, an impulsive response when enchanted by a beautiful thing. But twenty years later, alive but decayed, imperfect? Our Romantic poets die young, we do not hear of the heart's difficulty in loving what is the same thing but without the same corresponding feeling.

For Scarborough is as imperfect as so much else on the island, yet still consistent and alive. Not everything can be in bloom, and maturity or senility are as much features of a place as its youth or infancy. Whenever I booze with the young, they put the world to rights, recreate it again in their own image. But as ages progress, people speak most of their families, and of their memories, and some worry about the young. Perhaps, like fellow island-travellers Daniel Defoe and Celia Fiennes, I've being journeying with an eye to reforming the terrain, correcting its retail parks and suburbscapes with some kind of... what? Village folky Arts and Crafts revival? Reopening the mills and mines? Capping rents and abolishing second home ownership? Chance'd be a fine thing. Democrats of every age have found their people wanting.

Standing by Paradise, I decide to suspend judgement, to accept those imperfections, and let the road decide.

North, that's easy. Out of the guts and through the heart, and now towards the brain of the island. North along a cinder cycle track that skirts along Robin Hood's Bay. A warbler ponders on the outstretched branch of a wizened ash, whilst butterflies and sparrows momentarily fleck across the blue horizon. Sheep graze idly in the fields beyond, and a murder of crows harasses the thrushes.

I make Ravenscar, a seaside resort that was never built. Demarcated housing plots and road lines are the legacy of wishful thinking. Further along are the remains of the Peak Alum Works, a factory that'd take the piss from London's loos and mix it here, with local rock, to produce alum, once essential for dyeing fabrics. The azure North Sea to my right, and the knotted spinneys back left, I leap off the bike and push along the coastal path, surveying the abandoned guns and gullies of the Jurassic coastline, where dinosaur fossils some 176 million years old are still unearthed, fragments of another lost world. The Cleveland Way's a delight, though difficult with the gear, and the effect of pushing the bike across Stoupe Beck beach, up (!) and then down to secluded Boggle Hole is one of exhaustion and elation, the best of all feelings.

Breakdown on the edge of Whitby. The bicycle's become more disinhibited about expressing its disapproval. Like a doting spouse I've become adept at finding the right thing to tweak, but the remedy's temporary, and privately, doubts gather like storm clouds over its roadworthiness. It was never built for a journey like this. The back brake is increasingly ineffective, and the new chain's coming off all the time. Something to do with the gears, perhaps? There's probably a way of fixing it, but I don't know anything about bikes. My Dad does, fortunately, so I text him my lament. He directs me to two small screws near the chain that I'd never noticed before. After some fiddling and diddling, I get the chain back on and rejoin the road.

Tiers of stone arches with windows the colour of sky menace the old whaling-port below. The vast, ruined abbey would've already cast a solemn shape, distant for miles around, but the throngs gathered today are more intrigued by Dracula. The effect is less "children of the night" and more kids wailing over ice creams. I patter around beneath its broken walls under the vault of noon, then head down into town.

Nose around a small harbour and into the old town, whose streets cram, curve and knot like a ship's timbers. A man clumsily flaps a seagull's darting attentions away from his chips. The gull redoubles its efforts, and a screwball swoop along the promenade has greater success, though the now-weeping child might disagree. Along the West Cliff, monuments loom. One to Captain Cook, Middlesbrough's native explorer, and European "discoverer" of the already-populated lands of Canada, Hawaii, Australia and New Zealand. He journeyed into the grey corners of the map, as little-understood as Alpha Centauri, with courage and canniness. An indigenous Australian or Hawaiian will rightly despise his legacy, and their peoples undertook even more daring journeys in crude vessels out of Africa and Asia, but those histories are older than words. Still, marvel a moment at Cook's endeavour.

History is an enchanted mirror, reflecting our own distorted gaze. Look through the whalebone arch beside Cook.

> [H]ow then can this one small heart beat; this one small
> brain think thoughts; unless God does that beating, does that
> thinking, does that living, and not I. By heaven, man, we are
> turned round and round in this world, like yonder windlass,
> and Fate is the handspike.

Captain Ahab rages against fate, like that of Whitby's whaling trade, no longer a need for blubber and baleen, ambergris and spermaceti. One more obsolete, forgotten way of life.

The hills after the smuggler's bolthole of Sandsend are

bone-breaking. One summit after another, the road snaking so that one can barely anticipate or plan one's energetic bursts. Someone in Whitby must've tied a wardrobe to the back of the bike, because these ascents are devilishly cruel. The hot sun bakes my brain like a microwaved spud. I press on, thinking of people I love, that the love of others gives meaning to life. On, on, ON! til I pass a potash plant at Boulby, where, deep in an abandoned mine, physicists search for dark matter and cosmic rays in the most distant recesses of the universe.

Eventually I reach Staithes, where the scene changes: from flattening verdant plateaus, I now ride through one-trick ex-mining towns like Easington and Loftus, terraced housing cluttered along the main drag, dead collieries buried behind them. There's nothing here, everything's closed, the unloved buildings like the skeleton of a stranded whale. Laddish gangs gad around aggressively. A fifteen year old swigs a can of Stella outside an offie, the one thing open around, and confirms it for me, "nothing 'ere".

Whitby seems the exception to the rule along the northeastern coastline. Jovial as it is, Saltburn's fallen on hard times, its pier recently restored but inexplicably closed again. Redcar's even more depressed, a place that should be so much more than what it is today. Home to the world's oldest lifeboat and the first seaside fish and chip shop, it was once a mecca for holidaying industrial workers from the towns of the Tees. Despite a pretty coastline haloed in golden sands, everything in town's closed up for good. It's hard to tell what's still open among the poundshops and charity-shops, as many shop-fronts on the deserted high street have fake façades.

I chase down one local man and ask him what's happened. He talks of the area being gutted by the closure of nearby steelworks, and the loss of ICI Wilton, a profitable chemical works recently closed by asset-stripping venture capitalists. Something's failed badly, turning a once-prosperous town and seaside resort into a living ruin.

So it is. I've been in touch with an old work colleague, with family still in Middlesbrough. He puts me in touch with his mam, Jan, and at short notice a bed's arranged. The thought of a bath's consoling on the A-road out, populated with crushed mammals and car-crash debris. The horizon is one of lit chimneys, cranes and gas reservoirs, the air noxious and fumy. I pedal through the South Bank Estate on Middlesbrough's edge, a poverty quarter marked by CCTV posts, St George flags, slum terraces and loitering cops. Further into town, another story like Redcar: Victorian grandeur, slow suffocation, derelict buildings. Retail parks and malls being constructed with as much foresight as an air-drop of ketchup in South Sudan.

We meet by an old concert hall, and I follow Jan's car into Middlesbrough's periphery. Joe's dad is a steel-plater, but since the collapse of the local industries he now works across Europe, and is currently in Shetland. His two-up two-down on the Acklam Estate is empty, and Jan lets me in. We talk a while. She's a school dinner-lady, but speaks with pride of her two children, who've moved out of the town. Unemployment everywhere.

"They call them scroungers, but how are they supposed to get a job when there's none? And it's all zero-hour contracts, where you work fifteen hours one week, eight the next." The local news announces a huge growth in employment, but few round here credit the figures. "It's the young ones I feel sorry for", Jan says. "There's nothing for them."

Morning on the Acklam Garden City Estate, surrounded by cheery red-brick terraces, patriotic flags and, a little beyond, row after row of boarded-up houses, many habitable. Most I'm encountering in the North East are unhappy with the status quo, perhaps more so than even South Yorkshire, but cannot conceive it ever changing. They are like a defeated army, recently demobbed.

By the local estate parade, where I've been warned of "dodgy people" who might despoil a traveller of their possessions,

Gary's out with his young son. "Yer fucken mad, you are", he says, laughing at my alibi for asking. He flicks his head up proudly. "It's marvellous. Some bits are good round 'ere, some bits are bad, like everywhere." His mum and sister live round the corner. It's a community, he presses. Like Jan, surrounded by her sisters in the nearby streets, in spite of Middlesbrough's decline it's still kept together families and communities, and this is what people love about it, something impossible in most growing English towns.

But how does one live? Within the 19th century, Middlesbrough exploded from a dozy hamlet to an "infant Hercules" town of a hundred thousand, producing ships, metals and chemicals. Its Teesside docks and port were live-wired into global trade. But all this is another history lesson, and the last of those industries, ICI's chemical works at Wilton and Billingham, was wiped out in the 90s, with a rump of smaller firms operating in its place. Middlesbrough's population has been plummeting, but there's been no serious discussion about a responsible shrinking or ungrowing. Instead more retail parks, malls and call centres are promised, and receding memories of a future that's failed to arrive. We're all middle class now, right?

The sentiment isn't merely melancholic. Riding through Billingham among its belching chimneys and swerving juggernauts, air funked with astringent fumes, the Brunner Mond chemical-works later taken over by ICI inspired Aldous Huxley to imagine his *Brave New World*. Likewise, the neon-lit towers and flares I passed last night at Wilton inspired Ridley Scott's *Blade Runner*. Both dystopic visions of the future, tagged to the Tees. A "space age coated in pigeon shit" is how Owen Hatherley describes its town centre today, a 60s New Town built by ICI now marked by dereliction, a description given with a hint of affection.

Newton Bewley and Seaton Carew follow, disorientatingly bland suburbs, all cul-de-sacs, palisade gates and paved driveways, Sky dishes and CCTV pointing outward to the world. Places where one could fake one's death and live undetected... as John Darwin almost proved. This is the future that has taken its place, one which, despite its ugliness, has succeeded in offering what more people wanted more of, instead of needed. I press on into Hartlepool. Beside the deserted marina and "historic quay", site of the preserved HMS Trincomalee frigate, a binge of retail parks, fast-food drive-thrus, bingo halls and budget hotel chains. The effect is bizarre, compounded by its New York-style yellow taxis and the sheer emptiness of the place, as if a millenarian religious cult had massed in the town, built these totems and trophies to the consumer gods, then quietly disbanded after the Credit Crunch apocalypse failed to arrive.

An older couple potters past. Yvonne and Eddie struggle to explain the town's present condition. A massive steelworks and harbour have closed, leaving behind a "lot of poor" and unemployment. The retail glut reflects the magical thinking of the Blair era, that wealth could be simply magicked into creation, *ex nihilo*, just as if one could "create" energy into being, rather than harness or redistribute it from elsewhere. One needs credit for these places, now that the jobs are gone, but even that's harder to come by. Eddie points to the empty but modern-looking marina opposite, now owned by the council. There are no plans to use it. "I'd turn it into a big sports centre, with football, tennis, badminton." "Kids today sit at home in their rooms on the computer", Yvonne adds, describing their grandchildren. "It's just the age."

County Durham. The relatively flat scene is akin to the Cleveland towns, gelded by the closure of the mines. The takeaway and off-licence constitute communal life. After Blackhall, I pull over in Horden for clues. A woman old enough to have been a miner's wife during the Strike struggles to articulate its story. "They're all gone, shut in 85." What happened to the people here? She shrugs. "Nothing." Another man of similar age repeats the same. "They went out six miles to sea. They reckoned it cost too much money." He hurries off.

At (another) Easington, the village's school and council offices are boarded up, their windows smashed through. The pubs are closed, even the neat red-brick miners' terraces barricaded in places. One might expect this in Detroit or Chernobyl, but on our doorstep? The damage done is plain to see. An old boy pushes a broken lawn-mower down a back-terrace, and we chat. When the collieries closed, some miners were sent on computer courses, for certificates "not worth't paper printed on".

The terrain begins to steepen, then at Sherburn it collapses down again. Durham emerges from nowhere, secluded from sight in a deep valley. The town appears affluent in contrast to its neighbours, populated by aspirational student bars and luxury homeware shops, its cobbled lanes threading over a gushing river and up a hillock towards its vast, austerely-adorned Norman cathedral and castle. Young Americans babble loudly, and some-one busks with a violin.

I pedal on to Langley Moor, an ex-mining village on its out-skirts. Clarissa, a friend of my partner's, lives out here. As we drink beer and wine in her back garden, surrounded by light-industrial warehouses and a sports centre, she reflects.

"There used to be a slag heap there, a colliery down there, even a little railway bringing the coal." The pits and two-up two-down terraces have almost all been pulled down and eradicated, unlike Easington. A similar pride in a place that used to make things. "I do think it is as bad now as the 80s", she adds. I wonder how, still struggling to mentally connect up these scenes, past and present. "Lots of unemployment", her late-teen daughter says, her and her mate joining us. Many lads join the army. The local suicide rate is high.

Perhaps it's in the collapsing infrastructure, the true, hidden extent of poverty and unemployment. But as they talk, this sense of 80s-scale defeat is in something else. It's at the level of desire and feeling. Since York, the towns have been deserted. There are no pricks to kick against, just the stony silence and shame that comes with robbing Peter to pay Paul, with heavy drinking and anti-depressants to salve the pain. The local miners' gala is now a formalised piss-up with historical speeches, like the funeral of an elderly relative, as sheer hedonism blunts the boredom with special occasions for off-the-leash Saturnalia. We hear the radio news from the other room, distant headlines of London and a political elite rattling on about economic growth and employment, but it makes no sense out here.

Eden is a keeper of sheep. He works alone on his council farm, something I'd never heard of until this morning, beside a vast Argos distribution centre.

Long dispossessed from the land – Britain was the first world state with a majority-urban population in 1850 – an ignorant public has no idea what farmers do, myself included. The media often characterises them as ignorant, lazy and cruel, massacring foxes and badgers and engaging in the nefarious practices that caused Foot and Mouth and BSE. This is the first time I've met and spent time with a farmer.

"Nobody speaks for them", Clarissa says, as we drive to her brother's farm near Darlington. He makes a subsistence living out of rearing and selling lambs before they're fattened for slaughter. During the lambing season, he works all hours. Supermarkets continue to force prices down, whilst natural diseases ravage herds. A coat of wool earns the shearer 50 pence for a half hour's work, not worth the effort, except that the creature will become vulnerable to deadly parasites if left unshorn. Inside the farmhouse, Eden talks laconically yet ponderously of his work, as if formulating haikus. He's keener to extrapolate a common experience among workers, farmers or not.

He talks of an unholy mess developing. The modern farmer lives with low pay, stress and often sleeplessness. His farm's profitable, his tenancy granted by a more progressive post-war era that bought up and offered smallholdings to returning soldiers.

Some farmers are unable to make a profit at all, and are losing their land; many others are simply not passing down their skills, as their children witness how demanding the work is.

The average age of a farmer is 58. Eden's not far behind, and has no children to help him. Intensive factory farming and cheaper international imports are crushing their trade, forcing farmers to cut new corners. "People want to blame the poor for the situation they find themselves in." But it's akin to the blame levied against smallholding farmers themselves, rather than their economic circumstances. In this race to the bottom, multinationals cut costs and reap the profits, as slave-wage producers and barbaric mega-farms wipe out smaller producers. Eden and Clarissa trace out a common experience among other skilled professions, now being de-skilled, automated, but in the process bastardised, impoverished. The profit-hunting "law" of the market.

We lunch together, joined by John, their father. He's a local historian and teacher, and talks of the Workers' Educational Association, of teaching radical history to miners, prisoners and the motley enthusiasts of community centres. Much of the WEA's funding has gone, another effect of the cultural barbarism following Thatcher's civil war. He believes that active civil disobedience can wrest power from the privateers and politicos behind Eden's unholy mess. John cites and explains the bread strikes of the late 19th century, where miners' wives began attacking and harassing the travelling salesmen from whom they bought their food at high prices, eventually forcing prices down.

It's a blunt strategy, perhaps lending itself to a community version of *Supermarket Sweep*. But after I've left them and their endangered ways behind, I'm struck by something about the North East that I hadn't reckoned with before, perhaps because there's nothing like it in the South. It's their quiet, dignified pride in their work as a part, but not the keystone of who they are. Do not call these ruins or a people broken by political events. Here are a set of communities that have been abused and abandoned by outside forces, but that retain a distinctive toughness and gentle irreverence. There is less to laugh about here than in Yorkshire or the Midlands, but *hadaway man*, they're not down yet.

Back through Durham, then out to Pity Me, the highway scattered in truckers' refuse and crash debris. Bouncers lurk outside the boozers of Chester-le-Street. Settlements start to slurry, one into another. A female metallic figure broaches the horizon after Birtley, but Antony Gormley's Angel of the North is surprisingly small at its foot. Built over an old colliery, it has an oddly calming impact on its surrounds, as if unscrewing some of the terrain's pent-up sadness.

Gateshead is a town of contrasts. Victorian and early 20th century terraces border the scene, yet much is derelict and needlessly condemned. Its ugly yet ambitious town centre is marked by a combination of grand, self-important civic buildings, jutting beside a cheerless hotel to my left, and a semi-bulldozed high-rise block to my right, the multi-coloured walls of the exposed storeys providing an artistic counter-history of the flats. And then the road steepens, slithering beneath a great green arch. The image will be familiar to anyone fond of a certain brown ale. *Newcastle!*

In the local tongue it's *Nyucassal mon*, and arriving in its compact sandstone centre, much of it grandiose Georgian design, one has the feeling of entering a new country. Friday night, and the streets are chocker with lads in matching polo shirts and overweight lasses contained in small dresses, both of similarly neon hue. I quickly survey the city's minuscule, forgotten cathedral and explore its centre, a plethora of British Town Centre malls, stores and styles all well-represented, then drift back in towards Bigg Market, the eye of the storm, the Toon alive with hooting drunks and barmy banter. Track down the Rupali tandoori, home of the late Lord of Harpole of locally produced *Viz* comic fame. Forget Roget or Samuel Johnson, the Viz Profanisaurus offers a truly spectacular diorama of the English tongue. *Reedle, Alfgarnetstan, air biscuit* or *shiterature*?

The final ride's to Monkseaton, north east of the Toon. Paul awaits. He warns me in advance about his scary-looking house, surrounded by overgrown hedges and ferns. It doesn't disappoint. A kind gentleman welcomes me in, a man I've never met before, and another exhibit in the now-overwhelming case for a prevailing culture of goodwill. We're surrounded by taxidermied animals and more ferns as we sit in the lounge. Mr Beak swoops from one corner of the room to the other, an African Grey parrot who issues a caustic commentary of *bok bok bok* as Paul and I trade tales over red wine, pease pudding and stotties.

Paul's a public health manager, and his social insights spill out with professorial ease, but he agrees to show rather than tell, and that, tomorrow. Though only somewhere in his late 40s, he grew up in nearby Wallsend without a toilet or bath, surrounded by the noisy cranes of the shipyards. His story reminds me of those in Leeds. "I remember growing up and thinking council housing was posh! They had a plug in every room, and heating..." He is not sentimental about the past. "People lose perspective. The high-rise flats I saw as a kid were palaces, absolute palaces." And indeed, like Park Hill or Heath Town, to their first generation tenants they were. So what changed?

The industries were suffocated by international trade and a lack of investment, then killed outright by privatisation – if there's one English story, it's that. Wallsend's cranes were scrapped and sold to India by the 70s. The "deck-access housing" built over them by "Mr Newcastle", T. Dan Smith, replaced one set of slums for another, albeit with heating and plugs.

"Looking back, I dislike the way the government just closed these places down without providing jobs. They just left legacy populations. You had all these people who weren't going to get a job. That scene from *Abigail's Party*, they all work in computers? That never happened." What did instead?

Saturday morning in the Tyneside suburbs, and I'm feeling like Humpty Dumpty, post-pranged and pulverised. Paul suggests we take a drive. He knows the towns of the Tyne and Wear all too well, and like many others, issues a warning, only half in jest, of one particularly unloved place ahead. "Beware... it is a shithole."

Gold arcs the bay. Loser buys the ice creams as kids chase each other down the promenade, past Italian ice cream parlours, old maid Victorian guesthouses, castle ruins and the hulls of berthed sailboats.

The Whitley Bay scene is serene. We traipse across the sands. I chance upon a pretty shell, and let it roll within my hand, sensing its grooves. Paul recalls a different scene than the one today, of the sooty, stinking dock town of Tynemouth. He tells me how the Italian revolutionary Giuseppe Garibaldi came here in 1854 and was mobbed by adoring crowds. One myth has it that the Garibaldi biscuit was inspired by him accidentally sitting on an Eccles cake. Yevgeny Zamyatin worked on ice-breaker ships here a half-century later, then returned to Russia to write *We*, the dystopian image of a technologically sophisticated future without love or freedom, and uncredited inspiration for *Brave New World*. We drive out.

Southwick, Sunderland's edge, the source of so much disapprobation. Paul points out that the life expectancy here is around twenty years less than the wealthier parts of London. There are no unusual geological or industrial factors. Sheer poverty and its peripheral effects on health, diet and housing are its causes. This reheats earlier conversations about class. Is it not real, in the very way people live and die?

He has a better vantage to talk from. Whilst ruling out moralising delusions about reforming human nature or "improving" the Great Unwashed, Paul draws on his experiences delivering public health programmes to low-income communities. "Poor people cost more." They get ill younger and more often, their physical and mental health problems more likely to intersect, then impinge on others.

"Man hands on misery to man", as Larkin versifies. But a new management-speak and free market ethos has become the norm, one that turns communities and cultures into "asset-based development" and "additionality", "adding value". The meaningless verbiage of Public Choice Theory, the diseased management doxa crippling local government, health and social services. It turns ordinary people into rationally selfish "clients" or "customers", whilst casualising the workforce on insecure contracts, subjecting teams to regular surveillance to assess efficiency. It all becomes about the stats, often juked. Council services must now put in business "tenders", something previously and appropriately consigned to builders and plumbers, where the cost is the priority, not capability or people's lives. Paul talks of the competitive tendering for refugees, but as we home in on Sunderland, I realise we're trading in grumbles again, the most universal and least valuable of political currencies. What would make a difference?

"Conversations. Just talking to people." He recalls the successes of the NHS's anti-smoking campaigns of the 2000s. "Health workers would simply ask patients: do you smoke? Have you thought about stopping? Would you like some help with that?" And that was it. No guru required.

The car shifts into the left-hand lane as it approaches the city centre, and prevaricates on the third exit, its driver struggling to access the appropriate turn-off. From the passenger window, I scan the wasteland that separates us from the Wear, where the local Vaux brewery once stood. The site has been owned by Tesco for many years, who persistently insists on building a vast hypermarket against the council's approval. In the stalemate, nothing stands.

It's a symbol of Sunderland's uncertain status, built on glass production and shipbuilding. Only London Euston has had more unkind things said of it. Today's there's only "Nissan and call centres", as my mate Mark warned me. Paul remains in second gear as we survey the gutted scape, from run-down Grangetown to Hendon out in the east where Mark grew up, the homes of the poor often zone on where stink-winds blow, from west to east. Mark also told me about "Hendon bricks", not quite as weird as Wayne's chickens, but just as disquieting. Petrified sewage that sometimes surfaces on Hendon "beach", one of the few things Sunderland still produces.

Past the university, we park in a 70s mall car-park and mosey into the town centre. We're surrounded by many grand Victorian department stores, either derelict or filled with bargain chains. "All the shops are closed down", one lady tells us, as we wander around the pedestrianised centre, a city like Middlesbrough, all-too-aware of its faltering powers. We stop in Elizabeth's Tea Rooms, where milky tea's served up in at least four different vessels. An elaborate faff. It's lunchtime, but we're the only customers. "Have you seen enough?" Paul asks.

Not yet. Back in the car, we snake through the same subtopian drawl til signs appear for Bede's world. Jarrow town, reshaped by a large 60s urban project, with a now-familiar panoply of discount stores, hire-purchase shops and budget supermarkets. There's a random statue of a Viking opposite the town hall, where a plaque to the unemployed marchers who left Jarrow for London in 1936 has been inexplicably removed.

As we stroll around, a local senses something different about us. Nigel is a retired schoolteacher. He talks about the shipyards that once designed and built massive vessels for transporting Durham coal south to London, and about the unemployment march of '36 that followed when the shipyards closed, a result of an economic recession caused by financial speculation and a devastating programme of austerity cuts, overseen by a coalition government. Two hundred and seven of the town's fittest men were picked to take part. It took over a month to reach London, and their demands were ignored.

But like other major protests, its effect came later, in a kind of *never again* realisation that governments could, and would, ignore the poor, those they claimed to represent. It left a lasting moral indictment. Few consider it a failure, though it didn't succeed in its aims. Change is not often immediate. A completely different kind of Labour Party was elected in 1945 to that of 1931 under Ramsey MacDonald. But those 207 men today might be drafted into workfare supermarket jobs. Some would be too overweight or asthmatic to walk a week, let alone a month, not even regarding factors of motivation. Yet as Nigel reminds us, "all they asked for were dignity, recognition, and the chance to work". But it wasn't work for work's sake they asked for, but instead the right to live and work in dignity. Nigel tells us about the hunger marches of the early 30s and riots in Hyde Park. He's sees it all as of another world, but with foodbanks and riots of recent memory, I'm unsure.

We follow the signs back to Bede's World, an unusually enterprising cash-in on the local monk. Through a gate within a hedgerow, we approach the modest church and ruined abbey where Bede worked. It's early evening and things are closed but, just as incongruously, a group of drunk lads have scaled the ruins and clamber about the broken walls, twelve feet high. Bede wrote here in 731 CE that "man appears on earth for a little while; but of what went before this life or of what follows, we know nothing".

Bensham, Gateshead. We drive through one of the island's oldest Hasidic Jewish communities, and park by a partly bull-dozed terrace of early 20th century back-to-backs. Every window is barricaded, though some are double-glazed, and some of the houses look recently renovated. Like Middlesbrough, Rother-ham and other deindustrialised Northern towns, the houses were condemned in the early 2000s by Prescott's Pathfinder programme, a misguided plan to increase house prices and occupancy by bulldozing countless terraces in "low demand" areas. Its error was to persist in condemning and demolishing liveable homes long after their demand was in fact proven. Paul points out the recently repaired roofs and double-glazing of some. The money might've been invested into local industries to create employment, or the houses could've just been left standing as habitable homes. Instead we're amidst around eight blocks of back-to-backs, about a third demolished, the rest boarded up. Paul tells me that Gateshead's social housing waiting lists are empty, even after Pathfinder, because the government's spare bedroom tax now makes council rents unaffordable. "Look at it", Paul gestures. I've seen enough.

Back in Newcastle, we wander along the Tyne. The Sage concert venue squats over the river like a silver scarab beetle, whilst the scrubbed-up bricks of the Baltic mills are poised vertiginously like a near-lost game of Tetris. The regenerated quayside is pleasant but sterile. As we meander towards a boozer, two young men run past us, dressed in their birthday suits. One plunges ingloriously into the hacky Tyne, whilst another manages a front-flip. A big boozy crowd outside the Quayside Pub cheer in unison. "What's it for?" I ask one lad. "Oo gives a fook", he cheerily replies. The atavistic energies of the Geordie are irrepressible.

Over bottles of newkie broon, Paul gives a final crash-course in local accents. The Yorkshire lilts of the Middlesbrough Smoggy are contrasted to the pinched cheeks of the Sunderland Makem, as *make* and *take* become *mak* and *tak*. The Newcastle Geordie is a headier brew of assonance and elongated vowels. *Amganyam man!* Much of the Geordie dialect comes direct from old Anglo-Saxon English (to *gan* is to go), and it shares some Scottish features, whilst Middlesbrough retains some of the Viking influences of Yorkshire, where the Norwegians and Danes settled in some numbers. To the outside ear, these accents all sound apiece, but the local can tell one from another, or will make a big point of doing so at football derbies.

Unlike its neighbours, Newcastle's weathering the economic storm. We rove around its town centre, by its large university, pulsing nightlife and aspirational shops. Paul points out more local curios, from vampire bunnies built into the walls to the ruined Morden Tower where Northumbrian poet Basil Bunting read *Briggflats*, an epic capsule of life, of a man's and of a place's, and where Ginsberg came too, injecting a bit of Beat imagination. We drift from pub to pub til, by midnight, we're back at Bigg Market, where cops gaze irritably at pished partygoers passed out on street corners. Everyone's drunk. People queue with tickets for their choice of burger, chips or kebab (or even all three) at the Magic Flame. Seen enough?

Migraine in Ashington. Much, too much, red wine and beer. As a parting gesture of kindness, Paul drives me a little way out of Monkseaton to this small and depressed ex-mining town. There's no one around.

I'd been told that Ashington had been the biggest pit village in the world a century ago, employing ten thousand miners in five collieries. Then Thatcher waged war on the organised miners, and the productive mines were closed. The town's other product, aluminium, had also recently ceased production, leaving Ashington cut adrift. In the new era of liberated free markets, it was considered more viable to have whole communities on the dole than in useful work. A young man's tip in a newsagent directs me to the Woodhorn Colliery, the last of the mines still standing, open as a museum to this lost way of life.

"Close the door on past dreariness." "The will to work is the way to prosperity." "Nationalisation 1947. The New Era: Welfare Education Mechanisation." Queen-blue and claret banners hang inside, produced by local branches of the NUM, like Ellington, Seghill and Sleekburn A, all nearby. They are defined by their headline fonts, their sentimental and often heraldry-like use of borders and scrolls, and their emotive depictions of grey and miserable slum terraces, like those of Middlesbrough and Gateshead, a past they wished to put behind.

Their progressive, mechanised future failed to arrive, but there is a specifically working class English modernism to these banners that I hadn't anticipated. Rather than seeking to defend an unproductive and dangerous form of work, they sought to improve it. The banners were produced in the late 40s, at a time when much still felt possible. Rather than appearing as things back in time, they seem like the artefacts of ghosts of the future. What would demands for welfare, mechanisation, education or nationalisation look like today?

The scenes of the Pitmen Painters collected here present a way of life gone, perhaps mercifully too. There are blinkered pit ponies, wandering underground; a Friday fish supper; a Labour man addressing a packed-out pub of menfolk; a woman alone, the drudgery of domestic work before the era of cheap appliances; the death of a wife by tuberculosis. One image captures in cartoon format the life of a fourteen year-old miner, who wakes up at two each morning to put in a long shift on an unproductive seam, often where new miners would start until an older relative could negotiate something better. Returning home, he's too tired to bathe, eat or see his friends. He falls asleep as soon as he gets in, only to be woken by his mam to go back to the pit. "Slept it through" is the title.

But the paintings are intriguing also in how they were produced. The Pitmen Painters began meeting through a branch of the WEA in 1927 in an old hut, and by 1934 they worked with Robert Lyon to develop their paintings, which were then exhibited to the world. Harry Wilson was one miner involved. "Here I found an outlet for other things than earning my living", he said. "There is a feeling of being my own boss for a change and with it comes a sense of freedom."

Their hut was pulled down in 1983, and the last mine in the area shut in 2005, Howard, one of the museum's volunteers, tells me as I quiz him on the legacy beyond the exhibits. "Coal not dole", the striking miners demanded. Today even the latter's hard to come by. Paul had spoken of the local foodbanks struggling to meet demand, as numbers of people too poor to eat soar, often caused by four-to-thirteen week benefit sanctions. Jobcentres are aggressively sanctioning claimants for often absurd reasons, like attending job interviews or funerals elsewhere, or selling poppies for charity, and are themselves rumoured to be under targets to reduce the number of claimants. It may be some decades before Freedom of Information requests reveal whether the DWP or private firms like Atos have been instructed to actively impede as many people as possible from claiming benefits.

That basic right to freedom, to live and to live well, is not an expensive or unrealistic demand. Far more is spent on housing benefit to private landlords than on building new social housing; far more is lost in tax evasion and tax-breaks for wealthy individuals and corporations than over benefit fraud.

People in London or the South might think that I'm being too negative, "playing politics" over the veracity of the narrative. Come up to Easington and Ashington, and spend some time here, seeing, listening, talking with locals. Take a look at just how needlessly ravaged these places are, and think about the past and present political events that are causing this. Consider whether it is morally right that a person should freeze or go without food, or be punished for the crime of being poor *and* having a spare bedroom, or that they should be coerced into working without a wage, in a country presently the fifth richest in the world (GDP, nominal). If that is fine with you, continue voting Conservative. You may wish to close the book here.

For those of you who feel, like me, wearied and stunned by it all, a position of sceptical impartiality or knowing inaction is no good either, for these things will continue, whether we choose to look elsewhere or not. Trading our grumbles won't interrupt the processes that protect bankers and billionaires whilst consigning the vast majority of young and old to insecure, low-paid and drudgerous jobs. "Close the door on past dreariness", said the

Ellington miners back in 1950. What does a brighter future look like, and how will it work for us all?

There are murmurs of something on the other side of the border. *North*. North I go.

Out, along the Northumberland coast, keeping the cool vermilion sea to my right. Through Cresswell and its tangy brine, past ponies and cattle, the scene peaceful, then out to Amble, a harbour-village, the high street empty and still. "It is easier to die than to remember", Bunting wrote in *Briggflatts*, an intense and brooding lyrical reflection on this scape. "No hope of going back." But immersion too, as I continue north into a new kind of country, among the slowworm, and the bull, and the mason and his mallet, and one's youthful lover, and the larks, and "Words!", just words, the latter less useful to fathom this gentle desert scene.

Time slows, space expands. This region was once called Bernicia, part of the kingdom of Northumbria, a depopulated border-zone claimed by Norwegians, Danes, Angles and Irishmen, English and Scots at different times. Abandoned cottages, castles ruined, fields where foxglove, meadowsweet, red campion and purple loosestrife meet. The track scrapes through Warkworth, a perky old village marked by its floral front gardens, and a wizened castle that looms over the horizon, crucifix-outlined holes bored through its medieval keep. It still looks hardy enough to deter any invading Scots seeking the remains of the North Sea Oil profits.

Further north, I leave the coastal road at Alnmouth and detour inland, towards the old-fashioned and fusty delights of Alnwick, an old market town out of kilter with the ex-industrial settlements south. Another whimsical old castle, but the real treasure's locked inside an old railway station, now repurposed into a treasure trove of second-hand books. "It's very friendly, you'll like it here", says the assistant at Barter Books, as a toy train choo-choos over me, momentarily obstructing the wall-etched words of William Blake. She points me to the Black Swan.

Inside the accents are lighter and more nimble, with Irish inflections. "Different times", agree three men at the bar, trading anecdotes on haircuts whilst picking their nails and tapping away. A young woman beside me gazes wistfully into her smartphone whilst knocking back a large cup of wine. It's a Sunday and things are slow, between worlds. Nearby, a man starts to play the kazoo, riling everyone at the bar. Bland indie burbles in the background.

I'm missing my wife. Misery's a beast. The traveller rarely mentions the loneliness of the road. Phone calls are nothing to locked lips and a warm embrace. She'll be in Edinburgh in two days. I *will* be there to greet her off the train. I think back to Sandsend's brutal hill, and those words, that the love of others gives meaning to life. It's not gels or potions or ten-grand bikes that'll see one right, day in day out, on a journey like this, but a light within.

North, far from anywhere now. The disfigured ruins of Dunstanburgh Castle stalk the bay like the relic of an ancient and possibly nonhuman civilisation. I clamber around its collapsed walls, among sheep. But night's setting. With the last of the light, I pedal through Seahouses up to one last epic pile, Bamburgh Castle, still occupied by some titled worthy. I sneak around its battlements and pitch up tent beneath its walls. Two distant lighthouses momentarily illuminate the moon-silver beach and wine-black sea, which turns over and sighs. Wonder of the unknown road.

Surf bursts into the cramped, oily-nosed vessel, as it chugs exuberantly against the swell. Curds of briny spume splatter against those unfortunate enough to have picked a seat on the right-hand side. The passengers, mostly retired bird-watchers, cheerily commiserate and chuckle with one another.

The seas possess languages of their own, as do the skies. Our pilot navigates the tidal currents with an intuition akin to a lamb-farmer's collie, conversant with its master out on the field but deaf to table-talk. To our left, small black puffins with yellow bills, or tommy noddies as they're affectionately known locally, bob about in the straits that separate Seahouses from the Farne Islands. They will lay a single egg, and sit on it for forty days with maternal zeal until it's hatched. To our right on a distant rocky islet are a series of larger, sleek black birds, shags, stretching out their wings in the sun. Around and above us loom gulls in their thousands, navigating different tiers of wind with the minimum of wing movement. Razorbills and artic tern roam about in clusters of black and white, rising, casting shadows across the skerries. The pilot warns that anyone who lands without a hat will have their ears bitten clean off by the birds.

Gannets, bottlenose dolphins and minke whales gather here, but this morning the seals lollop and yawn atop the rocks. Guillemots cluster on another set of stacks, gadding about like flustered maître d's. Kittiwakes squawk nearby, half-pint seagulls. Rocks tang with shit, capping the skerries like snow. When a young gull is ready to leave the nest, one parent will gently encourage it down into the water, whilst the other boots it off the rock.

The lighthouse of Inner Farne approaches. The boat circles the islet, bringing into view the ruined remains of a 7th century chapel where St Cuthbert lived in hermitage, surrounded by the sea-birds who he's since been depicted with. Celtic Christians like Cuthbert preferred an ascetic exile, and lived in the most austere conditions. One can only marvel at the fruit of his reflections, alone among the birds. His body was later recovered and, to protect its sanctity from marauding Danes, buried by a group of itinerant monks at Durham, still incorrupt despite three centuries of being dead.

A little north is Lindisfarne, or Holy Island, which one can only reach by way of a regularly flooded causeway. There's just enough hours to get there and back. Pedal over the golden mudflats. A couple of miles on, a small village and visitor amenities are clustered together, a ruined castle in the distance, but most are here for the ancient priory, site of one of the earliest British Christian communities. Though its religion was Roman, its faith was forged in Ireland. Pagan Anglo-Saxons pushed out the earlier Christian culture from those parts of England where they settled over the 5th and 6th centuries. Retreating to distant islets and locales, missionaries like Enda, Finnian, Columba and Aidan maintained and spread an austere, monastic Christianity back to Scotland, then to Lindisfarne. Aidan was summoned from Iona by King Oswald to convert the heathens of Northumbria seventeen hundred years ago, just as Cedd would be summoned from Lindisfarne to reform the heathens of Essex.

No doubt there were political benefits to "civilising" wayward natives, or being spiritually attached to the old Roman church, but they would've brought spiritual consolation to their congregations. The first English illuminated gospels were made at Lindisfarne, using lapis lazuli sourced from the Himalayas, and some of the earliest surviving Anglo-Saxon writing and artwork was produced here, often surrounding the cult of St Cuthbert, its legendary abbot. The ruins of the priory, first gutted by Vikings, then Henry VIII, remain tranquil and picturesque, suited to meditation.

"Sell your cleverness and buy bewilderment", says Rumi, words as apt in Persia as distant Lindisfarne. I weigh on those words and chew them, as I cross back over the creeping tideline.

At some point along the highway I must've surely entered Scotland, for by the time I reach Berwick, the architecture changes entirely, and the locals have a lilting Scots twang. "You're beautiful!" shouts a young woman to her beau in a supermarket car-park, the last greeting one'd expect in the towns of the Tees or Tyne. The jerrybuilt miners' terraces and concrete crap of the 60s have no representation. Instead to my left and right are well-built hardy houses of thick grey brick, emanating a dour pragmatism that correlates to darker skies. The supermarket sells cheese from Caithness, Arran and the Mull of Kintyre, and McEwans and Tennants over Carling and Carlsberg. Even my change comes in a cheery blue Scottish note. I ride into the morose but intriguing old town, in search of a boozer, and my last night in England for some time.

Sitting by the old pier on a sleepy golden morning, I gaze at a distant lighthouse to my left, and the arched viaduct over the Tweed to my right. Sat beside me is the ghost of L.S. Lowry, occasionally peering up from his easel as he converts the glory of the morning sea into one of his Berwick seascapes.

I'm on the threshold between two countries, one beginning a journey towards political independence, the other scarcely aware of its own identity. The signs are already promising. After a cheap bed in a hostel bunkhouse, I rose early and popped into Wilson's bike shop. The bicycle, as usual, provoked mirth, but he fixed a couple of niggling issues and refused payment. He told me of the town's struggles since the loss of fishing and its industries, but spoke too of its generous, friendly spirit, as if its poverty were an insurance against losing that.

Bagpipes blare heartily from the town centre, and milling crowds shower the piper in small change. Edinburgh wool, black pudding and bampot bilingual tea-towels are each on offer. Filled with Caledonian Spirit (Irn Bru) and armed with anti-midge cream, I follow the A1 out, over the border. Signs and flags announce *Failte gu Alba!* "Scotland, here I am", I reply, with a fist to the air. Twenty-eight days! My welcoming party, a bald-headed geezer by a trucker's hot-dog kiosk, looks on sympathetically.

And och, the Lothian landscape soon whacks you over with its epic beauty. Through rolling back-lanes with fruity hedgerows and lush forests, I spin out, fattened lambs bleating left and right, songbirds cooing above. The sun hovers overhead, proud of its majestic perfection. Along hills that gently undulate through car-free serenity, I realise this is exactly the kind of cycling experience I'd dreamt of finding. Times and miles disappear.

From zingy pine spinneys, I buck back onto the coastal road, tumbling down into Pease Bay, where red cliffs give way to a sandy beach and caravan park. Modern geology was born in this place, when in 1788 James Hutton sailed out with two friends to Siccar Point. His claim is now common sense, but to assert back then that the world was older than four thousand years was heresy. As he pointed out the different layers of the cliffs, his friend John Playfair reflected that "we became sensible how much farther reason may sometimes go than imagination may venture to follow".

Thistle juts out from the quarry, beside an unlikely rural waste-plant where Manchester's recycling piles high. Nearby is Dunbar, an old town built around a wide and sober high street. A queue snakes out of Adriano's, where a production line that puts Nissan to shame deep-fries and wraps every conceivable food item one can think of, from haggis to pizza, all served with Irn Bru. Gut replenished, I pop into the Volunteers, overlooking the rocking boats of the harbour, for a drop of the local Belhaven.

Inside the cosy old boozer, a Londoner sways about on a barstool and issues small talk with depressed enthusiasm. "You don't fall far from the nest", he warns. Outside, another southern English couple tells me about the beautiful Isle of Harris in the Outer Hebrides, and complains of the emotional constipation of the English. There's something freer feeling up here I can't yet identify, something disarming, in a way unknown south of Buxton.

And so I head out of Dunbar, detouring out to North Berwick where, on a bumpy road that threads past the ruins of Tantallon Castle, I reach a twee harbour dwarfed by a vast Tesco, and an even vaster volcano, Berwick Law, that looms over the surrounding countryside. By Gullane, and a gnarled forest barely contained in a laird's drystone walls, I enter the conurbation of Edinburgh, glimpsing distant Carlton Hill and its ruined pillars, then Seaton Sands and the alms-houses of Prestonpans. At Musselburgh I see that same architectural style as Berwick, grey and gloomy, dignified and sturdy, symbol of another North European culture. Teenagers frolic by the river, reminiscent of those first heady evenings of summer when everything felt possible. Indeed again now.

Edinburgh takes a long time to reach, its low-rise suburbia dense and repetitive. But lo, the increasingly pot-holed roads and sight of black taxis indicates the onset of urbanity. Its Georgian centre is pretty, and unlike most English cities, without interruption by corporate phalli or neglected social housing. Into the city, surrounded by patient traffic and droves of tourists, I follow roads round until Josep's instructions begin to make sense.

A good friend from London, he's now moved up here with his partner Delwar. Over snifters of local whisky, Delwar talks of Laurie Lee's journey across the Pyrenees. Lee encountered things he hadn't yet words for. He needed "new forms for new sensations", as Virginia Woolf put it. This world I'm exploring is already mapped, photographed and transcribed. Much of the route could be undertaken using Google Maps. But the experiences of exhaustion and elation, bitterness and pride, are beyond my limited political and imaginative vocabulary.

What will come? Let the road decide.

CHAPTER 5

Freedom is Best

"No, but where are ye headen?" – Richard.

The next few days pass in a gentle blur, as Sarah and I maunder around Edinburgh, spending time together, absorbing the place. It's been twenty-nine days since I last saw her and despite regular phone calls and texts, her face and embrace restore the strength needed to enjoy being alive.

For who'd bet I'd make it this far? Not me. Reaching Scotland makes things that much more serious. There are mountains and midges, and an unpopulated wilderness to the north where bike shops and boozers will be few and far between. I can't wait to explore it. First, a few easy days with my partner.

Edinburgh is twee and beguiling, if at times too saccharine. Wide Georgian boulevards and poky squares and a grey garrison hulked over the centre give the lie of a grand medieval city, but Old Town and New Town are much alike, and Edinburgh's centre was largely designed and built over the 19th century. It is ambitiously designed and impressive, and peerless in many respects. The Scottish nation has a worthy and distinctive capital.

Even if, in places like the Royal Mile, Edinburgh feels burdened by its history, there's pleasure in meandering around it: the orderly squares north of George Street, past restaurants, hotels and freemason clubs, then through Princes Gardens and down to the Old Town, dawdling behind the tourists along the Royal Mile with its tartan and tat dispensaries, past statues dedicated to Walter Scott, David Hume and Adam Smith. The city is proud of its philosophical and literary history like no English town I've encountered. Beneath them, a high number of beggars, a more familiar poverty hidden behind its affluent old façade.

Drifting down through Holyrood, we locate the Scottish Parliamentary Building easily by its vast, experimental form. Pied-white and bronze, it's defined by funky-shaped windows and a prevailing cheerful incoherence, indicating transparency and benign intent. Access is easy, one can come along inconsequentially to hear a public debate or consult one's MSP. There are no machine gun-toting cops outside, nor anything reminiscent of the old school tie. We find our friends Kirsten and David in a car-park there, the site where arch-Presbyterian John Knox is buried, and, in the irreverent spirit of Hume, more commonly used as a cruising spot.

We spend a night with them, having spent two with Josep and Delwar. "Travel two miles out of the city centre and you'll see a very different Edinburgh", David tells us, as we're given a crash course in Scottish drinking and pro-independence politics. He talks of nearby ex-mining towns like Dalkeith, obnoxious kids rampaging round on dirt bikes, drunken brawls in the ex-miners club, air of torpor and frustration. The next morning, feeling blue having said another farewell to Sarah, I take to the bike again, and throw myself into Edinburgh, to find out what he meant.

Calton Hill, overlooking the city. Flat, low-rise suburbia stretches out to the Forth of Firth. I picture Balerno, Joppa and Drem, the peculiar names of settlements ill-matched to the blandscape. I ride back through Princes Street, heading north to the disconnected pebbledash estates of Drylaw. A girl in a bakery talks with tested pride of the place, describing all the signs of stability and community. But nearby Muirhouse is more obviously deprived. I pass through the grotty Pennywell arcade, where the only things open are a tatty pub, betting shop, offie, Greggs and a drug misuse team office. The supermarket closed some time ago.

"He was saying that I shagged his brother."

[Sounding disappointed] "Didye?"

"Aye. He was a fucken fag."

Groups of mid-teens wander about in a passive trance. An older man shouts at two of them in a drunken rage. The next time I see him will be at a nearby bus stop, holding a part of my bicycle.

Josep's a librarian here. He teaches local children how to read, and the library provides a safer, quieter space away from the turbulence of the surrounding estates. I peer through books on Scottish flora and fauna, as a group of young lads nearby play a football videogame supplied by the library. "What a fair mess eh?" says one. "That's a daft tackle, unnecessary, and now he's off", announces the game's CPU commentator. They all swear back in unison.

One lad takes out a lighter and tries to set alight another kid's coat as he plays. Another enters on a BMX and races about, ignoring the staff. Later, I ask Josep if they ever get any aggression directed against them. "Some of the kids just lose it", he says, after a time. "They're not able to control themselves."

We're sitting outside the library, in what might've once been a car-park, or recreation ground, now just an abyss of concreted nothing, distant high-rises, garage lock-ups and barren scrubland all around us. The effect is debilitatingly grim, and I point this out. As physical animals that live in our minds, the spaces we inhabit shape how we think and feel. But Josep replies that people do have the power to step out of these circumstances, and not be determined by them to repeat cycles of poverty. If he could back in Catalonia, why can't others here?

Last week, one local person's bike was destroyed by the kids here for no reason whatsoever, after he popped in to use the computers. As I unlock my bike I realise that someone's interfered with it. A flask and my bungee ropes have been nicked – luckily I took all my bags in with me to the library. Riding up Ferry Road and feeling pissed off, I spot my flask in the care of the heavily pished old "jakey" (the local phrase for a down-and-out alcoholic) who I'd seen ranting earlier. "A wee one left it!" he insists as I pull it out of his hand and issue a reprimand. There are the dregs of cider at the bottom. I think of the bored kids in the area, the easy cash opportunities and escapism provided by drugs, and their wider abandonment by parental figures. The library struggles to provide some sense of order and kindness on an otherwise miserable and violent estate. Its work is commendable.

I reach Leith, a port town now absorbed into the Edinburgh metropolis, but still retaining its own independent spirit. It's a bustling though evidently impoverished place, though by no means as grim as its early-90s immortalisation in Irvine Welsh's *Trainspotting*. The Banana Flats cotch over the scene like a piece of Thunderbirds' concretopia, as colourful as a stubbed-out snout. The old docks have now been gentrified by posh restaurants, luxury apartment blocks and a moronic Ocean Terminal mall, a non-place inflicted on Leith as a punishment for once having any kind of character.

I roam around the old port area, wondering if this gentrification has been good for a once heavily-deprived district. Into the lively Port of Leith boozer, I soon find myself in friendly company. Glenn, originally from Kirkcaldy, has been a delivery man some decades. He talks of the beautiful drive from Edinburgh to Inverness, of the marketisation of Royal Mail, and the changes in Leith the last few years. He's largely positive, and thinks the area's been improved a lot. Outside investment has done something for spaces and places that were once abandoned. Bad housing and troublesome tenants have been removed (down Ferry Road...), but there's a buzz about the place. Money has that effect.

Over pints of Belhaven we talk about the city, about the piss-poor performance of Hearts and Hibs, the local football clubs, and onto the popular topic of independence. Locals chip in and out as the hours pass ("How's life?" "Same old pish"). As Glenn sees it, "I'm very lucky to be from a prosperous country. But it's just a fluke of birth. This is a unique chance for Scotland to take control of itself." Like Kirsten and David, and most of the Scots I'm meeting so far, he's broadly in favour of independence, considering it inevitable within the next twenty-five years. "Whether it's this referendum or the next, it's not going away."

All those pints have rendered the bicycle unsteady. I make it back into town to meet with my last host in Edinburgh, Crìsdean. He's a passionate and well-informed campaigner for independence, and like many Scots, is angered by the centuries-long normalisation of Englishness taught and passed on as Britishness. We've exchanged emails over the last fortnight while I've been on the road, a correspondence fascinating and fruitful. Crìs has already supplied me with a plethora of information about Gaelic, Scottish history, and the culture of the Hebrides, and set up a number of contacts. I'm looking forward to meeting him.

Pedalling up Leith Walk, I reach Café Habana where a crowd of partygoers are drinking and laughing outside. It's one of the gathering points after the Pride Scotia event, and Crìs spots me outside locking up my bike. We head inside where Crìs introduces me to Paul, and over a few drinks we talk about identity whilst pop tunes and bright colours fizz the interior. As some gyrate, others gaze out into the empty distance, chewing on lower lips. It's a chance to spend time with another community that has fought hard for equal rights and, still incompletely, secured these through organised struggle.

Later, we eat dinner and drink wine back at Crìs's place among the suburban streets off Dalkeith Road. He recounts tales of serving in the Royal Navy, before getting kicked out and moving to South London in the early 80s, the gay co-op squats of New Cross, rioting in Brixton, bricks against the cops. Back then, overthrowing an unpopular government seemed possible. Thatcher was an "obvious evil", fighting an open war against the poor. But could Thatcher have succeeded with the bedroom tax, or privatising the health system? Now, however, there's no obvious holder of power. In England at least, polled public opinions on immigration and welfare are shifting rightward. Offshore firms and global markets steer people's lives, and the collective memories of victories like the NHS or public ownership seem forgotten, museum pieces like those of the Woodhorn colliery.

And now, sat in a cluttered living room, plates of pasta on our knees, surrounded by piles of polymathic books and pictures of Tibet, trying to make sense of all this. "Working in A&E often gave you a view of the impermanence of this life", he says of working in the NHS. Heart attacks, car accidents, people insisting they were too young for cancer, too young for this. Death doesn't wait for us to be ready.

When you say Britain, what do you mean? A One-Nation island? No, it's made up of many. Do you mean then the political state of the United Kingdom of Great Britain and Northern Ireland, theoretically established in 1922 after Irish independence, or the Act of Union of 1707 preceding that? Or the ancient Britons, or maybe the British Empire? A bit of them all, perhaps? Rarely is it spelt out, and instead a certain kind of London-centred, middle class Englishness has become the universal norm of British and Britain.

Over cups of milky tea and Gaelic songs on the radio, Crìs and his mate Ian talk about these infra-island idiosyncrasies. I ask them why Scotland has secured free prescriptions and free university education, and what's generally considered superior social care for the disabled and elderly, whilst the Sassenachs south of Berwick still fall for myths of benefit tourists and job-thieving Romanians. "All these things, they're at the heart of the Scottish psyche. When I look at the situation in England, it's much much worse." But Crìs sees some hope. "We could live in a more inclusive, fair and equal society.". The independence debate's generating these kinds of constitutional possibilities. It is with hope, and a sealed note pressed into my hand, that I leave Edinburgh, an unknown country ahead of me.

Back through Cowgate and along the potholes by Princes Garden, weaving through throngs of tourists. Out into Edinburgh's vast suburbia, the features begin to thin out, wider and flatter residences, a zoo, an airport, then total disorientation in the out-of-town corporate zones and science parks of Gyle, roads leading nowhere, absent of discernible features. Signs forbid cycles from riding the highway west. My jacket has somehow fallen off the back of the bike, and a retracing of my route brings no joy. I'm ill-prepared for the pluvial persona of the Scots summer.

Lost, cold, and with absolutely no idea what location I should even head towards, despair sets in. I left Cris's quite late in the afternoon. Will I be even able to get out of outer Edinburgh? After a time, I find myself on a canal path heading west towards Falkirk.

Without a map, I'm reliant on directions to gauge the route ahead. One jogger is breezily optimistic: "Falkirk? Just follow the path..." Who knows how long for. Another cyclist issues more distressing instructions, "very long, forty miles! Four hours! Phe-ew!" Well... I'm subject to fate. So I ride on, following the canal path by wheat fields and spooky tunnels, past randomly distributed pebbledash council estates and, as two teens tell me near Broxbourne, "plenty of green spaces to walk the dog!" Further along, two lads tear along the towpath on mopeds. Thereafter, the early evening path's empty, except for the occasional fisherman, cheerily failing to catch tench, carp or perch. "Good day!" I shout to them, with an awkward nod back.

But I'm still nowhere, and the darkening skies warrant upping the pace. I reach the outskirts of Falkirk by eight, pausing by its corkscrew boatlift, linking two canals. The scenery is rural and flat, with the small town in the distance. The parkland nearby is eerily empty and undramatic for all that's supposedly taken place within it. William Wallace lost and Bonny Prince Charlie won against the English crown here in 1298 and 1746 respectively and, along this way too, the Romans built their Antonine wall, as ambitious as Hadrian's but abandoned after two decades.

Against a dull and heavy sunset, only the cries and curves of the birds interrupt the scene. Then Falkirk, an incoherent Victorian market town, seemingly subject to some Sunday night curfew. Takeaways rub against empty shops. I finally find another soul. "It's alright", quiet, good pubs – the main priorities. "There used to be around seventeen factories open. Now there's one!" Familiar stories. Once a centre of iron, steel, then publishing, thriving on its canal connections and location equidistant between Glasgow and Edinburgh, things are quiet, "tough". Chemicals are the main industry over at Grangemouth. He hurries along, as if some prowling policeman might punish us for talking in the street.

Though it's around nine, the north hemisphere light sustains the gloaming much longer than down south. After Larbert and its PFI hospital, mobbed by cattle, I reach pebbledash Plean, a grotty ex-industrial town. A tatty chippie neighbours a neglected-looking health clinic and library. "You've tried the rest, now tries the best", promises the sign.

Inside, a lengthy queue of overweight young adults. Feeling famished, I begin to wonder what the "pizza crunch" on the menu might refer to. A cheeky smile escapes from the overworked assistant. "Half of that, with chips!" Others queue for sweet chilli haggis, gargantuan portions of chips and cheese, all accompanied by hulking bottles of Irn Bru, sought out with the thirst of Tantalus. Stephen Fry drones on incongruously from a TV screen in the corner. "What would you like hen?"

I find a bench outside and eat my pizza crunch, a deep-fried cheese and onion pizza coated in grease and salt. My fingers quickly slime up, and it takes determination to finish it. Irn Bru helps wash away the taste, explaining its popularity. Dance music blares out from a nearby car covered in tribal decals, two portly lads cramming more chips into their bodies than seems feasible.

Like the meanly proportioned terraced housing around it, this crap food indicates some internalised sense of social inferiority, a passive acceptance of it.

Leaden, I push my heavy body up a hill towards Bannock-burn, now a small and indistinct suburb of Stirling. I'm only two days shy of the anniversary of the battle here where the Scots, led by Robert the Bruce, beat the English and secured an almighty victory in their war for independence. Despite its obvious nationalistic significance, the only boozer I pass is named the Empire, proudly parading its Britishness with countless Union Jacks. Light fading, I ride into Stirling.

This small town, wedged with a forested valley, is more beguiling than Falkirk, and its combinations of old buildings and statues to Rabbie Burns, Rob Roy and other national luminaries adds to its Jerusalem-like ambience of nationalist significance. Stirling was once the capital of Scotland, and possesses the greater share of its triumphalist monuments. A nearby hall promotes a Ken Dodd show, images of oversized dentures and feather dusters only slightly dampening the patriotic airs.

I wander around the castle, gazing between its battlements at the towering Wallace monument in the horizon, situated by Stirling Bridge where Wallace won the first decisive victory for the Scots against the English in 1297. It was his only victory, and was largely aided by the bridge itself, which collapsed when the English advanced over it, drowning much of their army and dispersing the remainder. Wallace was roundly defeated at Falkirk the year after, and went into exile. It's his myth that's more enduring, and another retrospective fabrication of a kind, as authentic as the vast 19th century tower in memorial to him, built from public donations. "Freedom is best, I tell thee true, of all things to be won", Wallace is quoted as saying, in remarkably Victorian phrasing. "[N]ever live within the bonds of slavery, my son."

But as young Jamie puts it in the Portcullis later, "freedom isn't free". I'm drinking by the old prison, the only punter in at this late hour. I've opened Crìs's note, and found some very kind words and enough cash for a few, much-needed drinks. Jamie polishes cutlery and talks politics. "I think there's a lot of people who aren't talking who'll not vote yes", he says, a little dyspeptically. "People who don't want to look anti-patriotic." Nationalism equals liberation is a narrative that shouldn't be too easily accepted, he adds, and he begins to supply a bevy of persuasive reasons why patriotism cannot ever be allied with a progressive movement for equality.

He gives the case of nearby Bannockburn, stirring up strange behaviours. "Celebrating and re-enacting people's deaths... I find distasteful." The landlady sits with us. They take turns recalling aspects of an event the previous night. A group of men had been getting tanked up all afternoon, "doubles with their pints", a lot of noise from their corner, increasingly rowdy. They were getting out saltires, Scottish flags, "raving on" about Bannockburn. They were thrown out after a verbal altercation. The crew marched down to the battlefield.

She's unsure what happened to them next (it's a fair walk...), but the story reflects an uncertainty about what independence might deliver beyond pride. What of borders, or currency, or the NHS? "I'm proud to be Scottish, but..." Jamie says, hesitating again. "I don't know, I can't find the right word."

Uncertainty's been the recurring word. As I head past the dark outline of the Wallace monument, I scan the surrounding fields for a place to camp, but they're filled with livestock. "At night, all cows are black", goes the Yiddish proverb; still, no good if they trample down your tent. Desperate again, I pedal along the road to Alloa. It's around midnight, too dangerous for cycling. At last, a little off the road, I make out what looks like a forest. I venture inside.

A herd of sheep eyes me cautiously. I pack up quickly, not wishing to test my squatters' rights any further, and head east. To my left are the rolling Ochills, towering majestically above the flat farmlands that span out to my right, the first rural scenery since Northumbria. Beyond that, one can make out at matchstick-scale lines of pylons, petrol forecourts and bungalow clusters at Alva, Tillicoultry and Dollar. Each person smiles or shouts "Hullo!" One old dear tells me it's lovely here, "small", and I hear the accents change again, from the Edinburgh fuzz and the ponderous elongation of Falkirk, to a slower, glacial drawl. Livestock outnumber people, life's lived at half-speed. Alas, the rain whacks against me hard, soaking straight to the skin. Determined, I keep Loch Leven to my right and the Lomond Hills to my left, the rural scene giving way to the mighty Firth of Forth.

It's an increasingly undulating scape, as county Perth gives way to Kinross. Kids queue for chips and Irn Bru in Leslie, whilst in Glenrothes, a young man starts raging at the girls beside him in the car-park of a discount supermarket. Things seem straitened. "Why won't anyone ever fucking listen to me?" he cries, not even himself heeding. Leven's not dissimilar, a preoccupied pinched-scape defined by low-rise pebbledash council housing, squat 70s schools, its coalfields closed up, spent.

I cross into the Kingdom of Fife, the terrain becoming flatter. Signs point to luxury golf resorts and tourist coastal paths, the economic tenor changing. At Lundin Links, I detour off the major road and head into Largo, marked by a placid little harbour and a small tribute to Alexander Selkirk, the unruly anti-hero who inspired Robinson Crusoe. After a series of arguments with figures of authority, he was left stranded on an unoccupied island in the South Pacific, and somehow survived for four years. He loved it. As the captain of the ship that later rescued him reflected, "[o] ne may see that solitude and retirement from the world is not such an insufferable state of life as most men imagine".

Inside the Railway Inn, grown men clutch onto the bar as if gravity were suspended inside. There's a background fuzz of televised snooker that everyone ignores. Outside, two women trade gossip, the boozer reflecting the gender segregations of the local golf clubs. As I down the last of the mild, a retired American storms into the bar and announces himself.

"Hi! I am an American! Where's the men's room?! When I come back, I'll tell you all about myself!"

Stony silence. As he disappears, a taciturn local gazes up from his mercurial postulations and eyes me his disapproval.

After lunching among the briny marram of lovely Elie Beach, I ride past a succession of twee fishing villages, like St Monans, then Pittenweem, the smell of fresh fish on sale, then out through Anstruther, Cellardyke and Crail, a gorgeous village defined by its quaint cottages, lobster pots and a harbour where peeling timber boards are the last remaining signs of shellfish kiosks.

Has the place changed much in the last fifty years, I ask one old boy. "No no", laughs Jimmy. But pubs and shops have closed in some number. The price of goods is too high, particularly beer, he insists. "People are struggling." What about the tourists? But it's only a "summer trade", the winters bite hard. His explanation is also depressingly familiar. "The system's set up for those who dinnae wanna work, they just come over here." Who, the Swiss bankers, petrodollar sheikhs or Russian oligarchs? No, but these mythic hordes of European benefit tourists who no one's ever seen. I ask him if he has any evidence or experience to back up his view. "No, they don't come round here, no jobs." False, but at least consistent.

The sun's now setting over the Fife coast. The road's populated by one exclusive golf resort after another, until, in the distance, appear the steeples of St Andrews, the very home of golf itself. Into the austere old town, where American and Chinese students are showing their proud parents round. There's a small harbour, and a series of university buildings overlooking the sea. I'm most impressed by St Andrew's Cathedral, a picturesque ruin close to its centre. Once the largest building in Scotland, resplendent in gold and opulent icons, John Knox came and incited a mob to burn down its superfluous trappings. The hypocrisy of religious zeal has left behind a charmed relic.

I stop for a pint in the Criterion where, outside, and with the rain cleared, I get talking to Ben and Rich, two Londoners here for the golf. We talk a while in the early evening sun, Rich of Ireland, Ben of the Outer Hebrides and the best local malts. They marvel that this kind of journey can be done on a vegetarian diet of kidney beans, biscuits and tortilla wraps, and insist on squeezing my leg muscles for proof. Beery male company soon breaches intimacy!

North, the sun squeezing more light into the day than I've yet encountered. Why stop just yet? The evening's the best time to ride, cooler, imbuing everything with an ethereal gold. Out past the Old Course by the sea, its teeny little bridge where golfers queue to pose. The road gently weaves past Forgan and the RAF base at Leuchars, where grubby semis and a silent playground stare behind barbed wire. I race two lads on BMXs over the River Tay ("Och, you win!") and face wide Dundee before me. Dirty, tired, soaked, and knowing no one here, I decide to use the rest of Crìs's money to tumble into a backpacker's hostel.

A young Pole tells me about his course in International Relations, whilst Nick, an ex-bike mechanic from London, smiles in the hostel kitchen as he recounts his trajectory. He's taken a risk, a "big one", leaving all that behind to come up here to train as a comic-book artist. Dundee is the unlikely home of the schoolboy comics of the Beano, Dandy and the Broons. "One day I realised, I was running just to keep up, and that I'd be doing this for the rest of my life. I decided. I had to make the opportunity to get out." A practical vocation? Yes, no doubt, if that's what he loves. He's here, as am I, each pursuing our desires to the beat of the rhythm they impress on our hearts. Love can never enjoy the certainty of its object. Life is a continual striving, and love is the expression of its energy. Either that, or knock back crate after crate of discount lager, as another fella does in the TV room, dozing asleep, jerking awake, drool stringing from his cheek. Freedom is also a burden.

Late morning in Dundee. A young man from Andalusia traces a finger over a map. Philip's enthusiasm for this modest, overachieving city is contagious. Consider the ultraviolence of Grand Theft Auto, the first cash machine, or Snow Patrol and Brian Cox... Before I prostrate myself, I scan the setting. A British Town Centre of predictable hues, but with some impressively ambitious Victorian structures. Its population continues to shrink from that 19th century heyday of jute, jam and journalism, but the town has a high number of universities and research institutes, and carries a confidence about it that I found missing in Edinburgh. Its commitment to learning and high-skill technological development is proving successful, and indicates a more sustainable urban model than the low-skill retail park drudgery that defines the small towns of England.

With the northerly direction I'm taking, this will also be the last town I'll see for some time. I stock up on supplies, pleased with the bargain of a "showerproof" coat that'll prove anything but, and then ride out north, past a busy harbour, and into the county of Angus, where the Hindu god Ganesha greets passing traffic, a plastic silver statuette left atop a roadside bin.

Reprieve from freight truck fug comes at pretty Carnoustie, where boules, crossword books and littoral napping have the effect of ketamine on the gladly retired. People talk freely, and one old boy tips me on a lovely cycle route hugging the North Sea. I skate by golden beaches to my right, and fattened cows to my left, wistfully unaware of what cut of steak their hindquarters will make, and towards Arbroath, cycling awhile with Ian, an old fella who laughs about the "old ways" of the town he loves ahead.

We part ways besides its old harbour, where lobster pots are piled high beside signs advertising angling trips. "It's all shellfish, lobster and crab", a young boat engineer says, but some fishermen still make enough from their catch to sustain a living, so long as they're willing to do the boat trips so popular with tourists. The numbers are diminishing. The smoky scents lead to a clutter of seaside shacks, where Arbroath smokies hang for sale. Fishing used to employ the entire community. Men needed lines and baits prepared, as well as their fish processes for market, dirty and difficult work that their wives and children would do on the shore. Odd omens accrued, and to mention pigs, salt, rabbits or hares could spell certain death on the treacherous ocean.

That's long gone, a way of life beyond even their memories now. Outside the town's Wetherspoon's, Greg speaks with warmth and sincerity on the meaning of life. "All I want to do is help others. If other people are happy, then that's enough." What's life like here for young people like him? Ambivalent. He's been unemployed since leaving college with a sound-engineering qualification. There's little work he can get, but he's got grit, volunteering his time to local charities. "Living on the streets of Arbroath isn't as tough as sleeping in the fields of Africa." Desperation effects such optimistic calculations.

I take the hilly road out of Arbroath, passing poly-tunnels growing swollen strawberries. My legs are aching, and the road plods along through the green Angus farmscapes with some monotony. After some time, Montrose arrives quite from nowhere, a pleasant bloom in a coastal valley after a long series of wearying humps. Over a long metal bridge traversing the Esk, and into town. To my right is a large busy harbour, and the road threads through grubby workaday townhouses into a wide Victorian high street, statues of old worthies under the shadow of a russet steeple and mock-classic columns of grandiose character. An old port town, it's aged well.

Outside the Mermaid Chippie, I talk with an ill-looking young woman, brown tooth and index finger, hesitant gaze. "Not many jobs round here at all. Same as everywhere." Together we survey the scenery: betting shops, charity shops, payday lenders. I look at those old civic statues, and wonder what an independent Scotland can do for all this unemployment, ill-health and general unhappiness that also characterises a generational experience. "Never live with the bonds of slavery", said William Wallace, ventriloquised, but freedom isn't merely the right to vote, but the right to live, and live well.

It's all going off in the Royal Arch, a batty boozer with wild-looking old men sucking cigs outside. The landlady's pointed glare conveys I've come into the wrong place. But I stick it out, and don't regret it. I sink a pint of Tennent's sitting on a tall barstool and work through the local rag. Soon thirst compels more. Two inebriated fellas beside me, in their sixties at least, debate recent sexual liaisons. Conversation skitters from Bill Murray ("he's the cunt coming in", inexplicably) to pool. The boozer erupts in rowdy shouting when another refreshed punter insists he's the best in the bar. "No, I'm the best, I trained yous!"

Ben sits beside me. He was a chef in Bermuda for thirty years, but decided after retirement to come back home. His sister is a manager in the port. "Grain, potatoes, oil, it's busy!" but, like with other port towns, drugs arrive here too, and he complains to me of the problem among the numerous unemployed here. I share some of my observations. "If it's not broke, don't fix it", he replies, on the topic of political change, an attitude of serotonin-depleted resilience that can sink or save a man's marriage, job, even his mind.

Our chat is disrupted by George. Success in the bookies. He slaps down notes and coins onto the bar and buys everyone in the pub a drink. It's the first time I've seen it happen! Another beer comes my way. He's been out of work, he tells me, but he's making ends meet. People look out for each other, he adds, and it's obvious. He disappears to put some Elvis on the jukie. Everyone starts singing along to 'All Shook Up'. I'm talking to Richard now, another old boy equally refreshed. We talk awhile but he's unable to focus on the thread of the conversation, and eventually palms a fiver into my hand "for ye dinner!" and staggers back to his table. Scottish hospitality!

I leave the boozer shaking everyone's hand, and with sadness push north, past the wee towns of St Cyrus, Johnshaven, Inverbervie and Kinneff. It's a long and bumpy road, and the sun begins to set by the time I reach Dunnottar, where the road dips into the sea.

On the edge of the easterly cliff arise the ruins of Dunnottar Castle, appearing older than all human habitation. The low sun burnishes the bay, from teal-greys to gold, and the cool breeze and the wildflowers further enchant the scene, as I ramble down a steep staircase and back up towards the rough-hewn, immense rock that holds up the crumbled remains of a fortress on a shelving slope, a monument to the expiration of time.

After a nightcap in Stonehaven with Richard's dinner money, I drift out again, towards the wooded Highlands. Two miles up the military road, approximately nowhere, I notice my phone has no signal. It won't return for some weeks.

We, the most distant dwellers upon earth, the last of the free, have been shielded until today by our remoteness and by the obscurity in which it has shrouded our name. Now the farthest bounds of Britain lie open to our enemies; and what men know nothing about they always assume to be a valuable prize. But there are no more nations beyond us; nothing is there but waves and rocks, and the Romans.

I awake in the foothills of the Highlands, overlooking an old military road that presses north. It was built by the English to control the rebellious population, the first of its kind since those of the Romans here two thousand years earlier. For somewhere nearby is an old Roman marching camp, and near that, perhaps, the location of the battle of Mons Graupius, where Calgacus abortively led the most distant dwellers upon earth against the Romans. Ends connote margins, dissident spaces. Another Roman historian, Cassius Dio, claimed that the Caledonians "possess their women in common, and in common rear all the offspring. Their form of rule is democratic for the most part, and they are very fond of plundering." Even by the 6th century, Gildas, also thought by some to be from Scotland, claimed that the "island of Britain lies virtually at the end of the world".

It's quiet enough to listen just to the breeze along this a single-lane deserted road, fields and thickets to my left and right, kestrels, swallows and wagtails flitting above. Pause at the hamlet of Rickarton, where George laughs and shows me round his meticulously maintained front garden, fussing over petunias and begonias. Eighty-two years ago he arrived here, a young child, his parents running the local shop. The farmers have gone, he sighs, and he points out the unlikely remains of the store, and other local buildings, now ruins. Much of the land is still farmed, but fewer hands are needed, and in any case few could afford them. The lone farmer takes on much of the work himself, with his machines, working longer for less. George smiles with ease, with the tranquillity of the aged who've so long reckoned with fate's cruel ineluctability that it is no longer worth the concern. "You're young!" he says, closing up my questions. Obsolescence is the way. He insists I take a photo of him with his colourful flowers to remember him by.

Further along is Banchory, a small town on the cusp of the Cairngorms National Park. Outside town, a vast Tescopolis. It bustles in the way Banchory's town centre once did, and seems to have replaced its primary functions. All it needs is a hotel and a pub, and perhaps the old town could be closed down altogether. Inside, there's a school trip to the fish counter. The children each wear Tesco-branded bibs, whilst a worker introduces the array of foreign-sourced fish at the counter. "Who's brave enough to try this?"

I get talking to Joe and Jen outside, a retired couple from Ashington. They invite me back to their motorhome for lunch.

In a vehicle with more mod-cons than the average flat, they are more circumspect about the nobility of the mines I've passed. "It's not for human beings", says Joe. He remembers the tiny seams, the hot, black, hellish conditions, and his father, who worked down the pits from 12 to 60, urging him, "as long as I've got a hole in my behind, you're not going down the mine!"

So Joe took a job at the aluminium plant. Wages were lower but the work was easier. He managed to get out just before Alcan laid off its workforce a few years ago, taking early retirement whilst there was still money on offer. "It's going down", he says, circumspectly. It's unclear whether he means Ashington, the North East, or something else more broadly. With further austerity cuts likely to suffocate the rump of health and social care, Jen thinks that change has to happen. Joe agrees. "I think things are changing, where it won't be normal for people to lock themselves in their little homes, with their TVs, all alone. People need each other."

Scents of burning timber and pine tingle nostrils as I pass the paper-mills on Banchory's edge, and out through some increasingly rugged and rocky terrain. The scene is beginning to stretch out: longer sweeps of forests, of swooping corries and glens, of ascents into the hills that rise imperceptibly for some time, and that one can only measure by looking back, and surveying the verdant ranges behind. Inchmarlo gives way to Kincardine O'Neil, another enchanting hamlet with a name like a Hollywood actress. Surrounded by tall pines and distant peaks, nature is as awe-inspiring as the massive lumber lorries that narrowly overtake me.

Pause in the village of Aboyne. Two teens passing cheerily deal with my questions. Evie and Callum have a choice, a stilted one, as all young people do here, they say. Farming, of whatever's left ("wheat, barley and lots of turnips"), though reserved for "cliquey" families, or the services, that is, cleaning in the nearby Hilton, or the local cafes and supermarket, like Evie.

How does the future feel? They disagree on politics, but both –
again – consider that regional autonomy is the bridge towards
a more progressive future. By the large village green, a BBC Alba
presenter debates shots with a cameraman, and explains that her
team's tracing the story of Dennis Dinnie, whose weightlifting
record in the local Highland games remains unbeaten for nearly
two centuries. The landscape's pocked with these marvels.

In the deep, dense forests between Aboyne and Ballater, I spot
salmon leaping along skittering rivers, and red deer that return
one's gaze between spindly branches. The road continues to
ascend, getting steeper as it approaches the cluster of mountains
that make up the Cairngorms. At last I reach Ballater, a classic
Highlands tourist village that can be imagined by the unfamiliar
reader without much difficulty (picture haggis, Highland games,
tartan gift shop, plaque staking tenuous link to Bonnie Prince
Charlie, whisky distillery tours, golf clubs...). A man struggles to
board his bike opposite the Balmoral Bar, indicating a degree of
heavy refreshment. Lawrie gives me directions north, but warns
me it's "the second highest A-road in Britain!", and suggests
where to drink, which happens to be right where he's tumbled
out of, opposite us.

It's another kind of locals' boozer, if one accepts that "locals"
in these parts are now either English lairds or their gamekeepers,
or those working in the tourist industry, often not from the area
either. A waspy Winchester toff holds court at the bar. Tiring, I
follow the road north, out into the midnight hills. The roads are
empty, and after passing the huge Hilton, the quiet road snakes
up through a thick forest. With the little luminescence of my
bike light, I swipe away at the midges and, with my sleeping bag,
clamber into a jackstraw of gnarled, broken trees.

Next morning, Lawrie's warnings prove accurate, as the mountainous scale of the Cairngorms becomes apparent. The road
seems to follow the mountain ridge itself, affording awe-evoking

views to my left and right, great gullies and glens cleaved out of the earth, greens of every conceivable hue, and ripples of violet and yellow, the heather and gorse spilling beneath the glossy bracken. Wilderness it emanates, but there is nothing dramatic or desolate about it either. Stopping to take my breath again, I hear no human, airplane, car or police siren. But I can hear grasshoppers, songbirds and plenty of sheep, each engaged in their hypnotic call-and-response communications. Enchanted, I carry on.

I pass the ruins of farmers' cottages and shielings, brick huts where shepherds would rest. On one great hill I spy two stone staircases that lead up to an empty plateau where nothing else stands. There are rolling springs and streams, like the little lively Don leading to Aberdeen, where it joins the Dee. In one valley I can make out the entire imprint of a glacier, which once covered Scotland in its entirety, and most of the North.

In Corgarff, I meet another friendly Northumbrian out walking the dog. Gerald invites me into the old village hall for a coffee and to see his photography exhibited inside. Gazing out of the window of the dusty hall, Gerald warmly tells me how he came here eight years ago to ski in the nearby slopes of Lecht. He shows me photo-scenes of India, China and Saigon, of lichen in the rocks, and winter in the remote mountain passes like that of Lairig Ghru, nearby. "I never earned more than ten grand a year and I've travelled the world. Everywhere." Today he makes his living selling these photos, cutting trees, and teaching people how to ski when it snows. He wouldn't want to be anywhere else. "People ask me, 'What do you do for a living?' And I say, 'As little as possible if I can help it'."

But time-zones overlap. Whilst he was glad to escape suffocated Northumbria twenty years ago, he doesn't deny that Corgarff is an equally deserted shell. Its farming village failed to recover after the First World War, when most of its labourers were wiped out in the fighting. Much of the land now belongs to English aristocrats and is treated as a luxury playground. Gamekeepers keep the rivers and forests filled with sufficient deer, salmon and grouse for hunting, and many are supportive of their paymasters. "This area is very unionist", he adds. Round here it's "dead man's shoes": a job becomes available only when a father or uncle has died.

With such topsy-turvy arrangements, the young of Arbroath and Montrose go without work or a living wage whilst lords inherit vast lands and riches with which they buy political influence. "How can they call that a living?" Gerald wonders.

I ride through the Queen's vast estates by Glenlivet. The road has become almost vertical as it recklessly ascends another enchanted mountain. This is by far the most difficult cycling I've encountered, and I'm unable to ride for more than a minute at a time as I huff up hairpin hills and punishing climbs. Reaching the top of Lecht, I'm elated and shattered, like crossing a marathon line. Ski lifts wave and rattle in the breeze above patchy grass, patiently awaiting the arrival of the next snowy winter.

It's taken an hour to crawl up two miles, but two minutes to whizz back down a curving Moray hill, wind scorching the ears and eyes. I should be braking, but, crazily dangerous, it is so exhilarating. I was overtaken by lines of Dutch and German bikers up Lecht, but gravity has me overtaking them on the way down.

At the foot of the mountain is the village of Tomintoul, a tourist hotspot clustered along a single high street. In the town municipal office/regional museum – in the countryside, every premises has at least two separate uses – I talk to Laura, a young woman from the area who, like many, is outgrowing its restricted economy. Like Gerald intimated, there's little here: Speyside whisky distillery tours, Walkers shortbread, or hotel and bar work. "It feels so safe", and it's a lovely place to be alive in, but she wants more than service work, and cannot afford to live on less, and so, reluctantly, is leaving for university.

I seek the refuge afforded by cool beer on a tongue-toasting afternoon. The Glen Avon does not disappoint. My Transport for

London water bottle catches the eye of a Spaniard. He and his friend have left the capital to explore the Highlands by car. "It's so different to London, it's like… nothing…" Dan tells me, words fading into the vast scenery around us. Other guests exchange clairvoyant speculations on fishing ("there'll be clear water tomorrow") or trade observations on the local malts.

Half-broken by Lecht, the Bridge of Brown north of Tomintoul appears ahead like a Neolithic earthen pyramid, and I nearly pass out as I huff up its corkscrew curves. The views at the top are like those of a dream, expanses of a vivid green world that peter into infinity, then focus back into view: densely wooded deep valleys, streams that murmur into the breeze, and jagged grey peaks beyond. Being totally unfamiliar with outdoor pursuits or country living, I have no references for it. Like a computer screensaver that feels narcotically elating. Kestrels soar unfathomably high above.

It's evening now, and after pedalling through lush forests, a micro-universe of life, I cross the Spey and into the village of Grantown, a lattice of streets occupied by hotels, houses and a couple of pubs. I get dinner in the town's chippie. Margo tells me about the quiet quality of life in the Highlands, but the difficulty of making work pay. "For most it's related to tourism, hotels or places like this", and for most, too, it's a combination of some of these as well as more traditional kinds of employment. She directs me to Craig's Bar for a good nightcap.

Inside, boisterous Norwegians and Danes sample the malts. A sea eagle researcher on Mull sits with me awhile, tipping me on how to recognise different birds, using photos from his phone. Like astronomy, such a skill has no use in London: one sees pigeons, crows, magpies and runaway parakeets in the parks, but out in the Highlands I'm seeing more than my vocabulary accommodates. The landlord's English, a warm-hearted and gruff eccentric, our conversation delightfully silly. The barmaid, a Londoner, tells me how she and her husband chanced it here.

"They needed a butcher!" She works here, there and everywhere, but together they've made it work.

"Never felt happier." It seems a cliché, but these people I've met the last couple of days are living proof. "We are strong, aren't we?" she says to him, smiling, past last orders now. I gulp the last of my malt and, missing home too, pedal back out into the midnight woods, in search of some secluded mossy grove to lay my head.

The rain awakes me, pattering against the thin windsheet which still, for now, keeps me dry. The air is damp and cool as I clamber out, the morning wintry. Around me is dense woodland, tall, spindly pines and firs that continue in one direction for as far as the eye perceives. Some rotting, some wearing a floral blue mould. Trace the line of a buzzard over the forest, and absorb the chirruping, whooping and cawing of the birds engaged in their social affairs.

The land's more cultivated beyond the Cairngorms, as I pass Cawdor Castle and a large RAF base outside Forres. The road traverses Macbeth country, menacing crags and dense forests that exist by their own internal laws, inhuman ones, the icy ambience all the more appropriate. "I dare do all that may become a man; Who dares do more is none." The madness of desiring power, the cruel futility of murder. Military trucks rumble past into Forres, a small town sprawled into its surrounds. I follow a line of school children who trudge into the out-of-town Tesco, a heaving agora of communal exchange. Curiously, no one thinks to lock their bikes. Is it something to do with the New Age caravan park just up the road?

"It's a crazy place, but in a good way", says Jackie. She's surprised I even ask about locks. "It used to be small, it still feels safe, but...", her voice trailing off, a furtive scan of the vast carpark around us. "You used to be able to trust people, leave your backdoor open. Now the town has got much bigger." The nearby military bases have expanded the town in turn, but Forres, like Inverness nearby, is enjoying a kind of growth unlike its neighbours, still dependent on the generosity of tourists. It has a growing population and a sense of animation I found missing in the Cairngorms.

Another local man warns of "drugs" and "undesirables". And I wonder how to respond, how to articulate to him my new-found infatuation with the Highlands, trying to fathom its inscrutable gestures, wanting to lose myself in it, becoming transformed... or how to explain concisely that he is entirely wrong, that no one has the right to define another as an "undesirable", or decide what a drug problem actually is... But this testing encounter forces me to revisit my naïve assumptions. Perhaps human nature cannot be reformed, the grass is indeed always greener. Sancho's rejoinder to Don Quixote makes a little sense now. "It's up to brave hearts, sir, to be patient when things are going badly, as well as being happy when they're going well."

Enough. Past Sueno's stone, a 10th century Pictish relic left beside a highway, then the NATO airfields over the mudflats of Findhorn Bay, a haven of odd birds. I'm intrigued most by the Findhorn Foundation, a centre of spiritual exploration on the Moray coast. On the edge of a caravan park, a noticeboard advertises short courses in finding one's inner self, discovering Gaia, and sacred circle-dancing, each around £600. Books warn of the dangers of electromagnetic pollen, whilst enlightenment itself is retailed through crystals and playing cards. "Gaia loves our diversity and knows we can harmonise our perspectives to create a future that works for All!"

I join a small group of enthusiasts on a tour of the foundation, striving to keep an open mind. It began in 1962 as a venture by a bankrupt hotelier and his young family, consigned by circumstances to living in a deserted caravan park. According to our guide, Eileen Caddy would hear the voice of God whilst on the toilet, and transcribe his words. Initially God's instructions concerned the growing of vegetables on the barren sands, but then instructed establishing a religious community and farm using volunteers, seeking the higher spiritual awareness promised by Peter and Eileen.

It's now a scene of serene gardens, meditative yurts and huts produced from ecologically sustainable materials. Our guide, an older woman involved with the foundation for some decades, reflects. "I think we need to re-establish a connection with other forms of life... We're all part of one thing that expresses itself in many different ways." An American of similar age agrees. "I've come here to learn how to further that connection between head and heart. And I've learned a lot."

But some are more spiritually aware than others, apparently. I wonder who gets to make such judgements, and their consequences? One can't help but feel mixed about the place, and I decide to abandon my initial plan to camp at the site, which was already prohibitively expensive. Yet as I pass a group of meditating gardeners, I cannot help delighting in their discovery of inner peace, as much as I concede my own inner disquiet about its subtle elitism and insalubrious air of profiteering.

Findhorn village itself is only a mile up the road, out on the Moray coast. The landscape is quite wonderful here, with a rugged sandy beach and salty harbour cocked into the tides, an old-world village behind it. I talk to a local couple, out walking this sunny afternoon with their granddaughter. They tell me that the commercial fishing that once supplied the people of Findhorn with an income has all gone, after wealthy lairds inland bought up all the rights to fish. "If you want to fish in this harbour here, it'll cost you a thousand pounds or something, just for the day!" She complains about the local lord, a South African, now harassing locals with unconsented building incursions.

But they've heard about something big on the Isle of Eigg, out in the Hebrides. There's been meetings locally. They're now planning to buy out the lord, purchasing the land as a community trust, so that it remains in the hands of local people for years to come. In this way, by securing a degree of their own autonomy they can begin to work together to produce a brighter, fairer and more equally prosperous future, collectively.

She shakes her head when I ask about the local caravan park. "We think they shouldn't be allowed to use the name of the village. They have nothing to do with us." They dislike how the foundation has built itself up over an increasingly large area but refused to communicate with the village. The sentiment's echoed further west in Nairn, an ex-fishing town now also dependent on golf and whisky tourism. Another couple out walking the dog recount, with barbed humour, that "Findhorn's a place where very rich people go who don't know how to live their lives".

Walls of distrust. They have no first-hand experience of the foundation but, like much else, a certain degree of animosity and cynicism comfortably substitutes for a lack of evidence. I drift around Fishertown, with its fishermen's library and depopulated pubs, another glimpse at what's left when a way of life isn't stopped from declining and disappearing. A stoned-looking young fella by the town supermarket tells me "it's shit". He lives here because it's cheap. There's "not many jobs now", but he doesn't seem bothered either way. "There's a few industrial estates", he says, hopefully, but he's on surer ground when dispensing pub tips. Uncle Bob's is a cheeky upstairs boozer nestled within Nairn's older town. It's a pleasure not to think for a change, to goose around with a group of local women who insist on talking about holidays in Spain instead of dreary Nairn.

It's getting late, and I ride through flat farming landscapes up to Balloch, a village west of Inverness. A local lad ties up unwanted copies of the *Daily Record* and gives the skinny on the local life's quietude. His instructions are equally sharp, and I eventually locate the vast heathland of Culloden. It's easy to sneak through the enclosure into the preserved battlefield. Rabbits dart about in the evening gloaming, beneath lines of blue and red flags, marking the positions of the advancing armies of the British Hanoverian monarchy against those Highland clans that rallied behind Bonnie Prince Charlie, the Stuart pretender to the throne.

The last pitched battle on the island took place here on April 16th 1746. Unlike Wallace or Robert the Bruce, the Jacobite rebellion wasn't one of Scotsman against Englishman, but of one parasitic royal against another. After an invasion that reaches Derby, the Bonnie Prince and its clans retreat, deserted by empty French and English promises of support. It's here, Culloden, that the clans are truly decimated, first on the field, outmanned, outgunned, but later and more devastatingly by the law. Highland culture is effectively outlawed by the victors, from the wearing of tartan to the feudal obligations between chieftain and clan. The defeated clans were stripped of their lands and weapons; others later sold theirs to English aristocrats; others, like the clans of Mackay and Sutherland, turned them into private estates, willingly participating in the new economic order.

What was once in common, belonging to the clan, was now enclosed and under deeds of private property. Clans were kicked off their under-profitable farms in favour of sheep. They were first shunted into infertile crofts; others were dispatched to newly-built fishing ports. There was a kelp boom for a time, but that passed, and neither kelp nor crofting provided a liveable income. This would lead to the Clearances, completed a century after the catastrophe of Culloden. Wandering among the memorial stones to the clans of MacLachlan, McDonald, Murray and many others, I marvel that a collective way of life effectively ended on this field.

Rain starts falling heavily. I rejoin the road. Local man Sandy gives directions to Inverness. Like Jackie, he notes how the town's "getting big very quickly", through an influx of people from Glasgow and England, seeking a better way of life. "What can you do?" he offers, as we survey the uncertain moment. We both shrug.

Inverness once epitomised the very definition of distance to me. Listed occasionally on the weather forecast, substituted at times by Fort William, I'd pictured a timber hamlet dwarfed by vast, inhospitable mountains, menaced by bears, adders and wolves, with frequent snowfall in June.

Now I awake in its hostel, grateful for shelter after last night's deluge. After sharing breakfast with a Kiwi couple tracing their ancestors ("There's more Scots in Dunedin than Inverness"), I talk with Abe, a Londoner showing some European friends around the Highlands. "When the shit hits the fan, people can change", he says, with quiet conviction. "Look at the Second World War. In four years people changed the way they lived and worked. It can be done again." Hair greying at the temples, his face is expressively youthful on this point of hope. "People can be malleable. We can adapt, either way, something has to be done. Places like Bangladesh will disappear in floods, food prices will rise... When does action start?"

"I need to be outside sometimes", says a girl to her lover. "Too much time indoors and the stress just grows on you." Just south of Inverness is the gentle Loch Ness, a long grey stretch surrounded by mountains in a teal-coloured V. I reach it an hour later at the village of Dores on its quieter eastern bank, a row of young couples holding hands by the water. Further along the shoreline, a preoccupied man gazes at the placid water from a small hut, surrounded by colourful models of the local monster. Are the rumours true? "We just don't know", replies Steve, wearily. He's lived by the Loch in a van since 1991 to research Nessie's existence. I sense his disappointment. "More chance of it being a spaceship than a dinosaur", he sighs. Or a catfish, perhaps. He refuses to leave just yet.

At the bar of the Dores Inn, young Michael buys me another drink and tells me about his work as a skyliner, a riskier form of logging. "Aye it's dangerous, but I love it. Out in the hills. I see new places every day. I love being out in the hills man." He used to work in bars, then trucking, but was nearly killed by a stomach ulcer caused by consuming far too many energy drinks and cigarettes each day. Writhing in agony in hospital, allergic to morphine, he re-evaluated his life, and wishes he'd done it sooner. "Nothing's more important than your own happiness."

I head back into Inverness, past the River Ness and into its Victorian sandstone centre. Its growth has been somewhat unevenly managed, great rings of early 20th century suburban houses choking its centre, and north, the living guts of the place, the hypermarkets, hardware stores and retail barns that serve the entire Highlands. Out over the Kessock Bridge, suspended high above the Beauly Firth. Ahead is nothing but wilderness.

The road forks. Left, inland to Dingwall and Lairg, or right, along the coastal road to Wick. I chance the latter, desiring a different scene to the mountains and forests of the Cairngorms. I ride through the bleak Black Isle and along flat, desolate Cromarty, its barren and rocky heathland evacuated of life. Few trees and little green, little even to sustain the birds, far fewer out here. It's an unfamiliar, miserable terrain, a marked contrast to everything east and south of Loch Ness, and the Great Glen Fault that lies beneath it, the border between two ancient tectonic plates, and two very different vistas.

The traffic overtaking me is eye-wateringly fast, and the bleakness of the scape requires some resilience. I count one B&B about every fifteen miles, and the first pub since Inverness comes after thirty. Road signs and the hostel map had intimated some settlement, but none's evident. It's a landscape erased. Though the area was never populous, there were once corn-growing farms and villages here. But seventy years after the defeat of the Highland clans at Culloden, now mostly-English lairds began the Clearances, forcibly dispersing the crofters from their lands. Sons were coerced into enlisting in the British Army, whilst factors put whole villages to the flames over unpaid rents. Many had no choice but to migrate, to Nova Scotia and Manitoba in

Canada, to Australia and New Zealand, others to the industrialising towns of the Lowlands.

In their tongue, they called 1792 "*bliadhna nan caorach*", and the year 1814 "*bliadhna an Losgaidh*", the years of the sheep and of the burnings, respectively, indicating the direction of events. But there's a degree of complexity here, not mere malice. Landowners saw themselves as entrepreneurs, putting to work Enlightenment ideas of agricultural improvement, having little sympathy for the darker ages of feudal obligations. The crofters were living in abject abysmal poverty before they were evicted. Their Gaelic language and customs set them apart from the Scots of the Lowlands, and there was no expression of nationalist solidarity or outcry, for what was the nation? Since 1707 it was the United Kingdom of Great Britain, a political merger that would come to benefit the near-bankrupt Scots as much as the distrustful English. Yet thousands were starved, murdered and banished from their homes for the sake of immense profit for a few, and by any moral yardstick, this was an atrocity. If anything at all, the silence of the deathscapes of Sutherland and Cromarty indicates something of the ethnically, culturally and politically chequered nature of the island. Time has no monopoly on progress.

Since Forres, signs appear in Scots Gaelic, yet few people speak it. I was told in Edinburgh that Polish is now a more commonly spoken language at home than Gaelic, but the northern Highlands are its remaining heartland. I'm curious to learn more. I eventually reach Tain, a small oil town on the coast. There's a vast Tesco on its edge. Locals inside and out disparage the place, and insist on pointing me elsewhere.

What's there to hide? The small town itself is little more than a late 19th century high street with a couple of lively boozers filled with oil workers. At the Saints Bar, a young Geordie tells me about life on the nearby rigs. "It pays the bills", he laughs. An older man gestures with his index finger, tracing a line from left to right. "Not much here, this is all of it." Just the rigs. Wages converted into liquid refreshment, they seem to be having a good time of it. Refreshed too, I leave tough Tain behind.

Night's falling. The road is now deserted, compounding the limbo-like feeling of this desolate and featureless abyss. Past the Glenmorangie distillery and over the tranquil Dornoch Firth, leaving behind the plains of Cromarty for the coarser terrain of Sutherland, pocked with heather and ferns and, in the distance, sweeping ranges that overlook the barren vistas with the resignation of abandoned gods. Wheels of corn silage stand with the poise of Easter Island Moai.

Exhausted, I reach Dornoch, an old and charming little town by the sea. There's a web of sandstone townhouses, dominated by an enchanting 13th century cathedral and market square, an equally aged prison and, for today's purposes, a golf club, Chinese takeaway and two boozers. It's a Saturday night, and by the Eagle Hotel bar, three young women have returned home for a reunion drink. Jobs are few and there's little to do, and only one stayed behind, working in Inverness. The others have gone to university, "most don't come back"; but it's so quiet, and city trappings have their attractions.

Dance music blares improbably from a traditional, timber-clad bar. Lively tonight. I sit back with a well-earned dram, cotton softness suffusing my temples. In the loo, a refreshed, enthusiastic Finnish-Glaswegian identifies my pannier as the same make as his. Tommi refuses to believe what I'm doing, and insists on rewarding a lunatic with a fresh pint and a malt. We sit together with his two mates, Dave and Alan. They're up here playing golf for the weekend ("Sixth best course in the world!" "Aye but it's tough!"), making it an excuse to escape the stresses of modern life and have a laugh together. Drinks flow, tumblers of Talisker clinking across the table. Tommi and Dave have lost the day's game and been given the forfeit of running into the freezing firth in their undies. Dutch courage is called for.

"I need the escape", Alan tells me, the conversation taking a more serious slant for a second. "As a Scotsman, we have a pride that you can only know from seeing these places. The Western coast, from Fort William to Oban... I need to go out there. The mountains, the air, it changes you. I don't like my job. But the stress, it's gone." In spite of the shadow of the past and the uncertainty of the present, the landscape itself still has the capacity to enchant, reassure and bewilder. The effect is hard to articulate but we agree, therapeutic.

I awake at the side of a football pitch on the edge of Dornoch, head splitting from another night of Scottish hospitality. In the distance, the breeze sighs over Dornoch Firth, and one can hear the occasional whooshing clip of golf irons teeing off. It's a Sunday morning, and everything's closed. Elderly men in over-sized suit-jackets and well-pressed trousers join wives with neat perms and floral blazers, strolling serenely into the cathedral for the morning service. I cycle out through the old village, down by the street where the parishioners once set alight Janet Horne, the last woman to be executed for witchcraft on this island, in 1727. Up to the white sands of Dornoch Beach where, among the wind-swept dunes, a leaflet is momentarily unearthed by the breeze: "Faith Brings Hope".

This beach feels like the departure lounge to the ecstasy of a higher existence. Pedalling out by the golf course, the landscape softens into wheat fields and grassy vales, past jolly Enbo and along Loch Fleet, where the ruins of Skelbo Castle survey an expanse of sky, sea and forest, as shelducks and oystercatchers mingle on the mudflats. At the village of Golspie, a dog-walker issues a warning: "Watch out further north, it's wild!"

In the distance looms a towering column of a figure, situated on a wooded hillside. It's a one hundred foot monument to the first Duke of Sutherland, architect of the Clearances, built by public subscriptions though vandalised today. Another statue of the second Duke lords over Dunrobin Castle's teeny train station, serving only the turreted toy-town pile built by the Duke and Countess in 1850.

But who was this "judicious, kind and liberal" figure, and how did he and his wife amass the fortunes required to build their French chateau on the Sutherland coast? The Sutherlands evicted over fifteen thousand farmers from the late 18th century onwards, often violently, leaving them with a choice of starvation or emigration. They eventually enclosed around 1.5 million acres, a greater fiefdom than any in the British Empire.

Today things are not much better. Over half the land of Scotland is in the possession of 432 wealthy landowners, many banking millions in farming and forestry subsidies, windfarm rents and tax avoidance schemes. Like the English Duke, most have little connection to or interest in Scotland, hailing from the US, Scandinavia, Malaysia and the Arab world. Like the island's infrastructure, ownership is cloaked in secrecy and protected by an archaic legal system. Political freedom, of the kind the young raise up as the remedy of Scotland's ills, will mean nothing without retaking all this into common ownership.

I follow throngs of tourists down a wide avenue towards the castle. A lone bagpipe-player starts blowing the Bonnie Banks as a coachload of tourists disembark. Gazing up at the towers, I'm accosted by George, a Romanian tourist chewing on a sandwich, who bluntly announces, after cursory conversation, "You cycled all the way from London this? Oh my God. It's not quality."

Baffled by all I pass, I push on through the empty coastal terrain, til I reach Brora, a village defined by the scale of its derelict industries. Down by a small harbour, two old fishermen compare the catch. Jim and Campbell explain that one can catch saithe, cod, mackerel, ling, rass and coalfish in these waters, even haddock a little north at Helmsdale, all with a degree of luck and skill. For them it's a hobby. The only commercial fishing is in the odd lobster and crab, far less than the harbour's heyday. The North Sea trawlers devour anything worth catching. Gesturing to the saithe he's caught, Jim says that "locals don't eat them. Same with mackerel. I've probably thrown a ton of pollock back in, perfectly good. Now they're selling it at the supermarket counter."

He shakes his head. The town itself has suffered some kind of setback, though the evacuation of industry and activity has left behind few clues. "It was once large here. There was a wool mill, and a mine. Brickworks, fishing. Offices too. It's gone." Why? Jim blames the oil boom of the 1970s, drawing workers towards Aberdeen, where wages were three times local rates. Though a shortage of young workers is feasible in this depopulated part, it's unlikely any would've survived Thatcher during the 1980s. Jim reads it as a moral fable, instead of a political one. "It was the allure of big money, but it didn't last. Now things have got worse, for all of us."

Though Helmsdale's granite lanes and gallant clock-tower cast a more magical impression, there's a similar story of deindustrialisation on the back of land enclosures. Ros is out walking the dog. It's a very quiet place here now. Her concerns turn to the future. "There's not much for the young people. They all go to the university, they have to. Problem is they don't come back." She describes the disorganised contraction of the town. The main hotel is now for sale, as are several nearby homes, but few are looking to move here. Her daughter is struggling to sell a five-bedroom townhouse for a little over a hundred thousand. "Independence will help the likes of Glasgow and Edinburgh, but what about here?" They feel cut off, cut out.

I take a breather in the local Belgrave Arms. One odd feature of these remote villages is that they always have *two* pubs. I wonder if locals are ever allowed to freely move between them, or if some moment occurs, around the age of sixteen, where sons (women being only seen behind the bars of these places) are initiated by their bearded fathers into the drinking rites and membership of The Local. Entering the other boozer would be as transgressive as changing sexuality or, worse, football team. Inside, football's the topic. A man beside me finishes rolling a cigarette from a Godfather tin and slaps his hand against the bar. "Right, I'm off to put on a bet!" he announces.

Me too. Where to sleep tonight? The scenery is so flat and bleak that I'm compelled to crack on. There are few forests or hills to hunker by, just the occasional ruins of a crofting village, and the stony heathland is ill-suited for tent pegs. It may rain again too. I push north through the desolation. The one man I see is a hiker, Phil, attempting to hike to Land's End. He hands me a biscuit and warns of a "killer" hill ahead.

Crossing into Caithness, I soon discover what he means, and it takes all of my strength, and the last of my food, to wretchedly huff up the zigzagging hills into Caithness. Then Dunbeath, Latheron and Lybster, more ghost towns along the coast. The only sounds are the breeze and the occasional cry of a looming buzzard, or lowing cattle, the rustle of rabbits or whinnies of a stallion. An underwhelming retail park opposite a vast cemetery announces entry into Wick, the one thing approaching a town in remote Caithness.

"It's a shithole", says Kevin, a young man I pass. He gives the air of a man trapped, resigned to an unlucky hand. Not wishing to disappoint me, he points me to the town's Wetherspoon's, using takeaways and off-licences as landmarks. This was once the largest herring port in the country, and home to a number of shipbuilders. Today among the ghostly scene, a banner announces with hope dismayed that "Christ died for our sins". The day has come full circle, book-ended by the unheard appeals of a Jewish rabbi who was crucified for believing that God was love. I ask a young lad walking by the deserted harbour what he makes of the place. He looks around, then glares at me. "There's nothen. I'm getten oot."

Near midnight, and I leave the Alexander Bain, past the red cones of an airfield and through the village of Keiss. Though pleased at being able to procure a bowl of ice cream from the boozer, I'm feeling blue, worn out by all these things that I've seen and heard and can't make sense of. There is no one here, no lights on, little sign of habitation or existence.

The flat terrain is deceptively peaceful. Where am I now? Not far from John O'Groats I think, the very edge of a nation that, since Edinburgh, has felt all too burdened by its history, deeply uncertain. But though there's common talk of freedom, of independence, its problems are one with those of Yorkshire, the Midlands and the North East. Essential resources like land, infrastructure, and remunerative jobs are out of reach for the young, enclosed into private ownership, and most struggle to keep up with bare existence.

Though every sign suggests an island people subjugated and exploited – their poverty, anxiety and drudgery, is it not sufficient sign? – there's no obvious holder of power, openly lording it, no summit-statue to the hedge funds and offshore investments that own the island. Out here, the lie of an egalitarian democracy remains untroubled. People believe sincerely in voting their way into freedom. Power is everywhere and nowhere, as discreet as oil and aristocrats. "What can you do?" sighed Sandy. The question remains unanswered.

CHAPTER 6

Cruinneachadh

"Stay with life" – Father Michael, over the kyle.

A young weird circles the deserted tract of road, close to where I awake. A large rock is attached to the back of his rusty lady's bike, and he sports an old farmer's tweed blazer and dirty jeans, several sizes too large. At first I cannot understand him, his accent fuzzy and lilting. His head is rudely shaven, as if on a whim whilst shearing sheep.

"Ah ya seen it, the bambi?"

"A deer?"

"Must'a come offa road."

"No mate, is it hurt?"

"Aye, but I think she's still alive."

He keeps muttering to himself and continuing his swoops up and down the road. Ten loud whomps follow, a little down the way. "Put it out of its misery?" I ask, struggling to pack my bags in some haste. "Och no, s'already dead. I want the antlers. Might come back for them later." He gestures the motion of a saw with his hand, then mentions something about the police. "Why?" "Coat hangers." He looks at me with impish seriousness.

A moment later, we both erupt with laughter. "A ya got any tools?" It's unclear whether the implication is to enlist me in his coat hanger enterprise, or despoil me of my belongings. "Just a screwdriver and things, shit to fix the bike." He looks down as I talk, as if I've been reading Euclid aloud.

"Me, I don't bother. When it breaks, I drop it and get a new one."

"From where though? This place is empty."

He looks at me sympathetically, the way an adult does when a child has misunderstood some furtive implication. "I just do." He shakes my hand. "See you around."

In these remote and abandoned plains, mutual incomprehension is inevitable, even appropriate. Surrounded by shepherd-less sheep, gutted shielings and abandoned crofters' houses, the landscape combines ambient misery with a sardonic gut-laugh at the absurdity of it all. One can acclimatise to desolation, agree common terms.

Northeast of John O'Groats is Duncansby Head, the most northeasterly point of the island. Gulls wail about the stacks and skerries, the air briny and sharp. I survey the North Sea and the Orkney Islands ahead. Two brothers from Devon speak of Duncansby in mystical terms, whilst a dog-walker from Skegness tells me what's brought her here. "Look around you", smiles Vivienne at the peace, dwarfed by the terrifying majesty of our surrounds.

But what tourist trap awaits? John O'Groats disappoints morbid hunger. An attractive visitor centre sits between a food kiosk, souvenir shop and a jetty, with a small caravan park beside. A Victorian hotel looms over all with the grateful if desperate airs of an elderly butler, recalled to service after being dismissed for a misjudged comment. One can pay £8 to have a photo taken by the Official John O'Groats sign, or diddly-squat by the unofficial one of equal proportions, a hundred metres off. I spot one couple disagreeing over the best pose, and sense the opportunity for a vanity shot.

It's Richard's third cross-island ride, he says, as I snap the pair beneath the famous sign. Tirzah dutifully travels behind in a supply van. Lycra, hot breakfasts, lubricants, supply vans: it's a way of cycling I'm unfamiliar with, though seems more often the norm. "My last", he adds, unconvincingly. I'm unsure if he's doing the run for charity. I already met a bearded hiker setting out for Land's End that morning, Big Dave. "Going far?" I asked cheekily. There was Phillip too the previous day. Both were in their thirties, not-so-young men with a point to prove to them-selves. I'll later look up Big Dave. He'll be injured in a hit-and-run by a campervan a few hours after I meet him, and be unable to complete his journey, whilst Phillip, I can't tell. I'll later hear of two charity cyclists killed on the roads, and, of course, will see many other shrines to killed cyclists around the island. I wonder if in some ways these physical endurance tests, with their vague affiliations to major charities, are fulfilling a desire akin to pil-grimage.

In the John O'Groats café, Tirzah gets me a cup of tea, and we compare trajectories awhile, snooping over maps. My route's a little further. "I've never been", laughs one postcard-seller, as if I've asked her directions to the moon. Curiosity piqued, I ride out to Gills Bay to catch the cheapest ferry over to Orkney.

There's an air of apprehension at ports. People examine each other with an unusual degree of curiosity. The skies seem broader, the architecture of the clouds more suggestive. Small brown dwellings appear on the horizon, sparsely distributed along waves of gentle grassy hillocks, that slowly expands as we approach St Margaret's Hope, Orkney. I follow the traffic out in a dreamy haze when a man on the other side of the road beckons me over.

"Hey, you got a flat tyre?"

"Err no?"

"You wanna check that wheel!"

The back wheel is buckled badly, skittering around elliptically. It may well roll off, if it doesn't crumple in on itself first. How long has it been like this? I pedal on, hoping naïvely that the road will right it.

By the small harbour I meet Jim, a native Orcadian who enjoys laughing and fixing things. No, he doesn't have a spare back wheel. But he does invite me into his garage, a cavern crammed with old tools and timber, where he explains the arcane uses of various broken appliances. "I never lock it. No crime!"

He worked in oil on "good pay" for most of his life and is now retired, and seems immensely content. He points down the narrow back-street behind the harbour, and tells me about the English migrants to Orkney. He has no truck with them, and his attitude to politics is as laid back as his personality. "I've never voted, not once in 67 years. It makes no difference!" Another local, Betty, invites me into her "smiddy", a blacksmith museum she runs, giving a guided tour of its exhibits, another instance of unsolicited generosity. She shows me ceremonial horse yokes, worn around girls' necks, and other kinked local traditions. What would Pauline Réage make of it? The "brothel" sign semi-erased on an old farmhouse nearby compounds the polymorphous perversity beneath its kindly façade.

Orkney's strange like that. A relatively small series of interconnected islands, it feels separate from anything around it. One could easily disappear here, go off the map. Burrow into the sour harvest of life experiences, or start a new one altogether. The terrain is entirely flat and there are no trees whatsoever. I ride to the southern edge of South Ronaldsay to look round the "Tomb of the Eagles", where wizened volunteers let one handle bones five thousand years young, scurvied and arthritic, their skulls deformed, teeth ground down by the sand in their bread. To be thirty was old, thirty-five senility. What a life! One middle-aged local tells me that she didn't have electricity in her home until she was fifteen. "You could just press a switch. It felt like the world had changed."

My bicycle's no longer roadworthy. I call up Victoria, who has offered to let me stay at her place on the island. She sends out Russell, her son-in-law, to pick me up. Being perhaps the only road-users on this deserted island, we soon recognise one another.

We drive at speed across Churchill Barriers, man-made causeways linking Orkney's islands, the waters around filled with scuttled German boats. Russell talks of the Italian POWs who built the barriers, and takes me to a nissen hut repurposed into a chapel, interior painted with the intricate décor of a Mediterranean cathedral, also by the POWs. We pass the island's capital, the teeny town of Kirkwall, and out towards the northwest tip of Orkney. As the sun sets over the rolling terrain, Russell complains about the number of wind turbines. "It's an eyesore!" Only nineteen percent of the energy generated is used, an engineer told him once on the ferry. There is indeed a gentle, relieving pleasure in mocking the absurdities of bureaucratic institutions.

Victoria waves at us from a white house in Evie, overlooking a vast golden bay. Over dinner, she tells me how she and her partner John took a chance here in the early 90s, moving from Sussex. Though both have since worked in all manner of jobs, from teaching assistants, to special needs support service directors, to leading goose-hunts in the wilds, they don't regret it.

"Money's not the most important thing." When it comes to the enjoyment of life, of truly living and living truly, one must gamble with more than pounds and pence.

Four hours. A bus timetable on the dresser spells bad news. There's two options. Remove the broken bike wheel and wait four hours for the next bus to Kirkwall, and hope on some lucky star that there's a bike shop, and it's open, and they have the right wheel. Or call a mysterious number Russell left me. I finish up my tea and toast, and strike on the latter.

Steve picks up the line. He's the island's parcel delivery man, but fixes bikes on the side. After giving him vague directions – I have no other address details to give except "Victoria's, at Evie", which proves sufficient – he tells me lackadaisically that he'll be over some time in the afternoon.

I wander round Victoria's enchanted old house, full of quirks. Feral cats clatter in, dangling dormice, whilst outside, chickens cluck at ankles, and cows reflect one's gaze with the studious concentration of research scientists. Inside, the TV switches on, the kettle boils and the toaster pops, each of their own accord, a ghost reliving the dull and quotidian habits of a life.

Around two, a bright red van parks up outside the house. Steve's a brewing Hampshire man and another refugee from the rat race. With his family, they chanced a better life up here. "One day there was a project meeting, and they were discussing my project. And for an hour and a half I couldn't understand a word they were saying. It was all management jargon bollocks." That was the tipping point.

We smile knowingly at each other. "And, just look around you." The sloping hillocks that become, imperceptibly, one with the opal bay; the gentle babble of animals and birds; the breeze, untroubled by fumes and fug; the lack of coercion here to be this, or do that; and the bohemian nature, in all, of Orkney. This is not a refuge of second home-owning rich folk, but a sanctuary for those who despise all that, and have discovered something special up here.

He gives the bike a quick appraisal, before offering an unpromising diagnosis: "The technical word for this is fucked." He's amazed the bike's made it this far, but bundles the sorry thing in his delivery van, then returns around five with a natty new wheel attached.

I'm just in time to catch the night ferry to Shetland from Kirkwall. The local BBC News blares out into an empty waiting room, a local Lerwick man dressed in Viking garb and horned helmet being interviewed about the island's sporting heritage. Waiting alone for the boat to arrive from Aberdeen, I feel like I'm about to sail off the very edge of the earth.

A piercing white light reflects from the shore of Sumburgh Head on the southern tip of Shetland. Shielding my eyes from the rays, I make out tall grey townhouses arranged along the shore, with the spacious and sober grace of a small Scandinavian town. Thunderclap Newman booms from the cantina, their earnest, whimsical exhortation to *get it together now* failing to elicit any-thing beyond bemused grunts from the oil workers crowded on-board.

Lerwick is a busy little town, splayed across a hillside above a harbour. To the left of the small ferry terminal is a web of low-rise terraces and semi-industrial premises, many cut from the same morose grey rock as Sumburgh Head. To the right is a small power station, and a vast complex of warehouses beyond it servicing Shetland's various sea trades. Fishermen and oil workers stand sleepily at a small bus garage. Past streets named after St Olaf and King Erik, I stop outside a Chinese takeaway to better assess the horizon. A man in oily blue overalls strides past me, stops, and asks if I'm looking for work.

Down by the old harbour, Magnus says that Shetland's boom-ing from newly discovered gas reserves. "There's work here. You needn't be unemployed if ye wanna job, but there isn't much to do. People come here for a drink, aye", and his finger traces out a few pubs, each with colourful descriptions. "That one's rough", he winks.

It's also a hard place to leave – literally. The ferry takes seven hours to return to Kirkwall, and a further seven to Aberdeen, where the oil boom continues. Magnus looks on at the quiet early morning scene. "It can drive you mad". I follow the old harbour down knotty lanes to the Knab, a steep promontory overlooking the town crowned by an ugly school. In the distance, what looks like a prison boat is actually the floating home of five thousand gas and oil workers.

George is out walking, a retired local who sucks his two remaining molars diligently, ensuring they've not escaped. He used to work in fish-processing, a big local employer still, and hasn't ever ventured beyond Lerwick. "Aye, there's people in the country, but I've never been there." In isolated communities, imaginations of geographic scale increase exponentially. That said, "if ye gat a trade, ye can get work!" "Does Shetland need a philosopher?" He pauses for a moment, consulting his teeth. "If I were you, I'd write to the educational board."

It's a productive morning! I now know where to get a job, and a good drink, but what about the islands?

Shetland's a unique place, caught between Scotland and Norway in its singular fuzzy accent and cultural history. Until recently it had its own dialect, Norn, fusing the two, and its accent varies across the island. In a small bookshop opposite the town's equally small post office, I track down some local words for what I've just encountered. The headland where George and I stood chatting was a *noup*, overlooking a *voe* or inlet of sea, the sea sighing in its *vaddel*, clogging its *mijn*. I stick a Queen's head postage stamp on my postcard and send it back to the UK for the same price as posting it across London. I feel like I'm in some cold and rocky Scandinavian outcrop of the British Empire.

Such a feeling isn't as daft as may seem. For around eight centuries Shetland and Orkney were under the rule of Vikings, who had either assimilated or eliminated their native Pictish culture by 800, leaving a lasting Norse legacy that it hasn't lost, even after being sold to the Scots in 1469 as part of a wedding dowry. In the visitor information office, Robin explains that Shetland's independence comes first. "The SNP are too focused on centralising power in the South. It would harm us here, and Orkney, and the Western Islands." Why not just go the whole way? "No, we're too lazy! Our local government meetings are just brutal, but nothing gets done. We'd rather someone else did it!"

North of Lerwick is the Gremista industrial estate. The smell of dead fish is ripe, and seagulls howl into the late morning wind. I stop for a tea in a wooden kiosk, waiting some time in a queue of workers buying sandwiches and cigarettes. Chatting, more clues. Shetland is booming: oil and gas workers are travelling from across Scotland and northern England, like Joe's dad in Middlesbrough. Fishing remains viable, and fish-farming has also expanded. Yet none of this wealth seems visible. Were it not for all the burly blokes in overalls, much resembles the North East of England, or the former fishing towns of Fife. Where are the profits being banked? It's not a question that anyone can immediately, or willingly, answer.

Out of town, the landscape is unremittingly harsh and bleak. Shetland is also treeless, defined by punishingly steep hills. The terrain is barren and rocky, and the thinnest of layers of heather and grass give the impression of a lunar landscape, atmosphere only recently installed. Everything is rock, though little is quarried or mined, its geographic distance no doubt contributing.

At the deserted Tingwall, "field of the parliament", I'm reminded that Shetland is not a part of the UK but, like Orkney, enjoys a semi-independent status as a British crown dependency, still using its own medieval Norse legal code, udal law, alongside Scots law. There's a tranquil little chapel, whose cemetery stones share a preoccupation with skulls. I scatter onto Scalloway along another roughly hewn lunar road, aided now by the wind.

Though Shetland's second largest town, the scale of human settlement here is dwarfed by the industry and natural majesty around it. Next to a vast salmon-processing factory, a foreboding Brutalist cuboid disappearing into the bay, I survey the ruins of Scalloway Castle and a small museum commemorating Shetland's connections with Norway. Little else to this small fishing port. I find a book from 1801 with an apt description. "The sea is the proper element of Shetland men; they are bred to it from their infancy, and acquire a hardiness and dexterity in the management of boats that cannot anywhere be excelled." Once press-ganged into the navy, now sent underwater for oil, the sea remains the terrain of the Shetlanders. Edinburgh feels distant, London a world away.

The wind is now too fierce to cycle through, gales blowing me back as I attempt to advance further west. So I give in, and allow it to imprint itself on my back like some Norse deity as I whiz back to Lerwick. Back in this homely harbour town, I find a warm café to take refuge in. Emma shares a sentiment of Magnus. "It's slow here, too slow. Everyone knows each other. You're trapped, in a way." Easier being an outsider looking in, perhaps.

Feeling ill-equipped for this cold, rugged and bare location, and unsure if the bicycle can lend any further insight, I move into the lively Lounge Bar back in town, one of Magnus's tips. "You on the pushbike from Scalloway?" A friendly fella buys me a pint, and tells me about caring for his father with Alzheimer's. Locals crowd around the bar and each has something to offer on the topic, not suggested, of community. "I ken everyone on ma street", says the landlady, and others agree. "That's what we like here", says the man.

Not everyone agrees. But surrounded by fishermen, oil men, hoteliers, waifs and strays, I feel like I've found a second home. I'm not ready for a life drilling gas or trawling crabs however, and I head back to port to catch the evening ferry to Orkney. Watching the trails of surf from the deck, the twinkling silhouette of the power station and warehouses on the horizon, I wonder about those Vikings and their star-led navigations, the uncertainty of tomorrow, their strange and wondrous world of sea-gods.

For all its innocence and Norse affiliations, Lerwick's gentle music is in the same key as Wick, Montrose, Sunderland and Grimsby, other former Viking settlements. Back in the old harbour that morning, I remember Alnwin, holding his infant son's legs kicking over his shoulders. He, like everyone here, spoke of work as if it were here to stay. I wonder if the pubs of Durham and South Yorkshire would've offered similar sentiments, five decades back. Like those places, none of the profits are evident. Lerwick looks run-down and depressed, animated by a culture of heavy drinking. Today's Vikings are no Danes. Somewhere else on this island, the real loot's being hoarded.

Ignore Russell: wind turbines do have their uses. Surprisingly large and remote, one offered discreet sanctuary last night, as the treeless island was blasted by ferocious gales. The rotors zipped round like a buckled wheel, blades pucking the air, wafting me to sleep.

The morning is gentler, and it's a short ride from Carness Bay back to Kirkwall. The small town bustles with tourists, carnival-crammed into its narrow lanes, past boutique coffee shops, street puppeteers and horse-drawn carts, a muddled melee. Reaching St Magnus Cathedral is as difficult as navigating its bustling innards, and I'm soon spat out by the coarse, ruddy building.

West of Kirkwall is Maeshowe, site of a five thousand year-old covered tomb. Whilst Orkney and Shetland abound in native rock, the former's site of an unusually large and sophisticated array of ancient standing stone formations. Nearby Maeshowe's chambered cairn are the Standing Stones of Stenness, now just four of what would've been around twelve rocks arranged in a ring with a central hearth. Some are around six metres high, and they dominate the flat and featureless surrounds.

Their obvious significance is long lost, but the durable fixity of stone hints at memorial. The circle no doubt represents power, but of what? The collective group, the family, the tribe, the island, all for one and one for all? Of nature, the sun, moon and earth together in unity, summer and winter solstices, seasons circling. Or of time's very circularity, like the visions of the ancient druids, who believed that the human soul was immortal, and lived on after death by migrating to other bodies, reliving birth, maturity, decrepitude, and back again? Or all three, or none at all.

Remarkable that these stone circles are common in Britain and Ireland, and rare elsewhere. On one is a Victorian graffito, "W.H. 1880", a statement more simple than the stones, but no less effective. *Once, I existed, like you do now; and you'll become like me, sooner than you think, mere initials on a rock.* What is human life, when among these immortal stones? The consciousness that temporarily fills a physical mass, transforms through experiences, til sickness saps its fire, and death extinguishes it altogether.

A mile away is the more impressive Ring of Brogdar, overlooking a marshy isthmus between Lochs Harray and Stenness. Though its stones are smaller in stature than Stenness, it is greater in scale and power. Archaeology can trace its stones to every corner of the island, as if attempting to coherently capture the power of the island itself and focus it in some unknown direction. Its use was the stuff of speculation in the Auld Motor Hoose, Kirkwall, last night.

"You can make of it what you want. Nobody knows with any certainty", said one lady, as the four of us supped beers round the bar. The man beside her, pissed off by some earlier unheard grievance, glared sorely. I tried to access his thought. "Bullshit relativism! No, we're not special snowflakes, free to be whatever we want to be. Life's a fucking struggle. *This*." But he said nothing, and stewed on his Guinness.

The barman was a local lad, his toned-down accent reflecting a university education in England followed by inconsequential job applications, poverty, then reluctantly boarding the ferry back home. He volunteered that an elaborate cult of bone-mixing and preservation took place at the tombs here, with unknown religious importance. "They didn't keep track of whose bones went where. There were stages, higher stages. All the bones got mixed up." The individual identity of the bones was not important. What mattered was their participation in a greater collective power, an ancestral force that conferred order and continuity on the present. Past, present and future were intertwined in one circle.

In Scottish Gaelic a gathering or assembly is a *cruinneachadh*, stemming from the adjective *cruinn*, meaning round or circular. The gathering is a circle, an old motif of sociality and collective strength. For which part of the circle is the weakest? None, it remains strong at every point, a whole greater than its parts. To reach the higher stages, one proceeds from the lower, but if past, present and future are circular, then one falls from the higher back to lower again. It is a cycle of forces, and so therefore a circle, beginning and ending with where you are now, whether this subjective *you* be the consciousness of your great-grandmother or father, you who breathes right now, or your great-grandson or daughter in the unforeseeable future. Life's oneness is a collective strength of forces. The bicycle's circular motion reveals this bone ontology of life's majestic immanence.

I reach Skara Brae on the western edge of Orkney, a preserved Neolithic settlement and visitor attraction. A young Orcadian, Aiden, tries to explain this way of life to me. Remains suggest that they lived in roundhouses made of midden, a recycled mix of human waste and the remains of the dead. Their past gave solidity and bearing to the present. They lived on shellfish, some farmed cattle, and they carried no weapons, a peculiarly benevolent existence, suited to recognising nature's divine properties.

"It's extraordinary", I gasp.

She smiles. "It's brilliant."

"Were they happy, do you think?"

"We don't know, but they were peaceful. And they lived close together, in close communities. They didn't leave in a hurry either. Just one day, they went."

She looks at me and smiles. *Who knows?*

Morning in Thurso, back on the mainland. I arrived here yesterday evening and met with John, Victoria's gruff and friendly husband. He'd also picked up a French hitchhiker, Thibault, and the pair of us stayed in a cottage he was refurbishing, talking politics until late.

Over breakfast, Thibault gives John a brief but pointed glare. "You know about midges, right?" "What, those tiny, flighty, annoying little evening flies? ...So what?" I reply. "Oh no", Thibault chuckles, darkly.

"They're different here", John says, with a sudden, steely urgency in his voice. Thibault continues. "There was this guy... cycling like you. He stopped, not far from here. Durness, I think.

No protection. Well, the midges came, a great black cloud…" His hands arc outwards, knocking over a box of Coco Pops. "They had to sedate him in hospital. He'd ripped the skin off his face, his arms…"

"You've got no protection at all?" John asks in disbelief, dispelling the silence that has now fallen over the table. Apparently not. The midge cream picked up in Berwick is, by the standards of the North West Highlands, "mickey mouse". John insists on driving me to an angling shop before I set off, his transit careering heavily through the dirt-yellow pebbledash of Thurso.

"What will I need?" It's an open and desperate line of enquiry, but the elderly Yorkshireman behind the counter promises to try his best, then returns ten minutes later with a midge net, some angler's galoshes – effectively a tarpaulin sewn into the shape of trousers – and… some Avon Skin So Soft. "The SAS use this", he says with earnest seriousness. "Twenty-five of us went out fishing warm day, no wind like… Only four of us stuck it out… I'd put this stuff all over me face. Me face were black wi'em, but they weren't biting." At least when they find my bloody, midge-ravaged remains, my face will have a moist glow.

Sleet lashes against the transit, the roadsides sludging up gloopy slush. It becomes difficult to make out anything beyond abstract grey shapes. John insists on driving me up to Dounreay, west of Thurso, and I'm loathe to refuse. We pull over by a particularly dour nuclear power station and gaze at the gorse-abyss beyond. A heavy mist snags over the granite crags, a herd of harassed sheep drift in front of the verge where we're parked, and cross the deserted road. We've been staring in silence for some minutes, the rain perkily pattering against our warm, musky cocoon, like steel drums on some sunny ganja afternoon.

"I like to go out there", John says, after a time. "Into the wilderness." Where things are simpler, and some conclusive sense can be made of them. Like we find in other large mammals, prolonged company with our own kind causes its own stresses.

John's going off the map, out fishing in some remote hinterland for a couple of days. "Good luck", he smiles, patting my shoulder.

I climb up to Bettyhill, stopping for a moment at the summit of a remote mountain, where the view of the surrounding peaks and glens is as inspiring as a letter from an old friend, and as tranquilising as the first beer after a long day. A couple stands beside a campervan, imbibing the view. "I come here a lot. I just need to see this. It makes me feel real again", says one lady, the vermilions and fuchsias of the surrounding scape utterly indifferent to our speculations.

Bettyhill itself is a miniature settlement, speckled across a road that eddies over two glens. There's a small museum in an old church, where an enthusiastic old boy chuckles at my request for a student concession, "the first we've had". It tells the story of Sutherland's Clearances, and is populated by a party of Australians tracing their ancestors, forcibly evicted from these lands two centuries ago to make way for more profitable sheep. As one factor put it, "[s]uch a set of savages is not to be found in the wilds of America. If Lord and Lady Sutherland do not put it in my power to quell these banditti, we may bid adieu to all improvement." These banditti, poor crofters and farm labourers, were collected by enterprising planters and then put to work in Canada, New Zealand and Australia. And modernisation, improvement, progress and other abstractions continued, as the local people of those countries were cleared out to accommodate more profitable livestock. But who reflects on the moral atrocity of "stopping the boats" amongst the neeps, tatties and tartan flimflam?

These ancient, now unpeopled scapes resonate with that same solemn ambience of Helmsdale and Wick. Upon one doggone lonesome moor, west of Bettyhill, I discover a Johnny Cash Best Of CD and a dirty pillow, discarded by the road. To my left and right are small grey lochs, the rain and breeze causing them to deceptively glimmer, and between them, grey tors bursting through the barren heathland and glossy bracken. It is wintry cold, and the galoshes soon prove unfit for the task.

Ahead, a small village hugs onto a rocky descent into the sea. A priest strolls out of the village's post office, which also functions as a newsagent, café and community centre. He tells me that this is Tongue. Father Michael's accent is oddly familiar. He gave up years of being a secondary school headmaster in London to care for his elderly mother with dementia. I sense his grief, still. Not long after she died, he packed a bag, got into his car and opened up a map. Tongue, the edge of the island. He drove up here. He takes leave with a strange exhortation, after describing the ethereal beauty of Loch Eriboll. "We've left the young a terrible inheritance. The world, the planet, the social problems for the young. I'm really sorry…" His voice trails away, until his thoughts find temporary fixture in the kyle beneath us. He eyes me pointedly. "Stay with life."

The sentiment's repeated with anger by Dylan, behind the bar of the Ben Loyal hotel. He'll soon leave for an engineering apprenticeship in the Aberdeen oil fields. He singles out Westminster greed as undermining the common good of the union. "With respect, we produce and give more to the economy than we consume. I don't see why the South should suck it in. We make it, and all you do is sell it." The question of independence is not an end in itself in his mind, but a milestone in the journey to create a fairer society.

Over the kyle of Tongue, and the landscape starts to emanate a unique, dramatic intensity. There are no motorists, or villages, or cars. Birds stalk the higher skies, buzzards roaming with a stoic glare over the barren landscape. Scattered sheep spill out onto the road, requiring a sharp trill to clear a path. Ruined farmhouses are all that remain of a human presence. The horizon over the lochs begins to soar out into an almost infinite distance ahead. I feel far from anywhere, and very much at home amongst the savage serenity of the place.

Rain clears by the late afternoon, and the road curves around toward Durness. In front of me is a shepherd, his collie and a large flock of sheep that fill the road on every side, making passing impossible. The sheep well outnumber the pair, and could easily overwhelm them and break free were they to act collectively. But they wait for one young sheep to show the way, and one rebel sheep is far easier to control than a resentful flock. "Don't do it, lamb!" A horrible canine growl and the clang of the staff against a metal crash barrier sends the creatures into terror. I talk with the shepherd, an Englishman helping the farmer, driving a Land Rover ahead. "If it wasn't for the [EU] subsidies, we'd be wiped out." It reflects another desire for independence, popular not in Scotland but England, where hostility to the EU could lead to decisions that unwittingly annihilate the country's smaller farmers. He looks on circumspectly. "What can you do?"

Rainbows pierce through the early-evening sunlight. Azure Loch Eriboll is a small piece of paradise, and the narrow road hugs its concourse til it reaches Durness. The far-northern light is penetratingly white, clear, cutting through the mind's clutter, the cynicism that presents a worldview as inaccurate as a medieval mappa mundi, instead towards what really matters, love, pleasure and the thrill of discovery. The depopulated majesty of the loch and surrounding bens is extraordinary, defying conventional superlatives.

I explore an empty, unspoilt beach, then peer into Smoo Cave, listening to a distant subterranean waterfall somewhere within. Back on the road, a young French woman catches my eye, and I recognise I've seen her at several points along the road, hitching in the same direction. Camille's bewitched by the grandeur of the place, "like nowhere else". We gaze down at the bay, silent, smiling, words still being formed to match the scenery. We part ways, each without knowledge of where we'll be the following evening.

A group of locals take turns shooting at a tin can with an antiquated rifle just behind the beach. They cannot hear a word I say, but surmise my objectives, and point me to the nearest boozer. Lynn, Ang and Gavin smoke outside the Sango Sands bar, and dish out the local gossip. We get talking and I join them. "There's not much here", jokes Gavin, "but I work in fish, salmon. Fish farming, yer just out on a boat and feed 'em. Other times, like now, we're out all the day changing the nets." They are all content. "Make sure you turn left at Spar!" they shout out to me, later, too drunk to ride. Is it worth leaving?

8.30am. Flashbacks: cattle-trucked onto morning tubes and trains, fellow passengers bickering and barging each other, stress seeping out of sleeves and shirts. Buses in the sluggish South London traffic, kid behind you etching into the back of your chair. World of frustration, resentment and fear. Camped above the tranquil heather over Keoldale Bay, I realise the ruse beneath John's remark yesterday. The real wilderness is where I've come from.

I catch a small ferry over to the most northwesterly tip of the mainland, Cape Wrath. One of the local women yesterday spikily defended the place. "Tourist trap?" (as another on our table had intimated...) "Och no!" Her father has worked here some time, and she has a point. On the other side of the ferry hop is a veritable abyss, some 107 square miles of inhospitable wilderness. Its use as an MOD and NATO firing range has also made much of this terrain explosive. The odd unlucky sheep still proves that the unexploded ordinance is live, says another John as he drives our small group along a pocked trackway to the edge of Cape Wrath. Adders roam the lank grasses, and occasional groups of red deer appear in the distance. It's a rocky terrain that would've looked just the same as when William Camden travelled here four hundred years ago, finding a place "haunted and annoied by most cruell wolves". Its menace remains evident.

At the other end of the road stands a lighthouse. "Not everyone could do it", our driver says of the solitary lighthouse-keeper.

"It's his choice, but he loves it." As he welcomes visitors into the lighthouse, I disappear off down the cliff-edge, where a stony pathway creeps around the precipice. Among the lichen, cotton-grass and wildflowers, it's curious how nature can thrive even in cruel environs. In the distance is the morose snaggle-tooth Cathedral Stack and the rocks of Garvie, used as missile practice by the Americans until the people of Durness complained about the noise. A tree surgeon from Sutton climbs down the same cliff-edge and we share in the awe, bleak yet beautiful.

Back on the mainland, I continue following the stark coastline, among vast mountain ranges and ruined crofters' cottages, and little else. It feels like I'm exploring the limits of my own mind. Unfathomable, as if time had ceased. Strange memories and forgotten desires burden the mind as if transmitted by this barren scape, like the ocean in Tarkovsky's film *Solaris*, as if the abyss itself is aware and alive. Heather, gorse, sheep, occasional eagles and buzzards. I pass Handa Island, a home for rare birds, and Kinlochbervie and Sandwood Bay, with an unlikely golden beach.

Elated somehow by it all, I feel more alive than I've ever known. Some hours pass by like this, til I reach the little village of Scourie, where I stop for a pint in the quiet hotel bar. Leslie's from Birmingham, and came up to Scourie after the vague promise of a bar job. "I don't regret it. I couldn't go back. I can't do cities now... Just look at this place." Indeed. He knows of Czechs, Poles, Australians and many English people that've settled here, found a way to make it work. "Fish farms" is a recurring employer. Unaware of where I am, exactly, I ask for a map. Leslie points to a village on the western edge of the island, seemingly nowhere. "That's Lochinver. Lots of Spanish and French fishing boats come in with their catch. You might like it."

On a whim, I go for it. With only one road on this edge of the island, it's not hard to get lost.

"More remote from civilisation than when I crossed the Sierra Nevada... the very workshop of God", is how H.V. Morton described the scene after Scourie. It's a prehistoric landscape of glens and bens, lochs and rocks. But this "God" is also famed for his inexplicably cruel sense of humour. By the deserted hamlet of Kylesku, I spot an abandoned car by the road, hazard lights pulsing on the verge, windows down. The rain has cleared, and the afternoon is unusually hot. The familiar breeze has now dropped. I draw closer to investigate. A faint itch on the back of my arm. Prickly tingling around my neck. Some nuisance buzz in my ear. Now a fly, or several, tiny things, lodged in my eye like a fleck of persistent dirt. In a matter of seconds, my head is surrounded by a black mist of midges. With my other open eye, I just about make them out, swarming into my ears and mouth and down my sweaty shirt. In a manic flappery, I get that midge net over my head and pedal out as furiously as I can, a little sorely-bitten but grateful for the lucky escape. The fate of the car-owner remains less certain.

The road forks by the edge of Loch Assynt, and I take the narrower track right towards Lochinver. To my left, for some ten miles or so, the Jurassic-looking Loch Assynt gleams gold and black, reflecting the setting sun and a savage mountain range. Trees spurt out of crags with tropical plumage. The midges collide against my face like papery sleet. When Thomas Pennant travelled to Assynt two and a half centuries ago, he describes a scene of "desolation itself", of jagged mountains and a people malnourished, living in hovels. "[T]hey wandered in a state of desperation; too poor to pay, they madly sell themselves for their passage, preferring a temporary bondage in a strange land, to starving for life in their native soil."

I think of the foodbanks of Gateshead, of the sheer poverty of the North East, and consider the cruel blessing of these crofters to access a better life overseas. What use have the Chinese for a clinically depressed miner's son or daughter with less than five GCSEs? The people of Assynt were also cleared in the same rude fashion as in Sutherland and Caithness. Pennant concludes his travelogue with the report of a dream, wherein an ancient Highland chief warns how contemporary chieftains have become "rapacious landlords", exchanging the "warm affections of their people for sordid trash". Pennant's moral invective is instructive, though not in the way either he or his chief expected. Those crofters could've rushed the chief's mansion, overpowered his factors and taken back what was rightfully theirs. But they did not. And the sheep who succeeded them were noted for being unaware of their collective strength and easily cowed. Don't do it, lamb.

Shielded by forests, I reach a small thread of a town, its harbour resplendent in the late evening sunset. Outside the Culag Hotel, a smartly dressed man clutches his face, weeping. Nearby, a preoccupied fellow wanders out of the deserted fishing terminal. He sucks on a cigarette and gazes at the sea with the detached affection of a parent. Ian smiles as he attempts to explain how he found this place. "I love the place, it's so quiet. I come here as much as I can." He directs me to the nearby Culag woods for a place to camp, and points me to the Caberfeidh for refreshment.

Past a scrapyard of burnt-out coaches, I climb up into a deep forest behind the village. It's uncannily populated with life-size wooden fertility sculptures, orgies of midges beneath. I pitch the tent at the top of a remote hill, then drift back to the boozer.

It's a Saturday, and the entire village has turned out for a night of drinking. A local woman has died, and beyond the live music is a peculiarly charged emotional intensity. A young Australian singer has the crowd in chorus on the 'Bonnie Banks o' Loch Lomond', whilst one besuited bloke utters apt advice into the tottering ears of a stocious nephew.

"There's nothing more difficult than the relation between a man and a woman. I mean me, and your da, and whatever... we're all cunts. We all fuck up. Ye just got teh feel yer way through it. But..." and he points his index finger for a dramatic emphasis, the stagecraft lost on the lad, "don' be afraid to say ye've fucked up. When yer dogmatic, that's when things fuck up... stubborn-ness!" The last word is said with a weirdly high-pitched emphasis, as if intended as a quote. The man wobbles, and rests his weight against the bar. "Pride's one thing, but humility is what'll win yer the battle."

At the bar, a wizard-like man with long white hair and beard gazes out at the locals with a very specific kind of curiosity. Yes... a fellow member of the association of dreamers. His conversation does not disappoint. Greg introduces himself as a storyteller, and has just moved here from Aberdeenshire. "There's a differ-ence between being welcomed, and being accepted", he reflects, as I share my affections for the Highlands. "You're being wel-comed, and that's great. These people will talk to you, invite you in, buy you a drink. But there's a way to go with being accepted, when the locals see you as one of them. When they'll invite you in, confide in you."

As we head outside, Greg gestures to a nearby tree beside my bike. "Take a look at this tree. You see each leaf. It's like each leaf has its own opinion. Together, all these leaves have their own views, disagreeing as they go. We've got to take a look at the tree as a whole. What does it need? What brings it together?"

Eventually I track it down, a house with no number or obvious sign of habitation, along a small lane of white pebbledash hous-ing just outside of town. Mount Sullivan sulks gloomily in the distance. Soaked through by the rain, bitten meticulously by midges, ticks lodged in my arms, I'm all too grateful for Greg's offer of a shower and a cup of tea the next morning.

He opens the door, but before we can shake hands, Florie gallops up and jumps to greet me. Inside is an explosion of books, art and a life's miscellany, packed up in piles or screwed onto walls. As he potters about making tea, I peep through guides to mountaineering, folk poetry and radical Scottish his-tory. Three pieces of wood hang from the wall in the shape of a harp, next to an ink-drawing of a frigate. Greg talks of whaling and Herman Melville as I pick away at the remains of a tick lodged in my forearm.

"The most terrible creature on this planet? The human. Closely followed by the tick." He laughs heartily, then disappears into the kitchen again, where the boiling kettle whinnies. He returns, and resumes a tangent from last night, about Aberdeenshire and its oil boom.

"You know, I regret not taking up being a diver. This was back in the 70s. I was working in social services. I used to get four hunner a month, not bad money, but I could get five hunner a night just being a relief diver." Scotland's oil boom began in Greg's home county. Work was well-paid but dangerous: for just fifty minutes underwater welding pipelines together, a diver would need to spend a week in a decompression chamber recovering. "The real danger wasn't in the sea. These idiots would fall asleep at the dials. One guy was a total pisshead. A fella died of a heart attack in those chambers, they just ignored him. There wasn't much health and safety back in them days."

But, does he know of the "other way"? It was a rumour I heard in the pub last night. This morning, getting supplies in the local shop, a map was presented, and it did seem a theoretical possibility, though even the shopkeeper knew nothing of it. "The other way? To Ullapool? No chance!"

I decide to foolishly dispense with this local advice and instead pursue an obscure theoretical possibility, perhaps the one thing years of miseducation have gifted me. Rather than skirt over Assynt again, I pursue a southbound narrow trackway, just wide enough to accommodate a small car, that pulls out of an obscure corner of Lochinver and up towards Inverkirkaig. The trail cuts through dark corries, the green granges and russet moorland twisting after a time into vast mountain ranges, and amongst these ancient hills and forests, silent except for the whoops of birds, I begin to feel again like I could've accidentally travelled five centuries back. Burnt-looking trees, black and dry, burst out of the hillsides like the antlers of fallen stags. Hardy sheep psych each other up, dashing across the road in front of me. I trill the bell and laugh, the pleasure all my own.

The steep hills and broken road are difficult to navigate. One driver, seemingly lost, loses control of his car and drives me off the road. I tumble down the verge and crash into rough scree, body bruised and hands bloody. The young driver apologises, and I sense the sincerity of his guilt, but I'm pissed off and make this clear to him. Lingering pain hampers my progress thereafter.

Eventually by Loch Bad a' Ghaill the road splits, either west towards remote Reiff, or east back toward Ullapool. I take the latter, following a single track that bends around a vast and otherworldly loch before rejoining the main highway. Coaches and motorhomes overtake me at speed as I approach Ullapool. After miles of desolate rocky expanses, it is something special to clap eyes on an actual town, a place with more than three streets and at least one pub. Its white Swiss-style chalets gleam in the distance, and I soon find myself in a small modern settlement dominated by its passenger harbour. Two lads in the local Tesco advise me on the best chippie, and a local lady speaks of scallop fishing and the boon of tourism in an area with "not many jobs" left. I join a line of visitors gazing wistfully at the ocean, as together we wait for the ferry to Stornoway, the main settlement on the Isle of Lewis, on the Outer Hebrides.

It's as strange as Greg told me. The Outer Hebrides are fiercely religious. Aboard the vessel, a young woman laughs incredulously as she describes the protests by staunch local Presbyterians, outraged by the launching of a new ferry service on Sundays. She remembers brave locals wearing red shoes on the first passage, hoping to appease the Holy Ghost for disturbing the Sabbath with a peculiarly pagan custom of their own.

Stornoway is a much larger town than anything I've seen for weeks, more so than even Ullapool, and makes up most of the settled part of Lewis. It's morose in appearance, with grubby housing and shops lining the shoreline, beside warehouses, brown pebbledash blocks of one kind or another, and the looming fortifications of Lews Castle in the distance. Nothing is open, and most of the pubs have timber boards over the windows. I find two locals chatting furtively on a deserted street by the harbour, and inquire after the source of freshly-tapped ales. George points me to the Lewis Hotel, and says he'll meet me in there.

Over a pint of McEwans in this shabby but lively hostelry, we get talking about toleration. An odd subject, perhaps, but an apt one. "Religion's a problem here." George tells me about all the protests when the town's one Indian restaurant first opened on a Sunday. The island's isolation has allowed the perpetuation of an intensely ascetic Presbyterianism, long eviscerated by inter-cultural communication on the mainland. His accent is harsh and fast, a peculiar brew of Irish and Norwegian, lips pursed and jaw locked in a softened drawl, but with its own intonation and assonantal music. It reflects the Lewis-Harris Island's history, a Norse possession until the late 13th century but one where Gaelic had always been spoken. Many signs are in Gaelic, but the barman and another local reflect that only "about half and half" speak the language, with the others having a vague understanding of it. They speak of the island's quirks with a peculiar stubbornness to consider them as anything but ordinary.

Locals chase their pints with shots of cheap vodka and tequila, and the TV blares out Motown's best songs. It's a convivial atmosphere, but ill-suited for sleep. "What are ye gonna do?" asks George. The barman gets out a map of the island and points out the island's only other notable feature for the tourist: the stones of Callanish. It's around sixteen miles from town, and it's now half ten at night, but Stornoway's northern altitude and these summer months mean that the gloaming's still light enough to ride. I head out into the deserted lunar landscape.

The ancient stones of Callanish are known as *fir bhreig* or "false men" in the local tongue, petrified for the breach of some forgotten taboo. One legend has it that young locals would gather here on the summer solstice, when the morning sun appears to walk eerily down the aisle that separates the stones of Callanish, arranged in pairs in the shape of a cross for forgotten purposes, some five thousand years ago. In the morning light, the huckled remains give the impression that a cathedral once stood here, and, in spirit and concept, it once did. Wedding vows were exchanged on that solstice morning, and marriages consummated communally beneath the stones until quite recently. Well, legend has it.

"Only two topics can be of the least interest to a serious and studious mind", uttered Yeats, "sex and the dead". A characteristically deceptive comment. What else but some strange blend of the two has us rooting around these inexplicable stones, some three billion years old, at two in the morning, thinking about the fundamental interconnectedness of past, present and future as ticks tack and a deluge drowns the saturated land and fills a woebegone tent?

Though it's still early morning, tourists are already parking their hire-cars nearby, photographing the vast, flat, boggy peatlands of Lewis with the dedication of forensic criminologists. There are dozens of local terms for peat here, once cut, dried and burnt for fuel, even smoked. *Cruach, mòine, fòid...* No one in Stornoway could think of more than two or three. Zigzags in the hillside are all that remain.

A man with electric-blue eyes and a tufty shock of white hair drifts towards me, the rick-tick-ticking of his bike chain indicating ailment. We chat over bananas, and experiment with tools on his chain with the dexterity of chimps operating a space capsule. A man of similarly quixotic temperament, he's sailed to Callanish from the Elba aboard a crude, self-fashioned vessel, and his inspired if impishly dry humour suggests a lengthy deprivation of human company. He complains about the modern dependence on computers, and, quite spontaneously, begins outlining the philosophy of Abelard, a medieval theologian who sought, against the grain, to introduce some degree of reason into religious belief.

"They were total rebels back then. Constrained by this church that, how you call it, cut his balls off! But the systems of thought were so advanced, I still don't understand it. They brought Greek thought to us."

He smiles, and stops for breath. We both reflect on how useless our skills are in this manic information economy and the fact that, remarkably, one culture can instruct another, centuries, even millennia apart. Lovely Callanish was deliberately damaged three thousand years ago as new ideas overwhelmed old, just like the Stones of Stenness, dynamited by an insane Victorian farmer, gelded like Abelard's balls for the crime of existence.

After an hour venturing round the various Neolithic sites of Callanish, I retrace my progress through the flat Lewis peatland. Flat plains, stale lochs with a stagnant stink, distant telecommunications towers. This desert mirrors itself in the traveller's mind. Without the protection of mountains and trees I'm assailed by the roughest, toughest wind I've ever encountered, nearly knocking me sideways as I rejoin the Tarbert road south. Progress is cripplingly slow. I pull myself up the great mountain ranges that separate Lewis from Harris, an adjoining landmass south, forcing myself inch by inch against a jetstream-like headwind. There is nothing more miserable than cycling in a headwind. Except, perhaps, if it's also raining. So yes, it starts raining heavily. Such an inimical combination merits a term of its own. Pisswind, I call it. On the other side of the steep ridge, Harris' terrain is even more deserted and bleak, scarcely hospitable for even the few hardy sheep unlucky enough to be roaming round.

There's one ferry leaving Leverburgh on the southern edge of Harris today, sometime in the early afternoon. The mischief of the wind has slowed me down no end, and it quickly becomes unlikely I'll reach it in time. More worryingly, I'm aching in new places. A runny nose, migraine and sneezing attest to the onset of a bad cold. I'm not sure if I can handle another night in a damp, rain-filled tent.

I'm spent by the time I reach Tarbert, a small village with a couple of shops and a hotel, and the only evidence I've seen in some hours of human habitation on Harris. My options are either to wait here for a night, or…

"Ask for Big Michael", a woman suggests by the island's bus station. She points me towards the hotel. An inebriated, ursine Englishman sits alone at the bar. "We'll get you there young man!" he assures me, upon hearing my dilemma. He downs his pint and shows me to his car, whilst another local bundles my bike in the boot.

Rain lashes against the car as we traverse solitary straits at speed, the landscape intermingled with some of the most beautiful sandy beaches I've ever seen. "It can be clannish here. It's alright if you're a man, going into the pubs. People are welcoming. But for me second wife, it were too hard. She wanted to go back to England, and I said 'ta ra!'"

Leverburgh. The name's distinctly English, unlike the Gaelic and Norse names about it like Scarista, Seilebost and Geocrab. Sunlight Soap magnate William Lever sought to turn this part of Harris into a modern industrialised fishing port in the 1920s, but he died before his plans were realised. Leverburgh might well have become a Port Sunlight by the sea, a model fishermen's community, but today is just the rump of a harbour. Consoled by beer and whisky, a man from the Burnhams in Norfolk laughs at hearing the names of childhood places, and complains of being priced out of Chelsea-on-Sea. He's washed up here, via Dubai, in bar-work. Fishermen exchange part of their catch for beer. Life is slow, calm. The population of Harris and Lewis has plummeted in the last fifty years, the crofting and fishing long gone.

"You don't earn as much, but there's nothing to spend your money on either."

Aboard the ferry, Gaelic is the first language, a flowing and lyrical tongue. Feeling ill by this point, I follow the ferry-man's tip to seek out a small hostel on the other side of the bay, on Berneray.

There's a briny tang in the air but few sea-birds, and the overcast silver skies clash against lush marine blues, like a troublesome reflection in the palette of Turner. I pick up supplies in the village shop, where Bob and his daughter talk of the peaceful life here, privately glowing in the unlikely success of their escape from Lincolnshire. Peaceful white cottages cluster round a bay, and I follow a broken road towards an unscripted terminus. Beside the ruins of an old shieling is a sign for a hostel, as Bob instructed, and further down a trail I spy two thatched roofs over whitewashed cottages, overlooking a long sandy beach extending as far as the eye can see.

I politely tap against the red timber door of the larger cottage, then stumble inside, nearly tripping over the flagstone threshold. Inside are a family, a couple of guests and a delightfully warm fire. The air's ripe inside, boiled potatoes and toasted mackerel, abub with genial conversation. Hiking boots and waterproofs dry above the hearth, a tart muskiness emanating from their corner. Most of the guests are English, some walking around Berneray and North Uist, connected to this small island by a long bridge; others, like this young Scottish family, often returning here, for the tranquil landscape and the internal states it produces.

"People are ruled by their heart, not their head", worries Nigel, as I pour kidney beans into tortilla wraps. Regional self-government is the topic. For what end, I ask, fearing the onset of an anti-democratic diatribe. "It's true of Cornwall, or Yorkshire... The South East, sucking all the power, all the life." There's some material stability across the island, and the narrative of "economic recovery" does seem to be commonly believed, despite the lack of any obvious evidence for it. But middle class prejudices begin to come out, as if these folk with their qualifications are somehow neutral in their observations. "In places with poverty, where there isn't much chance of an education, you'll find people making uninformed choices." Another Englishman chides the obstinacy of Scots nationalists, not recognising the economic problems they'll face after independence. "It's not about that", I venture.

"What's it for then?" And it's the terms of that question, as much as the asker's inability to even conceive of its intrinsic answer, *the common good*, that troubles me.

The sun is out, and a gentle breeze drifts over Berneray Bay, coupling with the gentle murmur of the tides. I'm sat outside the cottage, sharing peppermint tea with a hiker who had "gone missing" the previous night. The guests were worried for her – the building itself quickly producing an intimate, familial care for one another. She laughs as she explains how, whilst rambling through the hinterland of North Uist, a farmer had asked for her help in herding some cattle. He repaid her in dinner and wine.

"It took me twenty years to find this place. Now I come back whenever I can. I just keep it open, I don't plan anything. There's something magical about here." She tells me of a man who stayed for four months, after a breakdown, possibly. He was silent, "just sat out there looking at the sea, every day". Some riddle solved, he left, relieved.

I wander out onto the white beach. The sea's turquoise, the sun's reflection flashing from it like white lightening. Amongst the sands I spy seashells, crabs, desiccated jellyfish, and gulls, scavenging like me. The granules crackle between bare toes. I wander up to the shoreline, and disinterestedly skim pebbles over the ripples, the sport of schoolboys and sages. In the water I spot a fragment of green pottery, possibly the bottom of a broken mug. It has "England" printed on it in small letters. The shard presents a question I can't yet answer. I drop it in a pocket, and push on.

Over a long causeway into North Uist, a rocky and flat scape with a little more green life to it than Lewis, populated by a familiar cast of sheep and ruined farmsteads. The road forks, on to South Uist and Barra, or left to Lochmaddy and the ferry to Skye. With people to meet in Armadale on Skye that Crìs has put me in touch with, and still feeling a little unwell, the choice's easy.

Dan and Rick also have dark memories of cycling through yesterday's winds on Harris. We trade nightmares on the ferry to Uig. Like me, they'd given up at Tarbert perhaps an hour after I'd left, but then, under some odd compulsion, decided to push on to Leverburgh around midnight, pedalling alone through the black banshee hills. We share beer and ice cream, and it turns out we've more in common, all of similar age, each seeking some escape from London, crushing vocations, strangled by the threads of the fates.

Rarely have paths yet crossed with other cyclists, but the experience usually evokes imposter syndrome. They laugh or grow pale when I describe my journey, or the distance covered that day, and scrutinise my bike and casual costume. "Cor, that's heavy!" they say, lifting the old frame. They find it peculiar that I wear no gloves or lycra, that I live off biscuits and beer and sleep in the wild, and that I remain in the same highest gear whether ascending or descending some vertical slope. Perhaps it is strange. But it's how I like it.

On the other side, we race each other down to Portree. Rick's recumbent struggles up Skye's gentle, forested hills, but picks up speed on the other side, disappearing into the horizon like a granny's mobility scooter with a Ferrari engine inside. To avoid confusion, I am now "Dan 2", a slightly younger relation to "Dan 1". We laugh together as we pass through Skye's verdant hillsides, the jagged Black Cuillin mountains in the distance.

Portree's a cheery little town nestled in a valley. As we arrive into the old town square, a bagpipe band fresh from success in the Forres games parades the lanes, blaring out the Bonnie Banks to gaggles of giddy tourists. Americans talk loudly of their surprise at the sunny weather. I agree to meet Rick and Dan 1 later, and go off exploring the little town. A local man tips me to check out the Lump, a small amphitheatre cut into a bosky hill overlooking the town and its harbour, used occasionally for highland games. A young lad helps me push the bike up its steep hill, and after stumbling around, I find a place beside the woodland that might conceal a tent.

We reconvene in McNabs, where Swiss and Dutch tourists knock shoulders with locals packed in to watch the football. The topic of my recent marriage leads onto a reflective foray on life experiences and goals. "Don't say this will be the only time, the one time", Dan 1 replies, after a period of silence. "What you're doing now, you can do again. People say too easily: *this is it*. They go travelling, then lock themselves into a miserable job, a miserable life. Don't feel obliged to be responsible!" he admonishes me, and Rick, and himself.

We tour the bars, pished and exuberant, cracking jokes and talking horseshit, til at last everything's closed. As a parting gift, Rick cuts off one of his bicycle wing-mirrors and attaches it to mine. We shake hands and part ways.

Back on the Lump, overlooking the bay, I watch the stars a little while, and think of something Nigel said, beatifically. "I thought I'd gone deaf. There it was... nothing. Silence."

Sweet piny scents drift out from the forests to my right, as I pedal through the heart of Skye. Over my left shoulder, the Lump overlooks a dozy bay. To my right, the dense woodland and intense greenery that distinguishes this place from the craggy barrenness of everything around it. Just wonderful.

Skye's popular with tourists, and its built landscape distorts towards their trade. Tartan scarves and Talisker distillery tours, coaches queued back-to-back, and why not? Skye's a lovely place. But that's never the whole story. In the supermarket yesterday, a young cashier addressed my idyllic take on the island. "No... there's nothing here", she said, scanning my muesli and chocolate milk. "It's difficult. You've got to go to another island just to go to college. It's a nice place but... not many of the young people come back once they leave." But there was no rush, no queue, and I quizzed her a little longer. What then? "Medicine, maybe..." A smile, uncertain. "To be a doctor?" "Och no, a nurse maybe." "Why, you might be good at it?" She looked at me as if I'd asked her to sprout wings and fly.

Perhaps I should've chosen my words more carefully. Or maybe it reflected another kind of uncertainty, of taking a course that might last some years, and take her irreversibly from her home. In the Aros centre, a middle-aged woman spoke wanly of the same things.

"Skye is heavily dependent on tourism. That's fine. But for us, who live here, the problem is when house prices go up." She complains of people from "down south", but in the Highlands this phrase incorporates the cities of southern Scotland as much as England. She draws a map of where she lives. On one side, herself and her relations, their houses passed down by inheritance. On the other, English newcomers. Glendale too, a "mini England".

Bloody immigrants! But in a way this isn't dissimilar to the English working class antipathy to economic migrants and refugees I encountered in the Midlands, competing for decreasing wages, housing and services. Economic inequality is the basis and cause of the problem. The growing social divide on Skye is a spill-on effect of the island's increasing wealth divides, with the gentry buying second and third homes when much of the population cannot even afford one. Curiously, the Gaelic tongue has taken on special significance here. Nigel and Fiona's family on Berneray were ensuring their daughters learned Gaelic, and earlier I'd talked to Louise from Drumnadrochit, who was doing the same with her children, recognising Gaelic as essential to the identity they wanted their kids to adopt. On Skye, Gaelic is similarly enjoying a resurgence.

"I have a bit of Gaelic. You're likely to hear it, especially with the older generation. Go into a pub, the two old men in the corner, with their dram or pint. It started to die out when I was young. But it's coming back now! A lot of the young can speak it." I've found it rare to overhear Gaelic. It's a more intimate tongue, varying in dialect and phraseology across the islands.

I pedal below the craggy sierra of the Cuillins, overtaking coaches clustered around Carbost, and then on to Broadford – with the very different name of Leathann in Gaelic. It's a small village with a string of shops tending to passing tourists. An improbable flea market plies a lonesome trade. Inside, I nose through dusty Victoriana and pap 80s novellas. A woman pops her head in, unrealistically hopeful that these items still have cash value. Luckily for her, she doubles up as an estate agent, and has a more nuanced take on Skye's fortunes.

"There's two ways you can look at it. They've got money, and people want to sell their homes for the highest price. Then, work here doesn't pay the wages you'd need to get a place. So...?" "Well, you've just got to inherit a place from your dead granny then?" "Aye..."

She sells "ninety percent" of her homes to people "from down south", and notices the effect of this migration even in the schools, where the Skye accent, as she hears it, is in decline. But until Skye can give its young people forms of work they can stick around for, and homes they can afford to live in, what else can be done? She shrugs.

But the acquiescence of the present gives the lie that Skye's history has always been untroubled. Glendale may be a "mini-England" today, but in February 1883 conflict between local crofters and greedy landlords escalated to the extent that the British government sent a gunboat to quell the locals. Though the era of the Clearances had passed, crofters were still being moved to smaller, less fertile holdings to make way for sheep grazing or hunting reserves, and many lived in extreme poverty. Landlords continued to increase rents and mercilessly evict those who couldn't pay. Inspired by Irish land struggles, crofters and their allies in Glasgow formed the Highland Land League, and began to organise rent strikes across Skye.

The unrest had earlier culminated in the Battle of the Braes of April 17th, 1882, where fifty Glasgow policemen brawled with several hundred locals whilst escorting five arrested crofters away. Protests spread to Glendale, where local people refused to be priced out of their homes and communities. They refused to pay rent and began occupying private land, and in January 1883 attacked and drove out local police officers stationed in the area. For a time, Skye was on the verge of revolution. The gunboat and its threat of violence forced the crofters to temporarily back down. But sympathy for the crofters grew, more rent strikes and occupations of private land followed, and five Crofters Party candidates won seats in the 1885 election, predating Labour as the first organised working class party. The unrest forced the government to grant a Crofters Act of 1886, granting security of tenure and leading to the reduction of rents and arrears. But the Act didn't go far enough, and crofters continued to strike, occupy and agitate, securing further meaningful political change through their determined resistance.

There is no memorial to the struggle, but like in Ireland, their story has been passed down in rebel songs, like the 'Coinneamh nan Croitearan', or gathering of the crofters, by Màiri Mhòr nan Òran (AKA Big Mary of the Songs – an unsurpassable moniker...). I only heard of it when I asked Cris about the *cruinneachadh*, the circular gathering, which in terms of a meeting or assembly is more precisely called a *coinneamh*. He also gave me a name and email of introduction to an organisation on Skye's southern tip that, in its own way, is reopening these questions of cultural identity and landownership. It will prove revelatory.

Towards Sleat the landscape transforms, from the lush vermilion hillsides around Broadford to a flat boneyard country of dust and rock, some burnt bronze by the sun. On the edge of the village of Armadale, I finally spot a sign for Sabhal Mòr Ostaig, a Gaelic college that began as a barn and a good idea back in 1973. Iain Noble had been inspired on the Faroe Islands, where islanders were asserting their political and cultural independence from Denmark through their common tongue. Ireland and Wales had discovered renewed political pride through their heritage and language, so what of Scotland? So began Sabhal Mòr Ostaig.

Children and parents chat in this mellifluous tongue as I park my bike up by the college's walls. In the distance, I hear a bagpipe group practising, occasionally silent, followed by the intemperate hectoring of their elderly tutor. I wander inside, peering around the modern, capacious building. The receptionist fails to understand me at first, and I have to apologise for my lack of Gaelic. After a few repetitions, she calls Ciaran, who comes out promptly.

He shows me around its facilities, from a library and extensive archives to a large cafeteria, down corridors of classrooms, and describes in detail this Gaelic resurgence. It seems strange to even conceive it thus, when Gaelic predates the arrival of Latin, English or French on this island. Ciaran describes two movements and forms of the tongue: a first Goidelic wave, that was dispersed by later settlers but remained in use in Scotland, Ireland and the Isle of Man; and a second Brythonic wave, itself dispersed by Anglo-Saxon settlers into Cornwall, Wales and later Brittany.

Sidestepping historical paradoxes, Ciaran presents the paradox of a "lost generation" of Gaelic speakers aged between 20 and 60 who were discouraged from speaking the language at school. He ties the programme for language reclamation with a parallel one of land reclamation occurring on the nearby islands, like

Knoydart, and Eigg, or even Assynt, where communities have cooperated together to rebuy the land from "absentee landlords who never visited the place".

Ciaran seeks out my views on Scottish independence. It's an opportunity to separate the common conflation made in these parts of rich English landlords and second home owners from the poverty and financial difficulties that many English struggle under.

"Don't judge the majority of people in England like what you see here. Many people I've met, that I know, are skint, out of work or not getting enough work, just as fed up with Westminster as you are." "We've got a sense of identity, it's coming back. So has Wales. But what about England? All there is is the St George's flag."

I struggle to think of an answer, and as he talks – this cheery man with the same outlook, age and passport as me, though born into an all-too-different culture – I rub a finger around the sharp edge of my own "England", fragmented, hoping in vain for some revelation. "I've only been to England twice. I've been to Germany more often. London feels like a foreign country here, but it makes all the decisions that affect our lives. Scandinavia's a more realistic model for us. Even if the oil runs out."

His face brightens. "When I was younger, a Scottish parliament was unthinkable. Then later, a SNP majority was unthinkable. Even a No majority, on the smallest of lines, will make a huge difference. It would force Westminster to grant the maximum devolutionary powers." The same discontent simmered across the East, and the North, but here it has outlet, on the more straightforward question of regional self-government. It has opened up a conversation about political constitution and the future that remains, in the present moment, totally inconceivable in England. "All the wealth is in London. When there's a recession, London can weather it. It's the rest of the country that's been made dependent on London that suffers."

On the other side of Loch Houm, back on the mainland, I sip a beer with Michael, a sunburnt cyclist and glaciology researcher I met on the boat to Mallaig. English, well-spoken, at Cambridge University, he's a friendly chap, but of the same outlook and background as those who've bought up much of the Highlands. I wonder how I can begin to explain to him all that I've learned of Scotland, its language and histories. I'd been taught *nothing* of this country.

A pallid nun and a flustered friend fan themselves on the ferry deck. It's hot and balmy, unseasonably so, and today Mallaig Bay could be confused with the Canary Islands. Handing me her binoculars, Jan points out the lines of the tides and explains how to tell a basking shark from a minke whale, but all I see are ripples in the sea. Unlike this assortment of English and Welsh dolphin-chasers, I'm crossing over to a tiny island of no more than a hundred, a place that virtually everyone has told me to check out.

After decades of being passed from one irresponsible land-lord to another, the islanders had enough. They worked together to buy out the laird, and return the land to those who lived and worked it. By 1997, the island was in community ownership, and its story has inspired dozens of other communities to emulate the Isle of Eigg.

Ferries only land twice a week, and their arrival is a big event. A crew of locals wait apprehensively as friends and relatives are discharged. It's a great place to converse with strangers. Hilda is the headmistress of the only school on Eigg, also serving nearby Rum, and takes pleasure in telling me about the island's many natural attractions. She invites me up to her place for coffee later, but with so much here, will there be time? A cheery collie chases an old red van as it approaches the jetty. "Things are a lot better now", the old postie says, reflecting on twenty-six years in the job here. "Lots more parcels" since the arrival of the Internet. Like Hilda, he remembers the time before ownership, but took a more active stance, working on the island's committee, and glows with pride at their unlikely, collective accomplishment.

At the other end of the jetty, a solitary fisherman contemplates the sea. His name is Ewan, and he's neither a man of Eigg nor a fisherman, but the owner of an architectural firm in Glasgow. We talk for some time. He's very familiar with the island, often holidaying here as kid, and he contrasts Eigg's rediscovery of "collective rights" against a wider backdrop of political defeat. "I think it's sad, that in the last thirty years, something has been lost. There was a move, after the war, towards egalitarianism, towards collective rights. Somewhere that changed."

He locates it in the disproportionate influence of the South East of England, sucking wealth and power from the rest of the island. Worse, the Labour party and most of the well-known left-wing figures and movements I think to name are to him indistinguishable from the Tories. "They all go to the same schools", he says, but he later qualifies his comment, meaning universities too. Just a bland consensus of aspiration and greed, of narratives that blame the poor for their own poverty, the disabled for being workshy. If we were looking back on the 1930s, he reckons, such jeremiads would be transparently ugly. But today, greed and fear secure the media story.

Ewan ties it all together into a wider cultural narrative of defeat, giving the revelations of child sex-abuse cover-ups by major celebrities and government figures as indicative of a wider collapse in the authority, and trust, of Westminster. "The whole thing should be swept away, swept clean", he says. But he zooms out, eyes still affixed on the sea. "I think things are much more fragile than they seem. Poke at the right hole, and the whole thing could come falling down."

I find Ewan's conversation remarkable. Though of different background and occupation, he shares many of the same political views as me. That was also true of Dylan in Tongue, Ciaran on Skye, and many others I've met these last few weeks. Their conversation is far more informed, reasoned and hopeful than the English gloom, where some effort must be made to advance conversation beyond unfounded fears about immigrants or the economy. Indeed independence poses real risk to the Scottish economy, but as is often said here, it's not about that. In England the past is more political than the present: the closed mines, lost ways of life and disappearing sense of "community". In Scotland it is the future that is most political. And that energy is extraordinary. For if it can happen here, it can happen elsewhere, with potentially revolutionary consequences.

Behind the jetty is a large house, incorporating a café, gift shop, and no doubt more inside. I venture in. Peggy and Ian chat in the shop, two elderly folk born and raised on Eigg. The topic of Gaelic is instructive. "We were brought up with Gaelic. I never heard English until I first went to school, I was seven!" Ian tells me, chuckling. "We think in Gaelic, it was our first tongue. Now, those that speak Gaelic do it in translation, they translate from English to Gaelic in their heads. For us it was our first language."

Ian no longer lives on the island, and has put his croft and house up for sale. People are looking to buy here but, as Peggy notes with sadness, if Ian goes, there'll only be one other islander she can speak Gaelic with. Eigg's new population is, like much of the Highlands and islands, either English or Lowlands Scottish. And there is a substantial difference, as moments like this reveal.

For only the third time on this journey, it becomes so hot that shorts and sun cream are necessary to proceed any further. The hot glow on my shoulders is delightful as I cycle out of Mallaig, this time heading inland. To my right, the white sandy beaches of Arisaig and Morar, and to my left, scattered woodland and bens beyond, cool and grey-capped, my constant companions since crossing the Great Glen at Inverness.

Just west of Glenfinnan I spot a stray cyclist in the road, struggling to attach something back onto his bike. Ben is a geologist from Switzerland. After tinkering together, we both realise we have no fixed destination, and so agree to combine our powers, laughing and trading stories as we zip up and down the undulating road to Fort William.

He tells me about his country's compulsory military service and unusually relaxed laws around guns, but what's most intriguing are his observations on his country's extensive democracy. Referenda are frequent, perhaps a little too so. To hold a public ballot, all that's required is a petition with a hundred thousand signatures. They could well vote to have Monday mornings off if they wanted. Votes can be on matters important and trivial, and poor turnout is a problem. Another is when a decision representing the welfare of future citizens loses to the short-term interest of the present. Anti-immigration votes are one such problem, with a vote narrowly passed in February 2014 to re-introduce immigration quotas, making it difficult for immigrants to work there, be they cleaners or consultants. Xenophobic populism is often better able to absorb concerns about low pay, housing shortages and a declining sense of collective power with its fantasies about swarms swamping and invading. Europe's history proves exemplary in the dangers of such rhetoric. Movements of people define our past, present and future, *everywhere*. They indicate the bare fact of our existence. There is no easy answer to the problems migration raises, except to accept that it is us, and will be us. It raises the question of what kind of life is fit for us, being fit for all.

I think back to Hilda and Ewan. "Collective rights" seem far more encompassing than a five-yearly vote, most struggling to remember the name of their local MP. It's about putting the people at the heart of government, and agreeing fair rules that ensure that all decisions are made for the common good, today and tomorrow. The freedom to become a billionaire while others haven't food to eat isn't indicative of a country one would call modern or civilised. Both should be abolished, like the slave-trader or usurious monk. But everyone shrugs, as if eradicating the class system were like abolishing bad weather, rather than a straightforward change in political and economic rules. No doubt they would've shrugged two centuries ago too, at the suggestion of giving the vote to all women and men, or six centuries back, at abolishing feudal tithes.

Later, as Ben cooks couscous on a stove in a small forest just outside Fort William, we carry on talking, marvelling optimistically at these many ways forward, gladly unaware of the future's more likely outcome.

As the morning mists clear, it transpires that we're at the foot of Ben Nevis, Britain's highest mountain. Together we scour a map. Where next? "Somewhere to the west, I think... or, maybe south!" Today I am in no rush, and decide to take a day off the bike, as Ben ventures on towards Strontian, possibly.

Past the bustling Braveheart car-park, I follow the deep glen that leads up to a large visitor-centre complex. Groups of men in matching vests clap and shout, psyching themselves up with Maori-style chanting. I stow the bike behind a tree, and grab one pannier to take with me, containing a few key valuables: laptop, phone charger, tools, and a cheese sandwich, made some days ago and previously forgotten about. The weight will prove regrettable.

I have to wade through five hundred European hikers to get inside the centre, where a local woman urges that I ascend only with a map, waterproof jacket, hiking boots, bandolier, a gallon of water, dried food rations (at least a fortnight's worth) and an oversized staff. With a dirty dinner shirt, DIY shorts and my knackered cycling trainers, I decide to scale this giant mountain on my own terms, against all right reason. Why not?

A queue forms behind a long line of Dutch teenage boys carrying scout flags, chanting *Nederland, Nederland!* After the past few days in the remote Sutherland scapes, the place is positively packed out. Everyone seems to carry oversized walking sticks, sensible shoes and a backpack. And here comes this Saaf Laandener, carrying a bike pannier with both hands, barely able to keep his balance on the scree. "What you got in it, beers for the top?" Asks one burly geezer as he descends. I wish I'd thought of it earlier! Still, that sandwich...

The path winds and zigzags up, and I stay behind this ant-like scout procession for some hours. The walk is tough and steep, the pathway often loose and rocky, and by no means easy to navigate. A hand is needed most of the time to keep tumbling off the side. These legs, happy to pedal away for all the hours a day can supply, soon struggle and ache. But camaraderie quickly develops among the walkers. I chat with a family of Chinese Londoners, also up here without an iota of experience or preparation. They rest, and I carry on, talking to the next group beside me, of all ages and backgrounds. "Nearly there..."

"No way!" a weary woman replies. OK, it does take several hours of walking along a Sisyphean path. Look up into the distance and see line after line of people walking up and down, into the clouds, and one will sigh with desperation. But the glen below has become so remote that the car-park is no longer visible, and the valley appears like igneous rock, flecked in white, green, brown and grey. Eventually a thick fog at the top obscures the view. It becomes unbearably steep. Small piles of rock line the route, mystic tributes to some unknown god. Despair, indeed. Stop here?

There's a powerful reserve of inner strength in each one of us, but one only discovers its presence in situations of desperation. It's like Allie described in Sheffield, that in confronting and then mastering fear, one feels more alive than ever before.

Temperatures plummet. The now minuscule number of hikers trudging ahead start to disappear in a mist. The slope is icy, the track unclear. Eventually, the outline of a ruined building appears, the remains of an old observatory, and dark figures, queuing up for photos. The summit!

The sheer number of visitors crowded will dispel some of the magic, but still, after three hours, the relief of being here is immense. Crows skulk across more distant crags just off the path, leering mischievously at this cult-like procession of people, struggling up and down this spur in the sky. The fog clears, revealing a sweeping view of the surrounding mountains and sea, an incomprehensibly vast panorama that swallows whole the gaze for some minutes. There is no human reference for such a scale. One man tells me that the fog clears just ten days a year. Wondrous.

I find a crag on which to cotch, and open up my pannier to the smell of ripe cheddar and salad leaves. Three lads from the Home Counties crash down beside me.

"Two hours thirty-three!" [Checks phone] "Look, I've got phone signal. Oh... fucking hell, Santander have rejected my mortgage!"

It's actually harder climbing down than it is up. One misstep and gravity will have you hurtle 1344 metres down. As I drink in one epic valley vista, my feet start to slide and the button on my shorts bursts asunder. The rocky wall catches my weight, and fortunately no one's around to see my bum, but my knee takes a gash and blood streams down my leg. I eventually make it down the mountain, clutching at my shorts and laughing at my folly.

Some local philanthropist has opened a boozer at the base of Ben Nevis. Whisky and a first-aid kit come not too soon. My mind's been electrified by these last two weeks, animated and expanded in ways I couldn't've ever fathomed. I was like Montaigne's innocent fool, who, having only ever seen rivers, thought they were the sea. The surge and struggle of these days indicate that here instead might be the ocean. After the traumas inflicted on northern England, and the uncertainty behind each conversation in the Scottish Lowlands, another way of answering the problem of the common good is being raised here, beyond the edge of the known Roman world.

Divisions of language, class and landownership are raising troublesome questions about this disunited kingdom without a king, eking out what feel like its final decades. People are coming together, rediscovering their histories, bringing back ancient ways of speaking and living, and connecting them up to the digital vitality of the new. It is only a small step, but democratic local assemblies and communal landownership are some of the first contemporary initiatives I've seen against the prevailing uncertainty. Ideas of independence, usually connoting self-sufficiency, are here being connected with community power and collective flourishing. Something extraordinary's happening. What will come next?

CHAPTER 7

Stravaig

"Life doesn't give you a user manual" – Christy.

Thirty-six hours since descending Ben Nevis. Rain lashes horizontally against thin trees clustered around a hiker's path through the fertile glen. The moon is full tonight, its reflection tottering lumpishly across a murmuring stream. Consciousness starts to return from the intoxicating fug of beers and shooters I've subjected it to all day, as the rough outline of a hooded man tramps through an explosion of socks, books and empty beer cans. Wait... where's he going with that tent?

Too late. I'm unable to stop my brother throwing his tent into the river in an act of drunken lunacy. But it is his birthday, and on a whim he's travelled up to Fort William to meet me. We're both soaked through, but it takes a little coaxing to encourage him into my coffin-like nest. My inflatable sleeping mat soon bursts beneath our shared bulk.

Next morning, my mind replays a horror film: boozing in the town Wetherspoon's from noon, then moving on... then...? One bar-room scene after another in my mind's eye. The Grog and Gruel, debating the virtues of Lancashire and Yorkshire with a group of northerners... "Yorkshiremen make for better lovers", did he really say that? The expressions of muted mirth in their partners. Then the Crofters, shouting at the TV screen in another pub, packed with football fans. That's when the doubles and shots started... it gets blurrier. Was that man playing a trombone at the back?

We should've walked back into the wilderness after that, still a little *compos mentis*... But led by loud music and a neon fly-trap, "late night disco" at the Volunteers... god, no, I was dancing! Legs stiff, hands clawed, like a constipated grandpa's midnight shuffle out of bed... Then outside, kicking-out time, a well-dressed man, asleep in a doorway like a baby, and a girl who'd been dancing, "bruised but not broken" inked on her wrist, struggling to follow her speech, a sad romantic event... then lost in the woods, and that bloody tent...

My tongue feels like leather and my cranium's about to explode. I gently tug his arm. "We've got to get out of here." We're camped in the middle of the main footpath to Ben Nevis, and already hikers are nervously veering round us. "Come on mate, we've got to go!"

It won't be easy. Christy's sprained his ankle and can hardly walk, never mind pedal. A bad buckle's appeared in my front wheel. We've awoken soaked and freezing cold. A plan B's called for.

In the tourist office, an Englishman suggests we hire a car. His face darkens as he describes his weariness of Ben Nevis, its countless tourists and their litter. "It's like a circus up there", he scowls. As we leave, a group of boisterous Americans ask for directions to "Edinburrow". I take consolation in the fact that the gods are making a little more mischief at his expense than ours.

We find a pub to recover our remaining wits in. Christy gets the number of a local fleapit hotel and disappears for sleep, and I stay out, enjoying the rest, nursing my wounds, and meet him later in the Crofters.

It's a Sunday night, but the locals are knocking back the strong stuff like Lucozade on a charity run. Few are able to sustain concentration on the football. One man lifts up his overhanging paunch and to his lady friend announces "I'm pregnant!" Another relies on hugging, handshaking or generally clutching onto passers-by to remain vertical. A woman has us searching for a phone that turns out to be in her pocket. Another gent looks on hazily, then sips a dark-coloured drink. His face twists and turns green. "That is shite!" He offers me his cola-flavoured vodka then heads out for a snout.

We look at each other with pained expressions. It's neither the first nor last time we'll be over our heads out in the Scottish wilds.

Spean Bridge and Loch Lochy pass behind us at speed. What would take two or three hours of gruelling, meditative cycling expires with little sensation in twenty minutes.

Still, for many the car is the only way to see the extraordinary terrains of the Highlands, divided by the Great Glen. Loch Ness lies in the centre, on a fault line between two tectonic plates. We pause at Fort Augustus, a touristy village given over to Nessie hunters like nearby Drumnadrochit, with placid canal locks and homemade haggis takeaways. It's a dark and misty day, clouds interrupted by an unusual white light piercing through the sleepy bay.

Without thinking, I lean again on my right foot, provoking a sharp burning pain. Trench foot has developed after all the cycling in the rain, and my shoes are falling apart. We stop in Inverness to pick up a cheap pair of trainers. The brand is Beckett and it is suitably apt. "There's man all over for you, blaming on his boots the faults of his feet."

But where to? Seeking wilderness, we escape the retail parks of Inverness and cross the Kessock Bridge, driving left towards Ullapool. The car is so smooth that at times one could be gently flying over the road's surface. It travels too fast to detect how the scenery transforms, of where forests or valleys become the start of rugged mountain ranges. One cannot hear the birds or feel the wind. Getting cold? Turn up the heating. Bored? Tune into BBC Radio Gael. And that steep mountain that, by bike, would require an hour's intense physical and mental effort? We just drove over it without noticing.

The sun is setting, and the empty Highlands road is rugged

and beguiling. Forests flank our sides, Strathgarve and Garbat, and we pull over to gaze dumb at some nameless bay beneath Dirrie More. Breeze stirs the cotton-grass. I clamber down to the marshy shore to kick about the spongey spume and examine the tidewrack for treasure. I offer Christy some samphire, but he's never heard of it. Together we chew on the briny marram, agog at this sublime universe unknown to us, lost yet enthralled.

Click! My spine cricks as I struggle to pull myself up from the reclined passenger seat. The windshield's fogged up, but with a sleeve's attention is rubbed clear, revealing the gentle Shieldaig Bay twinkling beside us.

The previous evening we poked around the lobster pots of Gairloch harbour, then chanced on the bay of Badachro, where the final post collection is 7.45am. In a well-placed inn we pored over the landlady's OS map, realising just how remote we were. Over Mount Torridon we then drove, through the dark night, stumbling upon the wee village of Shieldaig where we stopped for a final nightcap.

South is the Applecross Peninsula, a stretch of small settlements in one of the most remote corners of Scotland. Its name in Gaelic is A' Chomraich, meaning "the sanctuary", and until the early 20th century it could only be reached by boat. A rudimentary track of sorts has been built laterally over the steep mountains, the Bealach na Ba ("pass of the cattle"), but it remains one of the toughest roads to drive, a snaking single-track affair with eye-wateringly precipitous moments. Lunatics often travel here to cycle up it.

A middle-aged man in white-splodged overalls and a beanie attempts to rebuild a drystone wall. Until recently, he was a chef in a Michelin-starred restaurant in London. He considers himself a refugee of the rat-race, glad to have got out.

"I started coming here, just for a break, you know. Then I was coming here four or five times a year. There's something about the place. Eventually I thought, you know what, I'm gonna go for it. I'm so much happier here."

We drive down into a wide bay where everything's in bloom. The roads are gnarled and twisting, and we follow one trail to a dead end in the midst of distant peaks, then another that ends on an islet full of cantankerous sheep. I notice life in a distant cottage, and knock on the cottage window for directions. The face of a farmer's wife pokes out and, after issuing directions, appraises our rental car like a market-day heifer. After some moments of uncertainty, she affirms "it'll do".

Back on track, we eventually reach 'The Street', the only settlement approaching the scale of a village on Applecross, and from there approach the Bealach na Ba. The hairpin bends are terrifying in places, but we eventually reach the summit, where the view of Raasay, Skye and the more distant Hebrides is wondrous. The dramatic range takes the mind above its mammal cage, the transient preoccupations of the self falling away, like a character in a film that's come to an end.

The descent down is trickiest of all, the trail skittering over the abysses of Wester Ross til it tumbles down into the vast straths beneath. "Dread God and do well" is the aptly archaic motto of this time-stunted county, Ross and Cromarty. Beneath the heights of the Five Sisters range, we drive back through Drumnadrochit, where Christy insists on visiting the delightfully silly Loch Ness Visitor Centre, a labyrinthine gift shop with a small ghost-house-like museum attached. The story of Nessie has its insubstantiality revealed: a sensationalised media event of the early 20th century, aided by the testimonies of plausible locals. Harmless fun, and good for the local economy!

Where next? The car makes easy work of the rugged terrain. In the Scots tongue of the Lowlands, this kind of drift is called a *stravaig*, an aimless wander, where one takes pleasure in the moment of the journey and not its completion. After driving back to Inverness, we decide to complete the Highlands stravaig, crossing over the Great Glen to survey the Cairngorms and Grampians. The landscape is far greener east of the Great Glen, the road rising up and down through its bens and corries. Aviemore is as tacky as everyone warned, whilst Kingussie, Dalwhinnie and Laggan are rural hamlets, surrounded by steep verdant mountains, less dramatic than the rugged, Jurassic west with its brooding tors and glacial plateaux. In the evening sun we keep driving, listening to strange radio stations or the wind as the mood takes us, tongues silent, minds alive with recording these majestic surroundings.

Evening's falling, and we decide to pull into Pitlochry, a quaint tourist town not far from Perth. It has a couple of Tartanland-type stores over-catering for visitors but just about keeps itself in check, and retains a sense of character and joviality largely scorched out of Aviemore. We find a driveway on the edge of town to park up for the night, and a pub to settle in.

Our urban vocabulary has no terms for the summits, bays, forests, heathland, mountains and lonesome tracks that we've encountered these last two days. We can recount and explain a panoply of TV, film and popular music personalities, as remote from our mortal lives as the medieval saints, but present to us scenes like these, and we have only *hill*, *mountain*, *green bit*, *rivery thing* and *woah*. I've had to scour the works of Robert Macfarlane and online thesauri to learn those words, of dells, denes and tors, rills and gills, straths and skerries, glens and bens, carrs and scree, where previous travellers have pressed precious terms for safe-keeping. I think too of the people I've encountered across the Highlands over the last month, refashioning themselves and making new lives. Is it just escapism for the rich or some kind of luck?

We talk about the past that brought us here, the pointless jobs, and the secondary school that left boys like us more stultified at sixteen than when we'd entered aged eleven. A common story. Like many, Christy doesn't have a university degree. He couldn't tell you what hegemony or neoliberalism are. But he knows that what is right for one should be right for all, that a society's best interest is in acting together for the common good. In a few days he'll be signing on again in Brixton, another period of unemployment punctuating a steady series of minimum-wage service-sector jobs since dropping out of college. "Twenty-six years. It's a joke", he laughs, bitterly.

Yet not long ago he'd saved a young man's life, lifting him up and carrying him to hospital with a friend after he'd been shot in the street, escaping a gunman at a nearby house-party. He's a talented musician who can pick up and master any instrument in hours. His sardonic and irreverent sense of humour is peerless. My sister, too, a little younger than him and also without qualifications, is caught in a cycle of low-skilled agency secretarial jobs. She's also one of the most wondrously kind and easy-going people I've had the pleasure of knowing. There is no obvious social or economic place for either of them, except the service sector. Like so many, their talents and energies are going without use.

Should they have stayed on to university and trained to be GPs, IT consultants or entrepreneurs? If that's your position, reader, then you underestimate the socio-economic forces that give a young person the confidence, motivation, ability and sense of self-entitlement necessary to succeed in such occupations. The intangible feeling of deflation among the young working class across the island isn't a consequence of spending too much time on their phones, *having it too good*, or whatever guff's printed. Though both in their twenties, nothing indicates that either will be able to afford to move out of my mum's place in the next decade, except by other financial support from my folks.

What's to be said to them? What bit of Marx should I quote, comrade? That they're not unlike most young people I'm meeting on the road, skint, uncertain, looking back nostalgically to childhood, looking for points of escape? As he complains about unemployment I remain silent, and later, I realise that my brother mistakes my silence for disapproval. Even silence is treacherous. Understanding cannot be taken for granted. The road has no clear destination.

An old boy limps out from a small cottage, carrying a broom. "You... You!" he shouts, his voice starting to fail him. There's no one else here in the small Swiss-looking hamlet of Fortingall. "Och, I'll open the church, one minute!" He disappears back into the cottage, and doesn't return.

Luckily it's not the church we're after. Encased behind a brick wall is a yew tree, thought to be up to five thousand years old. It may be the oldest living creature on the island, and is certainly among the oldest trees in the world. It is strangely contorted, its centre exploded into an octopus-like array of wayward branches, each expressing a desire to thrive. Though many of its boughs bear the scars of Victorian souvenir hunters, it flourishes, and could remain alive for many more centuries.

The yew is an old British symbol of eternity, being one of the island's few evergreen plants, with medicinal, shamanistic and poisonous uses. It seems to have been an important motif of pre-Christian British paganism, whilst the Norse tree Yggdrasil may well have been a yew. One finds yews in many Christian churchyards, and its life-and-death giving powers are also reflected in its shortages during the Middle Ages, when it was used to make longbows. Though causing death, it never seems to die. Every five hundred years, it regenerates entirely, the core rotting from within, the outside growing new shoots. Its significance can be considered alongside lichen, or the rhizomatic growth of vegetable matter. Life propagates itself, clones itself and continually regenerates internally. Which is the original plant? This question cannot be answered, for it is the same and it is not. No use seeking purity, only the natural facts of what enable all of us to live, and live well.

Christy and I part ways outside Fort William station a little later. We issue farewells with a hug, a rare gesture for us, more accustomed to verbal sparring. For much of the journey we've been silent, our minds making sense of the intense and vivid scenery. Now, our trajectories diverging, conversation has turned back to London, and what we'd each sought escape from. He decides to detour via Glasgow, seeing what the old city might offer him.

I collect my much-abused bike. The mechanic's face manages to express both horror and a smirk as I tell him what I've been doing with it these last two months. I pedal out of town, back among the wind and the rain.

A brief ferry hop runs south of town, carrying a smattering of passengers across Loch Linnhe. On the other side is Ardgour, a hamlet on the western edge of Ardnamurchan, a vast and remote peninsula, untroubled by anything more than the most tenuous of human settlements. Using my compass, I head south, follow-ing a deserted road, passing Linnhe and the Glencoe mountains to my left and, to my right, an increasingly dense and verdant series of forests. The path snakes hither and thither then slides across a glen, cutting through gentle treeless undulations, popu-lated by eagles and deer.

Eventually I reach Strontian, an ex-mining village where the element strontium was discovered and extracted, along with lead, until the early 20th century. The element was used to extract sugar from sugar beet, a new and cheap form of energy for workers, and later into cathode ray tubes, powering their TVs. Its latest use is now most fitting for this Jurassic landscape, giving an insight into our Palaeolithic ancestors' ways of life. Absorbed into our teeth and bones through our drinking water, decaying strontium isotopes can be used to locate the era and birthplace of nameless, ancient bones.

No sign of that mining industry now. The village is nestled by Loch Sunart, and surrounded by tall forests of pine and fir. A young man is walking by the road, eyes dreaming before the distant peaks. He talks of the "good community" here, though he's leaving for university in Edinburgh, as "many do". How can one make a life here? His school friends will "stay here and farm... Sheep and cattle, you might've seen some" (I've not), but for those without land or interest in using it, university beckons.

The village shop sells every conceivable object in a chamber not larger than the average bathroom. An old gent behind the counter admonishes me in schoolmasterly tones to never mistake Ardnamurchan for an island. "It is a peninsula, pen-insula!" A little ahead is the Strontian Hotel. As with many rural locales, the village hotel often doubles up as the locals' boozer. Inside, the bar is packed with friends and relations relieved to be out of the rain. I talk to Britt, a retired Norwegian lady who has lived here for decades.

"It reminds me of home", she says, smiling. Trondheim, its trees and loch-like fjords, are mimicked here on this unusually wooded outcrop of the Western Highlands. She tells me she's the only other cyclist in these parts too, and introduces me to other punters, peeping in and out with conversational snippets. It's a close-knit community, and a pleasure to be invited into for a couple of hours. But I've made little progress on the road, and with worse rain forecast, I reluctantly push on.

The forests become denser thereafter, humid and damp. Deer block the narrow trackway ahead, and I watch otters skitter in the grassy verges. I'm quickly drenched. I catch a breather in the Salen Hotel, where a group of English émigrés chuckle at my dripping outline with sympathy. Their consensus is *stay and drink*, a persuasive argument, but the rainclouds momentarily clear, revealing a moody alabaster horizon. After ten minutes or so of drying out my shirt under a bathroom hand-drier, I ride out.

A steepening range pulls me out of the bosky glens of Salen, zigzagging up through abyss-like plains. Distant peaks snag the gloaming skies, deer and high-flying predators swooping along this empty vista. This twilight belongs to me alone, its dark blues and salmon tones fusing with notes of gold and fuchsia.

It's now late, and the road comes to a dusky terminus at Kilchoan. I stop in the local hotel for a nightcap. It's filled with drunken middle-aged men, some Australian and descended from this remote part. As I peel off my layers and recover over cheap Scotch, locals parley over common kin on Islay.

"Vodka! Vodka, and…"

"Coke for him, lots of coke."

Another old farmer wanders in, talks to an old boy, then whips out a harmonica. He plays some folky ditty for the boozer. "Never trust an Australian", he ends his set with, obliquely.

For a second we all glance at each other, men among men, drunk on beer and whisky, talking loudly about nonsense, setting the world to rights. And there's a slither of silence, no more than a second, where the sheer wonder of being in this remote spot, at this remote time, feels like a privilege greater than any in history. *To be alive at this time, feeling this, thinking this.* A stool scrapes against the granite floor, emitting the sound of stewed gas. An immense uproar of laughter.

I awake among viridian-like bracken above a single-track road. In the distance is an isolated farmstead, with no sign of occupation. Pleased with the isolation of this part of Ardnamurchan, I head out with the goal of reaching the end of that track, and the most westerly edge of Britain, Ardnamurchan Point.

The road's bumpy but exhilarating, and a little later, I pause at the visitor centre that stands beside a lighthouse, and relish the unfamiliar luxury of a hot cup of coffee to start the day. A local young woman smiles as she describes her life here, and like with Strontian and Kilchoan, I recognise a distinctive accent, softly spoken and very light, almost crystalline in its clarity and grace. There is no concern with being understood. Even the few visitors around this morning speak in hushed tones, nervous of disrupting the peace.

Bill takes my ticket and mutters to himself, as I follow a mum and her two chatty goslings up the turret stairs of the lighthouse. He follows behind me, issuing odd pearls of wisdom, most just out of my earshot. Unused to being heard, Bill speaks of time's circularity with a whisper, and ends his discourse with a polite, inscrutable chuckle.

He was the lighthouse keeper here for fifteen years, working full-time until all lighthouses were automated in 1988. He'd worked as a lightkeeper elsewhere before that, relieved of having to deal with others, alone to calmly contemplate the raging surge. Keepers usually worked alone, and fortitude was a prerequisite. As the Northern Lighthouse Board advised, "From his study of the sea, he will respect its immense power… A lightkeeper will not make a fortune but he will be at peace with himself and the world."

We stand at the top of the tower, surveying the isles of Eigg, Muck and Rum. The clamour of bored children perforates his eardrums, and in curmudgeonly reaction, Bill knocks the light beacon. It glides around a central axis, reaching the other side of the gallery, where it whacks the unwitting mum on the head. We look at each other in confusion.

Women and children dispatched, Bill speaks of the life of the lightkeeper. "We were often busy." Daytime responsibilities ranged from maintaining the lights and their paraffin, to checking the functioning of the foghorn (ceasing its usage was a grave mistake, he insists). They would maintain the lighthouse and helped produce local weather reports. At night, forced to remain at their posts, they'd gaze alone into the distant dark of the tumultuous ocean. "It's all changed." What has? "It's not what it was. I miss the boys, the craic." He points up to a series of small cast-iron lion heads, black, adorning the upper recesses of the gallery walls. "They used to be bronze", his words casting a wider indictment against the regretted obsolescence of his way of life.

Candy-coloured townhouses wink at us from across the busy harbour. An hour after leaving Kilchoan, our small passenger ferry approaches Tobermory on the Isle of Mull, the epitome of toytown twee. After strolling round the harbour, I pop into the island's cheery museum. Following waves of migrations that began over nine thousand years ago, from Celts, Vikings, Scots, even washed-up Armada Spaniards, today the English have made Mull their island-home. An English volunteer tells me that "eighty percent of people here are incomers". They've rejuvenated the depopulating island, she feels, bringing life and business. "They speak Gaelic in schools now, but few of the older generation can. You won't hear it here, it's like a private language!" Another English couple speaks of Bunessan on the other side of Mull, using terms ordinarily reserved for the after-life. After watching the boats over a pint at Macgochans, sur-rounded by yachtsmen, I seek it out.

South, past dense thickets and the clumpy ruins of Aros Castle, overlooking the Sound of Mull. At another village called Salen, I stop for supplies. A Yorkshire woman pauses as she stacks shelves to summon a fair description. "The new people, they keep the place going. They give it new blood. Like it or not, this place depends on immigration. I think it's a good thing." Indeed! Common sense, less commonly spoken. One should be wary of feeling too sympathetic for those views I heard on Skye: there are always two sides to any story, more often double that. This encounter's a reminder to check oneself for any moralising about *good* or *bad* migration, which I'd found myself falling into the previous days.

Next door, Anna draws a surrealist map of the island in the post office. "My kids, they're sixteen and seventeen years old, they love it here. They go away, but they say they miss the grass, the trees. You've got to be content to live here, that's what I'd say. You've got to have good people around you."

Finding fulfilment in objects or career milestones won't mean much on Mull, and I suspect that's what keeps people here, an island-gem that outstays all transient attachments. I follow a narrow track that bends between lazy cattle fields and enchanted forests. Road signs are stickered with love-hearts. The trail meanders around Loch na Keal, a bay the colour of lapis lazuli, flanked by sandy machair grasses to my right, and the looming shadow of wooded Ben More to my left. Rock pippets flutter over lazing sheep, and campers bronze in the late-afternoon sun, the teeth of distant islets like Inch Kenneth and Tiree gleaming in the distance.

The track twists again, snaking inland through dense pine forests, some lopped down in vast chunks as if by a drunken lumberjack, others that expand into the distance with labyrinthine complexity. I'm inclined to abandon the bike and go explore that woodland. Anna said that between Salen and Pennyghael ahead there was "nothing". She was mistaken. There is a banquet here for any imagination gorged and bored of concrete, queues and man-made noise. But I keep my head, and pedal on through the wooded trackway, reaching a clearing at Loch Scridain, a flat marshy bay where teenagers cheer as they catch sight of a rare sea eagle.

The road forks. Left, snailing back to Salen, or right, on to Bunessan and Iona. Choosing the latter, I pass wizened cottages along Scridain's southern edge. Sight of a closed-up hotel, corresponding to Anna's map, indicates Pennyghael. I pause for a glug of water on the roadside, when a man's voice booms behind me.

"Are you hungry?"

Do bears and wild-campers... in the woods?

Greg's supervising a barbecue outside the Pennyghael community centre. There's a lively party this evening. He turns over local venison patties and halloumi skewers, and waves off payment, pointing me to Sandra, standing by the entrance selling raffle tickets.

How does one end up in a place like Pennyghael? For her and James, her partner, a job came up on Gumtree. "Wanted: reliable couple for remote location." They'd just returned from travelling and had nowhere secure to live. It turned out to be caretaking for a vast country estate. They didn't know Mull but took a punt, and now love the place.

I talk outside to Marie and Philip, a middle-aged couple from Matlock. Their three children are now in their twenties, struggling to make ends meet in London and the North. They worry for their future, and have worked and saved to help them "get on the property ladder". It's the only means they know to secure a stable future for them – supporting them to get professional qualifications hasn't been enough. Though both consider themselves working class, they reflect on life opportunities they enjoyed that their parents, or grandchildren, are unlikely to know. "I wonder if it's all over, if it's a golden age that's come to an end", says Philip.

A peculiarly English pessimism perhaps, or a fair summary of the bottlenecked ambivalence of the political moment? I move around, talking to more strangers, conversation swerving from surveillance and the corner-cutting causes of the last recession, to the ethics of taxation. Tell someone you're a philosopher, allow a minute for teasing incredulity, and watch as talk takes a speculative tangent. But it's worth noting that I'm among largely the English, even those of the community settled some years now. Unlike the Scottish, many have been enlisted into thinking that the welfare of FTSE 100 chief executives *is* the state of the nation. Again, I notice the difference with my earlier conversations on Skye, Eigg, Arbroath and Lochinver.

As the night draws to a close, James warns me off Bunessan and tips me to an even obscurer spot, a place of some magic. The hill climb will be brutal, the road broken and treacherous, and there's a good chance I'll get lost in the forests along the way. "But", he insists, "there's nothing like it". Equipped with Dutch courage, I get on my bike.

"There's no point calling anyone on it. They won't hear a thing except the rush of water." He's right. Positioning an antiquated telephone box by the foot of a waterfall is a somewhat daft idea, but Mull is characterised by the charmingly inexplicable.

After several miles of calamitous cycling through moonlit forests the previous night, I'd finally whizzed past it, as the steep climb gave into a plunging descent. Carsaig Bay was as beautiful as I'd been told to expect. I camped by a Victorian boathouse, and watched the bobbing outline of a seal in the cerulean waters. A couple drank wine by a bonfire on the rocky beach, and invited me over. "We could hear your brakes a mile off", laughs another Englishman called James.

It was unfamiliar company. After months observing the negative effects of private landownership, property speculation, privatisation, and growing inequality, I was now socialising with the wealthy. At the barbecue, one property speculator proclaimed London's economic opportunities, boasting of his new flat in London's "regenerated" (or socially cleansed) Stratford. Another could not see that inheriting titles and land by birthright was unfair to those without them. By the Carsaig campfire was James, a confident and expensively educated company-owner, a friendly and amiable man. He explained how to identify the sound of a male tawny owl, and recommended the Fowey yachting regatta. Among travellers there can be a peculiarly benign egalitarianism, no matter one's walk of life. "So different from London", Fran said, wistfully poking the flames.

Then dawn. Ablutions, muesli, packing-up, farewells, and one tough mother of a climb back up to the phone box. Then I remember the second part of James' instructions in Pennyghael. Spotting the faux-medieval battlement walls of Carsaig House down a tributary track, I decide to make a house call.

Certain unusual ideas impress themselves on the mind. Once lodged, they refuse to leave. Shoo them away all you like, but they'll linger, pluck on one's daydreams and intrude on more mundane thoughts. A world once passably fine becomes intolerably dull. Over a mug of tea, James tells me about one of these unusual ideas.

To demonstrate his point, he asks me and Mary, his mum visiting the couple for a few weeks, to help unfurl a tatty paper roll. It is the size and weight of a medieval tapestry, and narrates a similarly epic tale. The image of a shabby sailboat gradually unfolds.

"The RX131." He saw it in a clothes shop in his hometown, Darlington, and coaxed the poster from a cashier. "I had to know where this boat was. And whether it could be brought back to use." He contacted coastguards, naval historians and port clerks for any information on the whereabouts of this quasi-derelict craft. RX represented Rye, near Hastings, but that was all. "It could've been anywhere on the South Eastern coast." Undeterred, James took an old bike on a train down to Brighton, and began his search.

"It's just amazing the people you meet, and the help you get." Eventually, on the verge of abandoning this obsession, he found the boat at the edge of a remote shingle desert, Dungeness. He wanted to bring the boat back into use, and had the desire, but not the skills. This desire to do good had flung him in many more directions, from abandoning an anthropology degree on ethical grounds and becoming a paramedic, and then into his current occupation, as a caretaker for deserted castles and country estates.

Carsaig is the second such job, the previous being a garrison in Edinburgh. "The parties we had!" Both were blagged through Gumtree, and required skills like woodwork, building and boating learned later, aided by modernity's universal educators, YouTube and Google. James takes me round the estate. There was once a village here, and in one dilapidated dwelling he identifies the remains of a post office, its dusty shelves and the stump of a counter. Carsaig now seems to be a private theme park for the upper class London lawyers who own it and rarely visit. "They live in their world", James murmurs, laconically.

One afternoon, following a boozy deer shoot, James was asked to prepare one dead deer into a wall-trophy. Knowing nothing of these things and finding it all unsavoury, he knocked back a bottle of wine and consulted Google. In the wee small hours, in this very shed, illuminated by a flashlight and the glimmers of the moon through the exposed rafters, James finally succeeded in separating the creature's sinewy head from its neck with a rusty saw. The wind howled again, rattling the timber door. James leapt around. Suddenly the creature emitting the most horrific gurgling cry. He ran for it!

Somehow the headless deer's larynx had bellowed a final instruction, unfathomable to human ears. He laughs in disbelief as we come to the end of a tour, by a hedged lawn overlooking the bay. "It's hard work but, you know, we get to wake up whenever we want. And if we want a day off, we can just take it."

Back at the cottage, we eat toast and finish our teas. The morning's quickly disappearing, but let it pass. The conversation of strangers possesses a degree of intimacy and frankness impossible among friends.

Wait, what time was that bloody boat...?

Eighteen miles in forty-five minutes. On Mull's rutted roads, such speeds would be boisterous even by car, but manic desperation, jammy toast and the formidable stamina I've now acquired has me huffing to Fionnphort just in time for the last boat to Staffa.

It's worth it. The day-trippers' vessel eventually approaches Staffa, an extraordinary islet far from anywhere. It appears like a three-tiered geological cake, the remains of a volcanic eruption. Black basalt columns dominate its middle layer, resembling a set of organic pipes that play out into the ocean, a harmony of ocean-swell and sea-breeze, with a layer of punky green turf on top.

Disembarking, I join a queue struggling over the grey brick-like stumps that comprise Staffa's base layer, and sneak round into a deep cave in the heart of the islet. Here in Fingal's Cave, countless have come to breathe in the gentle music of the tides colliding against the rocks within, reimagined by Mendelssohn, whose *Hebrides Overture* is inspired by an encounter with this place. I sneak under a barrier and crawl along a dark wet ledge deeper into the cave, linking the outside world to the dreams of Fingal. On some rocks I trace Victorian petroglyphs, the initials of ghosts also present at this private concert, and pause awhile.

One more distant isle intrigues me. An hour later, and another ferry now approaches a small settlement, no more than a coincidence of lanes, with an umber abbey aloofly apart. Little over a hundred people dwell on Iona, but thousands of pilgrims and tourists visit this place.

I wander by the ruins of a nunnery, now a community garden. Everyone has a contented glow and some greet me. Another invites me to the abbey's evening service, sensing I'm a pilgrim of some kind. Iona's large abbey is guarded at its front by two tall Celtic crosses, both over a millennium old. Iona was one of the earliest outposts of Christian belief in England and Scotland. It was established by Columba nearly sixteen hundred years ago, a follower of St Patrick in Ireland, who inspired his followers to become "'peregrini", fearless transmitters of his peculiarly ascetic, humble and pastoral Celtic Christianity. They travelled by sea, establishing remote communities on Iona, the Orkneys, Scotland, Lindisfarne, Gaul and beyond.

Columba and his monks developed some of the first writing, metallurgy and jewellery-making in Britain, and used it to transmit their faith in a belief-system so far removed from this cold damp edge of the world. The Book of Kells was probably produced here before being later transported to Ireland. Such unique and beautiful artefacts reflect far more of Iona's natural majesty than dour Isaiah or the parable of the unforgiving servant. In its Celtic crosses, the snake is a recurrent motif, a symbol not of temptation but redemption. God is love, love is life. The deity present is not a symptom of ancient psychosis or the rule of power-hungry tyrants, but the very island itself.

The abbey is large but modestly adorned. Another board narrates the "Statutes of Iona", given at a meeting of Highland chiefs on Iona called by James VI of Scotland (and James I of England) in 1609. It would have devastating effects on Scots Gaelic culture. Chiefs were forced into agreeing to the reduction of their households, including a ban on "vagabonds, bards, jugglers, and such like", an end to the practice of sorning (idle men wandering from house to house, offering entertainment in exchange for food and lodging – my precursors), told to stop their common people drinking whisky and wine, and instructed that, on pain of not inheriting their estates, their sons must be educated in English in the Lowlands. The statutes were intended to culturally solidify two very different kingdoms, but established in one swoop a cultural and class division between chieftains and clans, rendering it possible for such chiefs to happily abandon or evict their subjects from their native lands two centuries later during the Clearances.

Burdened by the ambivalences of the historical record, I seek succour in Iona's one pub. A visiting geology student, Callum, explains to me his pencil-drawn diagrams produced whilst stalking Iona, mapping every square foot. Surrounded by pilgrims, local boatmen, sheep farmers and a lively American tattooist, the social mix of the Martyrs Bay is pleasurably strange. "Multiple economies", chuckles the barman.

But I want to make something of the earlier invitation. Back in the abbey, a liberal and ecumenical community provides the service. I've not been to church since the age of thirteen, and never conceal my atheism, but the welcome is warm and opening. We sing hymns from a book together. After the chorus has repeated a couple of times I pick up the tune. A bowl of shells is handed round, and the pastor encourages the congregation to fill those shells with the metaphorical love of those we miss. "Could you be more generous in expressing that love?"

As we sing together, listen together, reflect together, there's a new pleasure in being among many, as one. "What do you want to leave behind, and what will you take home?" asks the un-uniformed cleric. I leave the abbey with my little shell now full, and remember something Mary said that morning. She quoted William Blake. "Hold infinity in the palm of your hand." Then another peculiar sensation. I hear, or rather, feel, a kind of rumbling sub-bass drone emanating from the earth beneath, that almost has me falling to my feet. Whatever it is, Iona's extraordinary.

I awake on the island's northern edge, my tent surrounded by undulating dunes and goats. A sunny Sunday morning, and I'm blue about leaving. I head down to the jetty for the morning boat back to Mull.

Two local ferry-men call me over, and kindly give me a free lift. "You know I don't go out much these days", one says, happily, as they talk of playing pipes and the Iona ceilidh last night, where I'd headed after the service, children and adults dancing to the beat of the drum. Then a nightcap at the Martyrs, still feeling stirred by the place and its inner peace. It's a hard thing to articulate. They carefully rest my bike against the harbour-wall and wish me well.

Past Fionnphort, fierce headwinds buffet against me, and there's a plague of flying ants causing mischief. They land in my mouth like little flecks of sand, and stick to my jeans and shirt. Puh! I pedal past lovely Bunessan, following the single island road back to Pennyghael, and then onto Salen. The track cuts through a deep glen shadowed by morose Ben More, til at last the road cuts itself free, whooshing through woodland where dragonflies clap against my cheeks, and swallows zip above.

The magic's dispelled by Craignure, a small and dispirited

hamlet built around the ferry-terminal. Phone signal returns and, with that, the rest of the modern world. Across the water is Oban, a Victorian harbour-town and tourist spot. It's alarming though exciting to see supermarkets, takeaways and dual carriageways, after the last few days in the late 19th century.

Like most Scottish towns, Oban's growth seems to have been attentively supervised. There's a promenade of shops and pubs that face the sea with dignified, jovial yet aged airs. Two old boys quiz me on my bicycle. Neither of us can understand the other, but they point me to a local tavern where, they assure me (I think), quality beers may be consumed in a convivial atmosphere. I'm given a friendly if vigorous pelt on the shoulder as I leave.

Hail Auley's Bar, a boisterous boozer where the footie's interrupted by beer-soaked inanities, profundities and obscenities, all hollered in indecipherable brogue by a crew of heavily refreshed geezers propping up the bar. The mother of monsoons is forecast, with imminent effect. Locals warn me in strong terms against going further ("are ye focken mad?"), but the wet-eared fool I am, I have an itch to press on, hoping my many days riding through the Scottish summer have toughened me up. Nope. Not for what's about to hit.

I'm only halfway out of Oban by the time torrents of rain, lashing against me, blind me into tumbling into the grassy roadside verge. The streets are already flooding. I put on my fishermen's galoshes, devour an emergency packet of Wagon Wheels, and force my brow down and into the pisswind, towards the long, deserted road ahead.

The occasional car passes, spraying a six-foot arc of rainwater over me. Poke your tongue out and lo, a free refreshing glug of Highlands mineral water! In situations like this you've got to laugh, shout obscenities, sing and do whatever else's in your arsenal. There's another unforeseen problem however: there's nothing here. After Dunbeg, the only settlement I pass is Taynuilt. My direction's south, towards Glasgow. Inveraray is forty miles ahead. Desperate to find any kind of shelter to dry out in before I camp, I make it my destination.

I push on through the deluge, past Ben Cruachan, and through dense forests. The road is lonesome and the horizon heavily misted. It takes every lesson I've learned these last two months in resilience not to surrender. For around four hours of purgatorial pedalling I pass nothing but trees. I shiver, soaked to the bone. Then, with night falling, I trace the outline of a village. Closer, a tatty hotel sulking over a waterside promenade and an abandoned funfair. Signs suggest Inveraray.

"Deflated" is how one lad sums the place up. I hoover up chips from a high street takeaway, overjoyed that it exists, and is still open. It seems like a place people get lost in, then struggle to leave. He optimistically describes a bus service that runs to Glasgow, but doesn't seem to have used it in some time. He points me to the George Hotel, the better of its two pubs.

I dry out in the hotel bar, changing into my last clean-dirty shirt, letting my shoes and socks air discreetly on a radiator. Sensation is beginning to return to my legs. Over beer and whisky I recover my wits, and an offbeat French couple debate the virtues of Aleister Crowley with me. It dries outside, and I feel rejuvenated, even relaxed.

But fate has made prior arrangements, and will not be disappointed. As I leave to find a woodland spot to camp, the midnight mizzling becomes an even fiercer deluge than before. The rain falls in great silver lines. I try to ride out of town but I cannot see a thing. Traffic nearly shoves me off the road. Desperate, I pass a cemetery, but Inveraray's eerie enough. Ahead, I just about make out a patch of grassland. I erect the tent as rapidly as I can, but that grassland gives way to a layer of stone beneath. My clothes bag tumbles into a deep puddle during the melee, soaking any still-potentially-dry clothes. By the time I get the tent halfway-up, its interior has filled with an inch of ice-cold water.

Suddenly, my body feels very heavy and sluggish. Without

meaning to, I collapse out onto my sleeping mat, still dressed, and cannot summon the energy to get back up. The water gods are out for revenge for Christy's tent-tossing hubris. What's next is even worse...

It's four in the morning, and I am doing jumping jacks on the front drive of a country estate. The sun is beginning its course over Loch Fyne, and the dawn light reveals a tent coversheet blown off and wrapped around a tree, two dripping panniers, and a young man shivering in a wet t-shirt and pair of shorts, leaping for his life.

In my haste to find shelter, I'd pitched down on what turns out to be a gravelled front drive. Collapsed, exhausted, it isn't wind and rain that woke me with a violent start, but a horrible feeling in my chest and limbs, like they've been crudely severed from my body and replaced with inanimate bricks, somehow tethered to my head. The most basic and profound panic envelopes my mind.

Think of losing one's passport or bankcards, or puking up a night's self-abuse in a cistern, unsure the convulsions will ever cease. Now double that in intensity. My arms starting to weary, I chance upon a discovery in my washbag that may just keep me alive. A little after six, I head off, my entire body tingling hot, sprayed in Deep Heat muscle-cramp relief.

Sleep-deprived and water-boarded, the scapes of Loch Fyne and the Argyll Forest pass by like in some narcotic trance, shimmering, bejewelled in emeralds and opals. The misty skies appear about to collapse into moody Loch Long, and I ascend up the Arrochar Alps with inhuman ease.

Eventually the green peaks terminate at a summit with the wonderful name of Rest and Be Thankful, named by the soldiers building this mountain pass back in 1753. Today there's a burger van and a busy car-park, couples eating burgers and bacon baps in their four-by-fours, an unlikely community of the lethargic. Drifting through them, seeking the best vantage for a view, I overhear shots of whingeing, about cyclists taking up road-space, about taxes paying for benefits scroungers, about theft, about wanting more burgers and fries to eat. I wonder if we can still rest and be thankful without some treat in our mouths, or checking our emails, or cocooning ourselves in air-conditioned vehicles.

"O ye'll take the high road, and I'll take the low road", as the old song goes. I skirt around Loch Lomond along an old track that parallels a monstrous highway, the lacustrine expanse obscured by flanking trees. "Is this it?" asks the head of a group of Indian tourists to me, confused. I'm not given permission to pass through a golf course, but find a way round. At Balloch, a McDonald's drive-thru, the first in an eternity. Then there's a frenzied dual carriageway into Glasgow. To my right, the grace-ful outline of the Erskine Bridge, and to my left, countless white pebbledash council housing blocks of Renton that give way to the mass semi-detached sprawl of Dumbarton. After Ardnamur-chan, Iona and Mull, I feel the pain of Rip Van Winkle, returning from the magic mountains into an ugly and confusing world.

The pain doesn't last too long. The scene shifts again, Dumbarton giving way to a distinctively Victorian sandstone, sturdy and dignified, which appears in gallant parades from Anniesland and increases in frequency as I pedal into Glasgow's affluent West End. This city more than anywhere else comes with a terrible reputation attached: violent, dirty, in terminal decline. As I reach the city centre I find instead a proud, friendly and ele-gantly European city, arranged in sober grids and spangled with civic marvels.

There are the signs of empire here: Glasgow was once the British Empire's second major city after London, where ships were built and the profits of uneven international trade banked. Some of the proceeds were distributed among the people, demonstrated in its vast museums that have historically been free, like the People's Palace, or Kelvingrove Museum, or in its many public parks and libraries, and the large botanical gardens that I passed along the Great Western Avenue. The UK now enjoys a resurgence as an international trading centre of finance, yet there has been no comparable construction of things for the public good. London also has its free museums, libraries, and public housing, but these are increasingly obscured by the conceptual corporate money-boxes appearing across the horizon. With its sharp industrial decline in the latter half of the 20th century, Glasgow doesn't have these, and so still possesses a visual reminder of this earlier paternalistic culture. This lively and chequered city intrigues me. I resolve to rest here a while.

Sauchiehall Street, the main drag. I'm resting against a wall, devouring a McFlurry and watching the crowds. My mind's still sharpened with the early-morning cortisol, but the passing throngs and their fuzzy accents muddle into a kind of glacial serenity. A middle-aged woman with a bright mohican and tartan skirt slaps a bodhran and caterwauls outside a bookies, passers-by doing their best to ignore her.

My camera was killed off by the night's rain, but in Argos, Kimberley is happy to exchange it for another without interrogation. She dispels some of the myths of Glasgow and adds a few of her own. "Haggis supper, Scotch pie, the chippie... Irn Bru!" What else does the visitor need? But no one knows where they bru it, or how...

I need a bed, a bath, a washing machine, and a cup of tea. Back along the Great Western Avenue, opposite the bus stop he's been directing me to over the phone, I finally spot the outline of a man waving enthusiastically. It's Tommi, the warm-spirited, affable golfer I met in Dornoch. He left me his number and instructed me to get in touch when I reach Glasgow. Thinking of reuniting with this cheerful man has sustained me all day.

In the kitchen, Tommi and his wife Michelle feed me cheese sandwiches and tea, and I gradually re-inflate back into my old self. He tells me how he came to this city in 1992 as a young foot-baller from Finland. Michelle has worked until recently in the higher echelons of business management. Their conversation's insightful, from the meaning of honesty to the death of the public sector and NHS by rip-off contractors and the growing waste on managers and consultants. "There's just air in the figures", Michelle says, reflecting on the more intensive contact she's had with the health service since developing multiple sclerosis. She feels a public sense of purpose in ensuring both patients and the health service get the best deal.

Her mind glimmers sharply from one topic to another, though what's best is the affectionate repartee between the pair. "You know what the difference is", Tommi says, on the topic of Finnish and Scottish cultural quirks. "At the weekends, people in Finland go out to their homes in the countryside, they exercise, they enjoy the air. In Glasgow they just go to the shops." "And drink!" Michelle's quip makes some sense. Glasgow's sober centre can be alternatively read as a warren of musty boozers, and earlier the other Argos staff tripped over each other's tongues as they rolled out pub tips.

Still, it's a friendly place. Tommi feels so, and reflects on how it's improved in the last two decades. But football still bears a colourful if troubled presence over the city. As a football coach with young people now, he's observed the Old Firm rivalry between Celtic and Rangers as one of religion between Catholics and Protestants. This sectarianism starts from an early age. "Ban religion in schools", he concludes, reflecting on the "indoctrination" he often witnesses. Orange Lodges still march through Glasgow, an island away from the catastrophic mess of Northern Ireland. To the love of Christ we can credit the Glasgow smile, the burning of Edward Littleton and the castration of Abelard, as much as the beautiful Book of Kells, or Father Michael's call to stay with life, or the tranquil power of Walsingham or St Cedd's.

Brought up in another distant North European land, but one that has not committed itself to an English-American model of unrestrained market capitalism, Tommi cannot grasp the inequality and ill health that characterise life for many, in the fifth richest country in the world. Surrounded again by gregarious and generous people – like everywhere else on this island – I can't fathom it either. I mean, who exactly voted for this mess?

I'm standing at the foot of a tall, narrow tenement block on Otago Street, a stone's throw from the bustling boozers Tommi and I toured the previous night. It's sandstone yellow, nestled in Glasgow's student area, and still carries a bohemian air, as I remembered. I'm not here to visit a friend. In fact, I live here.

Why did my mum and dad leave London back in 1988 to start a new life here? If there was one part of the UK during the mid-1980s with a worse reputation for violent crime and urban decay than Brixton, it was Glasgow. Heard of the razor gangs, or the Glasgow smile, or the Glasgow Ice Cream Wars? Four years earlier, the Doyle family were burned alive in their home for selling drugs in the wrong part of the East End. Glasgow had become a deindustrialised wasteland, plagued with heroin and unemployment.

Yet it's sometimes forgotten how difficult life was for people without money in London (and still is). Regular IRA bomb attacks were background music where the same Thatcher regime suffocating Scotland had deposed the city's elected left-wing government and overseen the rapid decline and dilapidation of its built environment. Riots had been ignored, estates had fallen into ruin and the transport system was collapsing, as events like the Kings Cross fire indicated. Patrick Keiller's film *London* of 1994 captured the decay of the city. London was

a city under siege from a suburban government which uses homelessness, pollution, crime and the most expensive and run-down public transport system of any metropolitan city in Europe as weapons against Londoners' lingering desire for the freedoms of city life.

They left Brixton for a better life, and returned a few years later, not through Glasgow's fault, but themselves run-down by the social isolation of the place. Friends and family were either in the north of England or the south of London. There's more to a place than just its comforts or the availability of work, particularly when bringing up small children.

Daytime television mews in the distance, the muzak of sociability. Should I ring the bell? Michelle said I should, just to find out if it's changed. I think of her courage, and reach up. No sound. A business-like knock. About a minute later, Martin languorously opens the door, and looks me over.

Curious how, in the mind, places once called home as a child still feel so expansive and large. I used to lie on the floor and gaze up at the ceiling, imagining myself unbounded by gravity, climbing over the doorways, leaping down upstairs. The ceilings are still very high and with coving, the rooms large and capacious, a common feature of Glasgow tenements. In the kitchen, I recall the same cupboard units I sat in aged two, in a photo my mum still keeps. Out of the kitchen window, I see steep steps leading up to a neglected garden. My brother and I would race across the garden in toy cars, stopping nanoseconds before the edge of the flagstone steps, terrifying my mum. But there's no madeleine moment. Photos can help us confabulate, fabricate stories of our lives that seem probable, and come to be taken as true. I leave Otago Street feeling as strange as I had expected.

Later, I meet Dave outside Glasgow's Central Station. With shoulder-length, immaculately conditioned hair, Cuban heels and a pointed beard, it's always been easy to spot this gentle metal guitarist in a crowd. After couchsurfing with me in London a year ago, he's offered to return the favour.

Dave's also returned "home" to a city once known as a child before moving away. Aged eighteen and bored of dozy Devon, he chanced it up here. After graduating with a good degree in 2009, the job market collapsed, and what little work was available was either in shops or call centres. He took the latter, and has remained here some years since. Computers monitor your bladder and provide a script to read from. It's hard to work out if he's being paid to use his mind, or his voice. "You get used to it", he sighs, wearily.

We cross the Clyde and walk down to Govanhill in Glasgow's South Side. At Eglinton Toll the highway widens to an expanse of disused warehouses and wasteland, interrupted by a gig venue and, later, a small string of shops, Turkish caffs and grubby boozers, Roma families playing in Govanhill Park.

He invites me into his tenement flat overlooking the park, situated in a grand square not dissimilar in scale to London's West End. Despite being built as housing for the Victorian working class – and the area remains one of the poorest in Glasgow – these spacious tenements are not "machines to live in", like the high-rise monstrosities flung up inconsequentially by the city council a century later, but homes, still occupied and desired.

Dave's flat is small, and some kind of cunning by the landlord has divided what might've been two flats into three or four. Still, it's by no means as overcrowded as many of these tenements used to be. He's glad to have this flat, and a job, and his music, the elements of freedom.

Like Tommi, he insists that Glasgow's secrets are to be found in its boozers. We hop on a bus into the West End again, spending the night in one pub by the Kelvin, drinking with his mates. Conversation is political, and often fierily intellectual. Dave reflects on Scotland's unique situation, and reaffirms the necessity of political independence. "Yes, it would be difficult at first, but it would be anyway. At least *we'd* be able to make those difficult decisions."

And for once I surrender playing Devil's advocate, a common strategy I've used to get people to qualify, expand or reflect on their stated opinions. I agree with them. And yet it doesn't feel like my struggle, my *we*. There's an entirely different structure of feeling up here to London, or the North, or the Midlands and outer London sprawl. Even unlike Dundee or Edinburgh, there's a distinctly Glaswegian Scottish pride here. Rather than race any further, I decide to slow down and tune in.

I'm propping up the bar of the Castle Vaults by St George's Cross, a cheap and cheerful local with its own two quid house lager. Its rankness outstrips all pessimistic speculation. Drunk men and women sing along to the jukebox, love don't live here anymore, along with a spirited attempt by one baritone to follow the airborne melodies of 'Good Vibrations'. Glassy-eyed geezers gaze morosely into the distance. Outside, two blokes struggle to paw and pull each other over as they brawl over the honour of a lady's stolen handbag. A crowd sportingly cheers both on.

It's a fitting place to reflect on the conflicting layers of Glasgow's civic ambitions and self-deprecating, lively communities. Across Scotland people have disparaged Edinburgh as a "mini-England". Look beyond the resplendent visitor attractions, and rings of serious inequality can be found. It's a place encumbered by its own apparent history. It's interesting to compare it then to Glasgow, a city also encumbered by its imperial Victorian past, but in a way quite different to the smaller capital.

A majestic fountain outside the beautiful People's Palace bears the inscription "Let Glasgow flourish". Surrounded by the flea-stalls of the Barras market and nearby Celtic pubs, Irish tricolours curtaining the windows, and the faux-Ottoman Templeton carpet factory nearby, the People's Palace feels like a good place to start.

Few places in England will mention "the people"; it's a country still ruled by private property. The Palace was built as a gift to the workers of the poor East End back in 1898, constructed over Glasgow Green by the Clyde, alongside new tenements and public baths. Reading, learning and leisure were considered as important for the welfare of the people as access to clean water or adequate accommodation, an understanding of human nature more sophisticated than that of the planners and profiteers of the 20th and 21st centuries. This would be "a palace of pleasure and imagination around which the people may place their affections and which may give them a home on which their memory may rest".

I wander around it this morning, talking to other locals and not-so-locals, picking up clues. Stephen told me why he thought Glasgow's now-notorious council high-rises like the Red Road Estate failed. He spoke of endemic damp and inaccessible plumbing pipes cast in concrete. He remembered high-rise spatial isolation, no shops or public transport nearby, lifts and doors never maintained, the scourge of unemployment over the 70s and 80s and the plague of heroin, the vacant wasteland beneath them. But curiously, he linked their demise to a cultural shift in the city. "I think there's been a rise in the individual, a rise in people looking out for themselves. Before you had patriotism, the nation, community. People see themselves as separate now."

It's an unlikely utterance in Glasgow, where desire for independence is feverish. Stephen qualified the point. This isn't a "choice" or failure on their part. Instead, egoism is coded into this new world, built into the shapes of its malls and gated apartment blocks, in the parameters of its apps, the features of its leisure, and the keywords of tabloid terror-tattle. It may well be that the desire for independence across Scotland, with its sympathisers across the rest of Britain, is expressing an atavistic desire for community and belonging, an attempt to articulate a desire for collectivity, commons, where all have equal stake and responsibility. Scottishness has replaced class as a point of resistance to a London-centred rule of the rich. It's one outlet for imagining a different future. "Nothing's been done... The recession fucked up people's lives. There was the bailout, but no vote for it. No one's gone to prison for it either. For the young, the people not working or studying, there's nothing for them."

I drifted on, trying to make sense of Glasgow. Consider the ultra-bland global-brand hotels and obnoxious office blocks of Argyle Street, or the catalogue malls and cinemas of Buchanan Street. Weigh those up against the Necropolis, where fifty thousand Glaswegians have been crammed into a hill overlooking the centre. There were once deer here, til locals hunted them to extinction after a TV documentary revealed their existence. Or consider that at least three major uprisings began here in the last two centuries. The 1820 Glasgow Insurrection demanded the democratic vote; Red Clydeside of 1915–17, British Army guns turned against revolutionary dockers; and 1989, where the first Poll Tax riots began a year before England's. The British Chartist movement was formed here, as was the first Labour Party. On the eve of the catastrophic Great War, two Scotsmen, Keir Hardie and Arthur Henderson – Labour's first MP and cabinet minister respectively – demanded "Down with class rule... Up with the peaceful rule of the people!"

Then there was John Maclean, a local schoolteacher who opposed the colossal brutality of the First World War, and spoke passionately and persuasively for an independent Scottish republic, freed from social inequality. Maclean believed that collective belonging of a nationalist kind would aid the creation of a fairer and more equal society. He's still largely unknown even in Scotland, but Soviet Union stamps used to commemorate him. He was killed off by sicknesses accrued as a hunger-striker in prison for the "sedition" of opposing war, in 1923. His fate, and that of early 20th century Scottish republicanism, is instructive when compared to the rebel "martyrs" of Ireland, "MacDonagh and MacBride // And Connolly and Pearse", the terrible beauty of violent nationalism shrouded around them. Scotland with its myths of Ossian, Rob Roy and William Wallace has never produced the same kind of bloodletting zeal. Why is that? Perhaps, unlike the religiously and racially othered Catholic Irish, some Scots radicals were incorporated into the British establishment.

Scotland was never actively occupied like Ireland. Or perhaps it suggests a native irreverence for pursuing intellectual causes?

Ride past the vast Tennent's Brewery to Dennistoun, where Union Jacks and the red fist of the Ulster Volunteer Force flutter freely from telegraph poles among bleak 60s council estates. Some of the lairiest pubs will be found in the East End, where locals will ask your surname to gauge your affiliation. Two fellas were "very confused", Dave tells me later, when in an English accent he gave his Irish surname. It's a fitting epithet, when brought back to the football violence that can erupt here. Tommi felt relieved that Rangers were now in the lower leagues, relegated following bankruptcy, thus ending for now the Auld Firm matches. Others felt it was only a matter of time before they'd be back in the top flight. And many indeed would welcome it.

"People make Glasgow" is the name of the city's underused bike-hire scheme. There's an unlikely cohesiveness to it, perhaps in its very tension. "You won't see any signs of obvious wealth here", Tommi said. It dawns on me in the Castle Vaults what this citizenship is. It's in the social manner of Glaswegians: open, agreeable, generous, unpretentious, unlikely to suffer fools gladly, and full of a sharp, irreverent humour. These are the conditions of its citizenship. I've been to no other city like it. There is pride everywhere, embodied not in its individuals, but as a people.

One heavily refreshed man turns to me, at least a minute after our last, mostly monosyllabic interaction. "Och, pesh!"

Ipswich, Ickenham, Ilfracombe or... Irvine. Drifting round the Riverside Centre, a pedestrianised shopping precinct filled with poundshops, CCTV cameras and British Town Centre chain stores. Some beg, some drink, some peer idly into the jewellery display of a pawnshop. As I follow the crowds, mind comfortably relieved of its contents by the scenery, an amiable woman hands me a leaflet.

Before I can even scan it, a burly, beetroot-faced baldie bundles towards the trestle table, fingers pointing with one hand, the other clenched into a fist. "Youse focken terrorists! Yer scum!" For a moment, it looks like a young man scribbling something on the table might deck the enraged fella. An older man attempts to conciliate, but this firecracker's already spent, and he disappears back toward Irvine's tatty high street, cursing at the top of his lungs.

I didn't mean to stop in Irvine, a deindustrialised town in Ayrshire that I found myself in after getting lost. I left Dave's early that morning, out past Govanhill and stately Queens Park. Shops mirrored social composition, from semi-open Internet cafes and phone repair kiosks to angling and gun stores, European restaurants and small supermarkets, red-brick tenements becoming detached Tudorbethan semis.

Outside Shawlands arcade, a guy had given up his morning to collect money for a local hospice. Sixteen year olds solicited for Sky TV subscriptions, local laddies in sharp suits and pointy shoes. The grandmother of one recognised him and began to tell him off. I veered off the main road a little after Barrhead, a could-be-anywhere blandscape of semis and hypermarkets. Gunning south, I found a country lane that matched the compass. Cattle grazed behind hedgerows, these undulating fields and docile villages reminiscent of southern England. A customised welcome sign announced: "~~Welcome to~~ Fuck yer Ayrshire". Then wreaths by the road, photos of a young man smiling, and a vehicle parked in a layby where another man of similar age is weeping, and then Stewarton, its pubs and shops with no obvious trade, and back into a familiar scene of dual carriageways and retail parks, lost in Irvine. "They used to build cars here, Volvo, TVs, Ferguson", contributes one old fellow beside the trestle table, hopefully.

Time to move. People around Glasgow told me to see this one place before I crossed back over the border. "Scotland in miniature", Dave's friend Neil called it, showing his photos. Tommi gave me the number of Bill, Michelle's dad. "Go there, call him", his instruction.

On the other side of the Firth of Clyde, I stop for a malt in the wee village of Brodick, on the isle of Arran. Locals chitchat lazily in the evening sun. "The boss man's here, watch out", announces one punter as a BMW parks in a nearby by-lane. "Yeah, I'd better do some work", the barmaid replies.

Me too. I give Bill a call. A warm-hearted gentleman picks up, his patter rippled with chuckles. He gives me instructions to find his place. The road skirts the shore of Arran's eastern edge, then pierces through pickle-green denes, teal bays and sweeping occasions of bracken and thistle. Reaching Sannox, I spot the Commonwealth flag, half-raised, he says, to mark the funeral of a friend. There's a cheerful sign too, "Welcome one and all". Up the pathway is a palace fitted inside a deceptively conventional-looking house. Bill opens the door with a smile.

A stone owl of Minerva, a surgical skeleton, a stuffed polar bear, various maps of the world, a ping-pong table, mounted antlers, paintings and witty epithets, framed, a salacious sculpture of a female nude, life-sized, repurposed as a hat stand, and countless photos of this bearded fellow wining and dining family and friends, all dressed to the nines. "Just silly things I pick up", he chuckles with the wave of a hand. I later realise that the home is an internalisation of his mental world: gregarious, adventurous, exuberant, reflective, a life well-lived.

Bill has two female friends over. They're all retired and hail from the Glasgow area, and seem gently fulfilled. Sherry is passed round, and as I describe some of my observations of the last few days, they reflect on their own trajectories.

"Back when we were younger, there was no such thing as stress!"

"How do you mean?(!)"

"Well back then... if you wanted a job, you could get one. I wrote letters out and went round for interviews. My mother joined me. She wouldn't let me work in a place she didn't like the look of!"

"I think we had more common sense, as a generation", adds Fay. "We just got on with it. You had to get work, you didne have a choice."

The young and not-so-young haven't had a choice either, really, though their observation on mental health does strike a chord, and echoes something other pensioners have repeated. What of this profound sense of unhappiness and unease among the young and middle-aged? "More pressures", says Fay. Life seems more difficult for young people growing up now. They recall the docks closing, and conversation turns to the future of democracy. They agree that something must change to empower the public, but what? Sherry passes round again.

A little later, with the ladies gone and Bill and I both tired, he disappears then returns with a large black tome. "A study of agent influence in nested agent interactions." Despite a successful background in business, Bill has repeatedly attempted to master this abstruse book. It's his son's PhD thesis in robotics. Two facts in that last statement make me feel immensely warmed and positive about the future ahead.

Fierce rains batter against Arran. Though today more often a home to retired Glaswegians, Arran was once the jewel of the Kingdom of the Isles, an independent political entity of Viking settlements across the Hebrides, reaching down to the Isle of Man. The scenery – if you can make it out in this horizontal sleet – is gorgeous. One road circles the island, with Goat Fell's peak at its centre, snagging against yarny clouds. These undulations make the cycling tough, certainly, but delightful, and never without surprises.

A ferry carries a small band of huddled hikers and bikers over to Kintyre. Grant and Anthony are braving it on their bikes today, a father-and-son duo from the South Side of Glasgow. "We might go to Jura, but look at this weather, it's peshing it doon!" Too rightly. But we share the destination of Islay, and the company's a pleasure.

As I huff up Kintyre's plain rolling hills, trying to keep up with young Anthony, Grant talks about Scotland's future. "Give it twenty years. Independence, this thing's in the post." Scotland's destiny is now different to England's, he thinks, economically, politically, as it has been culturally. A long-devalued partner with different ideals is thinking of going it alone. They do the same as we reach Port Askaig, on Islay's northern shore. Rain's lashing horizontally again, goaded on by gales. "There's no way you'll get us out in that", Grant laughs.

Pedalling over the stark, lifeless scapes of Jura, one could easily surmise that a hydrogen bomb was dropped here several decades ago. All around me are the ruined shells of shielings, perhaps even a hamlet – only the low-bricked foundations of walls remain. The Paps of Jura hover in the distance, mammary-like, apparently, for old shepherds starved of female company. There are no sheep, or farms, or homes today. Feolin is simply a house and a welcome sign, and the road to Craighouse, the main island settlement, is unsurpassably bleak. The gales try to force me back, but I'm determined to reach the end of the road, wherever it stops, for a taste of my favourite dram.

Craighouse eventually appears, a small harbour village dominated by the Jura whisky distillery, itself quite small. The door is locked. Soaked and seeking refuge, I knock and knock, ready to collapse. After a minute or two, a woman opens the door. "Come in, what are ye havin?"

Rachel, or "Tartan drawers" as her friends call her, pours out a little bit of everything inside the cellar-like room, from peaty Prophecy to the finest reserves. She's surprised by my knowledge of Gaelic and Scottish history, but I credit only the conversation of people I've encountered. She draws out the old Celtic symbol of infinity, a curling triskelion, "the past, the present and the future, all coming into one". She explains how common landown-ership, the revival of Gaelic, and the welfare of the young and old are all conditions for a meaningful Scottish independence. She talks of her friends in Israel, her time working as a nurse in Sheffield, and how George Orwell travelled all to the way to this remote, magical island in the late 40s to write *Nineteen Eighty-Four*. Jura's not changed one iota.

Hours disappear in the warm, cosy exhibit room, drink-ing drams and discoursing on many topics. "I must've opened this door to you for a reason", she says. Serendipity. Pedalling through Islay in a late-afternoon deluge is also best enjoyed after several snifters. Like Mull and Skye, it is remarkably green, the road weaving through woodland and occasional ruins of cot-tages, adding to an aura of mystery. Whisky distilleries abound with the same frequency as supermarkets in English towns, each producing the briny, smoky malts Islay's loved for, like Caol Ila, Bunnahabhain, Laphroaig and Ardbeg. I'm too wet-through to camp though, having learned my lesson from Inver-bloody-aray, so after drying out in Bridgend, a small hamlet in the centre of the island – which, more than anything, resembles that same triskelion-shaped symbol of infinity – I pedal round to Port Char-lotte, where Grant had told me of a hostel.

Yes, indeed! There's a drying room, essential, as the rain has snuck into both bags, soaking all my clothes. Among the expen-sive waterproofs and lycra, I can't help laughing at my own high street tees and shirts, the kind of gear one might wear to a night-club or the shops. In the lively Lochindaal Hotel nearby, a fiddler and a guitarist run through Scots folk to a small crowd by the bar. Alistair's sat next to me, a travelling sound engineer and whis-ky-sniffer. Like most Scots, he takes great pleasure in regaling an Englishman about the need for independence and John Bull's many historic sins. As we sip our malts, happily dry and beguiled by this unlikely kingdom, he says, after a pause: "There's no civil war here, no one's shooting each other". He downs the dregs of his drink and sighs. "This is an important moment for us."

Three teenage girls shriek with laughter as one hooded lad finally catches up with the other and leaps on his back. Both collapse into an empty road, one atop the other, laughing their heads off. It's a random burst of passion in this dour town, Ayr, perched dozing over the Firth of Clyde. Chippies nestle against deserted boozers, whilst a shabby Art Deco Odeon squares off against the derelict red-brick tower of a Victorian station hotel. "Music in town tonight", an old fella says to me, catching my eye, weary face loosening, a smile creeping up his face.

The day has passed in a blur of rain-swept mountain climbs, short ferry hops and the occasional papier maché demon left by the road. I carried on with Grant and Anthony, who I found in the hostel after my nightcap. They told me of a locally popular route known as the Five Ferries. With no plans otherwise, I joined them in the ride around Kintyre, Bute and Wemyss Bay, enjoying the conversation and companionship as together we braved the incessant rain and winds.

When you're in a monsoon, it is tough to make out what's around you, but let it be known that the dour Victorian seaside resort of Rothesay that we eventually reached has a very good public loo. So much so that a coachload of French tourists arrived to inspect the period ceramic urinals as I widdled on.

Back on the mainland, we shared Tunnocks teacakes, grateful for a transient dry spell. It was early evening and we'd covered around fifty miles. Worse rain was forecast, and I was lacking steam to carry on, feeling fluish after the days in the cold and wet. On their advice I hopped the train. Cheating? Yes, but wouldn't you? An hour later, the train has coughed me out at Ayr. Following the noisy lads up the street, I pop into Tesco for supplies, then head back out to survey the scene.

A man in his early twenties sucks away on an electronic cigarette outside a Tesco, eyes gazing into the limit of some troubling conundrum. He's on the dole, he says, in tones akin to the description of a chronic illness. His conversation is by turns sharp, frustrated and brightly intelligent. He reels away arguments and facts with impatience and uncertainty, as if trying to lift and unroll a huge tape-reel of repressed internal dialogue, locked inside the archive of a life paused and in-between. He tells me about recently turning down work in a call centre in Kilmarnock, the only job he's seen going recently, of how Thatcher's policies devastated the area, and the overwhelming need for total independence. We part ways amicably.

This is the last time on the journey that I start conversation with an unknown member of the public who turns out to be a well-informed, optimistic political radical – a kind of encounter that's been frequent over the previous weeks. I don't know this yet, but I sense something of it, in the aspects of a more familiar pessimism jarring with his prevailing argument. The border's not far now.

Dusk begins to settle over the Ayr suburbs. The countryside south is flat and heavily farmed, typical of the Lowlands, a landscape put to work. There were once several coalmines throughout the area too, all closed, like those of Patna and, further south, Dalmellington. A stone by the road states "in memory of unemployed 1922", another with "22 23" nearby, marking the defeated miners' strike and plummeting wages that followed. A funereal quietness hangs over this part of the land, and isn't dispelled until Dalmellington's Eglinton Hotel, where hoots and laughter bubble out from the boozer.

The pub is small and cramped, locals hulked around a narrow bar. They goggle then smile as I make my way in. Karaoke pulsates in the backroom, and it soon becomes clear that everyone's been here some time, enjoying the craic. Billy, a towering figure in his fifties, struggles to think of good wild camping spots nearby, and quizzes me on my journey.

As I'm packing up, ready for a midnight venture into the wilds of the Galloway Forest, the landlady, Rae, pops out. "Fuck it", she says with a cheeky smile. "There's a bed there if you want it, free." I'm stunned, and cannot help smiling, and laughing, and thanking her excessively, and coming back in. People smile and laugh in tow, and after changing into some dry gear in my cosy room upstairs, I head back down to join the community gathered here.

Billy introduces me to Alan, who chides me for wearing an unironed shirt, then signs me up to the karaoke. Luckily for them, and myself, there's already a long list of locals waiting to make havoc of 60s pop classics. Billy's daughter Shona captures its essence. "We're like a big family, people care for each other, we know each other, we look out for each other." Rae talks of the history of Dalmellington, a small Ayrshire town whose fortunes have been pegged to the rise and fall of its industries and mines. They closed in the late 70s, but people remember them. Alan's dad warned, "I don't want you going down that mine". Rae remembers going down on a school trip. "The lift, it were terrifying, so dark." "I don't know how people managed to work like that. For years they did it", Billy chips in. "Aye, and they were kids, some of 'em."

Billy disappears for a moment, then returns with a huge black t-shirt, which he gives me. It bears an unusual logo, that of the Scottish fire service. "Oh go on then", he says, chuckling, though I'm unsure what I've requested. And with that, he shows me round the building next door, Dalmellington's fire station, where he's been a firemen for twenty-six years.

"I've got to be ready all the time, I'm always on call." Shona agrees. "People don't realise. We've had family birthdays, Christmas dinners interrupted cos of it." She gives him a pointed glare. "Even in the middle of the night, as kids." It's a very difficult job. "You've got to have a weird sense of humour", he says, smiling weakly. It reminds me of nurses with their often blunt, dark humour. "I've seen all sorts of things, difficult things."

Billy hands round fire jackets and hats to me, Shona and her friend Leonie. It's like an astronaut's costume, the weight unbelievable. It gets very hot and suffocating in such gear, and that's before extra layers like the gas mask, breathing tanks and gas costume are worn on top. It's a wonder how they can even walk. The fire engine is filled with all manner of hoses, shovels and cutting equipment, and the interior looks like something from Robocop, filled with computer screens. Car accidents, suicides and gas leaks, to cattle getting stuck in the mud, these courageous people deal with it all. It's such vital work, yet from what I discover, these firefighters are paid little, and are struggling to recruit new people. It requires a degree of physical and personal strength that is rare, and extraordinary.

We return to the Eglinton Hotel bar, where the party's still in full throes. Alan passes another pint of Caledonia Best down the bar, as Rae regales us with her own tale of the fire brigade rescuing her horse from a quagmire. "He said, 'We've got to call out the assessor', and I said, 'Nae yous focken won't, tha's my hoss!'" I feel like I'm drinking with old friends, but then again, every night's been like that up here. I'll miss Scotland immensely.

CHAPTER 8

Among Ghosts

"These sixteen year olds, they've been indoctrinated" – Ruth.

Two priests stand before a congregation carrying candles. One glumly recites the words of the ancient sage and anonymous author of Ecclesiastes. "Whatever is has already been, and what will be has been before, and God will call the past to account."

The audience, mostly old, some middle-aged, bow their heads in silent unison. Some are thinking of their grandparents who came to this little town a hundred years prior, Gretna, a munitions factory with a village constructed as an after-thought. In more recent years, town planners have thoughtfully appended a retail park beside a derelict camping site. Locals still fondly commemorate the explosive "devil's porridge" produced here. In this not-so old church hall, they sing along to eerie-cheery ditties of the day, "Pack Up Your Troubles", "It's A Long Way To Tipperary", with peculiar obliviousness to the slaughter of the Western Front, as if no one knew, or as if it never quite happened in the way suggested.

I'm handed an electric candle, and follow a long procession of townspeople out of the church and into the street, where each candle is switched alight. A piper plays, a gesture less of memory than forgetting. Downward glare.

Time is a divisive subject. Some feel they're running out of it, others find relief in its termination, and some seek to rewind it, distrusting its linearity. In Carsphairn, a village south of Dalmellington, retired Ruth retold stories of working women and secret

Covenanter gatherings in the fields, whilst dismissing the rights of the young to contribute to the future.

There's something comforting about ruins, from the abandoned Polmaddy mining village to the Iron Age wreckage of Stroanfreggan Craig, which Ruth directed me to with a pencil-drawn map. But as I wandered around these dead places, I felt no closer to a truth about these islands than I had in twee Moniaive or ugly Dumfries. Futures passing, past futuring the present. Flavoured cider, retail parks, low-level bigotry, fear operations, a supermarket of the soul: are these the signs of modern Britain? Resting in a boozer that afternoon in Dumfries, surrounded by men silently nursing their mental wounds, I heard the TV blather about "sacrifice" in those trenches for the centenary of that war. One fella emerged from his Trappist vows and summoned the cheery young barman to call up the bookies and place a bet on a horse.

Outside the out-of-town supermarket, I got talking to local businessman Baz by the bike-stand. Since Glasgow I have returned to locking my bike up, after a few weeks of chain-free bliss since Forres. He worried that the political and cultural forces ranged against any progressive transformation are too vast to contemplate. Most times, messages go in without realising, fermenting for a few days before being expressed by the person as if they'd come up with it themselves.

"Most people will just look at the headlines of the *Mail* or the *Sun*, but not at the detail."

"Or where it comes from, and who is saying it."

"Ideas and opinions will get raised in conversations in pubs, not through the TV or reading."

"How do you reach that, how do you influence it?"

Baz smiled in exasperation. "I don't know!"

It's not that people always believe what they read – far from it, in his view. Rather, they take the presented news as the basis from which they construct opinions, often causing contradiction and confusion, like that building nuclear bombs will prevent human extinction, or that welfare causes poverty, and so on. Inside the supermarket, two cashiers told me that the service sector and farming provide most work here, though in Annan a weary woman described the precarious contracts of her care home. Gradually, I'm re-acclimatising to a certain experience and mindset.

Then through Eastriggs and into Gretna, early 20th century model villages, low-levelled and ruddy-bricked, orderly avenues and tombola greens: "Central Avenue", "Empire Lane". And then friendly old dears who invited me here, this church hall in Gretna, and placed this candle into my hands. "A time for peace, and a time for war... a time for everything", utters the clergyman, unsure if beginning or ending the sermon. Nothing of Gretna a hundred years prior, or thence.

It's been two months since I suspended time, turned off the clocks and went on the road. Always open and exposed to new experiences, each day feels twice as long as it did before. But time's about to lose its linearity as its trajectories tussle, and past and future become subject to bitter words and confused terms.

After the sensory stimulation of the Scottish Highlands and Islands, the border-zones blur without distinction. Gretna's Outlet Village could sit comfortably in Dumfries or Carlisle, Glasgow or Newcastle. Costa Coffee, luxury kitchenware, American outfits, Chinese gadgets. Car-parks are already full, and large families are gathered, quietly surveying the aspirational juicers and toasters in sedate appreciation of their matching pastel tones.

After waking in a public park, I gather my things quickly and sneak out. Heavy lorries pound along the M6. I follow a quieter lane parallel, crossing back into England, a state that does not announce itself with any signage or fanfare. Crusader knights stand on plinths on the frontiers of Carlisle, gurning aggressively. The city itself is compact and friendly. By its old city gates, I banter with a couple from Gretna, and then later a local woman, picking up clues about the mild affluence of this ex-Roman frontier post. The cathedral is eccentrically misaligned, its roof painted blue with gilded stars. Brian holds the position of architect here, and points up at its features, and describes a career in late 20th century town planning with the same zeal as his love of architecture.

He's surprised that more people in England aren't furious at the problem of landownership. Aristocratic families own vast swathes of the country, like the Cavendishes in Carlisle, or the Grosvenors in London. Inequality's flaring to Victorian levels, he fears, despite this being a country legally committed to equal opportunities and universal human rights. Should the poorest ninety-nine percent bring a lawsuit against Her Majesty? "It's no longer my fight, but for the young", Brian replies.

Preoccupations with history lend themselves to daydreaming. England's often dreamt of its Lake District. "You must go there", say one and all, except Baz, who warned me of coach queues and recommending cycling the coastline around it. "I wandered lonely as a cloud", Wordsworth witters, chief of a cult that has seen almost every social housing estate or municipal block in the country named, sarcastically, after a feature of this part of Cumbria. Derwent, Grasmere, Windermere, Ambleside, Bowness, Penrith, Keswick or Eden. Dreams are not visions of the future but confusions of past events.

The road out of Carlisle is fast and dangerous. Local football scarves commemorate two recently slain cyclists. To my left, industrial-scale barns and cattle warehouses, and to my right, fields of sheep, neatly gridded by hedgerows, devised not by Grandpa Joe traditions but cadastral cartography. Twenty miles and too many hours in the rain later, I reach Cockermouth, a small and shabby town on the edge of the Lakes. The streets are deserted, though life is found inside its motley boozers, where hikers have found refuge from the deluge. In The Bush, two dispense Daoist advice upon this topic:

"Once you're wet, there's nowt you can do."

"Yeah, you might as well just get wet."

"No, you might as well go out, get wet, stay out for the day, then go in."

Indeed. Outside, a wild-looking and inebriated man introduces himself as Patrick. His eyes light up during discussion of William Blake. "I was supposed to meet you!" he insists, shaking my hand and freely abusing a nearby driver for the crime of car-ownership. "I'm from this town, I love it here, but Dan, there's too many wankers", he adds, puzzlement writ large across his visage as he struggles to recall the purpose of his proclamation. Another local man sends me along a quiet back-route through to Keswick. This proves to be wonderful, without traffic and winding through fields accompanied by darting swallows and leaping hares, and through Embleton, and then by hedges of juicy raspberries that thrive in grubby lay-bys.

Out in the open, there's few mysteries to Keswick, another 18th century market town, lanes compressed into the shape of an X, and congested with middle-aged couples and young families, minds tormented over which of a trillion pub-restaurants they should sup in. Tea rooms, extortionate bed-and-breakfasts, camping stores and a pencil museum: a stage-production of tourist quaint, sold out season after season. Less whimsical Wordsworth, more the droll inertia of Magnus Mills. Liquor's called for.

"We only have two locals who come in here", a barkeep tells me in the Oddfellows. "They work in bars too. Only late, after the people have left." The town is dead between October and March, and he struggles to keep his outdoor-activity centre open. He works here most nights of the week to save enough to survive the quiet season. He feels content. His house "might now be worth something", he adds.

Tired but a little underwhelmed, I ride out into the night, a new heart-shaped bicycle light picked up in Carlisle failing to light any further than the edges of the road. The road is narrow and cars overtake tightly at speed. Rain begins to deluge again, and I abandon attempting to follow the road at Lake Thirlmere. I clamber up a hillside on all fours, tent slung around my shoulders, to reach a forest overlooking the lake, where I pitch up. The swooshing of passing cars soon becomes one with the pin-drop percussion of the rain.

Mist hovers heavy over Thirlmere, thick and tufty, prophesying the sky's collapse. The air is damp and cool, and my tent has flooded again, soaking all my clothes and food. I watch a queue of cars and buses snail past my encampment in what turns out to be a disused lumberyard. Some basic bike repairs are called for, and bored backseat babies eye me with avid curiosity.

For what is there to see? "The loveliest spot that man hath ever found" is a glug and fug of fumy cars. I see the same coach parties disembarking at the village of Grasmere, that reappear at Rydal and then Ambleside, a mecca of moneyed dreck, all the world here to discover an image of rural England that never existed, globally exported. Windermere is similarly congested. A coach swings into Bowness, but I avoid it, defeated by heavy traffic, made ill by the damp. I escape into Kendal, a small old market town nestled in a valley, bustling with shops and commerce.

"Oh it's mad out there. It was a battle just to get from the town hall. Holiday-makers!" She jokes to me as I find refuge in her small café. "He's in a death metal band. Death as in you've got to be deaf to listen to it", her friend bubbles in the distance. This ride back into England has been testing. What exactly is this place, after gorgeous Scotland? Semi-detached as social condition and political preference. Crusader flags fluttering over locked gateways and paved driveways. Traverse any road in a built-up place for one mile, and survey the full spectrum of wealth inequality, zoned, proportioned, embodied, uttered and gestured. This state of Englishness is at times awkward, at times awful. And then milky tea, hot soup, mischievous humour and warm, polite hospitality, of a kind like nowhere else, that can drive you crazy and yet charm you out of your pants. Love is never easy.

I follow a rural road out of Kendal and by the hamlets of Natland and Sedgwick. The lanes are wide enough for a horse and trap, but little else. Cumbria behind us, Lancashire sets out a vivid and pretty scene, thriving farmsteads interrupted hither and thither by slithers of early 20th century housing, and then plucky Milnthorpe, another midget market town relaxed about its unremarkableness. After Carnforth, my road skirts around a magnificent yet treacherous bay that disappears into the horizon, and into a faded but still charming seaside town, Morecambe.

I follow the promenade around the coast, past a wealth of faded Victoriana, some left criminally derelict, like the grand Winter Gardens, other structures enjoying a second life housing chippies, caffs and Chinese takeaways. There is the stunning Art Deco Midland Hotel at the edge of the prom and plenty, architecturally, to marvel at. But there are very few pubs, amusement arcades, boarding houses or hotels, and little evidence that the town still attracts holiday-makers. A statue of Eric Morecambe here is bittersweet, a reminder of the town's modest, fun yet aspirational past, of a world preserved by Alan Bennett, self-reportedly conceived in a boarding house here or Filey. A little after I visit, a local man is arrested for vandalising the statue, sawing through most of Eric's leg. Perhaps an act of self-wounding, or pecuniary psychosis, it's another symbol of the town's struggles.

They invented lettered rock and the helter-skelter here, but the piers have been washed away, the funfair closed, and the outdoor pools where Miss World was staged now filled in. "Bradford-on-Sea" they called it, back in its prime, enticing textiles workers with a little brass for some fresh air and frolics on the beach. At the end of the prom stands a large barricaded-up boozer, a chrome carbuncle of a café, and beside it a warm-hearted, bronze-haired lady named Sonya.

She's a local historian but she won't let you call her that. Her extensive knowledge of her hometown is matched by a modesty to underplay it, and in a more socially progressive country or era, I wager she could've long surrendered her job as a dole lettings agent to develop and publish her research academically. Sonya heard about my trip online and contacted me. We spend the next few hours talking about the seaside and drifting around, Sonya passionate and well-informed about her home town. We stroll by Heysham, following the coast around a wild and haunted tract, Toby barking and scampering in the distance. Her descriptions of ghost stories and teenage parties by 8th century St Patrick's chapel and a nearby overgrown cemetery are interrupted with laughter and shouts to call the mischievous dog back. We stop for refreshment in a deserted boozer. Sonya describes her work.

"Totally skint" are the tenants she works with, usually dependent on benefits and "trapped" in a cycle of poverty, debt and unemployment. I ask her about foodbanks, but she rebuffs the question with a pointed observation. "What good are foodbanks when people can't afford to pay their gas or electricity to heat the food?" She describes the situation of one tenant and the cuts to her housing benefit as a result of having a spare bedroom. She had begun falling into rent arrears, and was making desperate decisions about how to make ends meet. "It's a war against the poor", I tentatively conclude. "Did you not know?" she replies, anger and sadness in her voice.

But there's still spirit here, and plenty of things to discover. Sonya shows me a brick found on the beach, a remainder from an old brickworks. The stone reflects the town's spirit, adrift, a little lost, but still proud, lovingly kept and retained in people's memories, even when such love has been sorely tested. All across the island are stories like these, and wise, courageous, inspiring people who insist that these stories, these ways of life, are not so easily forgotten. "Electronical and mechanical wonders come and go but Punch and Judy last for ever", wrote Kenneth Lindley in 1973. Possibly, perhaps. Possibility's something.

Things appear different from a distance. I've friends and family who've been to China, Russia, Brazil and Japan, but none to the Isle of Man. Indeed no one I've yet met along the Lancashire coastline has ever even thought of going. The ferry journey is long and somewhat prohibitively expensive. At the other end is Douglas, a surprisingly large seaside town with a fetchingly grandiose promenade. It is a rendezvous of Rothesay and St Tropez, grand and ornamentally featured, its Victorian townhouses and Gaiety Theatre facing a sweeping seafront, adorned with lawns, benches and shelters. There are no derelict people's palaces, no chippies, penny amusements or Punch and Judy.

Nor would one expect it. The Isle of Man, known simply as Mann, is a self-governing state that is also a British Crown Dependency. It is not a member of the UK, and never knew Roman invasion. It stands equidistant from England, Scotland and Ireland, and establishes a unique space indebted instead to the Celts and Vikings. It has its own currency, the Manx pound, its own legislature, the Tynwald, and its own sitting parliament, the House of Keys, said to be the oldest in the world. Its political independence is a model for other British regions were they ever to consider it, but Mann is obscure, wilfully so. It even has its own tongue, Manx Gaelic, which has now mostly died out, and an extraordinary flag, the triskelion, three armoured legs against red, fluttering all along Douglas's promenade, terminating at its northern edge by the Hollywood-style lettering of "electric railway".

Trams are still pulled by horse, and the island has no speed limits or MOTs. It would seem that in this place, 1928 has yet to expire. Lindsey attempts an explanation. He migrated here from the suburbs of north London, and planned to remain only a year. That was some decades ago. "A lot of women come here. They say it's safe, no crime, no hassle in the street." How does it manage economically? It is effectively a "tax haven", whatever its government may protest. There is no capital gains tax, corporation tax, stamp duty or inheritance tax. The top rate of income tax is twenty percent and is capped at £120k. Offshore financial services, or call it what it is, organised tax evasion, contributes hugely to the island's prosperity, to the direct detriment of its island neighbours. Good news for the wealthy, and Lindsey speaks with cheery complacency.

Behind the promenade, I wander around a small town with familiar high street chains, a reassertion of English banality. Jeff wears an Isle of Man baseball cap, and years mowing lawns have eradicated his hearing. His accent is distinctly Manx, a blend of mild Scouse with a dull Lancs plod. Like many small islanders, his sense of spatial scale is bewilderingly magnified.

"No, I don't like Peel. I mean, I went to school there. I could've gone to Ramsey, but it was easier to get to. But I don't go there now."

"What about Castletown?"

"No, I'm a Douglas man!"

They are little over ten miles away, but Jeff resists the ordeal of leaving Mann's modest capital. I press on, traversing the small isle from east to west. The roads are safe, often flanked by striped crash barriers used in TT motorcycle racing, and the terrain's gentle and flat. I pass St John's, where the soils of Mann's seventeen parishes are brought for the annual hearing of the Tynwald's new laws, announced in English and Manx. A little further, the island slides into the Irish Sea. I call in at Peel.

There's a small town built into a sloping hill, much of a centuries-old fishing village still evident. One business sells kippers by postal order. I wind through its narrow sloping lanes, following the harbour round to a small jetty, where bikers and locals eat fish suppers and gaze at the haloed sunset sea. A Viking longboat has just docked, a team of young volunteers laugh and shout to each other as they struggle to tether it still. "This is where the life is", a local man, John, tells me, as he struggles ineffectually with a rod. "It's called fishing, not catching!"

His eyes dart around, his mind's fidgeting tamed once more by the sea. "They call it an island, but really it's a world." Few leave, bound together by kinship and a high quality of life. There are no signs of poverty or ostentatious wealth, and work is easy to acquire. But "there's a lot of racism here, some people would call it ignorance, I don't know". John and his wife went to a local church service recently "to get a sense of the community, but what is the community? It's a bunch of elderly people... calling themselves the community!" He looks at me again. "But... look around. People looking out for each other, helping each other out."

Inside the Creek Inn later, locals gather for a session of pub-singing, violin-fiddling and accordion-heaving. We're shouting along to the 'Irish Rover' and 'The Leaving of Liverpool' as beer spills out of rhythmically-oscillating glasses and onto a threadbare carpet. I'm drunkenly dancing with Debbie. "It's always like this in here, people playing music, just being open. I love it." Mann's secret is rather special.

I awake the next morning camped atop Peel Hill, overlooking the harbour and the ruins of an old castle. The ocean swell is invigorating, the breeze briny and cool. But the luggage rack's snapped, and pedals rattle fiercely. A local hardware store claims to repair bikes. Hopeful, I leave it with them and drift around Peel, wandering around the House of Manannan museum. A thespish figure booms out the story of Mann through a series of TV monitors. "Why else do we tell stories except to hand down the history of our time on this earth?"

By early afternoon, the bike's ready to collect. Its bearings "would've gone in days", and the mechanics are amused it's made it this far. There's great pleasure in confounding bike mechanics. The mood is equally upbeat at the Manx Agricultural Show, a little outside Peel. There are dozens of white marquees, some advertising farming insurance, others timber, livestock feed or local crafts. Long rows of tractors sparkle, reflecting admiring faces. Fancy-breed dogs peacock around a small field, whilst in another sheepdogs scarper round as a man issues gleefully mordant commentary over a tannoy. Burgers and onions sizzle, and children dart about, shrieking and laughing.

"I don't like honey with too much heather, it tastes... insipid", a bee-keeper tells me, taking me through the tastes of local produce, before proudly offering his own. He insists on distinguishing between "bee-keepers" (i.e. professional, authentic) and "keepers of bees" (dilettantes, hipsters fearful of stings). Others tell me of the best flowers and fruit trees that thrive along the rocky coastline. There's a tent full of memorabilia from the young farmers' club. People spot relatives inside photos decades-old, and the young seem not unhappily resigned to take over father's fields. Nearby, a lady from the National Farmers Union explains problems of "succession", and that for all the talk of an idyllic community here, farming remains a subsistence occupation. Being more socially and geographically isolated than their peers on the neighbouring islands, young people are still being pressed into farming, but the numbers are diminishing.

Back in Douglas, it's mid-evening and I'm sitting in the Prospect, situated in Mann's small financial district. Sat around me are workers my age, liberated from farming, complaining about their jobs. One's just thrown in the towel. A stream of blue words pass the table about a manager. The remainder feel trapped, by both the need to maintain an income and a lack of motivation to risk something different. Inertia's roots are deeper, historical, political and economic. "What a cunt", says a young man, but it's hard to ascertain who his remarks are addressed to, the girl leaving, the boss lurking or himself remaining.

But time's almost up, and I race back for the night-ferry to the UK. On some Douglas street I lose my heart, or rather, my new heart-shaped bicycle light tumbles off and clatters into a gutter. Fortune has a preference for equilibrium.

It's now midnight in Heysham. I ride along the coastline, seeking out a beach to camp on, but I spy a dark figure dashing in and out of the shore, movement disquieting, weird. Freaked by this ghoul, I pedal towards a caravan park snuggled behind a nuclear power station. The pylons buzz loudly, sounding like rain. I scale a small fence into a disused field and pitch up behind the cover of overgrown weeds. Boy racers zip about nearby. England never brings you down gently.

Lancashire lacks the charms of its neighbouring counties, but the welcome is warm. I rove about Lancaster, an imposing county town on the River Lune, marked by its old priory and castle, extensive university and a Victorian shopping centre, evidence of historic prosperity. Locals volunteer anecdotes of monks, beer and bunkum. The centre's bustling, and amidst the predictable brands and ubiquitous mall, a large crowd of protesters are demonstrating about genocide in distant Palestine. "Sometimes it's important to show that people in the world care", Valerie says.

Lancashire's also marked by its contrasts, from the droll early 20th century suburbia of Heysham to the professorial villas and Doric columns around Lancaster University, and out over the pretty plateaux south, among fresh wheat, grazing cattle and the breeze hit of manure. I queue up with a group of bikers and drunken lads for the ferry-hop from Knott End to Fleetwood.

At the other end, an athletic-looking cyclist rolls up a cigarette and seeks my opinion on scaling hills. Swifty's heading the same way, so we share the coastal track, deserted golden beaches flanking our right, and over-preened lawns, lidos and tea stalls lining our left. We approach Blackpool, the first of its three piers appearing ahead, and its surprisingly tall tower consuming most of the horizon. "Blackpool is the armpit of the universe", he warns, and parts course, hastily.

Alone I ride in, gingerly. What looks like a concrete fortress turns out to be the Castle Hotel. Then ruddy 20th century terraces, tastefully adorned. And thereafter, garish lights and discount chips, a cutthroat competition between dozens of small traders. Gangs of wasted hens and stags roam up and down the promenade, giggling, arguing and vomiting from one heavy-security karaoke joint to another. Hail Blackpool!

One person directs me to Shenanigans on "the strip", the closest Blackpool gets to Las Vegas, a green Irish boozer packed with pre-wedding partyers. "I've been here twelve years, and I've seen the place go down. I don't like it", says one Scottish woman in a chippie. The story's repeated. Groups of police stand attentive on street corners. The town centre is itself dated, its sprawl poorly managed. The streets are cluttered with pubs, clubs, chippies and countless poundshops. Nowhere seems to be making any money. "Not what it was", says the girl at Parma's ice cream kiosk.

I talk to a driver in a taxi queue. He's been doing this for some time, and worries that the town has changed for the worse. Not for the casinos, which, despite an initial outcry, have brought little footfall or fallout, but for a decline in families staying. "On Saturdays I might be busy, but it's Monday, Tuesday. I don't make much, but it's enough to live", he adds, an expression of stress now replaced with one of stoic resilience. The town is now dependent on stag and hen parties. "Without them, this town would be shut down." He's sceptical about its longevity.

But this afternoon Blackpool's in bloom. The streets and strip are heaving with families out for fun. I drift down the booming promenade, passing one gypsy palmist after another, licking my ice cream and enjoying the bustle. The social composition is multicultural, everyone out for the hubbub. There's no helter-skelter or Punch and Judy, but in every other respect Blackpool continues the seaside experience: noisily demotic, unapologetically hedonistic, cheerful and cheap. All this is built to pass and not to last, for who thinks of tomorrow? There's a three-hour queue for the Big One rollercoaster, the jewel in the crown of its Pleasure Beach. I ride out through shabby residential streets, happier with the place.

East on the road to Preston, a habitual scape of trade-supplier warehouses and semi-detacheds are interrupted with colourful handmade signs warning about fracking. A little ahead is a field full of tents. A wizened man with a bucket hat, white beard and golden tan beckons me over with a shout and a wave. "Haroo!" I pull over and approach. Silver Fox shakes my hand and welcomes me into their camp.

A campfire is being lit, and the local mothers who established the camp are serving food. "Any vegetarians?" they call out, momentarily silencing the serious discussions about the country's imminent ecological ruin. "Where are you staying? Come and stay with us", Silver Fox offers. I'm averse to refuse, but another stranger has offered me bed and booze up the road. They take time to explain to me the dangers of fracking, whilst Bob and others talk of scuffles with police, local government treachery, and the kind of quasi-justified paranoia one often encounters among seasoned activists.

Prospectors plan to test the ground beneath, reputedly riddled with gas reserves. Their previous endeavour caused earthquakes near Blackpool. The unpopularity of fracking is growing as people discover just how dangerous and expensive it is. Bob puts it succinctly. "The government says, 'Well it was bad in the US, but it'll be alright here', and we're like 'Hello!'" There's so much unrealised potential in wind and tidal energy, particularly for an island notorious for its bad weather. Yet the domination of energy companies over government policy is leading to a catastrophe, which, by the time it occurs, the parliamentary deck will have been reshuffled and no one will take responsibility. Undeterred, these militant protesters are leading an effective struggle fought through both illegal direct action and careful legal wrangling, challenging council decisions and planning permissions. Much depends on the success of their struggle, more than many could fathom and a knowing few concede.

A little later I reach Preston, an unpretentious town fugged in bus fumes. I pass rings of cramped Victorian terraces, Chinese takeaways, e-cigarette stores and bargain booze outlets, and then a modern university complex. I enter its centre, a large covered market and square populated by teenage goths. Its coach station is a lunar base of late 60s Brutalist extraction. In being listed it has been rendered useless, unable to have modern features fitted inside. Its interior is a cavernous void, a tatty barbershop and newsagent's beside empty rows of benches, a museum exhibition of social democratic futurism. Preston's in-betweenness architecturally, geographically and economically is a cipher of England more broadly.

I knock at the door of Carl and Andrea's, in the shadow of Preston North End stadium. A cat eyes me suspiciously from the window of their two-up-two-down. It's an apt location. Carl's a football strategist for the Welsh women's team, though does well to avoid talking shop. Andrea's hoping to be a vet, but has been unable to secure a loan through the rigmarole of the student loans company. Both hail from Northern Ireland, and their house is full of cats and dogs. After a few beers and shots of tequila, Andrea suggests a night out.

In the Black Horse we meet with Boydy, Frankie and later his girlfriend, and the drinks are flowing. Jokes and barbed banter pass thick and fast. In the Old Dog a young hippie insists that he never need buy a pint. I ask him to explain. He subdues his glottal reflex, and I subdue my judgement, and the outcome of a pint-downing contest has me covering the cost of his next beverage. Point proven, we continue, jiving among the neon lights, smoke machines and cheesy pop of the Attic. Beers become large spirits, someone discovers some maracas, and eventually we're crashing round the dancefloor, pulling shapes in arrhythmic manner. Over some minor impropriety later, one of our number is kicked out of the Loft, and we follow out, peeved, pished, but cheerfully exuberant. I'm unsure how we make it home.

Yes, I've become quite the lush, acquiring a new stamina for endurance drinking and cycling. There's method here. In pubs I can charge my phone and call home, find free heating in the dark evenings, and dispel my loneliness with the amiable and absurd banter of strangers. But it also relates to the need for pleasure, and observing how others obviate their boredom. Getting out of it, out of our faces, is a natural and universal feature of human societies. On this particular island, alcohol remains the traditional and most popular means of doing it.

Religious and socially progressive movements have often distrusted such pleasures, calling them escapism, against the supernatural dimension they prefer and term, peculiarly, "reality". Theirs is another kind of pleasure, perhaps. The necessity of pleasure marks this terrain, with its pubs, and breweries, and takeaways, and much else. For it's never just one drink, is it? Blunting one's ability to feel and see is essential to staying alive. For otherwise what is there, except white bread and margarine, corned beef, sugared tea and potatoes?

Touring through England on the way to Wigan Pier four-score decades before me, Orwell's description of the average unemployed family's diet was meant to appal his readers. Poverty and habits of class culture were effectively causing malnutrition. There was no use in berating their lack of wholesome choices. Even Orwell could sense the middle class snobbery of lecturing the working class on their feckless habits, something that now constitutes popular TV. People want something "tasty" like ice cream or chips, over brown bread, fruit juice and raw carrots. There's a psychological comfort in that, like in tobacco or beer, more desirable than mere appetite. They afford a momentary escape from the frustrations and uncertainties of living in an overcrowded and polluted social prison. "England is the most class-ridden country under the sun", Orwell wrote later in 1946, "a land of snobbery and privilege, ruled largely by the old and silly".

South of Preston, I pass the light-industrial terrain of Bamber Bridge, cycling along its long red-brick high street and by an ex-servicemen's club. Then through Leyland, once base of Britain's large publicly owned automobile industry. Trucks are made in their thousands now for Paccar, a huge American firm, the profits banked overseas. Three generations since Orwell and the Beveridge Report, seeking the end of squalor, ignorance, want, idleness and disease, the UK's returning to the inequality that characterised the 1930s. Describing that era in Salford, Walter Greenwood wrote of a "lost generation" denied "the natural hopes and desires of youth", like the opportunity to work, live and flourish. Theirs was an economy given over to immense cuts to social spending to appease an insatiable public debt. Conveniently, this just happened to rapidly redistribute wealth upward, plunging the population into a state of absolute poverty from which they only began recovering two decades later.

Wigan. The chimneys and workhouses of the Leeds and Liverpool Canal are now gone, replaced with poundshops, pizza takeaways and homeware barns. Wigan's always had a sense of humour about itself. A hundred years ago, you could take a look round the "Wigan Alps", though you'd be reticent climbing them, being huge piles of dirt from the coal industry. Factories and mills were built on the edges of towns on cheaper flatlands by canals, often plagued with drainage problems. Cheap workers' housing was built in masses by the mills, condemning families to damp and disease-ridden back-to-backs and courtyards. The word "slum" comes from the North, from places like Preston and Wigan, "slump" referring to wet mire until the 1820s, when it was appropriated to describe the houses built on top of it. "Wigan

Pier" was actually a wooden jetty used for unloading coal, and is also long gone, as is architecturally much of that old slum Wigan.

After a small suburban ring of narrow brown-bricked terraces, the town centre appears in a familiar garb of high street chains, pedestrianised zones, a small deserted mall and some dignified-looking Victorian council offices. There's no obvious dilapidation or decline, as with Barnsley or Rotherham. One local woman tells me of Wigan's history. Another man tells me how he met his wife, and shares tips on avoiding the town's street-fighting scene, which usually comes to life after last orders. The conversations are incongruously anodyne, suggesting time-zones out of sync, or rather, a lack of historical assessment of the present. East, through the suburbs of Hindley, Atherton and Tyldesley. To my left and right, a world pinched and pursed: red-brick terraces, bargain booze, chain pub carvery, a pile of debt letters on the inside of a "closing down" shop, a café here, a TV-repair shop there.

High-rises loom ahead, cast in primitive concrete. I join a dual carriageway, and weave alongside queues of coaches and cars filled with football fans, jokes and chatter audible. It's Manchester and Salford ahead, two cities that yin each other's yang. The textile factory chimneys have been replaced with rolling billboards. In Manchester centre, I pause at The Printworks, its ex-industrial interior refurbished as a mecca to the service sector, with a cinema and countless aspirational chain eateries.

> Heavy physical work, the care of home and children, petty quarrels with neighbours, films, football, beer, and above all, gambling, filled up the horizon of their minds. To keep them in control was not difficult.

And yet not everyone would agree with Orwell's dismissive, pessimistic assessment. Writers in Salford have spawned a kitchen-sink appreciation of profound feeling and struggle in working class lives: Greenwood, Ewan MacColl, Shelagh Delaney, Tony

Warren and the writers of *Coronation Street*, Morrissey. Of lives given colour and depth by loving relationships, with girlfriends, boyfriends, spouses, children, mates, pets, extended family. That all this is real, and deep, and satisfies a life otherwise dependent on drudgework, to which little thought is given, for *what else can I do?* And so the interest in media stories about outrages against children, celebrity trysts, and the common disdain for the emotional coldness that characterises perceptions of the middle class, their boarding schools, nannies and lack of affect. Here is a register of love that is not transcendental but immanent, *there*, *here*, somewhere. Few believe in love more than the English working class.

But in all this talk of history and wounds of the heart, perhaps I'm walking among ghosts again.

What is a ghost but the presence of the dead among the living? Flashing momentarily in the fissures of time and space, compelled to repeat itself, compelled to haunt until the present can release it from unresolved wounds. Time rarely passes linearly, but layers over days, upbringing indicating is and ought. Toasted white bread and margarine, fried chicken, energy drinks and chips. Discount supermarket booze, that Billericay widescreen TV with every show one might conceive of. The need to get out of one's face again, out of one's own vision.

Back in time again, a jungle of tiny houses in a dirty old town, where women are born three thousand years old, but, despite all this, there is a light that never goes out. And Lowry, dreaming, sees these ghostly figures: "I was sorry for them, and at the same time realising there was no need to be sorry for them because they were quite in a world of their own".

What? "Sorry mate, I was in a world of my own", says a young man outside Tesco in Piccadilly Gardens, later. He looks down into his hands, searching for the answer to a question he's yet to ask.

I stay the night with Jacqui, an inspiring cyclist and graphic designer who kindly offered a place for the night after hearing of my trip online. Next morning, we board a tram back towards the dirty old town. "Innovation, leadership and partnership", announces the council's candy-coloured cladding over derelict buildings. But what's most stunning about Salford Quays is just how effectively history's been wiped away. These new trams are speedy and spacious, and glide neatly into a starchitect's utopia: waterside luxury apartments and corporate and media offices, castle-like in height and scale, encased in reflective glass, an Archimedean strategy to deflect public scrutiny. There is a huge mall named ironically after Lowry, with a gallery attached, and then all around us, vast exposed spaces, bereft of people, paying lip-service to the notion of public space. MediaCityUK already appears strangely aged, its post-millennial optimism sapped and patina soiled. The "regeneration" looks in need of another transformation.

The still-extant old terraces of Salford, like Coronation Street, are just out of sight. I'll travel there later to pay homage to the Salford Lads Club, shuttered, and be pelted with crab-apples by three local lads, who mistake me for a postman. Their faces are dirty, and two seem to have learning difficulties. The streets around us are piled with discarded furniture, kids jumping around on fetid mattresses. I'll laugh at the time, unaware that I may well be among ghosts, time coiling inwards. The Smiths pilgrimage site, favourite group of the incumbent old Etonian prime minister. Irony's bitter pleasure.

Wandering with Jacqui, I find no sign of Britain's once third-busiest port. The cranes, warehouses and chimneys have all been demolished now. Old Trafford looms over the water, a symbol of Manchester's in-betweenness, City and United once sparked sectarian rages like Rangers and Celtic in another ex-imperial port. Now both indicate the moneyed corruption of the beautiful game, where celebrity players receive six-figure wages, clubs float on the stock market, and teams advertise all manner of consumables, from junk food to sweatshop trainers. But it's a city of contrasts: there is also FC United of Manchester, a cooperative football club democratically owned by its fans. The city that established industrial capitalism also established the cooperative movement – well, admittedly in nearby Rochdale, in 1844, but this proud city can overlook that.

Manchester has been far less systematic in its self-erasure and recomposition than Salford. Surveying the scene around Albert Square, one can trace different concepts and chronologies built and zoned into the city. Look up first at the neo-gothic town hall, its statuettes of kings and queens, then the Art Deco extension adjacent. Chin higher, consider the classical pretensions of the Central Library, worthy of ancient Rome, then beyond, the Midland Hotel, red-brick and brassy, catering for the new money of an upwardly-mobile merchant class. Lastly there's Bridgewater Hall with its wavy glass façade, cipher of the phoney transparency of the Blair age, relaxed about the facts so long as the figures looked good.

Surveying the horizon, this is no cosy cheek-by-jowl. Timezones grate, out of sync, each with a competing narrative of societal progress. If there's one thing that this ambitious city could be identified by, based on these features alone, it is the inglorious pursuit of money. Something of these merchants' Protestantism remains in its sincere insistence on the morality of work, that private property is the condition of social equality and freedom before God. This may indicate why today the Free Trade Hall is simultaneously a mediocre corporate hotel, the site of the Peterloo massacre of 1819 where protesters were killed for demanding parliamentary reform, and the apparent birthplace of all good music post-1976, if Manchester's post-punk chroniclers will be believed.

City made on textiles, built to the glory of profitable manufacture and the innovations of machines over men. Here, and nowhere else, Marx and Engels thought that the workers' revolution would spark alight. They'd meet in old Chetham's library, an eccentric medieval structure on the edge of the centre. It's the oldest surviving public library in the world, a worthy monument rivalled only by Salford, home of the first "unconditionally free" public library in the world, and where a working class library is now based. Jacqui and I leaf through WW1 poetry ("quite lost but sure of direction from stars" – Ernest Leech, 1917), sitting among their ghosts, Engels' peace, a momentary reprieve from the burden of running the family factory.

We loaf round Piccadilly Gardens and the Arndale, attempting to make sense of the high-rise, low-vision architecture. Jacqui leads me down the most insalubrious of back-alleys, Soap Street, its name typical of Manchester's gallows humour, and into a hidden canteen. "With Manchester, the grubbier it is, the better the food." Among students, street cleaners and civil servants, we scoff veggie curry and talk.

I ask Jacqui about time. "The gift of time", she calls it, but her beliefs jar against her way of life. She talks of her job for a telecommunications firm, difficult but enjoyable, or at least, it used to be. Routine's semblance is convenience, and nowt's easier than the path of least resistance. Orderly, organised and successful involves a lot of work. Facing her thirties, that path is less compelling, if it means missing out on more meaningful experiences. Community gardening, living on a boat, her speech takes colour when she describes the new sensations just beyond the threshold. Just not yet. It begins with the courage of a leap, the audacity of an act of unknown consequence.

The next morning I leave Jacqui and head back into the city, attempting in vain to make sense of it all. The garish hypermarket mush of Hulme "High Street", the unassuming terraces and cul-de-sacs of Moss Side, or leafy suburban Stretford, or Fallowfield and Northenden, 1920s scapes, students clustered around Rusholme, the "curry mile", the Holy Name church, then the luxury apartment block that now bears the name of the Haçienda, a once-legendary nightclub. Myths of Manc. "What a fuck up we made of it", recalls New Order bassist Peter Hook, unwittingly characterising Factory Records' legacy. The ecstasy and cocaine at an end, Factory closes, the band signs to London Records, signalling the re-demise of the city into bland corporate crapola, the capital's understudy. The danger of a life given to pleasure is its naivety about other people's motivations.

Manchester eludes an easy reckoning. Is it in the Foresters in Prestwich, among middle-aged men laid off from life, stewing in pints of mild and fried potatoes? M.E.S. locus... "No children, no exceptions" on the frosted door, a place to escape the wrath of the missus. A drinking society for the married and the recovering married. "He's getting a bit of stick in the White Horse so he's gotta come down here", the barmaid says without looking up, struggling on a TV-guide crossword, confusing me for someone else, perhaps.

None the wiser, I return down the Bury New Road, past used-car forecourts and vast Indian restaurants, towards the self-conscious bars in the hip-decayed Northern Quarter. A mysterious revolutionary outfit has summoned me as writer-in-residence. I'm unsure what this involves, so find a boozer and proceed to drink several rounds of strong beer and black coffee, and concoct an impressionistic polemic. Two hours later, I find my two contacts outside a popular café, and they lead me to The Castle. It's a rambunctious boozer, and pints pass down the long table with my name attached as I read new work to the Manchester Left Writers, a group of sultry young revolutionaries committed to conspiracies.

"Houses are for living in!" "Irony must cease!"

Self-taught and from working class backgrounds, David and Steve talk of finding themselves in a muddled class of precarious workers, subsisting on a meagre income of teaching and other things, but possessing the cultural markers and intellectual credentials previously associated with the middle class. They're unsure what that makes them, or what to make of class itself, and they reflect bitterly on the fissuring of class consciousness in their own parents' generation into fragmented concerns about migration. A specifically English phenomenon. When so much public debate eschews and at times even despises intellectual content, radical groups retreat into their own echo chambers. But together we drink heartily, look back in anger and set the world to rights. Perhaps it's apt here, in a city that has often mistaken itself for The North. Like Marx and Engels, the early Chartists, or the ballsy swagger of early Oasis, Manchester carries itself like no other city.

Now there's one issue with cycling drunk at night: blindness. Not improbably, I fly over the handlebars near Fallowfield after hitting a kerb. Jeans and jacket are torn but I am laughing my head off. Sometime in the early hours, homing south, I reach the outskirts of Manchester City Airport...

Down avenues all lined with trees, I find refuge in Wythenshawe. I'm hiding at Amy and Saad's, rest punctuated by the wail of low-flying aircraft. It's rained almost every day for the last few weeks, but this morning suggests if not armistice, then at least a truce.

Amy's a friend and a researcher, but the necessities of an income and the impossibility of undertaking research without institutional funding have her working the helpline of a holiday company. She hates it but loves Saad, and meeting this affable personal trainer has energised her. They're expecting a child and planning a future together. Both are learning Arabic, for this future in mind isn't clear, and may not be here. Dour rain, casual racism, McDonald's drive-thrus. They speak passionately of hope, glimpsing something beyond this.

I leave the city behind, pass the airport and the gated foot-baller villas of Styal, along country lanes that lead into Cheshire, and enter Macclesfield, a small town built on silk production. The mills are dormant, most now demolished, though one remains preserved as a heritage centre. The small workers' terraces are dwarfed by massive expanses of green around them. People dawdle around the town's small shopping precinct lethargically. One man tells me about the silk history of the town, and its now quiet, "pleasant" character. Umbro once made football kits here, and Zeneca still employs some. It's not altogether quite the "ghost town" I was warned of in Grimsby, but ghosts of another kind haunt it.

On Armitt Street is an old labour exchange where Ian Curtis, singer of Joy Division, helped disabled people find work and, nearby, the house where many of his haunting lyrics were written. I wonder if he attempted to exorcise the ghosts of this wounded landscape, or at least, to account for the inexplicable void at the heart of feeling where a teleological explanation about progress, modernity and the future was once embedded. It's an undertaking like that of Lowry, to meticulously record the emptiness, peopled with undead noises.

I find the crematorium where a memorial to Curtis stands. A groundsman leads me there, chuckling about how "weird" it is that it's now an international shrine. By the stone are two moody young Italians, Arens and Alyssia. Alyssia shows me photos of the chapel, whilst Arens draws attention to the outline of the brooding sky. "Love will tear us apart" – such a disquieting, contradictory phrase, etched on the headstone. There are plectrums, coins, flowers and photo tributes, and I leave the electric candle from Gretna, feeling stunned, wiped away. And then out.

I've arranged to meet Seth, secretary of the Didsbury Mosque and Islamic Centre, situated in an old church in leafy south Manchester, in an area once known for its large Jewish population. The mosque was established in 1967 by Muslims seeking a larger space for their growing congregation. He sees no clash

with the building's original function, and he reflects circumspectly on his faith. "Everyone's allowed in. We both worship the
same almighty God, there's no priority, Christian or Muslim."
There've been some attacks against the place, but he emphasises
conciliation: "That's between them and their gods".

Seth shows me around the prayer rooms, and explains the
names and rites of the different prayers, the five pillars of Islam,
and the "zakat" that Muslims give to charity. The mosque has
been financed by anonymous donations and, unlike Christian
churches, there are no conspicuous plaques or memorials to the
wealthy dead. He challenges me on the topic of faith, and though
some testy thoughts are beginning to coagulate, I have nothing
to satisfy him. He hands me a glass of fresh juice, and issues a
final thought: "Next time, ride on a motorbike!"

Later at Amy and Saad's, we eat together and pick at the uncertainty that forms a general experience across the island. Time
draws near to closing its loop, repeating an experience like that
of the 1930s, and the Salford of Greenwood, whose characters
are often drawn depressed, preoccupied ("these dreadful feelings
of aimlessness, of this perplexing sensation of being lost, out
of place").

Among the lovers, I begin to wonder if Greenwood's got
it wrong. For there is a light that never goes out, and love and
friendship are, if not altogether enough, then something. In
Arabic they are *hubb* and *mawaddah*, physical love and caring
love, as I grasp it. In the Qur'an, one reads: "of His signs is that
He created for you from yourselves mates that you may find tranquillity in them; and he placed between you affection and mercy".
Love, that rubber ring, something more pleasurable and escapist
than even alcohol or prophets. And I think of her that I love, and
a yearning for home hits me unexpectedly.

Morning in Cheetham Hill, and I am craning over an old scroll.
An old gentleman a little distance away clears his throat, and

begins his approach. "Those? 'Relics from a defunct culture.'" This Torah scroll once featured in Adolf Eichmann's collection. It found its way back to north east Manchester, into this Spanish and Portuguese synagogue.

Alan enjoys taking guests on a tour, wry observations accompanied by hearty laughter. The morning light filters through coloured glass, illuminating scenes without human or animal, consistent with the prohibition of idolatry retained also in Sunni Islam but not Christianity.

Both religions have been worshipping here for centuries, but Manchester particularly has a large set of Jewish communities. My grandpa's family left Germany to settle in this city, leaving behind violent anti-Semitism to join Manchester's growing and diverse Jewish community. Free trade's elevation of wealth above all does correlate with a degree of religious toleration. Like previous migrant groups, many of their distinctive customs and names have disappeared, undetected, into banal Englishness. In my case, Cohen is now Taylor.

Alan talks of Zionism, the movement to establish a Jewish homeland in British Palestine that flourished here in the early 20th century. Its success now troubles the community. Alan's worried about rising anti-Semitic violence, related to ongoing Israeli state violence against Palestinians. Synagogues are tightening security, and his friends and family feel increasingly concerned for their safety. He reflects with both concern and circumspection. "They think one Jew is responsible for another Jew... But we're all the same. We all want peace, we all want to see our children do well."

Through the suburbs of Prestwich, Heaton Park and Whitefield, past stores selling airguns, British-Chinese cuisine, spiritual wellbeing and cheap alcohol. Manchester continues in this mood for some time til the landscape clears its breath, coughs out some green expanses, then begins again with the bland affluent suburbia of Bury.

I wheel around this small but respectable-looking town, in an incoherent stew of Victorian pageantry and pseudo-plaza malls. One Londoner complains about local house prices. A council-funded brand consultant emails me to ensure I insert the correct hyperlink to a voluntary goodwill campaign being rolled out. Such is Bury.

A grittier story of suffocated decline emerges among the mills and dales thereafter. One sees it in the spindly brown-bricked chimney that stands alone, in the large sooty shells of old factories, in the sturdy sandstone terraces that marks out these ex-textile towns, like Summerseat, Ramsbottom, Edenfield and Rawtenstall. The latter is dominated by a huge Asda, and the remaining retail streets are visibly struggling. Josh and Stephanie are the first people I see aged below sixty.

"There's not much going on. Look at the shops, I remember when they used to be all open. This used to be an alright place."

"What changed?"

"Unemployment's a problem, there's just nowt to do."

"'Cept on a Saturday night, people come out and get pissed."

They're in their late teens, and plan to escape by way of university. Forensic science, sports photography, eminently practical. Eyeing my panniers, Josh warns that Burnley's worse. "Be careful. There's gangs." Their faces look mithered, like others. "Trouble" is a word Josh repeats. And yet though the situation's sour, our faces crease in laughter. Black humour suffuses conversations like this, issuing a barbed counter-commentary over the absurd outward conformity of our actions.

Burnley begins not long after Rawtenstall ends. The road dips into a deep valley where a surprisingly large town stands, unremarkable and without landmark. I pass the Charter Walk mall and a disorientating array of ugly retail developments, a collage of crass. One local woman speaks with tested pride. "There's something about it, it's... home." Another, less hopefully, "Unemployment, there's a lot of unemployment. I've been looking for a long time. I might as well give up." A derelict town hall faces a large retail park on the other side of the motorway. This sentence, or that of Rawtenstall Asda, indicates why these towns are now collapsing, yet just about staying alive.

Beneath the chimneys of the old mills, notice the bright-lit billboard, advertising a new mobile phone. There's a petrol station, self-employed tradesmen queuing, one or two chatting. Between the old terraces, trace the occasional onion-bulb and minaret of a mosque. These small towns like Nelson and Brierfield doze in their dotage, their populations depleting, even their malls near-derelict. Textile production has been exported to Asia, in exchange for cheap goods and furniture.

A change of scene thereafter. The road north to Barnoldswick intimates the loveliness of the Dales, a trail of rolling fields with clusters of sheep and cattle. Veins of emerald and azure thread the scape as hedgerows and streams, the brilliance of the sun casting beauty on whatever it reaches. Woodlands fade out into the distance, and kestrels hover overhead. Through picturesque Gargrave and Coniston Cold, surveying the sunset behind me at lovely Airton, then up through Kirkby Malham, its grey gritstone church casting an avuncular, benevolent presence over the gentle terrain. No mills now, just the fields, the ancient trees and drystone walls. And drowsing amongst those, beneath limestone walls, is little Malham, a village with a youth hostel, where I dry out my clothes from the day's familiar rains. I give my partner a call. With the pleasure of hope in my heart again, I'll be seeing her shortly.

The following days pass in a blur of verdant dales, distant sheep and fudge-box panoramas. I traverse Craven, past brook and briar, a region of North Yorkshire where much of the island's milk and cheese is produced. After Hetton and Cracoe, there are lung-bursting climbs to Appletreewick and into Nidderdale, the greens and blues of the dales shifting into sparse expanses of bracken, heather and distant tors, like that of the North West Highlands.

Pateley Bridge is a cheery and chintzy village clinging to the 1940s. The climb out is a veritable Kilimanjaro, a vertical ascent in torrential rain that restricts all vision to a metre ahead. The peaks of these dales are quite unlike any postcard representation and few see them, savage and enrapturing. After the Sunday drive and second home scapes of Kirkby Malzeard and Grewelthorpe, I reach the old market town of Masham, once a trading post of dairy production. Catering for local desires, Masham's large square is lined by boozers serving up sauce from its two local breweries. There's even a large church from which one can still repent one's nocturnal sins the following morn.

Beer-brewing and cheese-making both involve establishing the right conditions and then waiting long periods for invisible things to ferment. They are exacting arts, requiring careful experimentation to create and maintain the conditions for one object to transform into another. The English do not produce any spirit to a particularly high standard. But pubs in every town sell different beers, and the number of breweries is high and growing. Beer's the thing, not mass-produced lagers, but this warm, flat, brown and bitter brew that once alone boasted the title beer. Today they call it real ale, as if there were some other alternative. Both beer and cheese subdue the mind, fill the belly and smudge out the edges of one's mental horizons. The nights are long in the country. Things ferment by their exposure to unfamiliar elements in these scattered settlements, out of natural necessity.

Stoats skitter over lawns, deer trample through nearby woods. Cousins, uncles and aunts clink glasses, sing songs and dance til the early hours. Two days pass in Masham with my wife, gathered for a family wedding. And then, no sooner than a blink, it is time again to part ways. The sadness of separation barely equals the joy of reunion. Ahead, the road.

It is thought that the practice of keeping sheep began in ancient Mesopotamia and Persia. Sheep were herded and bred for their wool, meat and milk. The Romans found them on their military adventures, and brought them over to England. By 1000 CE the island had become a major centre of sheep-breeding. In many ways the sheep had more rights than those who herded them, free to roam the common land.

"Many thanks do we owe to the sheep", wrote Pliny, "both for appeasing the gods, and for giving the use of its fleece". A world understood teleologically, a landscape given by a God to service Man's promethean ambitions. Forests were steadily cleared for these sheep to roam. One can only speculate on the internal clutter also cleared in the minds of a people given to the keeping of sheep on a cold damp island, on the edge of the known world. Pensive, attentive, averse to speaking lightly, irreverently amused by the predictability of animal life.

Creatures of cities for some two centuries now, the seas and fields appear deceptively tranquil, "authentic", "natural". Dales like these are now cleared of sheep, but the production of wool shapes the nearby towns, like Harrogate, Halifax and the once wool-production capital of the world, Bradford. Wool was fed into the machines, and potatoes into the workers. "The last and most important of all raw products that play a revolutionary role in history", wrote Engels of that humble potato. And turnips, and sheep, and bricks, and iron, and a population, herded, and there you have it, Harrogate, Bradford, Halifax.

One man checks his watch repeatedly as he complains about his hometown, Harrogate, an old spa resort now markedly affluent. He is grateful that the demotic sounds and smells of the covered market have been replaced with a small mall. Not far from the delightfully named Idle, Friendly and Slapbottom, is Salts Mill, once the largest factory in the world. It sits on the River Aire in Shipley, just north of Bradford, the centrepiece of Titus Salt's model factory and worker's community, Saltaire. It was dirty, dangerous and difficult work. Writing back in 1844, six years before Salt's project, Engels described the Mancunian working class as little more than "machines, pure and simple", raised from a position of "silent vegetation" by their work. Salt in his own paternalistic manner sought to improve life for his workers in an era before the welfare state. Saltaire had relatively capacious, elegant terraced houses, with washhouses, a school, hospital, gym, library, even a concert hall. No pub in sight, of course. These moralising reformers couldn't allow the workers *too much* pleasure. Today the noises and smells have been banished for quaint serenity, with the mill converted to a shopping and restaurant complex and art gallery. One resident complains of the "dark and poky rooms", of "traffic" and "parking". I look agog.

Bradford also retains some similarly marvellous if under-loved Victorian buildings, crowning a surrounding terrain of run-down suburbia, car-wash forecourts and takeaways. A middle-aged local in a poundstore uniform tells me that if he could change anything, "I'd have the buses run on time!" We gaze up together at a nearby clock tower, til our reverie's interrupted by one gang of young men chasing another down the street. "You can get yourself in trouble", he adds, "but you've got to go out looking for it". Further down, a new square's been built into the city centre, benches facing its fountain, people sitting and talking. A local policeman stands alone, surveying the scene with detached pensiveness.

"There's a lot of drug dealing going on where I live, but it's low-level. You get the odd speeding car, dodgy behaviour, but it doesn't harm anyone."

"So better the lesser evil?"

"Yeah... Bradford used to be in major decline, real bad. Now it's on the way up. They knocked down the city centre ten year ago to build a shopping centre, but the developers ran out of money. The council just left it derelict. Now Westfield are building it."

Which is all strange, and true, and a somewhat ignoble

situation for a once mighty city. By the city's Media Museum I talk with a Polish lad, his accent fusing Warszawa and West Yorkshire. He's about to start university in Manchester, but came here nine years ago with his family. He's lived in different parts of England but likes Bradford best, though warns against cycling through postcodes six and ten. There's a lot of gangs, and racism's a problem. But he smiles. "Keep on!" he shouts out to me as I leave.

I exit Bradford through its south eastern suburbs, past near-dilapidated factories half-heartedly converted to one commercial end or another. Then west through the post-WW2 council housing estate of Buttershaw, ambience akin to the ex-mining suburbs of Nottingham. There are empty expanses of patchy-grass wasteland, a local boozer where bored kids roam around and, by Brafferton Arbor, an unlikely blue plaque I've been told to look out for, that remembers the playwright Andrea Dunbar.

Her work and life mirror this decline of skilled and unskilled textile work, as much a way of life as any other, and, with it, the slow collapse of individual and communal relationships. For there was always something greater than mere "machines" in those factories. Her characters were never given a fair chance to flourish or an opportunity to become capable of shaping their own destinies. They worked when work was there, and stayed and suffered in poverty when it was not, and when the industries were finally privatised and sold by the 1980s, none saw a share of the proceeds. New Labour arrived and gave a cursory facelift to its more wretched quarters. Net curtains quiver, stirring an otherwise deserted scene.

In Halifax nearby, another compact ex-industrial town totters with uncertainty. A young couple share a McDonald's dinner and tell me "it's shit". What compels them to stay? "I can't leave. I've got a shitty job. It pays just enough to live, but not enough to live here. I wanted to go to uni, but they said cos my mum and dad both work I can't get a loan. So I'm stuck..."

Are these new experiences? Perhaps not, but inequality's particular burden on the young is novel. Understandably, they are often angrier than any other social group, and of course, the energy of youth contributes, too. Yet unlike their parents and grandparents – in England at least – there's rarely any expressed belief in an alternative. They've not known trade union victories, haven't heard proud affirmations of being working class. Instead they know of chavs, Tony Blair, *Benefits Street*. It's a new kind of class poverty out here, not merely economic. The consequence of a strategic recapture of public ownership, expressed in a kind of individualistic, working class Toryism that is symptom, and not cause, of their disempowerment.

E.P. Thompson wrote *The Making of the English Working Class* whilst staying in nearby Siddal in the early Sixties, when the mills were starting to close. "The working class did not rise like the sun at an appointed time. It was present at its own making." One can talk of the working class now, but in an era of zero hours, zero current balance, zero time, the possibility of a successful strike feels less plausible than a lottery jackpot. I'm among a grouping that has even forgotten its own name, absent at its own unmaking. For class was never just an economic status, as Thompson saw, but a shared outlook, a commitment to solidarity. And without that, what separates sheep from their keepers? Don't do it, lamb.

Sheep, machines, vegetables or working class – men and women have taken many shapes among the mills and dales. In the razed valley of Luddenden Foot, I drink tea with Kirsty, who has offered a place to couchsurf. She tells me of the dales, of a life travelling the country, discovering and retelling its stories in museums and schools. Enigmatic, contradictory, we gaze out of her cottage window at the dales, unable to fathom the mysteries of the island.

You'll not find lager, wine or gourmet burgers here. No damask wallpaper, leather sofas nor chandeliers. It is minimally appointed, nestled at the edge of an ex-mill town. As with any boozer on this island, here the world's best ideas have been forged, toasted and forgotten.

Against a common Northern narrative of industrial decline, new things are being tried in ex-industrial towns like Hebden Bridge, where even a ubiquitous boozer like the Fox and the Goose is a cooperative. Nearby, mills are being repurposed into alternative technology centres and artist studios. Even the town hall is collectively owned by the community. Coffee shops sell organic cakes for dogs. It's eccentric and perhaps merits lampoon, but these pleasures are innocuous.

The only graffiti is a stencil of Sylvia Plath, resident of nearby Heptonstall, a steep old village Kirsty shows me round. Plath attempted a life here with Ted Hughes, from nearby Mytholm-royd. Not everything ventured succeeds, but "even among fierce flames the golden lotus can be planted", as Hughes would tell her, and later wrote on her gravestone, misattributing it to the *Bhagavad-Gita*. It says something of the scape around it. "Dark and gloomy" is how Kirsty remembers it, where once sight and sound were ground down by the buzz of the machines. Bus seats and asbestos were manufactured in Old Town, with deadly consequences for some. Those factories are gone, the scene serene.

Todmorden's bookended with derelict industries. One could easily break into these ruined buildings and roam around inside. Scattered papers, pigeon shit, old overalls covered in moss and mould, rusted wingnuts, each evidencing not the passage of time but its failure to pass. But here an organisation called Incredible Edible has turned these vacated spaces into community gardens and orchards. The idea's spread across the island now, admittedly more likely to be perpetuated by the reforming middle class, but it indicates another urban possibility instead of retail parks and supermarket "regeneration". In towns like Tod, or Burnley, Padiham and Whalley that I pedal through, populations have shrunk, and I sense a mood of confusion, as people and places become superfluous, "nowt to do" round here. Feeling left behind or left out, I find people to be taciturn, reluctantly vocalising thoughts. Out along narrow country lanes that wind and undulate through Old Langho, Dinckley and Ribchester, I eventually reach the quiet 20th century suburbia of Longridge, a more affluent commuter node.

A young couple points me to the Towneley, their wry smiles indicating likely disappointment. Product as described, I sip brown beer and watch Burnley FC get demolished by Chelsea on the big screen, til at last the call comes in from Steve. He's a citizen of the London suburbs now, but still comes back to Longridge occasionally, and the coincidence today is fortunate. After a spell as a university lecturer, he began as a teaching assistant for children with learning difficulties at a secondary school. He speaks with pride in the work he does. Over beer, rice and smoking herbs, he reflects on that journey.

He thinks that smaller classes are the way forward, and that old-fashioned "chalk and talk" can actually be more effective for the often tired, stressed and easily distracted young people he works with. Parents have been shaped by a consumer language of choice that undermines the authority of teachers whilst shoving even greater pastoral responsibility on their shoulders. He worries that the profession has become de-skilled, with teachers no longer teaching, only instructing how to pass the exams of a rigid curriculum. His colleagues are overworked and stressed, with 60+ hour weeks not uncommon. Running extracurricular activities is now expected, as is intensive performance-surveillance and increasingly unrealistic parental demands. But there's a wider issue, one that well-meaning teachers cannot address alone: "That you can have a Health Secretary who is not a doctor, or any cabinet minister who doesn't have any experience of these areas... is incredible. These people have been in politics since leaving university. They haven't done a day's honest work in their lives."

Weighed on by incompetent, vainglorious and danger-ously self-serving officials from above, and demanding yet increasingly detached parents from below, what powers does the well-meaning teacher have? Children are being taught to pass exams at the expense of their capacity to think creatively and critically. For what use is thinking? The goal of managerial systems has been, since the work of F.W. Taylor, the enhance-ment of worker efficiency, quantified in grades, league tables and Ofsted reports. And in this schema, everyone seems to lose, though few would dare openly come last. "It's scary the way schools are going now. They're like massive farms to churn out office workers."

Steve speaks of a prevailing culture of fear that he observes parents socialising their children into. "They don't think it's safe." The world has become a place of danger, rife with terrors without (paedophiles, gangs, terrorists, viruses) and within (poverty, school/career failure, ugliness, getting old). Refuge comes in individualistic pursuits, like video games and never-ending TV dramas, and beliefs in cooperation and solidarity become increasingly unlikely, even luxurious. But we must take care with the past.

Earlier, Kirsty told me about her grandpa. Each summer he was left with "ten and six" by his parents, and he'd go out on his own, roaming around Snowdonia for weeks at a time. He'd sleep in fields and church doorways. "He absolutely loved it", she recalls. Like the mills and dales, there's at least two different ways to read that story.

Preston, again. A driver pulls out of a minor road and, not seeing me, ploughs straight into the bike's side. My panniers take the bulk of the collision, though I fly over the handlebars. She curses, then drives off.

Cut, bruised, but just about OK, I wearily continue on, back towards the Irish Sea. At Southport I rest, a Victorian seaside resort ringed with convalescent homes. Seafront Art Deco glimmers nearby neo-classical pomp, cenotaph and arches, Victoria, Empress of India. Italianate roof awnings cap chintzy yet unscathed parades. The only reminder of the demotic buzz of nearby Blackpool takes the form of an inebriated old fellow, holding himself up against a pub sandwich board, swaying and rocking against the tourist tides like a shipwrecked sailor.

Amusement arcades, bargain mushy peas outlets and ice cream kiosks. There's the obligatory miniature train causing chaos along the promenade, passing a large warehouse filled with penny machines and one-armed bandits that cheekily calls itself "Funland". A long boardwalk then passes over a waterside bar where a cheery crooner burbles through the songs of Cliff and the Beatles, "we're all going on a summer holiday", as a pre-recorded Casio keyboard bounces in the background. Old dears sway and shake their ankles in unison, the grey flank of a lumpy field passing itself off as a golf course behind them.

I venture around Sefton Dunes a while, so lost I find myself in an artillery shooting range, where a military official escorts me to safety. Then well-heeled Formby, now reaching the wider conurbation of Liverpool, soon confirmed in the accent transformation at Crosby, the flat consonants of Lancashire now blended with the Celtic flow of Ireland and the singsong peaks-and-valleys of Wales. Good old Scouse, exuberant in its elongated vowels and mucal blockage. *Sound!*

Cast-iron figures jut out of Crosby beach, under the shadow of the port of Liverpool. Dog-walkers pace the sands, and gulls squawk over the sighing sea, forms winking over the sunset. I cross into Liverpool's North End, where traditionally the poorest neighbourhoods have clustered around the still-active docks, like Bootle, Anfield, Walton and Norris Green. Though the Bootle scene's largely derelict, a smorgasbord of smells greets the traveller: the claggy greasiness of New British Oils, then malty barley tons, followed by the baked bovine grease of a pit or pet-food plant, and lastly, a noxious chemical works, where I pinch my nose, dip my brow and pedal a little faster.

Containers stacked like Lego behind me, and a bar graph of marine-coloured glass ahead, signalling the centre. Liverpool is surprisingly compact, a sober melange of Victorian mercantile ambition, civic pride, 20th century modernism, and ill-fitting corporate glass of more recent extraction. I ride out into the eastern suburb of Wavertree where I'm staying with my friends Sandra, Dermot and their family.

It's a pleasure to eat and drink with old friends, where one doesn't have to begin again with an account of one's life story. We eat and drink with the TV news droning in the background. Sandra talks about her work coordinating a rehabilitative probation service. Across the country, prison and probation services are becoming increasingly run for profit by private companies. Rehabilitation isn't profitable, but it saves far more public money and social misery long-term than overcrowded cells.

"I don't use the word offender, I see a person, and I see something that was out of order." For Sandra, the point is to turn people's lives around. It's common for the people she works with to have multiple problems, particularly prior mental health issues disorders, which often begin from a young age. Early strategic intervention would save vast amounts of money, if that must be the wretched standard everything comes down to. The country's prisons are now overcrowded, and violence and suicides are rapidly growing. Sandra sees a "prison service at breaking point".

A government minister appears on the TV to blame the "violent" prisoners themselves for their frustrations about overcrowding. Victorian attitudes? "Nothing is assured", Sandra concludes, tentatively.

But I'm about to meet an unlikely man who'll do his damnedest to shake up all woebegone words. As the news presenter shuffles his papers, a figure bundles through the door, leaps out of one denim jacket and into another, flicks back his hair, then peeks inside. "Come on Dan!" We're off to a lock-in...

In The Edinburgh last night, we talked til the witching hours as punters hushed and hurrahed through a Dadaesque pub quiz that no one seemed to win or lose. Dermot talked of growing up in Liverpool's North End. The older docks began to close when he was a young man. Seeing the writing on the wall, he quit docking and worked as a building site electrician for many years, and was successful at this until the late 1990s. Suddenly no contractor was willing to hire him. He had a great record, always did his work well without mistakes. "Hundreds of applications", he remembers. He was never told why, but began to suspect something.

He'd heard of an open secret in the industry. There were others like him, skilled workers, unable to get any jobs despite ongoing vacancies and countless applications. Some were active union members, others only tangentially involved in workplace struggles, like him, back on the Jubilee Line Extension walkouts. Somehow, he'd been blacklisted.

In 2009 the Information Commissioner busted the Consulting Association, a blacklisting firm with at least three thousand workers on its books. Forty-four companies subscribed. Blacklisting is not illegal in the UK, and the only crime was the infringement of data-protection laws. Ian Kerr and his wife ran the organisation, collecting tip-offs from building contractors and police Special Branch, as well as combing left-wing bookshops and publications. One could be struck off for collecting a petition against local homelessness, or raising health and safety issues with a site manager.

The impact on workers and their families was devastating. "'How do you know?' And the problem is, it's very hard to prove." They were accused of paranoia, but here was true conspiracy. After some time, Dermot found work in perhaps the least popular trade going, nuclear waste disposal. In his spare time for the last few years, he's researched the impact of blacklisting on families, the divisions caused by both the loss of income and the lack of recognition of a legitimate grievance. He's just had his dissertation passed by Ruskin College, Oxford University.

Fitting to debate this in Liverpool, a city like no other on the island, except Glasgow, in its unwavering faith in the welfare of its people. It has repeatedly defied the dictats of Westminster and its fear-mongering allies in order to live its own story. Dermot wants to show me some of it. Resuscitated by black coffee, we head out.

Liverpool neither totters nor sprawls. Walking through the cluster of old and new university buildings on the edge of the centre, notice how wide, airy and light the streets feel, uncluttered by people, billboards or discarded plastic. Ahead looms a concrete ziggurat crowned with a large funnel, the Great Pyramid of Giza as imagined by HAL 9000. Dermot directs me into the Metropolitan Cathedral, known affectionately here as "Paddy's Wigwam", built for the city's large Irish Catholic population. It was paid for with their donations.

> They did it with dolls and with raffle tickets;
> they did it with pools and bingo;
> they did it with socials,
> and tired old men standing outside churches
> in the wet with a bit of a box in their hands.

Norman Cresswell poetically captured the opening of the cathedral in 1967, now exhibited inside. The stained glass casts an ethereal quality of light across the circular hall, a place of worship unusually bright and hopeful. We head out, meandering down Hope Street, where the city's neo-gothic Protestant cathedral stands in total contrast. Refreshment's found in the Casa Bar, cooperatively run by Liverpool dockers, and decked out with Communist memorabilia. There are photos of the Spanish Civil

War where many Scousers volunteered to fight fascism before it crept over the continent, a mural noting their names and occupations, from labourer to professor.

We pass the old Unemployment Resource Centre on Hardman Street, a community-run institution that gave free advice to a city blighted by redundancies and industrial closures during the 80s and 90s. It closed a decade ago, and a plaque commemorates its original function as a school for the blind. A metaphor there, perhaps. It's temporarily open for the Liverpool Biennial, and so we snoop around its peeling, rotting interior, ignoring the drearily postmodern and apolitical exhibits.

"There's no straight line with Liverpool, it's always been great highs and lows", Dermot remarks, as we exit. Thatcher's government sought to abandon the city, a "concentration of hopelessness" as Geoffrey Howe put it, blacklisting the city from the priorities of the suburban south. Instead the city council took on Thatcher and won, setting its own "illegal" budget, building thousands of new homes and schools, parks and sports centres. Their militant, Keynesian gamble was validated, but the city was vilified, rendered a byword for social dereliction and crime. Its Militant Labour populism probably kept the city alive.

We drift through the remnants of Liverpool's diminishing China Town, and past the bombed-out church, now a community garden where students are doing yoga. Into its grand Victorian centre which, more than Bradford, seems cherished and in use, be it the Central Library, or St George's Hall, the Great North Western Hotel, or Lime Street Station, all clustered marvellously together on William Brown Street. Navigation is easy, the people friendly. Even the new Liverpool One mall is surprisingly pleasant to explore, and crowds enjoy themselves on benches, leisurely chatting. Dermot points out the "To-Lets" and the shells of cinemas on Bold Street and Lime Street, predictably suffering a loss of trade, but the centre remains spirited and buoyant.

We explore the regeneration of the Riverside, Pier Head and

the ambitious white marble of the Italianate Cunard, next to the baroque Port of Liverpool building. "The Edmund Gardner!" Dermot says, pointing to a brightly coloured boat parked in the old Albert Dock, now regenerated by galleries, restaurants and faceless chain hotels and conference centres. He disregards the rest of the scene. "I serviced that", he says, beaming.

Beyond the obvious markers of gentrification though, it's remarkable how little Liverpool's changed these last few decades. The old Albert Dock was caught in a similarly elegiac moment over thirty years ago in the TV show *Boys from the Blackstuff*. George, a blacklisted trade unionist, recalls looking out at the same waters, forty-seven years earlier, when he began working on the docks. His speech stirs up memories of an optimistic post-WW2 socialist movement, and its disappointment then and since. "They say that memories live longer than dreams, but my dreams still give me hope and faith in my class. I can't believe that there's no hope, I can't." The scene's end is melancholic. Thirty years on, Liverpool's had a face-lift, no doubt, but the social content of his collectivist entreaty is less easily dismissed.

My companion insists on regularly assuaging our thirst in the city's many hostelries, among these being the Philharmonic, Doctor Duncan's and the Baltic Fleet. As the beer tickles, Dermot reveals just how primitive nuclear waste disposal is. "They basically just rub the rods very hard with a cloth, then put the cloth into a barrel and into the sea." These barrels eventually decompose and leak, and Sellafield on the Cumbria coast is now one of the most polluted parts of the island. Radioactive rods must be first cooled in ponds before disposal, but these are often open-air, and Dermot has seen birds fly in and out of these pools, carrying a stronger radioactive dose than Alexander Litvinenko. There seems to be an active and continuous contamination of the surrounding landscapes happening that few outside the world of nuclear energy are aware of.

Does it matter? Among all these ghosts, perhaps what defines

England against Scotland most is this obliviousness about the future, even scepticism. It's as if time has stopped, or was never there. Nothing yet suggests a rude awakening. It is a dangerously deluded scepticism.

"Realise that happiness is freedom, and freedom is courage", speaks Pericles through the pen of Thucydides. The words are now displayed in the city's slavery museum. Like Hull, London, Bristol, Plymouth and Glasgow, Liverpool was heavily involved in the transatlantic slave trade, and profits were banked here and built into the grand Georgian structures around the city. Liverpool particularly thrived, its vessels transporting around half of the three million black Africans seized and sold by British traders. The city exploited its new canals and transport links to gather textiles, crafts and guns to trade with enterprising local traders in exchange for their captives. Slave cotton from America fed the machines of the Lancashire textile towns, and trade profits from slave tobacco, sugar, coffee and rum fed the expansion of the island's Industrial Revolution. No descendant of the slave trade has ever been compensated, and slavery now takes new forms.

But Liverpool is more transparently critical of the slave trade than most. "Faced with what is right, to leave it undone shows a lack of courage", claims Confucius, in words I stumble upon in News from Nowhere, an independent bookshop on Bold Street, as I bore deeper for clues. If freedom's secret is in courage, the courage to demand the right to freedom, then such courage also consists in doing what is right; that is, in respecting and defending one's fellow as an equal, deserving of dignity.

Dermot's back at work, and I roam around the city, talking to strangers, assembling clues, but feeling empty. In one takeaway, a woman from the Wavertree foodbank appears on the radio and requests that the Prime Minister visit, find out "just how real hunger is". Over a beer in the Dispensary, I leaf through a yellowed tatty tome that Dermot had put aside. Not Confucius nor Thucydides, but Peter Taaffe and Tony Mulhearn's forgotten 1988 polemic, *Liverpool: A City that Dared to Fight*. It is melodramatic, optimistic and bitterly prognostic:

> The collapse of British capitalism... will be enormously compounded by the coming world recession. This in turn will result in a sharp deterioration in the living standards of big layers of the British working class. In their millions they will move to defend their rights and conditions... in the miners' strike and above all in the study of the Liverpool experience these workers will find the weapons to carve out a new world.

Wrong in many ways, and right in others. Economically, theoretically, even culturally, free market capitalism is in a process of accelerated growth, its momentary glow like that of a dying star, glowing and intensifying even as its untapped zones of accumulation disappear, spent. But politically it remains the only option. In Liverpool, I think I see the glimmer of a sea-change.

Courage, the courage to be free, the courage of stepping forward, alone, declaring a consensus wrong by one's contrary action. It would be easier for the Militant city council, or the striking dockers, or blacklisted Dermot to just not bother, to remain passive and submit to an entrenched and immovable set of political facts and norms. Passivity is wise, and there are good reasons for simply *preferring not to*. But there are those whose dreams still give them hope, and with that hope, the courage to stand up for what is right.

Courage, the courage to be active in one's refusal, and pro-active in one's thinking of alternatives. The courage to live up to common ideas of equality, fairness and toleration in one's relations with others, and to avenge the greedy and hypocritical whose actions damage those ideals. Few of those ideas began popular, and many were conflated with madness or criminality, but through protest, persistence, education, courage and generosity, they are now taught in schools as facts of life.

England sleeps, dreaming of dead things. There is an anger, sadness and hope beneath its surface vaster than any North Sea oil field. Courage calls for strong heads and hearts. All of us can stand up and act to demand what is right, and defend our common interest. That's not to say that courage is the "*genius loci*" of Liverpool or other such writerly nonsense – acquiescence in a disappointed fate defines the prevailing mood here, like the rest of England. Nor does courage naturally win out in the end. Time has no monopoly on progress, we've seen enough of that now. But times like these call for persistence in dreaming, and hoping, and standing up for what is right. For what else is there, except boozing, and love, and the Liverpool One mall? Even Cains Brewery is closed down now. Times like these demand a generosity of courage.

CHAPTER 9

Annwn

"We've got the knowledge here, we've got the potential" – Joel.

In a corridor of brickwork gloom and kaleidoscopic coloured glass, something unusual seizes my eye. A message, concise, its cursive eerily affectless. "All you had hoped for, all you had, you gave."

Here, back in 1917, a girl named Molly died. Her parents were moved to leave behind some tribute to their two-year-old daughter, who history otherwise forgets. There's a flash of sadness inside me reading it, standing in their place, as imagination blindly summons the image of that woman or man who knew Molly and her bright life cut short. It's reminiscent of Thomas Browne and his Norfolk urns, and of an affirmation that fulgurates, still, centuries hence, time's concentric circles misunderstood as dates: "Ready to be any thing, in the extasie of being ever". Giving the little one has. Alone in a taciturn mausoleum of medieval ambition, levitated beyond sense perception for a second, searching for something I feel but cannot see. These places are still charged with something.

Behind my shoulder, a loud and enthusiastic American interrupts a friend, industriously photographing the nave and ribbed vault of Chester's rusty-russet gothic cathedral. "Look, I spent my first British pounds!" She beams, proudly displaying some souvenir fudge. I take it as a sign to leave behind England's ghosts, and cross over into a greener world on the other side of the Welsh border.

Chester's halfway along my planned trajectory. I left Sandra's this morning, past prim Princes Park and the smart low-rise estates of Toxteth, built by its Militant Council with money it didn't have. I passed the vast Cains Brewery complex in the Baltic Quarter, now derelict and awaiting conversion into a service sector mecca, and crossed over the murky Mersey, as grey and brooding as the clouds above it. Birkenhead spread out sluggishly around me, its rusting warehouses, dilapidated clock-towers and car-wash forecourts easing into the Wirral and its indistinct early 20th century suburbia. Cod-Victorian conservatory roofs peeped over six-foot spiked fences. Juxtaposed to Ellesmere Port is twee Port Sunlight, a model workers' village where profits were paid not into fair wages, which might be wasted by the idle, booze-addled poor, but into a gallery, church and concert hall, paternalistic pastimes for the Lever Brothers' soap factory workers. I schlepped around its village greens, curious, then moved on.

By lunchtime I reach the opulent suburbia of Chester, a *Daily Mail*-constituency cathedral city, mock-Tudor medley mobbed with tourist-shoppers. The past still pays a good penny. After dawdling around the cathedral, I sit outside, supping on muesli, and get talking with an English student from the South Coast, who shares her love of the place. She remarks on northern hospitality, as most southerners do in the North, as if freed from some burdensome class obligation. Not far from a major international bank, the wisdom of Ecclesiastes adorns a scroll carried by two statuettes: "The profit of the earth is for all". An ex-soldier dressed in desert fatigues rests on his knees, body crumpled against a wall, braying "How Great Thou Art" to Chester's indifferent shoppers.

Further along, a shaggy fellow with a Wallasea brogue addresses me. "You'll like this", says Eddie, shoving a note into my hands. "It's got a happy ending…"

Most days he stands by this pedestrianised junction, handing out proseytising leaflets. Why? "Me dad used to whack us with the belt, and me ma' wasn't far behind. The fear, the fear of darkness... I was a drunk, a womaniser, I was violent", his voice starting to hush from its earlier clamour. A mate at the car factory where he worked spoke of his faith, and something of its redemptive promise clicked. He recalls the service he accompanied him to, tagging along, sceptical yet curious.

"And I was listening to him and I was just stunned. I was looking down by the end, at the darkness in me, at the love of the Lord. And me mate, he brings me to talk to the priest... It was like a spiritual experience. He said, 'Do you want to be a Christian?' And I felt that darkness coming out of me, pulling out of me, and I had Jesus in my heart."

He gestures to his chest, and raps it firmly with clenched fist. "Jesus, he's here all along, he's inside." Eddie describes a faith like William Blake's, of a joyful self-discovery that recognises the infinite in oneself, and in everything that surrounds. Like any belief that is genuinely felt, he is correct in his faith, as is Seth, and Alan, and those who've exchanged the paradoxes of ancient books for more modern material. Faith demands a certain kind of courage, if it has been tested or discovered anew.

But it is not an essential or indeed common staple for living. The road to Wrexham over the national border is neither strewn with gospel leaves nor Johnny Cash CDs but countless shards of glass and plastic, and the ossified remains of small mammals. Traffic signs double in size to accommodate the Welsh script.

Wrexham itself is modern, compacted, neither unpleasant nor distinct, with an unusually high number of pubs. My partner's grandfather gave up his nearby farm and traded the proceeds for the wine, women and song of this fair town. The Fat Cat was a dive situated between a bookies, bus garage and supermarket, everything an old boy needs, but has now closed down. I drift around, finding out odd little facts and stories on street corners. Mr and Mrs Roberts sit with their shopping, watching the traffic, the first of many to reflect sceptically on Welsh nationalism. Then into the Elihu Vale for refreshment.

The town's bustling Wetherspoon's is decorated in football shirts, not rugby, and few speak or read Welsh, neither the elderly Roberts nor the two lads I make conversation with outside. Solitary and sullen middle-aged men hold up the bar and keep the fruities filled with change.

Past the retail parks and new-build cul-de-sacs on Wrexham's edges, the terrain blossoms. Along narrow lanes through the rural hinterland, then following the Llangollen Canal (pronounced 'Clangoclen' – one soon gets used to the new pronunciation). On my right, the placid waters and cheerful narrowboats chugging along at walking pace; on my left, the mottled ochre, mocha and pomona of flanking thickets and briar. Children fish along the towpath, which whizzes over an aqueduct and, momentarily, back into England. Even these tall branches can't obscure the glorious setting sun, but one interminable tunnel by Chirk proves so lengthy and unwise to cycle through that for a time I cannot even make out the narrow path and nearly totter into the waters. The tunnel is alive with strange murmurs and spooky babbling. At the other end, I discover its source, a pair of young lads fishing who have been mightily amused at my progress through the tunnel, as I am too.

I stop at Chirk Bank, nestled in border country. There's a new degree of hushed reserve among those I pass and chat with, an absence of the ribald jokes and cheeky joviality that had animated the North. Though not friendly, neither are these places hostile to outsiders. No Little England or Cymru zeal. People living in England will register with Welsh GPs a few miles away to benefit from their free prescriptions, and most weigh up national identity with the same diffident scepticism as any other aspect of that most loathed of all island things, politics.

I'm staying with Sandra and Ken, my partner's aunt and uncle, not far from her granddad's old farm. Cottages have been built over fields where his livestock once roamed, though one field still houses a caravan where eccentric skunk-smoking, Triumph-tinkering relatives reside. There's some polite disapproval over the dinner table. Wine flows.

Ken recalls 1960s Manchester and the City Architect's office, mapping out the pipework and plumbing of innumerable buildings of cast concrete, those visions of social progress through futuristic planning that have borne the scorn of meaner times. Sandra shares tales of her work as a nurse, and travelling to Calcutta to assist Mother Teresa. She saw crumbling roads, leper colonies, and rampant tuberculosis. She saw luxury cars, routine bribery, and a city metro system with TV screens that no one except the rich could afford to use. Two cities, one layered above the other.

"And then I came back to Wrexham. And the streets were clean! And the buildings weren't falling down. And there were no lepers on the street corners, taken out by organised criminals and left there all day without water." In twenty years, has the world become more like Wrexham, or Calcutta? "It seems like things are just getting worse and worse", she says with sadness. Planetary resources and people's lives are consumed too quick, snuffed out for the sake of a remote few getting rich, with their free markets, accountants and property portfolios. A scarcity and precarity of a kind that many describe, even when, materially, such scarcity has never been known, and the UK remains one of the wealthiest states of the world. One that, fittingly for its medieval constitution, is almost entirely populated by the dispossessed and disenfranchised. With that most unlikely of things, faith, she reanimates. "God is love, God is in all things", she says, smiling.

After dinner they retire to bed, and I think some more on those words. Instead of dismissing such beliefs as another opiate, I wonder instead about other forms of faith, like an unflinching belief in the equality, dignity and goodwill of others. So much has been transformed as a result of beliefs in these, even in living memory. Ken spoke of his mother washing him in a tin bath;

Sandra, of growing up on a farm, water drawn from a well. What of this shower that I use now, with its gentle gradients of heat? The washing machine that cleans my clothes, the Internet that connects my phone to the rest of the world, and which brings any idea, work of art or friend of mine straight to my screen...

We are lucky to be alive today, and we have no idea what is possible. Everything will change, regardless of our involvement, but how it changes is within our power. The next few days prove instructive.

Bore da, a chroeso i Gymru!

The separation of Wales from England is particularly marked in North Wales, more distant and resistant to waves of Germanic, Norse and Norman migrations. Offa built a long earthen wall between Powys and his Mercian kingdom in the 8th century, like Hadrian and Antoninus in Scotland did before him, fearing those barbaric foreigners over the mountains. The English have ventured over several times to subdue the Welsh, imposing castles, governments, languages, and later mines and factories to control the people and put them to work. But out in the North Walian terrain, among its taciturn yet thoughtful people, England feels remote, elsewhere.

It's not in the cheery seaside resorts of Rhyl, Prestatyn or Llandudno that one feels Wales' uniqueness, but in the quieter villages of the Vale of Llangollen and Snowdonia, of Anglesey and Pwllheli, a name surely invented by cunning locals to bamboozle strangers. Varying in its verdancy but consistently gentle and pretty, the north is as sparsely-populated as Wales' mysterious centre. I cycle through this lesser-known hinterland over the course of the day, following an ancient holloway to Holyhead, built on by the Romans as the outer northern course of Watling Street, and in more recent times by Thomas Telford, he who reshaped so much of Scotland, these invader-civiliser-engineers.

Through sleepy Llangollen, brought to life once a year by an international singing competition or *eistedfodd*, I reach the small town of Corwen. Outside the Eagles bar, a group of locals rehearse for next year with bawdy renditions of 'Livin' la Vida Loca' and 'Lady In Red', but their inebriation and frequent issue of profanities might well disqualify them from receipt of the crown of the bard. I drink up and push out.

A statue commands the soporific scape, beckoning eyes to bow down at its gallant pose. Owain Glyndwr, the last authentic Prince of Wales, almost retook Wales from the English back in the 15th century. He raised his revolt at Corwen in 1400, and seized much of the country from the English, establishing new universities, an independent parliament and a separate legal code. A heroic warrior and an uncompromising negotiator, he was later recast by Shakespeare as a mercurial weird, able to summon 'spirits from the vasty deep'. That otherworldly deep is resistant to exegesis, and no local can satisfactory explain themselves. 'What do people do for work round here?' 'Jobs', a man says flatly at the Eagles, without even the slightest ripple of barbed irony. Glyndwr's worthy independence has not yet been fully realised, six centuries hence.

Curiously it's the language, scenery, pronunciation and fidelity to this prince, and not those since, that'll mark North Wales from its southern half. Through Conwy County, where Welsh remains the first language, I pass green moorland (*rhos* in Welsh) that starts to tug towards the sky, and distant Snowdonia. It is a very verdant landscape, the sun gilding the edges of the afternoon clouds, casting serenity over the fields, forests and cattle. The terrain's blue-veined with gills, gurgling streams peter through woodland and tumble down waterfalls.

The Welsh tongue has a number of different nouns for these, from a tiddly *pistyll* to the deluge of a *ffrwd*. They vary depending on whether a waterfall is in the North (*rhaeadr*) or South (*sgwd*). Sadly in Snowdonia, many of these are locked away in security fences and quid-box turnstiles. Serious rain is forecast, and I decide to pull into the hiker's paradise of Betwys-y-Coed, a string of hotels and camping shops at the foot of Mount Snowdon. After paying for the pleasure to peer at Swallow Falls, a fine *rhaeadr* west of Betws, I stop at a small hostel annexed to a pub.

I drop my bags in the communal kitchen and rustle up a bean salad. At the table, two Karens and a Nicola stretch out wearily and sip wine from plastic beakers. They've just returned from hiking up Snowdon, and their walk has raised thousands for Macmillan cancer nurses. Rob sits with us, and protests with laughter at his failure to ascend the mountain. He and his father-in-law attempted it this morning but were rained off, but there's less at stake – this is their annual male-bonding trip, and better progress was made in draining pints thereafter. His companion's in bed, but Rob's thirst remains unquenched, so we head into the pub for more drinks and trade stories for the night.

Rob talks of underfloor heating and his love for his wife and two sons, whilst the barman issues fishing tips between chatting up female guests. Rob glows with a contentment not only attained by double-digit drinking or, later, spliffs shared in the beer garden. It's of loving appreciation, of appreciating what one loves in one's life. "As soon as they come into your life, you're not number one… You're thinking about them all the time, worrying." We talk of our partners with sad and happy fondness, with the frankness of passing travellers, sure they'll never meet again. "The first year living together was the hardest", he recalls. "After that, marriage was easy."

Last orders. We rejoin our Macmillan friends back in the kitchen, continuing this Snowdon symposium over wine sneaked over. The women speak of decades-deep disappointment. "You've got to love them as a best friend. Everything else, it changes. They start getting lazy, snoring, farting, then they get a belly." One texted her husband after reaching the peak. He replied with the cricket score. "I wanted to say F-off!" Rob insists on convincing them how he'll be different in the future, still young and capable of reform, but their eyes suggest familiarity with all apologetic reasoning.

The road forks at this place, Capel Curig, blanketed in bosky dells, emerald-like, interwoven with vermilion brooks. One is quiet, flat, along gentle terrain around Snowdon. The sensible route, a few stirring vistas no doubt, with easy traffic. The other cackles and howls as it twists itself over the steep range, tugging itself past cludair (Welsh for 'scree') up towards a snarling sierra horizon. Inspired by last night's conversing, I take the tougher trail.

It's hard going, but I overtake queuing double-deckers packed with hikers, as I climb up Pen-y-Pass, standing on my pedals, huffing, gasping, til my head's right in the clouds, struggling for air – or is the view breath-taking? – looming jagged scarps before me, maroon heather hillsides – tor explosion! – then the road plunging down, *fast!*, whizzing at race-car speeds, flashes of shrub and sheep, laughing, singing, hairpin bending, brakes no longer responding, nearly catapulted into the cosmos by road detritus at Llanberis.

Tiers have been cut neatly into the violet mountain, some for slate quarrying, others for the Snowdon railway that threads from here to the top. Comparing the crowds clustered here to the occasional enthusiastic stragglers at the apex of Pen-y-Pass, train remains the preferred option. I leave behind Llanberis and its languorous lakes, and hereafter the forested scape becomes flatter and monotonous, til it terminates at the Menai Strait. I cross over onto the Isle of Anglesey.

My body's struggling to pay the bill for last night's festivities. The nausea's brutal, and the rain threatens to wash me into the Irish Sea. I find a mediocre hotel and a toilet where the remainder of my stomach disappears. A little further, I pause at a place I cannot even begin to comprehend, let alone pronounce: Llanfairpwllgwyngyllgogerychwyrndrobwllllantysiliogogogoch (or Llanfair PG for short). It is a large, somewhat unattractive-looking village, its name concocted by rascally Victorians at both tourists' and the language's expense, and fitting for an experience of intense hangover existentialism of Raskolnikov-like proportions. I wire around queues of coaches, reaching Llanfair's visitor centre, where I pick up clues about Anglesey.

The island is surprisingly large, and defined by the dour port of Holyhead on its western edge, the Victorian resorts of Benllech and Beaumaris that I reach later on, and the remains of a once intensely industrialised zone of bronze and copper mining and slate quarrying at Amlwch and the Parys Mountain, a forgotten world like that unsentimentally dramatised by Caradog Prichard in *Un Nos Ola Leuad*. There is a large nuclear power plant at Wylfa facing obsolescence, with a new one planned nearby. A well-meaning stranger who'd offered a place to bed in Holyhead has bailed out at short notice, though fortunately a friendly man in Bangor has offered a place to stay. Rearranging my plans a little, I head towards Llangefni in Anglesey's flat, depopulated centre.

It's a small market town, largely built during the Victorian era when Anglesey boomed from mining. Whatever profits were made in a place close to once the world's biggest copper-producer were invested elsewhere. Mike's the only man I see wandering Llangefni's deserted high street. He's the first soul I've seen in some time, and after a purgatorial morning inside my own head, his conversation is like a reprieve from an unjust sentence. He calls the place a "city", a statement that would be ludicrous anywhere except rural North Wales, and he speaks of spatial distance with a dissonance akin to George of Lerwick, or Jeff of Mann.

"Things change", he reflects. "That's how all the cities are changing now, but there's nothing you can do." He traces Anglesey's shifts in terms of social composition. "Five years ago there was one fish-and-chip shop here. Now there's an Indian, a Chinese. But there's not much there for those people, and they're not around long." Yet from his descriptions, there's not much left for "his" people either. "Good jobs" have gone at Holyhead after Rio Tinto recently closed its plant. Copper, bronze and bromide are no longer produced here. Secure factory work is now precious and in short supply. The Kellogg's factory was spoken of in reverential terms back in Wrexham, and in Chirk, the Cadbury plant. Mike sees change as historically inevitable, but when pressed on the topic, neither of us are sure why. Profits could've been reinvested into making a sustainable future economy on Anglesey, perhaps through skilled engineering and manufacture like on Mann. Instead, like so much of everywhere else on this island, it's largely spent, dusty, left behind.

I reach Anglesey's eastern edge, and stop for chips at Benllech, a somewhat tatty-looking but well-loved little seaside town facing Red Wharf Bay. A horse-drawn carriage trundles past a Tesco Express, and a drunken father attempts to prevent his overexcited children from pursuing it, bored potty in the Sunday beer garden. Two bearded bikers sit beside me at the Golden Fry, surveying a caravan park and the azure seas beyond.

We gaze down at the golden crescent of sand pursuing the bay towards Menai. The beaches of Anglesey, or *Ynys Mon* in Welsh, were site of the last stand of the British druids and a burgeoning band of refugees, fleeing Roman rule. By 60 CE, nearly a century since Julius Caesar's first invasions, Roman legions advanced to the edge of the island, and sailed over to Anglesey to crack down on these dissidents. Tacitus describes how the Roman auxiliaries, many recruited from British tribes, became terrified by the druids' power, who were grouped in circles, "hands raised to heaven", casting spells on the soldiers. "[A]mongst them rushed women who, like furies, wore funereal clothing, had dishevelled hair, and brandished torches." Paulinus ordered them to advance, and the soldiers proceeded to massacre the ragtag rebels, burning many alive. Sensing the untrammelled danger of this hostile empire, Boudica led the Iceni uprising in Norfolk shortly after.

"All things Begin & End in Albion's Ancient Druid Rocky Shore", wrote William Blake, later. He considered all major world religions as a unity, each indicating possibilities for human liberation through the imagination. Little reliable documentation is left that indicates their beliefs, but Roman writers are consistent in noting the druidic observation that the soul is immortal, and migrates between bodies. "You have a tradition, that Man anciently contain'd in his mighty limbs all things in Heaven & Earth: this you received from the Druids." For Blake, the intensive imaginative liberation and natural understanding of the druids preceded and made possible all other liberatory beliefs.

There are some beautiful parts to this landmass, like South Stack or Penmon Beach, and Beaumaris south has its Victorian charms, with cosy boozers and a genteel jetty, boats bobbing in the Menai Strait. A couple bickers, objectives colliding, communicating on different registers. Sip and sigh, frustrations. Outside the George and Dragon, two young latchicos strut, pout and contort robotically as dance music blares out of the Bold Arms opposite, til their mother shouts at them to "come on!"

I cross back over the Menai onto the mainland, soon reaching the university town of Bangor, opposite Beaumaris. Simon smiles and lets me in. He's a friendly linguistics expert who maintains an online encyclopaedia of global languages, Omniglot. In his neatly adorned kitchen, he explains that Welsh place names are descriptive, capturing the features of a location in its name. Consider *Aberystwyth*, the mouth of the River Ystwyth, or *Betws-y-Coed*, the prayer-house in the woods. It's in contrast to English, where place names are often possessive, with *-bys*, *-hams* and *-ings* connoting the farm, people or property of some Anglo-Saxon lord. *Reading*, the people of chieftain Redda; *Woldingham*, village of Wealda's people. Indicating something of its generous culture, there is no possessive "have" in Welsh, only a generous "with".

Simon's enthusiasm is infectious, colourful and hopeful. "It's like music", he says, making syntheses, identifying commonalities, building up from shared premises, in rhythm with one another. "There's no right method", but the goal is common, one.

Now tell me, *dach chi isio panad*? No, OK, try then *ych chi'n moyn dishgled*? I wager even the reading of these words will cause alarm, which is why I am assuaging consternation with a cup of tea. In North Wales, the first statement is correct; in the South, it is gibberish.

"It's like they think we're a county of England", a lady later tells me in Portmeirion, quietly seething. In the last two days I've found the division between north and south unexpected and remarkable, a divide incorporating different dialects, scenery, histories and industries. *Llaeth* or *llefrith*? *Gogs* in the North have one phrase for milk, whilst *hwntws* of the South choose another. The English cannot pronounce either. Wales' duality is more commonly apparent in the North, where many speak Welsh fluently, if not as a first language. Most trace a line at Machynlleth on the mid-west coastline as its internal border, where, south, a different dialect of Welsh may be heard – though most speak English.

Yet throughout the country nationalist feeling is tepid, and in surprising contrast to debates in Scotland, total political independence seems, for now, unthinkable. Out of the modest suburbia of Bangor, following the Menai through flat country into the old garrison town of Caernarfon, it's hard to imagine that this place was once plagued by terrorist explosions and arson attacks against English-owned holiday homes, tax offices, Conservative Party associations and symbols of royal power for a period in the late 1960s. Some attacks continued well into the 1990s. Analogous to the IRA, groups like Meibion Glyndwr and Mudiad Amddiffyn Cymru sought Welsh political independence rooted in a broadly anti-capitalist, socialist struggle. People either joke or talk in hushed tones of the plot to blow up Caernarfon Castle.

The scenery ripens with strange myths. I leave behind Caernarfon and push back into Snowdonia, following a southern trail via the village of Beddgelert, the moody Snowdon massif on the horizon. Snuggled into the mountains, it's a haven of hikers and bikers out gallivanting for the day. Coffee shops here trade in cupcakes, cappuccinos and tall tales of Gelert, the plucky pooch of Prince Llewelyn who was slain by his master after being found next to the bloody carcass of his infant son. The child was still alive, and that blood belonged to a wolf, not long vanquished by loyal Gelert. Llewelyn's guilt is another vernacular (and again, bogus Victorian) staging of a common island fixation with dogs and wolves, some evil, like the black hell-hounds that haunt Essex, Suffolk and Dartmoor, others miraculous, like the Latin-speaking wolf who discovered the decapitated head of Edmund the Martyr near Hunstanton, saying "*hic, hic, hic...*"

I cut through coppices around Beddgelert, then nose down a quiet road back down to the tatty treats of seaside Porthmadog. I break off the coastal road, venturing into the fairy-tale folly of Portmeirion. Imagination unfettered, architect Clough Williams-Ellis brought into existence the toy-town towers, temples and townhouses of his imagination, all in the candied colours of French fancies. It is a little piece of the fantastical landscape gardens of Capability Brown or William Kent, brought into the era of bully beef and formica: inexplicable randomness, carefully measured, indeed fulfilling its promise to amuse and delight.

This odd experiment in dramatic artifice huffed along some-what unsuccessfully as a mid-20th century seaside resort, but is recognisable as the setting of cult 1960s TV thriller, *The Prisoner*. It now trades off its connections with Number 6, the handsome would-be rebel who finds himself trapped in "The Village" and unable to escape, as various different characters in the role of nasty Number 2 attempt to coax out secrets even he's not aware of. "I am not a number, I am a free man!" Some less charitably compare his fate to childhood memories of typically wet summer holidays indoors in North Wales' many holiday homes.

Another myth requires a ruder shift in ambience. Cue late-afternoon monsoon. I am beset by a horizontal rainstorm that deluges the long-deserted coastal road south. Almost every visitor remarks on it. Two thousand years ago, Tacitus wrote not inaccurately of the "extreme moistness of the soil and atmosphere". The climate was associated with sickness, rebellion and melancholia. Dr George Cheyne diagnosed the "English malady" as an affliction of climate-related melancholia, leading to suicide among the aristocracy. "The Moisture of our Air, the Variableness of our Weather... the Rankness and Fertility of our Soil, the Richness and Heaviness of our Food." Rain, ceaseless bloody rain, was driving people mad. Just consider the disappointment and despair of those early humans migrating north and west here, in search of a better life, chasing rumours of a distant Eden... The bloody rain! Fittingly, the island now has dozens of regional terms for it, and countless superstitions.

Refuge! Foul weather is the topic of conversation in the Stag Inn. I've reached Dolgellau ('Dolgecly'), a remote market town composed of gloomy granite, narrow lanes and a deserted market square. The barmaid inside apologises for the weather as she serves up a fresh pint of Brains.

Raining old women and sticks: that's what the Welsh call this kind of cruel, vigorous deluge. It's warm and dry inside, and I peel off my jacket and galoshes and let them drip by the bar. The jukebox specialises in the tragic, and locals partake in an inebriated *eistedfodd* to 'Yesterme, Yesteryou'. The barmaid's a Manc and her acerbic wit is refreshing. "There's nowt round 'ere 'cept the minimum wage." The local meat-packing plant just closed after losing a supermarket contract – today's "British disease" is BSE– and the oil-pipeline work that drew her, gone. She looks longingly into the window beyond my shoulder, neither happy nor sad, as another beside me rabbits on about rugby. "It's not worth goin' up t' Bangor or Aber[ystwyth] fer more money. What yer pay out in travel, it don't add up." Minimum wage just about works.

"Like the sound of crying" is how Peter describes the murmur of the rills, veining the dense woodland south of Dolgellau. Once again, I'm too soaked through to camp. Fortunately there's an old youth hostel nestled in the wilderness nearby, several miles up a winding trail little wider than a footpath. At YHA Kings there is no phone signal, shops, houses, telephone wires or, really, much of anything recognisable at all. Yet this desert of humankind is abundant with life. Even the trunks are crystalline...

Encircled by trees, knotted in verdant bonds, I welcome in the misty morning amidst mysterious woodland. Sun shimmers against rippling brooks, flittering branches make a shadowplay on the forest floor.

In the fusty hostel, passing travellers enthused on their sources of escape. Parents talk about their children, each incontestably unique. Account managers and civil servants muse over wild hunting birds, comparing notes on the shapes of stratocumulus. Lycra-clad cyclists compare their measurements, find life validated by statistics. "Land's End to John O'Groats in twelve days, we were just looking down", one brags over breakfast.

Travellers vent burdensome thoughts, sometimes confessing to strangers what couldn't be confided in friends. Regret for the road not taken. It is no coincidence that the earliest forms of written literature on this damp and lumpy island were collections of personal stories. Consider the *Mabinogion*, the earliest British prose literature in the Welsh tongue, produced in the 12th or 13th centuries out of earlier oral stories, or the *Canterbury Tales*, an English travelogue where the scenery rarely gets a look-in.

Conversations fold into silence, and are then enveloped with sarcastic, cheery resignation. "What *can* you do?" Peter sighed last night in the communal sitting room, boxes of board games stacked around our knees. There's a certain pleasure in making one's peace with a disappointed fate, of mastering one's misery. "*Amor fati*", Nietzsche called it, a love of fate, his final discovery before madness completed its circuit. "Mustn't grumble", they sometimes say round here, foreclosing the possibility of change, political, personal, maybe both.

A kestrel soars above me, brooks babble and branches brush by. I breeze through the Dyfi Valley and out towards Machynlleth. Burrowed inside an old quarry is the Centre for Alternative Technology, a complex established by a cooperative of enthusiastic volunteers to experiment with more sustainable forms of living. It's been here some decades now, and retains a bohemian feel, as gaunt yet wholesome youths stride about in oversized woolly jumpers, and vegan broths and bakes are served in the restaurant. The site is itself reached by a water-powered cliff railway, and after perusing its lavender gardens, I take a stroll with Joel.

He points out a self-built timber-house, insulated with earth, and explains the production of carbon-negative sheds made of lime and straw. One structure is heated by burning grass, wood chips and animal shit. Another exhibit makes the case for how the island might become zero-carbon by 2030. Joel reflects on the global situation. World leaders have successfully fudged international summits intent on restricting ecological destruction, condemning mostly poorer countries to obsolescence as the seas rise and islands disappear.

There is no convincing sign that the powerful petrochemicals industry will either self-restrict its activity to sustainable levels or be forced to by international decree. Yet Joel believes that change remains possible. Money might be made of the island malady: buffeted by harsh winds and stormy seas, it could sustain its energy needs through offshore windfarms and tidal turbines. A programme of state investment could establish them on a comprehensive scale, like that which put running water, gas and telephone lines into people's homes. It wouldn't require any major shift in attitudes. Most are now happy to recycle, use energy-efficient bulbs and turn off unused appliances, behaviours that provoked scoffing two decades ago.

Muse on faded utopianism in the Red Lion. Embeiged on all sides, the Brains beer is sluggish and heavy like the late-afternoon atmosphere, inside and out. It's more refreshing fare than the daddocky dandelion coffee in the Quarry café nearby, a twee joint lined with local art and yoga ads, and gives an opportunity to survey another side of Machynlleth. A dedicated crew of middle-aged men of ruddy complexion stand shoulder to shoulder, holding up the bar. One offends the other, and a furore's afire, voices raised, til a more catatonic member of their number is swifty ejected. "I applied for loads of jobs before I got this one", the weary young barmaid tells me. "Look outside", she says to one of the barflies. "Bet you can't wait to get to Egypt."

Sylvie originally hails from Brighton, but ventured up to Mach to live and work at the CAT. She's kindly letting me couchsurf at her place, and we meet beneath the little town's clock-tower. She tells me that many in the town – though probably not Red Lion clientele – are former CAT volunteers who have since settled, working in its many green trades. Sylvie helps produce solar panels, whilst others are university lecturers or work in eco-thinktanks. I enjoy their idealism, though sense a culture and class divide between the younger, predominantly English reformers, engaged in the laudable business of saving souls, and a sceptical local populace.

We prepare and cook a feast of allotment-grown grub, baba ghanoush, couscous salad and roast marrows, and with her five housemates, talk of hiking, camping and protesting, and encounters with Silver Fox on anti-fracking demos. The night disappears in debates about the future, in an ex-miner's terrace front room, walls papered in OS maps.

Accelerating resource depletion, desertification, climate change, sea pollution and rising tides will jeopardise the ability of the Earth to support the same number of inhabitants it does now a century hence, let alone the ten billion supposed for 2100. There is no convincing sign that these problems will be stalled, let alone reversed. In their faith, these idealists remain persuaded that change is, if not likely, then a worthwhile possibility. Their demands are modest, rooted in the local and national, but even the most moderate demand for ecological sustainability, a shift away from fossil fuels to renewable energies, or the popular ownership of energy resources is, in our current moment, totally revolutionary. And for that reason, so much more worth fighting for.

The road out of Mach strides through slumbering country, a viridian dream, past the ghosts of furnaces and quarries. A little after, Aberystwyth. The town combines a still-lovely Victorian seaside resort with a modern university, and bundles in a ruined castle and old market town. The result is a neatly meshed network of lanes composing its sober centre, where Nonconformist chapels two centuries aged still outnumber pubs. I wander around, imbibing this eccentric place, before venturing back up a steep hill to the Brutalist university complex, where I find Nia in the vast arts centre.

Nia's a friend of my partner, and convenes Aber's annual horror film festival, a shock-and-gore event with a cult following. She's also approaching the end of her PhD research in film adaptations. In Aber, one feels cut away from the cage-like claustrophobia that impresses accelerating productivity as a means of escaping one's existential crisis. A gilded career or property ladder each offer secular images of supernatural ascension. "I'm too lazy and selfish", she jokes, when I quiz her on the usual kinds of teaching and research activities esteemed most virtuous, where success amounts to another kind of failure. "I just really like watching films, and thinking about films."

They'd have her scalp for such sincerity in certain research seminars I've frequented. "Very problematical", someone with a PhD in Lacanian semiotics would put it. It jars with the modern virtue of busyness, of bragging about one's activities and indispensability. I like it.

We amble along the old promenade by Cardigan Bay, past a choir singing the same trenches schlock as Gretna. Wandering back into the town, locating the Ship & Castle. We're with Nia's departmental colleagues now, coffee traded for stronger stuff, talk of cult TV actors and obscure film trivia pinballing around the table. Then it's midnight, and we're wandering back through the starless, silent Victorian terraces, conversations animating these empty streets, colouring this splinter of time.

Twenty-four hours later, and I am lying beside a five thousand year-old chamber, or *cromlech*, out in rural Pembrokeshire. Stars pulse like polka dots, and the soil is wondrously cool. After a day on the road, I've decided on some downtime with half a gram of MDMA and the splendour of the night sky above me, by a Neolithic wonder, singing along to Marvin Gaye as he plays out of my phone.

Having traced the plough and located the pole star, I feel inordinately pleased with my growing awareness of the stars. I grind my upper and lower molars rhythmically, making a mental note not to chew my lower lip clean off, enamoured by these oneiric visions.

I remain like this for several hours, exploring the cosmos with my mind's eye, searching for my place in that remote galaxy, realising there is none. Merely matter, momentarily conscious, beside what Dylan Thomas called the "sloeblack, slow, black, crowblack, fishingboat-bobbing sea".

I've sneaked into Carreg Coetan Arthur, a cromlech on the Pembrokeshire Coast near the Preseli Hills, source of the bluestone brought to Stonehenge and treasured by ancient islanders. Wales' unique rock has been transported across the world, from

the slate of Snowdonia and copper of Anglesey to the gold of Dolgellau, contained in the Queen's wedding ring, to Preseli's magic
dolerite, and the vast coalfields further south.

"Only mystery makes us live", Federico Garcia Lorca once
wrote. Psychotropic stimulants are just one of many subjects
that inspire confused comments among the islanders. Several
strong pints of beer are regarded as well-earned at the end of a
tough day, but an occasional dose of MDMA or acid? There is a
prevailing, ancient need to get out of our heads that alcohol only
incompletely satisfies. Tonight I seek mystery, to explore like a
stranger again the frontier of my own imagination.

How little can we bear mystery, without seeking to dissect and
dissipate its spell, and yet here's a poet's quarry. Mystery's the
marrow of the *Mabinogion*, the aforementioned compilation of
medieval Welsh stories, vividly reanimated by a wise and humor-
ous narrator. There are the "four branches of the Mabinogi",
describing various magical dealings between mortal men and
a subterranean Otherworld, the *Annwn*, to the demi-gods,
dragons, shape-shifters, and the exploits of mythic King Arthur.
Annwn also means "very deep place", an underworld. This subterranean magical realm could only be accessed through mysterious caverns, secluded mounds and remote islets. It was a place of
pleasure and eternal youth.

The landscape is a recurrent feature in the *Mabinogion*, from
Dyfed in the South to Gwynedd in the North. The Western
coastline I passed today, linking the two, was also mysterious,
animated by its gentle eccentric characters and quaint villages.
I left Aber in the morning, heading south, eventually reaching
Aberaeron, a twee harbour spot, bunting crisscrossing the lanes.
In Y Popty, the local baker spoke of the "easy ways", describing
a certain kind of spirit living here. I ventured around the old
harbour, licking homemade honey ice cream and strolling
through the kind of untroubled environs Dylan Thomas brought
to life in *Under Milk Wood*.

Seemingly every town in Wales has some claim to his legacy, but New Quay south has a stronger case than most. Here Thomas stayed as he drafted up that work, "a cliff-perched town on the far edge of Wales". It's a more touristy spot than lovely Aberaeron, but one can still imagine fishermen's spectres along the narrow promenade overlooking Cardigan Bay, like Nogood Boyo or Captain Cat, "observing the salty scene".

Another kind of cat was on the prowl in the modest, isolated town of Cardigan. "Big cat shock sighting in woodland!" was the local scoop. As with other small towns, communal life is not to be found in the tourist traps but at the supermarket, opened with an innocuous line of inquiry. The workers I spoke to live far south in Carmarthenshire though, and seem to have been threatened into work after long unemployment. One cashier held the line up as he told me about the "real history" of the area: the Rioting Rebeccas. His colleague joined him as he narrated a peculiar tale of local rebellion.

Back in the early 1840s, most were farm labourers, and rising taxes and food prices were making even a minimal standard of existence unaffordable. Common and waste land had been enclosed by landowners across southern England since 1500, evicting farmers in many places in favour of cattle and sheep. This enclosure accelerated over the 18th century through various parliamentary acts, and had reached Wales and Scotland by the early 19th century. William Cobbett's *Rural Rides* captures some of these grievances during the 1820s, as a once-familiar countryside became marked by evictions and poverty among farm labourers, a result of low pay, artificially high food prices and rising taxes. Unemployed and dispossessed farmers were forced into workhouses being built across the country. A new series of tollgates were the final straw.

The rebels took their unlikely inspiration from Rebecca, of the book of Genesis. "Let thy seed possess the gate of those that hate them." Transplanted to carnival effect, men dressed as women, blacked out their faces, and went on the rampage, tearing down tollgates, workhouses, and any undefended property of the unpopular gentry. Eventually the government capitulated, the cashier told me, as he scanned through my sustenance, muesli, tortilla wraps and kidney beans. Later I discover that it did not, but the folk memory of the Rioting Rebeccas is one of proud defiance, a victory for the common (wo)man. It cannot be said he was mistaken.

From Cardigan I took a lesser road through old St Dogmaels, a small village with a ruined abbey nestled into a hill. I grabbed chips and the local news at Bowens, then climbed out into the hills of rural Pembrokeshire. Fairies made mischief with my bicycle, the back wheel repeatedly coming loose and falling out as I huffed along these undulating hills, slowing me up no end. It became late, too dark to cycle, but with surrounding fields filled with livestock, camping wasn't feasible. Cars sluggishly steered around me, passenger lights on, OS maps spread out over laps. Others randomly stopped in the narrow lanes, lights on, but no activity inside. What's going on?

"Are you OK there?" I asked one driver, a little nervously. It was approaching midnight, and cycling these unlit roads is dangerous.

"Yes, we're just doing a treasure hunt", said the elderly driver, enthusiastically.

"Good luck!"

I reached the edge of Newport, spotted the sign for this ancient cromlech, and snuck inside its privet-hedged sanctuary. It is secluded and cosy, and after pitching up tent, I rubbed a generous line of powder into my gums, and laid back. What matters it, the truth of myths, when what they construct surpasses wonders of a more natural order?

An Irish-American colonel raises a spyglass to his eye and surveys the craggy bay. Assailed by squall and storm, Fishguard is all-too-far from Bristol, his first destination, or South Carolina, or Wexford, two places he has called home, or France, who dispatched him and this unlikely army of released prisoners to invade the British Isles. A blank shot is fired by British guns overlooking the bay, an attempt at cursory resistance, but they are staffed by disabled ex-militia and little fight is given. The initial lack of resistance by the Welsh and English will be spectacularly misunderstood by the French later. For now, it'll do.

Luckless Colonel Tate lands at Carregwastad Point, a few miles shy of Fishguard. It's a cold wet February night in 1797. It's unlikely that Tate knows of the *Deisi*, a southern Irish people that invaded and settled much of the western Wales coastline, after the Romans evacuated their forts at Cardiff and Caernarfon. Modern history often speaks of continental migrations, but Ireland's had a counter-influence on British culture, especially in early medieval times. Celtic Christianity was the first kind the island knew, and the Irish Ogham script – a series of lined notches, usually on wood or stone – has been found beside Latin across Cornwall, Devon, Wales and southern Scotland.

Posterity forgets Tate's adventure. Opportunity quickly descends into farce. His forces, composed of released, well-armed prisoners, roam the nearby farms, drunk on looted wine. The local militia flee. It's unclear what happens next. Some myths have it that local farmers, most women, run through the rampaging Frenchmen with pitchforks and round up the remainder. Others, that the hungover forces mistake the red bonnets of a mass of local women as British Army uniforms. Either way, their Gallic bender ends days later, surrendering on Fishguard beach to a lethargically assembled band of soldiers. Britain is spent by war, on the verge of bankruptcy, and burning up with revolutionary desire. Had Tate been gifted with a little more strategy, and the island's Victorian empire, a plague on the peoples of India, Africa and China, might not have been.

The last invasion of this island is perhaps also its most ludicrous. Those who are not too drunk to walk are marched to

Haverfordwest and Pembroke where, in a final twist, two local women enchanted by their new *amants* help thirty to escape. They steal the local lord's yacht and sail back to France.

Claimed by most, property of none, Pembrokeshire's an apt place to consider ownership and belonging. Tate was an American whose Irish family, hailing from Wexford, were killed by pro-British American Indians in the War of Independence. He fervently believed in Irish republicanism and revolutionary democracy. The French didn't simply plan to squash a rival naval power, but planned to invade via Ireland, crossing through the North, where wage-slaved workers were expected to join them in the common cause of *liberté, égalité, fraternité*. Now, as I drift from this Neolithic burial chamber into the pretty Pembrokeshire countryside, locals tell me, half-jokingly, that this place is called "Little England". Few would openly admit to understanding Welsh here. Further down the coast at Milford Haven, much of the UK's energy is sourced, in the form of liquefied gas. The country's energy comes not from local winds or coal, but Qatari oil.

Twee Newport. Retired women beneath pastel-coloured cottages gossip about their neighbours, sipping organic lattes. In a convenience store I hear about St Baynach, a deranged mystic who claimed to commune with angels nearby. In Fishguard to the south, now a pleasant town defined by that same sweeping bay, locals talk gruffly of their histories. At grubby Goodwick, adjacent, one can take a ferry over to Wexford, passing Carreg-wastad Point.

Rain's hitting hard, and my back wheel continues to slide out of the frame. Twice I tumble into the grassy verge along the undulating road to St Davids. The coastline is teal-grey and surly, the road peopled with modest farmsteads. The English malady's paining me, and last night's sleepless revelry has broken me in two.

St Davids is the island's smallest city, and comes across as a touristy village dominated by a large bone-white gothic cathedral, attracting most visitors, surrounded by parkland and the nearby River Alun. Inside, an elderly volunteer explains the faded ochre outline of a male figure, adorning a ribbed pillar holding up a stratospheric vault. Many of these were forcibly erased in a fit of iconoclasm by Puritan soldiers during the Civil War, and St Davids has been attacked many times throughout its history, by Vikings, thieves, earthquakes, ambitious bishops and bad Georgian restoration work. "It was a mistake", he says, melancholically, of the iconoclasm. Local worshippers depended on images to understand biblical stories, narrated in foreign tongues of Latin, then English, that they couldn't understand.

Villages composed of sober terraces, post offices and pubs define the route east, through Solva and Roch, reaching the old market town of Haverfordwest. Paint peels from townhouses tottering over narrow lanes, a warren of discount stores. In the Fishguard Arms, where a barmaid has "mum" tattooed mnemon-ically on her forehand, Jeff speaks proudly of his prince's prof-ligacy, of Charles Windsor's girlfriends. "Our princes have always had flings", he smiles, raising a beer to his bearded mush, before complaining of "interbreeding" in the English aristocracy.

Forget glucose gels and protein soups: there is no better performance-enhancing drug than a pint or two of warm, hoppy beer. The roads are traffic-filled and a little treacherous now, as I pedal at speed past the fiery chimneys of Milford Haven, past yacht showrooms and McDonald's drive-thrus. A particu-larly English ugliness is interrupted by lovely Pembroke, an old county town still caught in the shadow of its castle. Girls in glittering frocks rock tipsily outside the George Arms as a hen party limo awaits, Europop blaring. The ruins of churchyards are traded for an abandoned-looking military base further south, where the loneliest burger kiosk awaits nobody. Rain and wind batter me down, faced inward, hunkered in waterproofs, scarcely making out the road ahead, praying the back wheel will stay in place. It's now dark, but there is no time or place to rest. At last, I reach Tenby.

Declan's instructions are clear, accurate and concise. It's a flavour of the man. I buzz in at the foot of a modern apartment block, snuggled between a string of chippies, candy-rock outlets and a dozen not-dissimilar drinking dens, each with some claim to Dylan Thomas. Tenby's a magnificent seaside resort, encased in castle walls and golden beaches, its tightly webbed lanes woven around a quaint market square, and back out to chintzy promenades and Victorian boarding houses. Declan welcomes me in.

I got in contact with Declan through the Couchsurfing website, a free online community where one can find sympathetic and free places to stay, or host other such travellers. Cycling ten hours in the rain makes everything wet, and one cannot dry out in a tent, particularly one held together with sticky tape. Declan and his partner Dorie hail from Ireland, and work as engineers in the oil refineries of Milford Haven. It's "a dump", they laugh, though well-paid work, and a major employer in the area.

Conversation turns to travelling America, and speaking to God through a payphone at Burning Man festival. Declan's friend Matt, joining us, wonders about utopias. "What do you think of Communism?" Should individual freedoms outweigh the wellbeing of the collective? Is an island as old as this capable of sustaining new experiments in people power? When judged from our own myopic moment, history is always surprising, and few make less convincing clairvoyants than historians.

"That's where you're heading", Declan says, gesturing at the all-too-distant headland. I'd been thinking it was somewhere in Somerset or Devon, but on the other side of Carmarthen Bay is the Gower Peninsula. It's some distance.

I reflect on this image over the course of this long, exhausting day, up cliff-hewn hills and through winding thickets, the epitome of unreachability. But it's hard to feel miserable when surrounded by beautiful things, from the sunbathers and seaside snooze of nearby Saundersfoot, or zigzagging up the dingles and denes off Amworth Beach to the hay-bale villages of Marros, Pendine and Laugharne. One loses count of the butterflies, flecks of azure and tangerine, beside war memorials festooned in lichen and moss, the birds and breeze in melodious chorus. Soon spent by these hills, I pause for carbohydration in the village of St Clears.

"I'm shackled here", says Neil, as he generously apportions chips into paper bags and passes them out to customers. He's only half-joking. There's a queue extending far outside his little shop, but he takes pleasure in languorously conversing with his regulars. "If I left for three months, I'd lose all my business", he says, struggling to persuade himself of an epic exploit around the world he's imagined for some time. He'd tell himself it was worth it, were he ever to chance it, but the shore's a safer prospect. Outside, an ancient lady pushes a modern Methusaleh in a wheelchair. "Best of British luck!" she shouts.

Indeed! It's a cheery day, no rain for a change, and Neil's chips must have some narcotic secret ingredient, as I begin racing up hills and through traffic without complaint. Even the splattered mammals and birds that co-populate the hard shoulder to Carmarthen acquire an ebullient aspect. This castle town is like Pembroke and Caernarfon before it, still dominated by English fortresses that overshadow small and pleasant market towns. The accent's changing, now harsher and stronger in its intonations, and memories of Welsh-speakers are starting to fade.

In Nott Square, a young man rants to his bemused relations. "I did standard infantry, rubbish!" Another fella, sharp-jawed and heavily tattooed, attempts to distil the unusually warm and friendly essence of the place. "Carmarthen is like Spain... Swansea, people are in your face. Here there's a niceness about it, it's slower." But he can't afford its rents, and dwells in the ex-industrial towns further south, where I head next.

The road skitters south through Kidwelly, by the forests of Pembrey, and out to Burry Port. The terrain is mostly flat, scaped with quiet farmsteads interspersed occasionally with a warehouse or a cluster of two-storey terraces. I've no fixed destination in mind, with the loosest of plans to camp on a beach somewhere along the Gower Peninsula, til a last-minute Couchsurfing shout-out bears fruit, and Sarah texts me with a bed in Swansea.

Destination changed, I thread through Llanelli, past a vast Tescopolis, a Traveller caravan-site and a rust-horizon of derelict industries. On the Isle of Machynys, the once-colossal South Wales Foundry and St David's Coal Pit have been totally erased, replaced with a complex of aspirational housing overlooking the tranquil Gower estuary. Blackberries grow freely. I drink their sour juice and compare these two states of Wales, of the affluent old castle tourist towns like Carmarthen, St Davids and to an extent Cardiff later, and the rustscapes of Llanelli, Llangefni, Milford Haven and the towns of the Valleys and Newport later. The latter have had far less money invested into "regeneration" than even the Northern towns. Little wonder some clamour for self-government.

Swansea reiterates the rule, corticed in retail parks and cramped terraced housing. Yet it is animated by something else, a source of income that has picked up Coventry, Nottingham, Sheffield and Dundee: students, and lots of them. Sarah's a Psychology student here, and invites me into a boozy house-party. I put away my gear and join the crowd in the kitchen.

There are students here of every subject, from zoology and medicinal neurochemistry to the psychiatry of psychopaths. Their perspectives are fascinating, often considering human life as if they were entirely separate from it. Some work in call centres to supplement their inadequate maintenance loans. Others sell drugs, and I encounter a liberal consensus on substance use. One's selling morphine prescribed to her grandmother, who insists in a kind of Blitz-spirit asceticism that she doesn't need painkillers. Several work in the vast Amazon warehouse on the edge of town, minimum waged, "you're watched all the time".

Another's just picked up a part-time job traipsing South London streets, door-to-door, recording attitudes to the Metropolitan Police. She's not heard of Mark Duggan, but soon will.

A group of young men juggle poi in a cramped backyard outside, entranced with narcotic zeal in the glowing, gliding colours. Everyone has some intriguing case to make. One young man fills my ear with local industrial history. Another on Dylan Thomas. One insists on the genetic nature of mental illness, til Sarah corrects him, arguing that this would rule out the validity of rehabilitation and therapy. Against the reductive blather of nature *or* nurture, some synthesis is required. She speaks passionately and intelligently, they all do, even if we're now all drinking deep from a bowl of paint-stripping grog passed around, concocted by some perverse mixologist.

I call it a night around two, leaving behind this Swansea symposium. A young man hacks loudly in the backyard, then vomits. "I'm OK", he groans, unconvincingly.

I'm back on the promenade, resting my elbows on a black filigree balustrade, surveying the salty scene. This time it's England in my eye-line, obscured in parts by the rocks around the Mumbles, a jaunty little village beside Swansea. A golden band of sandy beaches can be traced along the curving line of Swansea Bay, populated with dogs and frolicking children, giggles reverberating. To my left, the "ugly lovely town" Thomas remembers of his birthplace, little recognisable now. Swansea's docks and smelting works have disappeared, and the seafront is now lined with office high-rises and chain hotels.

South Wales might've remained like the rival North, were it not for the iron ore, coal and minerals discovered here in vast quantities. Industry was eased by the sea, with Swansea and Newport rapidly expanding into trading ports. Some bastard form of this legacy remains, like the gargantuan Amazon distribution centre outside Swansea, where mail lorries thunder out onto the M4 at heartbeat pace. Melancholy words adorn the concrete balusters of busy flyovers, "Smoke your life away", "I'm sick of this shit", paeans to no one about nobody. I thrust inland, through the ex-industrial towns of Skewen and Neath.

The road steeps and then drops, each valley ringed with sharp smooth hills like an ice-cube tray. I climb up through the villages of Tonna and Resolven, hillside terraces that hang over the busy highway to Merthyr Tydfil. The Resolven Miner's Welfare Club, built and maintained directly through the wages of miners, now stands derelict, half-heartedly barricaded with scrap timber. Little seems to be open. Chinese-and-English takeaways, perhaps, indicating a shared palate with the Midlands and North, from where many migrated during the early 19th century to work the South Wales coalfield. Few shops otherwise, and no one around, making it impossible to find out just what's happened here, or even where I even am. Blackberries grow freely along the Neath Canal, another industrial legacy seemingly abandoned, and the atmosphere is ghostly.

Iron became coal, coal became dole. The last Welsh deep-pit mine in Hirwaun closed in 2008. The isolated locations of Valleys towns like Hirwaun, Merthyr, Tredegar or Ebbw Vale makes them ill-suited for the call centres, distribution warehouses, retail parks or supermarkets that now constitute employment in much of the Midlands, North or Scottish cities. Hirwaun's pebbledash terraces are cramped and stunted, pointedly under-proportioned. Like Heath Town or the Arbor, or the interwar red-brick suburban estates, cloned and repeated on the outskirts of every major English town, they have class disempowerment built into them, proportioned into the smallness of the windows, into the feature of a cellar over a loft. There's a Tesco garage open – at last, something! – and a pub, the Glencynan, which is friendly enough, and I hear a different kind of accent to Tenby or even Swansea, far more oscillating in its intonation, an uplifting singsong.

After climbing out of a steep valley and over a sharp ridge, I plunge down into another, nestling Merthyr. It was once the largest city in Wales, with the largest ironworks in the world, at the heart of Britain's industrial revolution. Now it has the honour of being the most difficult place to find work in the entire UK, plagued by high adult-mortality rates and health problems. Road signs warn scrap thieves not to bother.

The old miners' hall has been destroyed by fire and abandoned, and the town is a mess of residual dereliction. I cross the River Taff into a small town centre, where everything seems permanently shuttered. A nominal attempt at regeneration has been tried, pulling down some old buildings and pedestrianising one or two streets, but no social or economic Plan B has been prepared beyond this cursory face-lift.

A dazed-looking man stumbles out of a chair at the deserted bus station. He is disarrayed by his drink, and his body wobbles as he struggles to keep his beer can steady. A retired couple drifts ahead, the first sober-looking people I've encountered in some hours. "The mines are gone, jobs. It's quiet here. Have a good time", the man murmurs morosely. His wife stares silently with sharp disapproval, as if I'd gatecrashed a funeral.

A Britpop cover band blares from inside the Wyndham Arms, while outside a young man drunkenly argues with his girlfriend, who storms off. I ride on, past an impressive Carnegie library and town hall, and beside that, a large Wetherspoon's pub called the Dic Penderyn. Inside, pot-bellied gents in cheque shirts and denim put the world to rights. Topic of discussion is a recent child-kidnapping. "We haven't heard the full story", announces one with confidence. Silence. The fruitie jingles behind him.

Something's indeed gone missing. The Red Flag of the organised working class was first raised not in Paris or St Petersburg, but in this Welsh valley town. Spring, May 1831. Miners and iron-workers took to the streets, forced by desperation into an uprising against low pay. They were serious in their challenge to the gentry and factory-owners, burning down debtors' courts and giving out repossessed goods to the poor. Their flag was dyed in blood, and their symbol was the loaf of bread, representing what they'd been denied. Potential allies were persuaded not to join them. Divided, uncertain, though initially putting up a good fight, they were later overrun by Scottish and English soldiers. Some were imprisoned, others were sent to Australia. One was scapegoated and murdered by the authorities, young Dic Penderyn, falsely accused of stabbing a soldier.

The Valleys remained politically hot. Eight years later there was another uprising in Newport, this time led by a broad alliance of Chartists. It was again violently crushed and dispersed. Early syndicalist and Labour movements fomented here, with Merthyr returning the Labour Party's first MP, Glasgow's Keir Hardie. But that heat and anger seem to have been turned inwards, spent. Smug Lord Kinnock, a millionaire windbag elected by a Valleys town, its dreary cipher, still blaming Arthur Scargill for the defeat of the miners.

"Just the other valley", Bethan texts me. But after the last couple of ultra-steep climbs out of each valley basin, Aberdare feels unreachable. In "WKD'S Best Kebab Shop (2010)", I fuel up on quasi-thawed fries as the Turkish owner calls me brother and damns the town with faint praise. Fool I am, I decide to ignore intuition and check if my phone's GPS knows another route over the steep ridge. It does, and it is apparently some miles shorter too. Great, right? Perhaps, were it not in fact a vertical trail of broken rock scarp, still marked as an unclassified road, which is too dangerous to walk along, let alone cycle. I realise my mistake only after I'm halfway up out of Heolgerigg, and out of pride push on, pursuing this madcap route over and down its lonesome precipice.

Just about alive, the road becomes even enough to cycle on again, and I nose down into the cramped miners' terraces of Abernant and into Aberdare. Bethan smiles patiently as she lets

me in. I'm quite late, and her dad, a local teacher, laughs sympathetically as he recalls which road I've taken, and shares memories of it breaking his motorbike.

His father was a miner, and he's managed to trace ancestral
stories of Gloucester tailors and Pembrokeshire farmers, who
came to the Valleys in its booming industrial heyday. Bethan
serves us some pie, and she tells me about the socialist history
of the Valleys, and the working men's "halls" built out of miners'
contributions, like that in Resolven. They were places of learning
and leisure. Today one or two survive as boozers, but most have
been razed.

Bethan believes that a particular kind of left-wing Labour
politics remains alive here, in contrast to the "right-wing Labour"
east of Offa's Dyke. They reflect on the Valleys' in-betweenness
now, the cooperative beliefs and communal modes of mining,
Methodism and a general social fixity now loosened, undone.
People simply had to rely on each other for survival, be it in the
pit or in maintaining and caring for a large family with very little
money. In this way, forms of solidarity and cooperation were
coded into the architecture of people's lives, just as today one
finds the opposite coding.

Men came from across Wales and western England to the
Valleys. They worked the earth, going into it, under it, inside its
hot, cramped bowels. This was Annwn, the underworld, a place of
corpses, bones and shit, a place of darkness, death and the past.
One had to come through death and the past to reach Annwn,
that realm of youthfulness and flourishing. These men came here,
brought their families, and crawled into the earth, mining iron,
working the iron, mining coal. These were hard, dangerous jobs,
where employers were happy to pay starvation wages and bank
the proceeds elsewhere. But they were jobs that gave confidence,
a wage and an opportunity to prove a masculine pride and partake
in an intergenerational masculine solidarity, following dad and
granddad into the pits. It's worth noting that most miners' sons

recall how their fathers had urged them *not* to follow them, despite that allure. With the exception of the Rebecca Riots, communities of organised miners led all the major uprisings here, from the Merthyr Uprising and the Newport Chartists to the growth of the British Labour Party. The mines have gone; so too a sense of pride, community and solidarity, a shared way of life.

Mark cranks back on the rear wheel of a battered, spattered, beloved Raleigh Pioneer. "The cones..." he begins, but recognises my confusion. "Don't worry, it's all done." He wipes his oily fingers on a rag inside the breast pocket of his blue overalls. "How much do I..." "Nothing, don't worry", he replies curtly, with a smile. "But, tell me. Why do you want to go there?"

The antipathy that exists between neighbouring settlements always delights me. In Aberdare, a cheerful ex-mining town that bounces with throngs of young and old, the mere prospect of travelling to Blackwood is just plain stupid. Outside Dare Valley Bikes, I eye the passing bustle, and let Mark get on with keeping the town on two wheels. Aberdare's got a worthy musical heritage, embodied in Caradog, a blacksmith who led a 460-strong male choir to international success, introducing a characteristically "Welsh" choral music to the rest of Britain. But it's a spikier modern story I'm seeking, and so against Mark's strongest recommendations, I pedal out through Mountain Ash and Ystrad Mynach, then down to another ex-mining town.

> Life lies a slow suicide
> Orthodox dreams and symbolic myths
> From feudal serf to spender
> This wonderful world of purchase power.

Naked, perhaps the sebum-sturm angst and clunky wording jar, but it is the delivery of those words by the Manic Street Preachers that makes them vivid. The four band members would meet in the Dorothy café, now a Halifax bank, and plot their revenge on the asinine and anodyne of mainstream pop. Blackwood's high street heaves, not as slumped as other valley towns. Traffic slugs past a lengthy parade of shops, down to a car-glugged supermarket and retail park on the edge of town.

Not far from here is Tredegar, where the real founder of the NHS, Nye Bevan, grew up. It was the closest point that this island has come to democratic socialism – not close at all, granted – and its apogee has disappeared into the horizon behind it. Bevan went down into the pits aged thirteen, and attributed his political education to the library of Tredegar Workmen's Institute. Great thanks should be conferred on that building, but fittingly for these parts, the building was closed in 1982 and later demolished to build a car-park.

Bevan was a passionate believer in a specifically British socialism, where class and wealth inequality would be eliminated like some archaic, medieval custom. He called for an end to the austerity that had crippled wages and living standards across the 30s. "We have been the dreamers, we have been the sufferers, now we are the builders." And despite war-damaged infrastructure, scarcity and national debt, and with an undereducated populace weaned on a starvation dole, people like Bevan did build a more equal and fair country. There was much more to be done by 1960, when he died, but over fifty years on, it feels that this project has been thwarted and in places reversed. The working class confidence that could state with conviction "This is my truth, tell me yours" has disappeared, and the constituency Bevan appealed to no seems longer sure of itself.

I pop into Blackwood's Miners Institute, restored after dereliction in the 1990s. "There was nothing after the mines", a local woman tells me. But her conversation zones in on the present. "I'm worried. There's a generation of young people, some around thirty, who have never had a job in their life. And what'll happen when they get older, and these people retire then? There'll be no one to do the jobs, cos they won't have the skills." She thinks the retirement age should be lowered to give young people a chance, who round here are experiencing a gen-eration-deep underemployment in service-sector jobs. Yet she's highly sceptical of attempts to "incentivise" employers to set up shop and employ local people either, citing a raft of failed local initiatives. What, then? She pauses and gazes out through the door behind me, where a large Asda is visible on the other side of the road.

I think of the lives wasted, wasting away, then of the decades – no, centuries – of popular struggle across Wales, of Owain Glyndwr, the rioting Rebeccas, the Merthyr Rising, the miners who built these institutes and formed the backbone of the Labour movement, that anger and despair palpable in places here, given the form of a pop song by the Manics. What they shared was a refusal to tolerate poverty and injustice. They had no thought of "winning", something few could even recognise, let alone hope for, but shared a refusal to tolerate, a commitment to resist. In those moments they were free, no longer dominated by fear, resentment and despair, but energised, taking things into their own hands, acting as if transformation were possible, as if an underlying foundation of equality, dignity and freedom is what every man and woman should be entitled to.

Drizzle. Facing south, I follow a busy road down into Caer-philly, another town overpowered by a vast medieval garrison. Beneath the battlements, Celwyn asks me to take his photo beside his bike. Like others, he's surprised I'm surveying the Valleys and Blackwood, his hometown. He does not have the luxury of being a visitor. The dearth of jobs has sent him to Leicester. He points me to a route along the River Taff, along an old railway line through hamlets, fields and then parkland, into the salubrious suburbs of north Cardiff.

Something's astir. Black military helicopters circle above. Bushes rustle with strange activity. Suddenly, a six-strong squad of armoured cops approach me. One raises an arm into the air.

"I'm sorry sir, you'll have to go back that way", he says, politely, finger pointing to a makeshift footpath. Fair enough.

Cardiff's on a security lockdown for an international summit. Platoons of English police prowl round like an occupying army. Whole streets and roads are divided by thick metal security gates and fences. A paranoiac air hovers over an otherwise pleasant-looking, modern city. I amble round, past its large castle that has successively protected invading Romans, Normans and Englishmen. Around St David's mall, a colostomy-bag construct of a common kind inflicted on most British towns as some form of collective punishment. Toward the old docks, a new BBC building occupies itself with pride, whilst the golden façade of the Millennium Centre murmurs, a brave and ambitious structure still interested in story-telling. The Welsh Assembly stands close, more modest in its aspirations, reflecting the region's lack of certainty about its desire for self-government. The district feels modern, clean, with only the imposing red-brick gothic of the Victorian Pierhead building standing among these glassy gewgaws like a disapproving uncle. The bland, ugly, modern apartment block blooms freely here.

I sup in Kitty Flynn's, where a local girl tells me about Cardiff's large homeless population, and how family binds you back to where you didn't want to be. Her sense of being tested, that life itself is a bitter test, or of being shipwrecked yet still docked, is akin to Kevin's in Wick, and there are countless others who will tell this tale. Back over to the aspirational suburban terraces of Roath Park, searching for an address given by text. I spit into my hand to slick back my now-overgrown, dirty hair and straighten out my shirt, as I hear a dog barking enthusiastically inside the hall of a towering townhouse. A male voice curses it, then the same dog barks again, twice as loud.

Ropo breaks free at last, and attempts to engage me in the fox-trot. I've got two left feet, so he gives in quickly, and Sebo laughs, and invites me in. I'm couchsurfing with this young Chilean photographer and his partner Hanni, a university researcher. We cook together and chat.

"I got used to it and started to like it", Sebo tells us, recalling a long summer spent living in the mountains of Chile. "I was just on my own." Indeed he was, and a strange acceptance of fate, amor fati perhaps, brought him back into the valleys after months living off hunted rabbits, wearing no clothes and not seeing any other soul. Something ineluctable. Because, as he points out later, on a topic much removed from this, but connected, as all things are, such inexplicable journeys and events only make sense after their occurrence.

Garagelands, Victorian townhouse bedsits, tatty phone-card kiosks, tropical colours of graffiti and pan-Asian takeaways, blueprint hotel high-rises and an English police presence outnumbering the populace. Cardiff's little like anywhere else in Wales I've experienced. It is openly multicultural and multiracial. Pubs are few. It is busy and bustles freely.

For the last few days the back brake has rubbed continuously against the wheel, hindering progress. My attempts at blindly tweaking and adjusting things are failing. After a quick fix at Punk Bikes, I hope for the best and ride back into the centre from east to west, by the affluent parkland and terraces around the Millennium Stadium, a UFO tidewracked on the Taff. Through the Victorian terraces of Canton and Fairwater west, then out along a quieter country lane to St Fagans, just outside Cardiff.

There's a vast open-air museum here that commemorates Welsh folk life through dozens of reconstructed buildings from the last millennium, from Tudor villas and Italian gardens to 17th century farmhouses and early 20th century post offices. One can buy bara brith 1910-style from a working bakery, snoop around convenience stories, or straggle around the 12th century church of St Teilo, where gospel stories are explained not in prayer-book digits or Latin epithets but through huge ochre illustrations, emotionally inexpressive yet evocative, like the characters of Robert Crumb.

Even the Oakdale Workmen's Institute has been pulled down and rebuilt in the plain air here, with its modest sober library and dark oak-panelled meeting room. It's a far more temperate leisure setting than the boozy working men's clubs of the Midlands and the North. They were largely for men only, and the CIU didn't extend full membership nationally to women until 2007. Meticulously preserved and rebuilt, brick by brick, from its depressed Valley town where it would have been bulldozed, a supermarket or car-park built over it perhaps, there's a sadness in seeing it here like this. Working class culture, solidarity and learning as a historical exhibit. One wonders what of the early 21st century they'll rebuild here to mark our culture. Perhaps the supermarket or the fast-food drive-thru, or the digital architecture of a social identity through a smartphone. Collectivity and solidarity still there in much diminished form, the living room the locus of leisure and pleasure, people more free to be themselves, alone.

I'm in no rush today, with no desire to leave the city just yet. I ride back into Cardiff, exploring record shops, comparing curried pastries (Pooja's: best on the island), and drinking beer and hoovering up gossip in Roath Wetherspoon's. On a whim, I trace an old friend on Facebook and send him a message. Last news was he was living here. He messages me back a few hours later, promising an address. I drift from one pub to another, reading, writing, thinking, waiting for news.

I find him in the Andrew Buchan's at last, looking unusually tanned, smart, even well fed. His name is Jimmy, and he remains impossible to get hold of, unreliable yet affectionate and generous in his apologies. We're a world away from London's pub rock circuit, Deptford, Mare Street... Jim could never hold anything down except a beat, as we played in quiet boozers like this, walls asserting fealty to the classic rock greats. Though we joked about everything, some had hopes of making it. Jimmy was a talented guitarist and singer, and he still plays up here in a band. He introduces me to another musician, who now produces jingles and news items for a business TV channel.

After getting himself clean, Jimmy got a job at the council. "I wanna keep this one", he smiles. He looks back on those London days with ambivalence. He recalls working with one major drug-dependent musician, producing great songs, getting nicked, and the itch, "it just messes you up for days, you haven't got any life". Back to his flat in Roath, a popular student area, conversation continues over 1960s pop LPs. "I don't read the news anymore, it's too depressing", he says, sweeping away politics talk. Instead, he lends my journey a more disquieting thought. "We can't just say it's all bad, man, we have to think about what could happen."

Dawn. The sky hangs heavy over this steely, security-shocked city. A few more clouds and black helicopters and the whole cumulus'll come crashing down.

Cardiff jerks to life, and Jimmy dashes out to work. My back wheel is still misaligned, and my amateur repairs are making things worse. I head back out to Punk Bikes for a second try. With a cable tugged and a brake pad adjusted, this rickety, rusty but lovely old thing makes it back on the road without the previous scrapes and groans. "Thank you, friend", I whisper to it, patting the handlebars, before swerving out the way of a stationary bus.

I follow the mid-morning traffic east along Newport Road. The scapes become increasingly dispirited. Daubed on timber barricading a recently closed college, "too many empty buildings too many sleeping rough". Shrubby terraces hidden in suburbia, golden arches, retail wastelands. I think of Jimmy's words, of that persistence in dreaming.

This is a war for room, to breathe and move. Today's contestants are teetering supermarket juggernauts, transit vans, and the estate cars of Germany and Japan, driven by dozing local cabbies dipping their toes in the bus lane. I am Don Quixote among the Huns. Even the pedestrians don't dare cross the roads. It's clear whose coming last today, the fool on the pushbike refusing to ride pavements. I'm not into breaking pedestrians' bones or those of their pets, and adherence to an unwritten fantasy of road decorum has me wallying around three-lane roundabouts with the majesty of a mayfly. This A48 is a hectic helter-skelter of speedy driving, and I come on and off it, catching my breath before rejoining the maelstrom towards Newport.

There's a quieter route parallel, through Neighbourhood Watch terrain. Desiring to remain alive to see Bristol, I chance it. "Do you want THIS?" leers one poster in Old St Mellons, the devil in question being new housing. A cycle lane cuts by derelict warehouses and gas reservoirs, the pathway strewn with cracked sinks and cisterns, countless broken things.

At the other end is Newport, an ex-industrial city that boomed through iron and coal, its docks trading with the rest of the world. Far more than its neighbours the city's industries and sense of self have collapsed, and it is the most deprived and abandoned-looking place I've encountered. Past the struggling estates of Duffryn, the cycle lane oddly detours right around the centre, ominously. I rejoin the road in, past tracts of derelict warehouses next to cramped and sooty terraces. Buddleia bursts out of rusty-padlocked factories. Most city councils would've turned this into parkland, but not here. Further in, past a glut of retail parks where even the poundshops look nervous. I nose up the main shopping drag, past pensioners and strung-out young men, cursing and laughing. There's some beautiful structures here, like the derelict Kings Hotel, or the ambitious civic centre, but its red-brick parades are mostly long-languished as to-lets or discount offies.

I stand by the equally derelict Westgate Hotel, where on a wet

November night in 1839 around five thousand Chartist sympathisers gathered from across the Valleys, and marched into town
to demand the democratic right to vote. The British Army, locked
inside, fired down at them, killing twenty and injuring many
more. I want to stop and talk to people, discover what exactly
wounded this city, but a man right by me is stopped and frisked
for some time by a large group of cops. People hurry away.

I cross over the Usk, where the scene is bleaker. Junkies totter
on crutches, little older than me. Two young men swear and go
to chase me, for simply looking too long, too agog, at the shoes
that hang from telephone wire above a barbershop, one of the
few units open on a shabby parade. I'd feel pissed off and jaded
too were I abandoned here, as many are. I pass "hotels" on these
terraces, where single mums, groups of working-age men from
Afghanistan and the Levant, a Roma family, and a trauma-
tised-looking older West African man stand outside, gazing emp-
tily at the road. There is a high number of refugees and asylum
seekers here. Sending them to a city blighted by unemployment,
poverty and heavy drug use seems particularly cruel, without
money, shelter, opportunity to work or train, or do anything
really at all.

I pass another pile of fly-tipped waste on my way out. "They
just don't care", says a passing cyclist, gesturing at a broken TV
set. And I feel more distant from my fellow islanders than I have
for some time.

As Patrick Keiller writes, the "United Kingdom is a rich country in which live a large number of poor people". Newport is
one concentration, amongst many. Its sense of abandonment
and uncertainty isn't unique to this part of Wales – I've seen it
everywhere. But I think of Scotland and Jimmy's exhortation.
This bleakness and defeat feel so overwhelming and complex
that many capitulate to cynicism and indifference, repeating lies
they've read that, under even the mildest questioning, they come
to abandon as contradictory. But what could happen? People

have a social right to adequate housing, education and employment, and a liveable income, and a right to forms of support too, when things go wrong. This right includes a life free from preventable sources of anxiety. A right to live, and live well. But it seems this right has been forgotten, and time's movement stalled for the struggle of the day-to-day. I wonder what might restart it.

The scenery transforms again, with characteristically British pace and incongruity. Berries grow in hedges beside quaint cottages. Narrow lanes peter through wide expanses of wheat and cattle, punctuated by the sedate villages of Redwick and Summerleaze, and I pull over in Magor, where a noticeboard advertises watercolour classes and cricket clubs. Nearby flows the Wye, these pretty pastoral vistas once seen by Reverend William Gilpin, so good he coined them the name "picturesque", his roving eye "kept constantly in an agreeable suspense", a counsel that remains valid. "We travel for various purposes", writes Gilpin, "to explore the culture of soils, to view the curiosities of art, to survey the beauties of nature, and to learn the manners of men, their different politics and modes of life".

I cross the old Severn Bridge. Two cops interview me suspiciously halfway along, sceptical of the idea that I might just want to stop, suspended by the not so agreeable view. Then over, into England.

CHAPTER 10

Cunning Folk

"It's just intuition" – Jason, with the headless lady.

Dawn, and light's gilding the edges of heavy grey curtains. A ray escapes through a central parting, enrapturing the dust mites and specks in a weightless whirligig. I wriggle my toes and rub rheum from my eyes, and scan the unfamiliar room.

After crossing the Severn yesterday afternoon, I joined forces with a Romany Traveller riding a horse and trap at Aust, and we gently rode together for some time south in serene silence, attempts at conversation hamstrung by his quite possibly feigned deafness. The araf slow road-signs and rugby posts became a distant memory, and after losing track of my route, I found myself in Filton, on the northern outskirts of the Bristol conurbation. Getting lost again, I eventually found myself approaching the centre, passing the grand Georgian townhouses, crescents and squares of the city's slavers in Clifton. A sense of animation and affluence continues around the university area. After stopping for some frozen soy yoghurt in a hip café, surrounded by vintage clothes stores and bijou boutiques, I locked away the bicycle and strolled around a while.

I sat by the College Green, facing the modest cathedral and groups of young people lolling around, picking at the grass, a light-hearted ambience. And aside from a frequency of colour to the buildings, a light-golden Bath stone quarried locally, there was something else I began to feel about Bristol too, that seemed if not unique, then significant. It was the lack of a preoccupied air of doom like that I'd encountered in struggling towns, the toxic-stress atmosphere of most urban settlements in fact that I'd passed through.

Art galleries, hipster bars and a dockside facelift haven't been imposed on the city from outside like a benefits sanction or TV diet-intervention, like other ex-port cities. Bristol doesn't need cynical schemes to "create" wealth by redistributing public assets into private hands. No, for even in Easton, or Stapleton nearby, or St Pauls and Stokes Croft, Bristol's working class communities, there's a kind of confident, civic animation that reflects an unfamiliarity with terminal decline.

And so after circling this cosmopolitan city, I looked up a man named Jackson, who'd offered me a place to stay in Easton. We stayed up late, debating global politics with cups of herbal tea in our hands, as his friends played records. His flatmate Joe told us about studying international relations, a course funded through part-time care work. Jackson's a music teacher, and has also had first-hand experience of Newport, when a youth music workshop was interrupted after warnings his car's satnav was about to be nicked. He'd invited two friends over to arrange the logistics of a club night. Instead politics distracted them, and over the course of the evening, a shared outlook and age-range interlinked ideas into a common disaffection.

"There's this peculiar mix of nowhereness that politics in this country is heading towards", Nathan said, in broad brizzle, an accent that oozes and drawls, unlike nearby South Welsh intonation. It's a grey and uncertain moment, an in-betweenness I keep encountering, where contempt for the major political parties is matched by a suspicion of political ideas themselves. Whatever electoral success a new wave of nationalist or left-liberal parties accrue, it may not be enough for young frustrated people like these, stuck in dead-end service or care jobs, too educated and informed to tolerate hypocrisy and lies, too skint to be bought off with council flat mortgages (if they're lucky) or income tax breaks (if they can get enough work).

But their anger is light and spirited, still largely operative on the level of ideas, unlike the real destitution of the North East. There are work opportunities here, and money can be made. I sense that for someone of my age, class and culture, Bristol would be a fine place to live. Comfortably alternative and laudably idiosyncratic, multicultural without fussing over it, it reflects some of the island's historic virtues. But unfettered discontent, without a direction, is soon spent.

"Come up with a solution, any solution, and I'm gonna agree with ya." Two Jamaican men approaching retirement walk past, deep in political debate. Bristol's strength and its paradox doubly revealed.

I leave Jackson's living room and pedal out of Easton, crossing over the thundering M23 road dividing Bristol. Around Montpelier then over to St Pauls, among graffitied and shabby Victorian townhouses, tumbledown squares, Caribbean takeaways. There's a relaxed air to the city, without aggression or arriviste pretension. Stokes Croft and Nelson Street are vast public galleries of innovative stencilled and spray-painted artwork. There's a refreshing independence in the air too, one that led to riots against the opening of a Tesco back in 2011, standing up for local businesses. It's some contrast to urban disorder elsewhere since, more often among shoppers scrapping over sales-day gadgets.

Stokes Croft, where trustafarian hipsters, junkies and artist-activists commingle, is the exception that confirms the rule. Sat outside Hamilton House, a 60s Seifert-school shit-show repurposed from office to community centre, I sip organic barista-blended coffee and survey the scene. Architects debate the specifics of community pilot projects next to beetroot-cheeked locals berating the mothers of their estranged children. "They always want to talk about how your day's been... Eighteen years is a life-sentence." Bearded arts graduates gleefully exchange impressions of the poverty exotica of a familiar Brixton council estate. "Communist style, really grotty stairs, the most amazing décor I've ever seen." Then the Palestinian Embassy on Broad Street, another sign of the city's publicly supported counter-culture. Then down Corn Street and around St Nicholas' covered market, bohemian atmosphere, green juices, blue cheeses, hobble-cobbled.

I follow the harbour along Welsh Back. Where Welsh slate, coal, timber and stone were once unloaded and stored, the area's now marked by aspirational restaurants and bars, and a health club. Look up at the Byzantine brickwork of the Granary building, or the sober grids of Queen Square behind it. Tourists mill around Brunel's SS Britain steamship, in the shadow of Clifton's pastel terraces tiered above. No handwringing museums or soul-searching apologies to the slave trade on which Bristol thrived, trading locally produced brass for a human cargo. It's untroubled by history, and hasn't thought to cauterise it either.

I stop for a pint on the old Grain Barge, now a hip craft beer joint, this decade's take on the bourgeois wine bar. A lady complains about her au pair, and the toils of owning property in the Mediterranean. "This is my life", says a woman beside her. "Work work work then go home." I smile, bemused. Its placidity indicates complacency, yet Bristol is enjoyable, and I profit from Jackson's advice to seek its identity not in buildings but people. There is indeed sincerity in its naivety. I suspect most have no idea just how unnecessarily impoverished much of neighbouring South Wales is.

I scope round the town again, dashing up a doorway to inspect a feature, asking a stranger for the time, and then an opinion, then peering up at the late summer skies to judge the weather, the superego of the island.

Over the Avon is Bedminster, a built-up suburb marked by an Asda-McDonald's mutant-monster, and a long parade of suffocated shops along East Street. Like Lawrence Hill and Fishponds, Bedminster indicates the other side to Bristol, a more common island story: poverty, uncertainty, a lack of direction. I follow the course of a drunk, sucker-punched by circumstance, harassed by kids on race-bikes, who eventually finds refuge in a chippie. Further along, aboard a cycle of not dissimilar size to mine, a strung-out fella dozes off, the wheels giving away and shaking him awake. His belongings, what few they are, have been crammed into a Sports Direct holdall, and after a time his phone falls out of his hand and fragments against the floor. He curses, picks up its parts and drops them in a pocket, and slumbers once more.

Pat sings the praises of Bristol. He confirms my findings: a city laid-back, liberal and vibrant, unlike anywhere else. I'd decided to give Bristol an extra night after his offer of a bed. Over dinner we talk the city, and our lives. After the stresses of London and Cambridge, he considers it a beacon of light. Hesitant to sour such approbation, I ponder if Bristol's beacon indicates neither a way forward, nor even a way round, but instead a kind of cosy sanctuary from the peculiar nowhereness of its surroundings. The alternative's an easy place to stop. Reaching the new is something extraordinary.

The crude etchings and illustrations along the trackway intimate the intellectual discoveries made in these parts. "You see but R blind", captioning a linear ray emanating from an eyeball, spray-painted onto a warehouse fire-exit. "BBC corrupt" opines an iron bridge, beside algebraic notations, "longitudinarianism" and "binary eclipses", narcotic ciphers etched with impish humour.

The trail from Bristol to Bath basks in its eccentricity. Its recondite reveries are rudely interrupted on the edge of Bath, its canal surprisingly depressed by the dereliction of Stothert & Pitt, a crane-building company that was asset-stripped and expunged by Robert Maxwell in the arse-end of the 80s.

The city thereafter returns to sober grandiosity. Largely composed of the same golden stone as Bristol, this old spa resort is ambitiously arranged in Georgian neoclassical terraces. Tourists disembark from coaches in their hundreds. They peer up and photograph an image of nice old England that its government projects internationally, and that the wealthy middle classes of China, India, the United States and southern Europe find immensely and unconsciously reassuring: the centuries-fixed stability of inherited wealth.

Bath's town centre is free of the malls, offices and apartment blocks that the 20th and 21st centuries would otherwise inflict. Intrigued by the name, I pop into the Bath Scientific and Literary Institution, an old centre of learning and ideas where even the air feels antiquarian. Paul and Bob are hospitable, offering me coffee, quizzing me on my academic research and educating me in local discoveries.

The planet Uranus was discovered here by William Herschel in his backyard in 1781. An amateur dabbler and professional musician, his enthusiasm for experimentation led him to discovering infrared radiation. Joseph Priestley discovers the element oxygen, William Smith the existence of new dinosaur species and, a little out of town, Edward Jenner innovates vaccination, responsible for the prevention of countless millions of deaths. Something in the water?

Even the introduction of Arabic numerals, algebra and the number zero into medieval Europe can be traced back here. Adelard of Bath was a 12th century monk who studied across Europe, the Middle East and the Muslim Arab worlds, before returning home to translate landmark works by Euclid and al-Khwarizmi into Latin. Through these then-lost geniuses, Adelard helped introduce geometry and algebra into medieval Europe, supplying the conceptual apparatus upon which, today, our modern computers and digital technologies are based. It's yet another instance of the multicultural composition of our basic mental functions, like the Roman alphabet we write in, the Arabic numerals we count with, or Norse and Germanic tongues we speak.

Not far from Bath are Wrington and Malmesbury. Again,

they relate back to intellectual discovery, being the birthplaces of John Locke and Thomas Hobbes, two English thinkers whose empirical philosophies would transform modern European thought, committed to reason yet undertaking its realisation through experimental study. With time to survey one, I push out to Malmesbury.

It's a hot afternoon, and the country lanes after Bathwick are gnarled and winding. Flanked with fruit bushes, blackcurrants bursting to the touch. "I can't believe mothers just get them from the supermarket", an old boy in socks and sandals remarks, his wicker basket containing enough berries for a W.I. jampionship. There's variety and beauty in these Wiltshire scapes, intensively farmed but tranquil. The air is ripe with freshly tilled soil and horse manure, and curls of golden corn dry out in the breezy fields. I wile down one narrow lane after another, broadly orientated north east, passing cornfields and hamlets, dry-stone walls, wildflowers and songbirds, ramshackle cottages and exclusive private schools, through Grittleton and on to Foxley, at last reaching Malmesbury.

Thomas Hobbes was born in this old market town. It's not known if he ever spent much time exploring the beautiful countryside around him, though sensual pleasure is diminished in his treatises on politics and natural science. He considered human nature as little more than a "war of all against all", our natural lives "nasty, brutish, and short". Only the unopposed rule of kings would give us a little security. Conformity and drudgery were the prices of peace.

But he's mistaken for a precursor of the ugly social Darwinism now used to justify the "hard work" and meritocracy of the upper classes. Though humans are, like all natural things, fundamentally interested in preserving and increasing their own power, this power is best realised through cooperation. "The greatest of human powers is that which is compounded of most men, united by consent", he also wrote. Hobbes could never convincingly overcome his prior philosophical discovery that the most natural of political constitutions was democracy.

The town doesn't commemorate its sage, unless one counts a popular butcher, "Thomas of Malmesbury". But it's a pretty place, higgledy-piggledy rows spanning centuries in their sundry styles. Friendly locals in the Co-op tip routes and warn about traffic from the Dyson headquarters nearby. I rove around the edge of a partly ruined abbey, talking awhile with a young nurse. Even she's upbeat about work and life! Such contrasts, these. After a couple of pints in the Smoking Dog, where a local plasterer proudly recounts near-death experiences as a travelling Manchester United supporter, I pedal on.

Everywhere blooms. I spin through Brinkworth, under the shadow of a large hill with a white chalk horse etched into its side. I reach Wootton Bassett, a small town on the outskirts of Swindon, its name associated with Union Jacks, hate mobs and military corteges. It still retains the form of a village, clustered down a single high street. In a Chinese chippie I'm given child-rearing advice, iced water and more route tips. It's as if most get lost, but do not seek to get back. And why should they, when so much of this part of the world is lovely?

The day draws to an end over Broad Hinton. I leave another slumbering village, then pedal out over sloping wheat fields, burnished by the west-sinking sun. I reach Avebury, a hamlet squatting in the centre of a vast Neolithic festival complex, the largest surviving stone circle in Europe. It is actually composed of three extensive stone circles, one spangling a large outer mound and, within, two circles of towering stones. The complex connects to vast human-constructed earthen mounds, or barrows, at Silbury Hill and West Kennet, the former being the same size as the pyramids of Giza, and Avebury bears an obvious kinship with the better-known Stonehenge nearby. Most stones still occupy the spots they were placed in, five thousand years ago.

Surveying the peaceful scene, my eye traces the outline of the Red Lion pub, a few thatched roof cottages on either side, and a couple of closed stores. The Henge Shop is the only obvious concession to Avebury's druidic significance and its New Age attraction, a 20th century re-imagination of a lost belief system. Inside the boozer, sullen-looking couples dine under diagrams of ley-lines. One barmaid giggles about the "mad" who gather here for the solar solstice celebrations. Suitably refreshed, the gloaming tangling in blue, I go out roving. The area is peaceful and deserted, the sun's last rays casting an ethereal glow over the grand ancient stones.

I slowly venture round them, inspecting each stone with my hands and eyes. I marvel at the lichen coating them, some centuries alive, and ponder Avebury's purpose. Ancestor worship, astrology, or focal point of seasonal social gatherings? In some fissures in the grey-blue rock, visitors have left behind coins, feathers and string bows. After around half an hour of slow perambulation, I begin to notice a remarkable sense of physical relaxation, accompanied by a gradual intensification of my bodily senses.

Recognising the mischief of lysergic acid consumed upon leaving the pub, I elect to pitch up tent beneath a solitary sarsen before I become any further disorientated. Spine resting against the cool stone, I watch the gloaming sky become midnight stars with euphoric rapture. My mind is ensnared in a thought experiment. If these stones had sense perceptions, what would they have seen in the preceding five millennia? Each scenario is exhaustingly explored, and I cannot sleep. To tire myself out, I undertake another long stroll around the stones, gazing up at the eye-watering luminescence of the stars.

A flashlight flutters in the distance, a crystalline orb increasing in size. I panic. Won't I frighten witless this nocturnal sortie, a deranged young man rambling round in the dark, gazing at the stars...? So, quite naively, I venture out to greet them.

Jason and his girlfriend are very surprised to bump into another person among the stones in the wee hours. After a cursory explanation of my cyclogeographic adventure, they seem relaxed, even sympathetic. They're both pagans who've driven up from Cambridgeshire, out "dowsing" tonight, using a small birch to follow the course of a ley-line. He doesn't quite grasp my scepticism, and insists that "eighty percent of us can do it".

For much of the conversation, his girlfriend appears headless. Jason speaks warmly of Avebury. "There's a lot of love in this place. It's about marriage, fertility. Stonehenge to me feels about the past, about death and remembering." As he describes various ley-lines I begin to fear that I'm hallucinating the entire exchange, until he talks about life in his town, anodyne features I couldn't've imagined.

"Mysterious things do happen here", he says, with a smile.

"The stones make me hungry and tired. 2012 AD." The graffiti inside the gent's cubicle at Avebury captures the mood of the morning. Fatigue and insomnia have left me more sceptical about the purportedly divine origins of prophecy claimed by mind-fugged messiahs.

Still, I don't regret pressing the mind's escape key last night. All my life, like so many, I've escaped into my work and fantasies of a better life that would accrue from it. My shabby appearance and nomadic lifestyle have shaken things up. My material belongings feel impermanent, and even human relations and lives, more fleeting and transient. My world back home goes on without me, and everything I am experiencing is so different to that old terrain, that I have no map or words for it. Our obsessions conceal our insecurities. I feel broken open, neither happy nor sad.

In the village shop, an effusive old ma'am tells me about the area, Kennet, named after its local river, and heartily encourages me to head south. The lanes are quiet, the morning cool and drizzly, the flanking fields obscured in tufty mists. It's a serene panorama, if funereal.

Villages like Honey Street and Woodborough pass, enfolded in dingles and spinneys. I bundle along the Pewsey Downs, skin chilled by the mizzling, past a large group of Indian tourists. On one side of a hedgerow, the majority pose with a smile; on the other, an orderly line of young men urinate in unison with not dissimilar happiness. I struggle to share road-space with rumbling military transporter trucks passing between the area's various military bases. The army still uses old Imber village for urban warfare practice, and there's a vast old underground MOD bunker at Burlington. I follow the shopkeeper's instructions, mind focused only on reaching the next destination and not passing out on the verge. The road ends at another vast Neolithic complex, even grander than Avebury, comprising wood circles, a huge, inexplicable mounded cursus, and Stonehenge.

Christianity's conflation of paganism with devil-worship still taints secular understandings of Stonehenge. If it does not hum with dark menace, then its solemn sarsens become subject to all manner of mystic speculation. But archaeological excavations suggest that it was used as one of the central gathering places of prehistoric Britain, some five thousand years ago. A glacier-made ridge had coincidentally aligned perfectly with the solstice, pointing directly at the midwinter sunset in one direction, and the midsummer sunrise in the other, suggesting to their minds some divine significance. This was not an altar to prophets or holy spirits separated by continents and millennia, the "playsome whimsies of monkeys in human shape", as Hume puts it, but a place of wonder about the natural world. Over five hundred years, it was built in stages, with cremated bones buried communally under the bluestones, and social gatherings at the summer and winter solstices, meeting and feasting together.

Its festival usage ended around 2500 BCE, they think, following the arrival of the "Beaker people" from Europe. They instead buried their dead in barrow mounds, and used their metalworking skills to craft jewellery and arms. The intrinsic collectivity of the stone circle was lost to the individualism of metal. In the horizon, I measure those sarsens and bluestone posts, with strapping lintels straddled improbably over them, and beneath survey an unearthly traffic of visitors drifting concentrically in some group trance. Just as, many thousands of years ago, these Neolithic people came from across the island to feel a sense of connection with a vague and erroneous image of their ancestors, so do we today, many thousands of years hence. Our ancestors will probably be found doing the same.

What will they make then of the vast new visitor centre? It combines the aesthetics of a McDonald's drive-thru with a discount supermarket. Coaches queue in dozens, tourists in thousands, to enter, pay an exorbitant entry fee, then queue to board more buses that drive half a mile up to the monument. Heritage as an entertainment experience, of a kind quite unlike Avebury, Carreg Coetan Arthur or the Ring of Brogdar. "It's not even that bad today. Sometimes we get eight thousand", a worker tells me, as he ushers us along, our tickets timed.

Business is good. A palisade of selfie-sticks are raised before the sarsens, audio guides crammed against ears like a shield. I wonder what those Neolithic visionaries would make of the modern spectacle. No religious or intellectual movement has accompanied the recent automation and digitisation of our animal life, apart from catastrophilia about the environment. A crow mocks the scene with a beady eye.

An old gent of unkempt appearance approaches me, as I stand outside the fencing. A strange grin creeps up from one ear to the other as he draws closer, his self-shorn hair and chin complementing his incongruity. "I deprived English Heritage of many pounds yesterday", he murmurs to me, conspiratorially. Why, I ask, puzzled. "We hate them round here. The land should be free to roam."

This rebel is at war with fences, car-parks and coaches, and the wider tourism industry flogging England's ancient culture to the highest bidder. His weapon is the newspaper letter and a bony index finger, with which he points out to passing strangers an apparently free but ineffectual path that wheedles round to some distant hump overlooking the stones. He's a mine of Neolithic notes, this unlikely rebel, and I wish him well.

My road takes an occidental turn now, cutting through the chalky downs of the Wylye valley, and into Warminster, an old military town. Time and trade have become sluggish. A coffee-shop owner also complains of mass conformity, of how people are becoming brainwashed into an unthinking dream-world of international brands and loyalty cards. The subterranean source of this gripe is the opening of a local Costa, a chain brand that's killed her trade, but in the process of clue-collection I'm reminded to look deeper. Down Warminster's chintzy lanes are foodbanks and tucked-away poverty, and stories of disappearance. One man tells me that the only "life" here are the soldiers, suggesting that the town's hidden poverty is felt by its abundant elderly folk. But by the standards of Northern England and South Wales, Warminster's more out of breath than in terminal decline.

A little west is Frome, a more buzzing market town. Though it too has a Costa, along cobbled Cheap Street are windows displaying aspirational homeware, wholefoods and artisan cheeses, and the centre boasts regular street markets. Relatively younger, well-heeled and awash with middle class creatives, Frome's the kind of place other towns' ambitious politicians aspire to. But this is the wealthier corner of the island, equidistant between Alex James' farm and the estates of the Duchy of Cornwall. And then Shepton Mallet after, a more anaemic town like Warminster. Much of the country's cider is brewed here, but there's a prevailing sense of deflation. I follow the traffic out of town, where cars queue to park closest to the bustling retail barns of the Townsend shopping park.

I'm now in Somerset and, a little disappointed by the scenery, decide to detour north back towards Bristol. The ride through the Mendip Hills is challenging but exhilarating, with its emerald flickers and gentle breeze. The small cathedral city of Wells rewards the effort. Steeples soar over a wide market square, and its early English gothic cathedral is exemplary, even by this island's standards.

A panoply of stone figurines are cast into its vast ornate façade, illustrating a complex spiritual hierarchy of prophets, angels and saints. Once painted in bright colours, they are now the tone of earth. The air hums as an orchestra rehearses a sequence from *Star Wars*, and across a prim lawn is a monument to Harry Patch, the last surviving veteran of WW1. He waited for the queen's centenary telegram before telling the world of the "legalised mass murder" of that war, of all war. He said he'd lost all faith in the church. The monument is sarcastically garlanded in plastic Union Jacks, a legacy of a subsequent century of deafness, blindness and dumbness.

Wells is lovely, but the best lies a little ahead, overlooking the Somerset Levels. "Great British eccentricity lives and thrives here", Ellie's mum will rightly put it.

A funfair flashes on the edge of town. The heady thumping bass and laughter of drunk teens contrasts with the spiritualist stores, hemp outlets and prophetic promises of Glastonbury's colourful centre, hushed and earnest. Instead of cut-price beer and biscuits, here one can choose from cauldrons and crystals, or gurus offering mystic rituals. Gary and Karen are here Gawain and Lilith-Karenina. It trades in tarot and runes over tattoos and phones, and for post-pub grub one seeks organic flaxseed polenta over doner kebabs and korma.

It's a joy to people-watch here, everyone dressed up in velvet waistcoats, corsets, wooden staffs, yard-high heels and pony tails. In its relative isolation and conformity of eccentricity, one could take oneself entirely seriously here. Buskers howl and mages laze in the slow evening sunset, expressions inscrutable.

Ellie lives a couple of miles away in nearby Meare, but is all-too-familiar with the town. "Glastonbury is not like any other kind of community", she says, as we prepare freshly picked tromboncino from the back garden. I'm grateful for a place to couchsurf and the chance to wash my clothes. She speaks with affection and scepticism for her hometown, a place that can feel small ("everyone knows each other") and a little daft ("everybody's a therapist"). She recalls visiting a local business that promised guided meditation. A little into the session, the guru insisted she accept that he was the direct reincarnation of God. Here, too, such eccentricity is viable, even commercially sound.

I recline my head on the soft grass, and gaze up at the clouds. Fluffy, shape-shifting cumulus clouds glide gently over the horizon. We are skying, a term invented by the painter John Constable to afford dignity to the practice of studying the clouds. "I have done a good deal of skying... The sky is the *source of light* in nature – and governs everything." On an island defined by its rain, and with many terms for it, the practice of skying is an ancient science.

The forecast's optimistic – how we even ally our moods to meteorology! There's a pleasant breeze billowing up Avalon, overlooking the plains where locals still say that Jesus walked with his uncle, Joseph of Arimathea, on some tin-trading trip. The apocryphal image inspires Blake to imagine Jerusalem in England's "green and pleasant land". In the distance is Wearyall Hill, a wooded ridge over the Levels, and Ellie tells me how Joseph once struck his staff into the hill, causing a thorn bush to magically grow. It's a wonderful muddle of folk Christianity and druidism, imbuing the local environment with special powers – even if, sadly, some have taken to vandalising the tree in recent times.

We're up at Glastonbury Tor, overlooking the town. "This is the place where things happen", she tells me, from Christmas celebrations and first dates to family reunions. The ruined hulk of a 14th century church tower looms at the top, covered in centuries of etched graffiti. St Collen, a 7th century monk, is also claimed to have met the fairy-king of Annwn on the Tor, after being invited into their castle. Collen resisted the food and drink offered, which if consumed made returning to the human world impossible, and in conciliatory spirit threw holy water over his hosts, making them and Annwn disappear. As we drift back into town, there's more batty lore of ancient ley-lines, King Arthur's bones and holy grails. Children giggle in the distance, the late-morning sun a delight.

A little later, I'm surrounded by pirate DVDs, incomplete jigsaws and broken blenders. The crap on display at a car-boot sale just outside Bridgwater acts like a decompression chamber after all these quaint quirks. The town itself follows suit, its derelict pubs, rusted warehouses and knackered town centre evincing many signs of deindustrialised decline, though the Tuscan columns and portico of the neoclassical Corn Exchange are a nice contrast. Nearby, a humongous Asda imitates the scale of a medieval cathedral.

Surveying a vast car-park, Andy's finger traces the former uses of an array of dilapidated premises. "We used to have industries here. We don't make anything now." Though only in his forties, he recalls cellophane, sweet wrappers, pistons and military clothing made in each of these buildings. Though he doesn't suggest it, his point is made by Clarks Village in Street, just south of Glastonbury. A shoe factory has been replaced with a large designer outlet mall whose advertising, faux-heritage lanes, bunting and hanging baskets all flog a phantasmagoria of village life. It confirms Andy's point that the UK is now a place that buys and sells things made elsewhere, and that this buying itself constitutes a leisure activity. Only J.G. Ballard has intuited the attraction of these new out-of-town shopping-experience zones. They can be placed alongside the supermarket, the chain hotel, the Wetherspoon's, tabloid newspapers' coverage of sports stars' personal indiscretions, images of upper class Westminster politicians implicated in scandals, and the Facebook social persona, as all of a contemporary structure of feeling, one that is remarkably dull.

My thought returns to the conversation. What happened, I ask him. "Foreign competition." He speaks with pain, but not xenophobia, locating Bridgwater's decline within a wider story of industrial and social collapse. The British people were let down by their own government. "We just sell things, we don't make them." He gives the example of nearby Hinkley Point B where he works, now publicly owned and under nationalised ownership – by the French: *Électricité de France*, EDF. Andy considers the island's loss of engineering expertise and manufacturing power as symptomatic of this decline, though is sceptical of any state-invested programme of reversal. With a fifth of current power stations due to close within the next fifteen years, the island faces an unprecedented energy crisis, coupled with rising demand. In place of long-term solutions, there has been much short-termist fudging. Though it is unlikely that the lights will go out, energy prices will become far higher in the future.

Bridgwater hopes to benefit from this mess. Its hope is in Hinkley Point C, a new nuclear-power station whose construction is currently estimated at £24.5 billion. The UK government has already guaranteed to its French and Chinese investors that British users will pay double current market rates for their new electricity over the next 35 years. Electricity is not a choice: one depends on it, and its usage is better redefined as a tax, as James Meek has argued. This agreement effectively grants foreign states the right to tax future British wages at exorbitant rates.

What about the young? Andy broods. Like the island, they lack the skills to make, build, maintain. Their future is uncertain. "The 16 to 24 year-olds, they don't have a chance. The older ones are not retiring, not giving up their places. I guess they can't

afford to. But then when they get older they can't get a job."
He turns away, and surveys the scene again. "They're building
houses around here, but I don't know how people can afford
them... It's a shame." Another local man of similar age works in
the supermarket, and as well as describing deindustrialisation,
sees hope in Hinkley. "They're building a new one", he glows,
thinking only, and perhaps rightly, of the short-term benefit to
the town, and not the high bills, poverty wages and toxic mess
it'll also create.

It's a hot afternoon, and the crickets whir on the grassy verges
as I pedal through the Quantock Hills, a sumptuous array of sloping heathland and thickets. King Alfred conducted an English
guerrilla war against the invading Vikings in the nearby swamps
of Athelney, whilst Coleridge composed the "Ancient Mariner" in
a cottage in pretty Nether Stowey. As I approach Old Cleeve then
head along the quiet trail to Minehead, the azure of that "painted
ocean" glimmers.

Minehead is a Victorian seaside resort, untroubled by recent
decades, with a vast Butlins holiday camp appended to its eastern edge, which once brought an affordable measure of luxury
to holidaying working class families from the 1950s. The park is
quiet when I pass, and the sea-facing parade has fallen on hard
times. Once a bustling concert hall, the derelict Queens Hotel
now plays to the ghosts. But it's still pleasant in all, as one passes
the neglected amusement arcades and approaches the town
centre. I get some chips and head on, tired and tempted by the
town's taverns, but tugged toward the wilds ahead.

Evening sets over Porlock, a twee village at the foot of one
of the steepest hills on the island. In the Royal Oak I'm warned
to avoid the main road, a vertical ascent perilous even for cars,
and told to trace a narrow obscure toll road. "I wouldn't do either
myself", booms the landlord, mirth spreading across the bar.

Gadzooks! No sooner do I begin climbing out of Porlock Weir
but my front brake goes awry, now dragging against the wheel

rim. For the remainder of my journey it will continue doing this, and I find no way of fixing it other than disengaging it with my hands. I'm unsure whether to surrender here at the foot of this Everest, but after a good hour's vain tinkering, determine to push on.

Even the sun abandons me, and the moonlight's insufficient to trace the broken trackway past West Porlock and up the old toll road. It threads through an overgrown wildwood, whirring and whooping with the clamour of mammals, insects and birds. My loneliness is burdensome, but it is too steep to cycle now, and I am approximately nowhere, somewhere on Exmoor's edge. I push on through this knotted forest, singing silly songs for courage under the full moon.

What is the difference between the grey-black road and the night-sky horizon ahead? They blur into one confusing vista, too dark to see ahead with the bike light. The single lane zigzags past livestock fields, til, around an hour later, I reach the summit of Porlock Hill. It's some time until I find a strip of field not occupied by cattle or sheep. Completely lost, feeling a million miles away from habitation or human being, I listen to the breeze and bleating, and gaze out at the distant spangles of Cardiff and Newport over the bay. Wonderful.

There's something new in the breeze, a cool, autumnal bite. It's now September. The days have expanded and contracted again, my horizons broadened too, and I've acquired what feels like a love of the island. I journeyed out on an unsuitable bicycle, with two panniers packed with nonsense and a body unfamiliar with more than ten-mile exertions. I did not expect to finish. That I made it up to the Midlands was the first surprise. Edinburgh followed. Now Scotland, Wales, and most of England is behind me. If I can do this, any adult of sufficient health and naivety can.

But the hills and headwind never get easier. Porlock nearly broke me last night. As I cycle through Culborne and up, up, *up!* into the vast heathland of Exmoor, the aquamarine Atlantic glinting to my right, I wonder how on earth I'll survive the W-shaped peaks and troughs that lie ahead.

There is only one road, and one way ahead: west. I plunge down into Lynmouth, a fudge-box Victorian seaside resort with a dainty harbour and array of pasty shops. Feeling already worn out, I cheat and take the small cliff railway a hundred or so metres up to Lynton, towering over Lynmouth harbour. The holidaymakers cheerfully empathise.

Lynton's characterised by the same chintzy cream-tea cafes and sedate scenery. Local business-owners huddle outside Ethel Braithwaite's bakery, plotting against local taxation. Further ahead, the Valley of the Rocks approaches the sublime, an arresting statement of nature's randomness. A pyramid-pile of scree and tors burst out from the earth, tearing through the ocean horizon and into the sky. There's a majestic coastal road west, wiring by briary thickets, crescenting over plunging bays, with punishingly steep ascents. I stand on the bike, pedalling in the lowest gear up some interminable twisting hill for forty minutes, brakes dragging, bags sagging... just to plunge down the same distance again in forty seconds. This rigmarole repeats twice an hour. Up Martinhoe, down to Hunter's Inn. It's the most difficult and exhausting cycling I've done. But surrounded by jade forests, with a soundtrack of swallows, sparrows and the sighing sea, one cannot complain too long, and something beautiful always captures the eye.

After the smaller seaside village of Combe Martin, I reach Ilfracombe. It appears drab and dour, even in the fine weather, a faded parade of takeaways, boozers and the odd gift shop. A once-popular seaside resort, it seems to have blended into a prevailing English small town homogeneity: spiked fences, discount supermarkets, bargain booze, St George's flags, over-preened front gardens and an air of frustration. Down Fore Street, I find the old harbour and snoop round. In one chippie, a man gets confused over my questions, and starts interviewing me for the vacant post of assistant (still awaiting that call-back). At the Pier Inn, an ursine gent from Cirencester mishears most of my words, in a tawdry comedy of errors, as I struggle to glean where I am or where I'm heading. I head out, confused by this intriguing yet tart resort. A huge bronze statue of a pregnant nude bearing a sword by entrepreneur Damian Hirst further intimates its incoherence.

Westward, the road is flat and smoother, vaunting through Braunton, then on to Barnstaple along an old railway line. The Tarka Trail cuts through the country where Henry Williamson set his otter story, among clay pits and river plains by the Torridge and Taw. Barnstaple carries a similar gloom to Ilfracombe and Bridgwater, sapped by industrial decline and the desertion of holidaymakers in the late 20th century, and an inability to fashion a new identity. Globalised capitalism's race to the bottom has made Fethiye, Faliraki and Fuerteventura cheaper. The terrain remains serene and rural, as I reach Instow and Appledore, lovely villages bobbing on the sea. Bideford too, where Walter Raleigh landed the first tobacco on the island, is a slowly aged town, dry-docked into dotage.

Tammy lives in the nearby village of Weare Giffard. It's nestled in a valley where Friesian cows stroll beside a streamlet, and the evening sun projects splodges of gold and mauve against the windows and walls of a string of houses. She's a gardener from this area, and feels happy in its slower ways.

She reasons like Aristotle, recognising the seed as a would-be shrub, or a pile of aged timber as a preformed table, yet to become. "I've always been a country girl... Falmouth's the biggest place I've ever lived in!" She laughs, recalling her work as a cleaner in the house of a wizened Cornish speaker. "What can you believe", she asks rhetorically, later, on the subject of the media, her conversation sparkling with a scepticism for received wisdom, and a determination to find out things for herself through direct experience.

I'm couchsurfing with her tonight, and glad of the opportunity for hot food, a shower, and good evening conversation. She tells me about Cornwall and Devon with the aid of OS maps, as we sit and eat a fresh veggie stew in a vast, crumbling cottage. Henry Williamson would sometimes visit and play piano here, she's been told, and there's a pleasantly musty smell emanating from its decaying rugs and walls. A wacky primary-colour scheme, long-faded, adds to an aura of genteel decay. In this part of the island, along a strange and gruelling trackway, such eccentricity feels not exceptional, but its essence.

Kernow a'gas dynergh! It appears then disappears quietly, a sign as unobtrusive as the old cottages, barns, blackberry bushes and oak trees that surround it in Hartland. It marks the threshold of what was considered a separate country until the 15th century, Dumnonia, Cornwall, with its own tongue, trades and mysterious ways. The Anglo-Saxons would call it "West Wales", alongside "North Wales", the name "Wales" connoting "foreigner, servile" in their tongue. A region where earlier settlers migrated to, "Britons" as opposed to 'English' Anglo-Saxons. Cornwall's modern situation proves to be equally muddled.

If this is a new country, then its first frontier town is typically muddled and underwhelming. At Bude, coaches park in unison, ejecting passengers into the amusement arcades and souvenir sweetshops. The beach is more pleasant, ambience reposed. In the visitor office, a local woman suddenly pauses, mid-speech, fishes out a map, presses it into my hands and then apologises. "It's no good, you won't find it on any map." "Greenaway Beach?" Another lady overhears her, recognises the description of some idyllic spot near Trebetherick. "My haven", she smiles. "Where we always went as kids", replies the first. Neither can agree its location. My mission is to find it.

It's the first of many I'll uncover, small sparks of magic from the Cornish rock. Before Bude, I found intimation of those at Morwenstow, an old-fashioned hamlet burrowed into the rocky edge of the verdant Hartland Peninsula, on the North Devon coast. It was my first stop of the day after leaving Tammy's and losing myself among Devon's back-lanes. Robert Stephen Hawker provided for the spiritual needs in this parish of St Morwenna two centuries ago. Among his varied duties, he would climb down those precipitous rocks to rescue drowning sailors or recover their remains. His hobby, unusual even among the clergy, was the regular smoking of opium in a specially constructed wooden hut, overlooking the bay.

This eccentric English mystic pulled great verses from those pipe-dreams. "Window and wall have lips to tell // The mighty faith of days unknown." His words exude a love of nature, exuberant and alive, God's handicraft. Two hikers ask for a snap as they pose beside the graffitied hut, grinning with their dogs, the aquamarine sea-sky horizon behind them.

But no road is ever straight, no story without inconsistencies. Past the buzzing cream-tea café, a sign near St Morwenna's urgently appeals for foodbank donations. Further down the coastal road, I pass a humongous military surveillance complex, where massive satellites leer like exposed skulls over the dunes, dishes directed to every part of the globe. The complex is locked behind rows of barbed wire, and ironically one is not allowed to photograph the GCHQ base. In the name of public protection, security agencies monitor our motions and communications. They detain without trial and distribute spies to bug dissent. Such behaviour in a parent, teacher or partner would be abusive. Here, the government calls it anti-terrorism.

Still, as I ride in and out of Bude, I see a landscape transform, from the undulating fields and forests of Devon to the rockier, bare and exposed dunes of Cornwall. Its population has always been small, concentrated in fishing ports or mining villages. Many of these settlements have been inhabited for millennia, often bearing unfamiliar nomenclature of local saints: Austell, Erth, Ives, Enodoc, Mawes, Buryan or Endellion.

Threading back inland, I pass Dimma, rejoining the coastline at the village of Boscastle. Tourists tailgate, dawdling along tight lanes. I nose into its large Witchcraft Museum, offering a fascinating folk history of charms, artefacts and clairvoyant devices. There are ouija boards, mandrake roots, crystal balls and stone phalli. I'm intrigued by exhibits from two bizarre "black ops" campaigns by the British Army, one to spook superstitious Nazis with fake Nostradamus books, another, three decades later, to tar Irish republicans with Satanism by leaving black magic paraphernalia around Belfast. The fact is not the belief, but in its being believed.

Magic involves trickery. Until the early modern era, the island's largely agrarian communities would rely on cunning folk to provide medicine, counsel and reassuring clairvoyance, a museum worker tells me. I ask her to define their witchcraft. She smiles. It was a "way of seeing the world", of recognising "a divine creative energy" that is nature, and that permeates nature. In its wonder, it doesn't seem so far from Hawker's "Eternal Land" or Blake's Glastonbury-Jerusalem: a human attempt to confabulate meaning into an unpredictable world.

The sun starts its descent, egg-yolk rim indicating the way ahead. I stop at St Nectan's, a waterfall-shrine hidden a little off the road. It takes its name from a Welsh mystic who, after having his head cut off by two cattle thieves, staggered alone, head in hand, back to his beloved meditational spot. Then Tintagel, mecca of Arthurian myth. The sight of its ruined battlements in the horizon is impressive, above a shark-tooth isthmus cast adrift from the mainland, harassed by the surging sea. It was constructed in early medieval times long after Arthur's supposed existence, when still connected to the land. Its severance diminished its utility, and it was soon abandoned. Still, a beautiful site, whatever the facts.

Arthur is another beautiful, historical myth, embellished by the quasi-fictitious histories of Nennius, the *Mabinogion* and Geoffrey of Monmouth. His later Victorian renaissance by Tennyson supplied a chivalric ideal of colonial stiffness. It's not unlike the ancestral-astral adorations of Neolithic Avebury and Stonehenge, where past, present and future melded into a circular vision of reality. Arthur's ancient power presents both an ideal of former glory, and a quasi-Christian image of fallen grace. These stories gave meaning to lives lived long before ours. Uprooted from our traditions, dispossessed of the island's wealth, today's communities still dream of the otherworldly, now scrying through black screens at more modern cunning folk, dancing in glamorous costumes or selling the latest lifestyle hack, happiness cure or revolutionary truth.

But where is Greenaway Beach?

In Boscastle and Tintagel they had no clue, but one of the women earlier had mentioned Trebetherick. After Tintagel, the landscape is a pell-mell of tres, pols and pens, through Trevalga, Pendoggett and then Polzeath. I reach the small village overlooking Pentire Point by nightfall, the sun admiring its ruby reflection in the violet waters of Padstow Bay. A man in his fifties is taking the air. Dave begins by telling me where the grave of John Betjeman can be found, but he turns conversation to politics.

"You know the Scots and their referendum, I think if you gave people the vote here, they'd choose to be separate from Westminster." Dave is no Kernow nationalist: he's from Somerset, and it's wealth inequality that angers him, bitterly played out here in the extremely high cost of houses, a result of a booming second home ownership by wealthy outsiders.

"People are fed up. It's causing problems", he adds. "People from the South East with a lot more money. The South West, it's quite a poor place, really, dependent on tourism. A backwater..." Like others, he blames London. "That's where the numbers are... but they don't recognise they're supported by the rest of the country." He catches his breath, sighs, smiles, and then points me to the nearest pub.

First, Betjeman's burial place. It's snuggled in St Enodoc's churchyard, in the beautiful Daymer Bay. It's surrounded by a golf course, and sloping sand dunes (*towans* in Cornish), and the spiky marram catches one's feet. On the other side of the old gate, one feels apart from the world in space and time. The "hillock hides the spire", as Betjeman instructs, and past thyme and saxifrage is the old little church, with an unusual coned tower, and Victorian fustiness inside. Between the 16th and mid-19th centuries, the church was buried by sand dunes and virtually abandoned, except for an annual service in which parishioners would climb down for worship via the roof. A magical antidote to the 'tinned minds' of Betjeman's era, and since.

I've found where the second home owners drink, it seems, in the Oystercatcher at Polzeath. Horsey-hoarse accents debate the rules of cricket and disparage everything from the great unwashed to emotional softness. "You don't buy and sell idiots, you don't buy and sell chavs, like you do here", one man spits.

A friendly barmaid laughs at the question of speaking Cornish – who would bother? She's intrigued by Greenaway, and the question bounces round the bar. The landlord thinks he knows it. I follow his vague directions ("left, left, along the path behind the houses..."), edging along a jet-black cliff path til it stops abruptly at the edge of the land. Below is a secluded bay, hidden from all but knowing eyes. I uncap a small bottle of Jura whisky beneath the stars, and raise a toast to Greenaway Beach.

Shelducks soar over Padstow Bay, wings flickering against Pentire Head like animated ticks. They squeak at each other cacophonously, oddly oblivious of one another.

It's morning in Rock, a village dominated by recently erected luxury houses. These cod-shanty spots grate, their names asinine, bled of regional characteristic. Gull Rock, the Nutshell, Cap'n Spreadsheet's Cove. "This is a second home county", says a wearied woman in Padstow's information office, on the other side of the bay. "Local families struggle to get on the property ladder." I ask about alternatives, but she eyes me blankly.

Gavin is a local fisherman, a huge strapping fella in yellow dungarees. His scarred hand shields a cigarette from the wind as he explains his catch. "Bass and Pollock... mainly sold overseas. I wouldn't eat it", he laughs. "Tourist fishing is the best income", his eyes cast down, as if addressing a deeper and more troubling doubt. Outside the season, the town's "dead". He scans the harbour with its bobbing boats, and tourists droning among baby-clothes outlets, pasty shops and miscellaneous Rick Stein shite, and sighs. "It's very expensive to live here." His family have passed their properties down through inheritance, now reaching stratospheric prices. He sees himself as one of the lucky few. I wonder where the snakes hide in this aspirational game of ladders, played with loaded die.

Sinister hills await. I fuel up with a veggie pasty and brace myself. Like Devon, the North Cornwall coast zigzags horizontally and vertically like some crazed Escher scape, up St Merryn, down to Porthcothan Bay, snaking around Trevose Head, then back up and along to Newquay.

A lengthy expanse haloes a wan, swollen town. Fudge, lettered rock, pasty shops and amusement arcades in abundance. It's easy to have one's fill of seaside resorts, many alike. I pop into one pasty outlet to seek out the town's character. An older local speaks candidly. "It's very hard to make a living here. A lot of people have three or four jobs. But it's all zero hours. You might work in a shop..." She interrupts herself mid-flow, to check we're still alone. "But if it's quiet they'll send you home and won't pay you. The supermarkets only call you when you're needed, so it might only be a few hours. It's very difficult."

She seems worn-out and stressed, like so many other service workers, but seems more relieved after giving her story. She sighs, but the sigh is followed by an ellipsis, and then a self-correction. "What good does it do...?" And in that pregnant silence, a possibility appears and then vanishes. "I don't really think about it", says a younger man in another bakery (I'm hungry!). "All this town has is tourism", he adds. Drifting down with the crowds, I look out over Newquay Bay. Two hunky life-guards jitter distractedly on Towan Beach, supervising a scat-tering of sunbathers. "Lots of first aids, surfboard to the head, sprained ankles", one says animatedly, whilst his friend jokes about looser morals of Newquay's nightlife. Swings and round-abouts, as the island saying goes.

Seeking an adrenaline burst of my own, I leave the W-shaped coastal trail for the roaring A30, a speedy highway that tears toward Land's End. The similarity of crash barriers, concrete bridges and shattered debris along the hard shoulder instils a sense of reassuring sameness, a salve for an overstimulated imagination. I hug the edge of the road as transit vans, jugger-nauts and tractors squeeze past me, speeds piquing my energy. It's exhilarating yet dangerous.

I reach Hayle, and join a quieter lane snaking around Carbis Bay and into St Ives. It's an old fishing town, with a dinky light-house, crumbling jetties and shambling fishermen's terraces clad in cheery colours. Cobbled lanes web between with sentimental names, like Love Lane and Salubrious Place. Its appearance is more Corsica than Coventry. Though there are grumbles about encroaching chain stores in the local health-food outlet, the town has preserved an independent character more effectively than Newquay or Bude. This is in part by catering for wealthier Middle England like Padstow, but beyond the bistros and brasse-ries are some great pubs and characters.

After refreshment in the old Sloop Inn, overlooking the slum-bersome sands of Porthmeor Beach, I follow a local man's tip and find the Kettle and Wink at the back of town, beside an old Art Deco cinema. Joe regularly works behind the bar, and shares a similar story to Newquay's lifeguards, young men free to move as they choose. "Last year I went to India. It was amazing. This year it's Asia. Just booked my flights." He finishes pouring a pint of Proper Job, brewed nearby. "I came back in May when the season was starting. It's just what you do, bar work, restaurants." Without dependents, and quite probably with family support, work in the services isn't universally a prison-sentence.

A local poet picks up a microphone, coughs officiously, then addresses the lively boozer, packed to the rafters for an open mic night. "When dreams become reality, what else is left to dream? Be careful what you wish for, life isn't what it seems." One salty seadog takes the stage and croons Tom Waits; another local author climbs up and, with folk guitar, announces: "I think boyfriends are irrelevant, because of what's happening to the planet. This is about the planet, and it's called 'Foolish Man'." A young couple sitting next to me leap up, and for ten minutes enrapture the attentions of hippies, punks and wandering minstrels with their tales of wounded love.

The young people here are sun-kissed and glowing, and there's an ambient joy to the place. The night drawing to a close, I venture back through those narrow lanes, and chance my luck on a stretch of grassland overlooking the town, nicknamed locally "the Island". It's silent and deserted tonight, the sighing sea and stars excepted. I pitch up beside an ancient chapel, and fall into a heavy sleep.

West Penwith, national character area 156. It pokes out into the Atlantic like an outstretched toe, distant and ungainly, as remote from London as the Western Isles.

St Ives is behind me. This morning I'm alone in a level expanse of heather, bracken and furze, glossy and sweet, bordered by the blue Atlantic. The West Penwith Peninsula is under some kind of spell, where the frequent grey chimneys left behind by the Victorian tin mines dotted through the deserted wilderness stand with the same wizened composure as ancient tors, scattered equally indiscriminately. Pocked around and beneath are standing stones, dozens of them, some in circles, others stowed away down broken tracks, where cromlechs and quoits mark the tombs of long-forgotten dead.

Others defy rational description, and solicit wild speculation. One could leave behind a bicycle or car down one of these narrow tracks for just a few hours, and return to find it corroded, coated in lichen and inexplicable glyphs, rooted down rock-like in this preternatural peninsula.

It's less hospitable than the placid panorama around Zennor suggests, a little west of St Ives. Middle class artists could settle in numbers in that town, like Ben Nicholson and Barbara Hepworth, safe with its railway links back to civilisation. Zennor, St Just and St Burian are stranger and rougher.

D.H. Lawrence hoped to establish a writers' colony in Zennor, "a Promised Land... of the spirit", back in 1916. He and Frieda lasted little over two years before being forcibly ejected by paranoid locals, suspecting them of being German spies. *Women in Love* tells only some of that story. The village is built of dark granite, spartan and morose, the same inscrutable rock that composes the peninsula beneath. Zennor feels comfortable in its own isolation. The view from Zennor Head is lovely, and in its small church I find a memorial to John Davey, died in 1891, the last man to speak and know Cornish as a first language. *Re dheffo dha wlaskor...*

Above Zennor, the outline of tin-mine chimneys, shafts and engine houses flicker occasionally in the distance, and the road skitters by the remains of Carn Galver. Copper and tin were fossicked and mined across West Penwith until the late 19th century, and in a handful of places, up to the late 20th century. Phoenicians and Greeks would sail across the Mediterranean to reach Cornwall and trade for those metals, three millennia ago, the very metals that fed a new Bronze Age in Europe. Herodotus, Ptolemy and Strabo mention the distant Tin Islands. Other Greek myths recount Hyperborea and the Garden of the

Hesperides, places of divine beauty, hidden at the treacherous northwestern edge of the world.

The rocks of Penwith weren't just cut through. Detouring off the single coastal track at Morvah, I head inland, and struggle to trace a trackway between barren hillsides. Like the North Western Highlands, so much is stone and little flourishes. With the aid of a local guidebook instruction, copied whilst nosing around Tate St Ives' bookshop, I eventually locate Men-an-Tol, a dough-nut-shaped hollow stone or *tolmen*, stood between two pillars. It resembles a large eye but also a portal, like that narcotic glyph on the road out of Bristol. *You see but...* Once upon a time people would wander miles to this tolmen to be treated for spinal pain, ague and rickets.

Incongruity recurs later on another deserted hillside, where after half a mile trudging through bracken and scree, I locate Chun Quoit and the remains of an Iron Age fort. The only other living thing around here is an Australian woman, the first person I've seen for hours, robed in New Age garb and "completely lost". The encounter's awkward, the pleasure of solitude interrupted. We exchange directions, and move on.

Back on the road, I pedal through the austere granite dwellings of Pendeen, built to house the workers of nearby mines, some remaining open until 1990. The last of these, Geevor, is now a visitor centre. Rhonda tries to piece together the area's more recent story.

"It was a way of life. A generational thing, father and son", she says, wistfully. Though mines like Geevor had reserves left, they were closed, their workforces and dependent trades left to slowly die. But unlike South Wales or the North, little of that community remains trapped here. Farmers now sell their land to great profit with Cornwall's high property prices. Pockets of serious deprivation have shifted inland to Camborne, St Austell and Truro. She's sad to think of the deeper cost, the disappearance of those ways of life.

"There were the three main industries: mining, fishing and farming. Even farming's in decline... There's just no money in it." Once capitalising from it, now Cornwall suffers from the unfair terms of international traders, like the rest of the island. The market speaks: copper from the Congo, greens from Peru, fish from Vietnam. Each time one shops, one wins and one loses, often simultaneously.

The southwestern edge of Penwith is a little more populous and verdant than the savage plateaux passed earlier. St Just is one such pleasant town, though Sennen is complicit in the crass theme park at Land's End. See *Arthur's Quest* in 4D, or experience *20,000 Leagues Under the Sea* through a sedentary, cinematic extravaganza! It's hard to make a buck out of the majestic fury of the Atlantic otherwise, and most visitors skip the dross to survey the skerries and zawns of the jagged Cornish coast. A group of Chinese students tell me cheerfully of their own island story, and an apprehensive mum awaits her son and his crew of cyclists, completing LeJog.

It's now early evening, and the sky is welling up a heady golden-bronze. I keep off the major roads, riding through St Levan, past Porthcurno where the island's underwater communications lines with North America surface, and up into St Buryan, an isolated farming village, and inspiration for Peckinpah's farfetched bumpkin-paranoia flick *Straw Dogs*. The road twists adder-like, up through the village of Lamorna, still popular with artists and unusually forested behind its smuggler coves, as I huff up the steepest of hills towards Mousehole.

I stop to see the Merry Maidens, a wide stone circle, or the petrified remains of nineteen young women who committed the sin of dancing on the Sabbath. Behind a hedgerow I hear a gentle but plaintive female solo, singing words I cannot understand. I rove round to find its source, but all paths are obstructed by gnarled briar, long-inaccessible. Another hallucination of an overheated brain?

The sun glowers with less intensity now, a faded, tangy ochre. I ride into Mousehole, a charmingly old-world fishing village, then back up, and down, into the town of Newlyn. Fishermen's terraces totter over the steep hillsides, overlooking a wide bay that crescents around to Penzance. I stop for chips and mushy peas, then mosey round its large harbour.

Newlyn is still one of the largest fishing ports on the island, despite its remote location. A local fisherman strolls out from a large warehouse, and pours a crate of icy waste off the concrete wharf and into the murky waters. I catch his eye and, after brief patter, am invited into the large "market" inside. A group of ten men stand at different stages of a conveyor belt, some pouring freshly caught fish onto the moving line, others ensuring that these are then weighted and deposited in the correct trays. Once full, these are taken away for sale. One man tells me that they catch "everything" here, and reels off a list I soon lose count of. Another shows me the fish in each box and tells me about their capture. All are cheerfully bemused to find a stranger asking about their work. As I leave, the first man tells me that their future is uncertain. Like Andy in Bridgwater, there's both a tragic resignation and an element of external blame to his judgement. "European competition", declining stocks. A way of life still living, but not immortal.

I'm exhausted by the time I reach Penzance, and in need of a wash. The offer of a bed has been cancelled at short notice, but fortunately there's a youth hostel on the edge of town. Supplies first.

In Lidl, a young woman is also surprised by a stranger's curiosity. Asking a stranger about their views of the area, the community there, or the quality of life more broadly, remains a radical question. She talks of difficulties facing young people here, of housing prices and homelessness, and of the still-strong power of the stone circles. Another man in the Co-op, older in years, reflects on the hidden poverty and difficulties for locals in the area. He and his wife work three or four jobs each, from shop-work to cleaning. He speaks passionately of the need for a Cornish regional assembly, not for the sake of a language that virtually no one speaks, but to speak up for the communities of Penwith. "These politicians in Westminster, they don't have any idea how it is in our distant corner." He chuckles, lugubriously. Who in England does?

At some point in its prehistoric days, this island changed from none to one, and later into several. Between Penzance and the distant Isles of Scilly, there used to be a vast plain of farms, forests, villages and churches. A great flood of the latter half of the first millennium CE washed most of that away. William of Worcester thought some 140 churches had been lost. Guidebooks now take glee in describing the underwater church-bells that trill on a stormy night, summoning their ghostly parishioners into an otherworldly mass. Signs of a sea-sunk forest are still apparent east at Marazion too. "Noah's woods", the poets call them. Atlantis, Ennor, Lyonesse – this drowned world remains the stuff of legend.

A group of us are sailing to one of the last remaining vestiges of the underwater kingdom of Ennor, now the Scilly Isles. On the other side of the deck, a man makes out a minke whale. He peers again into binoculars, then hands them to his wife. The morning is bright, the squalls calm. After a two-hour voyage, we approach St Mary's, the principal of the five populated islands.

We dock into Hughtown, a compacted spit of low-terraced cottages, a brief high street and harbour, crammed beneath the vast garrison of the Star Castle, built in the late 16th century to deter European invaders. The only construction offered by the 20th century is a small hospital, spread across a nearby hillside. This small habitation is virtually the only settlement of an equally small island. Cycle for ten minutes in any direction from its centre and one will tumble into the Atlantic, and a subtropical greenness defines the place.

A gathering by the harbour seems pleased at our arrival,

and it becomes clear that most work in the tourist trade. The expense of ferrying my Raleigh over has forced me to lock it up in Penzance and hire another. The mountain bike Mark hands me in his shop is a smooth ride. Its wheels are not buckled and it has working brakes, after all. He's been here three years, and describes how the island has shifted from farming and fishing to tourism in recent decades. It's an isolated, self-contained place. "Small, very small. It's a very different way of life", he says, with a little uncertainty.

The Scillies are little like their mother island. Surrounded by warmer ocean currents, there is no frost in deepest winter, nor have badgers, foxes, moles, voles, squirrels or snakes snuck onto the isles. Narcissus flowers bloom in winter, and the Scillies are home to an unusually large and varied population of birds, like puffins and shearwater, and a popular spot for birds migrating through, like hoopoe and wryneck. There are very few cars, and those I pass are unusually corroded.

For a teeny island, there's much to see. I explore the ruined fortifications overlooking Hughtown, guns once trained on Spanish, Dutch, French, German, Royalist and Parliamentarian men. Beached boats slumber in the shade of trees, others with upturned hulls rest against artist shacks and ruined walls. On the northern edge of the isle, I stumble down an unmarked coastal path. At the foot of a BBC transmitter, I find the remains of a Neolithic village.

The early afternoon is balmy and hot. I clamber into Halangy Down, site of an ancient burial chamber and, nearby, the foot-high remains of drystone walls, where circular roundhouses once stood. Each bordered the other in a shared sociality. They cast pewter, worked iron, farmed and traded tin with the rest of the known world. The pleasure of Cornwall is that these Neolithic sites are so common, and so commonly deserted. The frequency of rocky outcrops, belched from the earth, has made it relatively easy to take and adapt the stones for human purposes. There are no entrance tickets or audio guides, nor a visitor car-park. Some enjoy the solitude. Marianne's hand rapidly sketches the view of Samson Island across the turquoise bay, and as we talk about the landscape and its colours, she speaks with expertise of sea hues. "It's pure viridian", she concludes, beaming.

Cycling St Mary's is blissful, a little piece of the South Pacific. There are very few houses, and even its airport is more heathland than Heathrow. I stop in Old Town Bay, the town itself vanished, beside a house beguilingly named "Nowhere". Eating a cheese roll over a sapphire lagoon, I wonder if this might be the isle that inspired Thomas More's Utopia, surrounded by shipwrecks yet deceptively tranquil. Two heretical bishops were exiled here in the 4th century, Tiberianus and Instantius, accused of cultivating free love and promiscuity. One wonders what became of those two Iberian Gnostics, and their untimely commitment to mortal happiness. With its hatred of ostentation and embrace of poverty, did the Scillies inspire More to imagine this island's first foray into Communism? Probably not, but it's a frabjous thought, and on a sunny afternoon on paradise, such thoughts come freely.

Hughtown Museum's wizened curator is also doubtful, but insists on not confusing Scilly with Cornwall. Both, he explained, are owned by Charles Windsor, Duke of Cornwall, whose duchy incorporates parts of Cornwall, Devon, Somerset, Wales (and even Kennington, South London), confusingly. He pays no corporation tax on this wealth, and banks a fortune in EU farming subsidies. The curator takes this for granted, as if it were fitting and proper that one man should be granted exceptional power by virtue of genetics alone. But the setting is too pleasant for acrimonious discussion.

On the return voyage, day-trippers talk pets and private property, with peculiarly aggressive one-upmanship. The English! Such talk is unknown on CalMac ferries. Reunited with my bike and baggage, I venture back into Penzance, in search of evening refreshment.

Along the harbourside, past deserted quayside benches, then up Market Jew Street, a Victorian Anglicisation of marghas yow, "Thursday market", and now Penzance's major thoroughfare. The Georgian Market House dominates a modest town centre, Humphry Davy's statue presiding over unprepossessing chain stores with an air of aloof, naïve importance, like Robinson Crusoe over a collection of coconuts.

Up Causeway Head, backing away from the high street is the older and more salty, bohemian end of Penzance. The Farmers Arms is lively and rambunctious. I sup local Skinners and chinwag with burley locals. One takes the piss out of "those la-di-da people with jumpers on their shoulders", talk turning on second home owners, them-and-us. A jukebox plays reggae, psychrock and post-punk, whilst darts are thrown with little success. Drunk and tired, I have no heart to go further. X marks the end of the road.

A fortnight now separates Peckham from Penzance. I'm unsure how much I want to return. The bike's become my home. Sarah I miss, but my old workaholic ways, and the massive, money-orientated city that everyone seems to despise? Not yet. There's still pleasure in being the visiting stranger, sussing the terrain, gathering stories. But there is nothing west or south except the sea, only east, homeward.

After a night camped on the edge of Penzance, I follow a coastal road along Mount's Bay. On my right, St Michael's Mount looms sternly on the horizon, its castle walls heaped atop the island rock. To my left is a sprawling retail park-supermarket complex, a malicious act by property developers against the natural splendour of Penwith. I cycle through Marazion, an old fishing town now trading on its tourist twee, pursuing a gentle road that skitters by Praa Sands and Prussia Cove, a secluded zawn cut into the coastline.

Helston's whitewashed council estates gleam in the distance.

The town has no pretensions about royal charters or Michelin-starred chefs. Its unfussy high street is made by and for the Cornish. In Rowe's bakery, a woman complains resignedly about the abundance of dowdy charity shops, and serves the most delicious pasty I've ever eaten. Other local women bumble amiably about "community" here, and I'm instructed that, based on my years, I must head on to lively Falmouth. I ignore their counsel, leaving town and veering south, into a vast, unoccupied wilderness.

Past a small airfield, the narrow road threads through a barren, flat and featureless expanse of heathland and hillock. The Lizard's composed of an unusual serpentine rock, fine for ornamentation but ill-suited for vegetation. A fierce headwind dogs the ride across the deserted peninsula, and it is some miles before I reach its southern terminus at Lizard Point, the most southerly part of the island.

A lighthouse guards a treacherous tract of sea. The cliffs are precipitous and jagged. Three lifeboat stations, two signal buildings and one persistent Italian experimenting with the invisible have left their mark. Marconi pioneered and transmitted the first radio signals from the Lizard. Radio, television and the mobile phone owe their origin to these experiments on this bleak, remote headland. I savour the scene, and then turn back inland, heading east.

Mushroom-like bulbs appear on the distant horizon. Closer, at Goonhilly Downs, the forms of a vast complex of sixty or so satellite dishes appear, receiving signals from around the globe. King among them is Arthur, a huge parabolic dish built to receive the first orbital satellite-relayed transmissions through Telstar, back in 1962. Half a century on, over two thousand satellites orbit the earth, only half still operational, whilst NASA reckon some 21-thousand pieces of debris, each over 10cm in size, orbit our planet. Space has become like our oceans, atmosphere and land, another receptacle for discarded rubbish. But Goonhilly's tranquil violets contrast against the buttery furze and indigo flowers.

On the outskirts of St Keverne, a village on the eastern edge of the Lizard, a monument commemorates Michael An Gof and Thomas Flamank. Michael was a blacksmith, and he began a popular uprising from this village in 1497, ostensibly against high taxes levied disproportionately against the Cornish to pay for a war against the Scots. In effect, they were also fighting against the enclosure of semi-independent Cornwall into Tudor English rule. Flamank, a lawyer, joins him at Bodmin, and their force gathers around fifteen thousand disgruntled labourers, yeomen and local gentry, marching towards London to present their grievances. The rebels fail to persuade the rebellious Kentish men to join them. Demoralised yet defiant, they camp at Blackheath, like Wat Tyler and Jack Cade before them, that South London field where every popular uprising has had its swansong. A lack of strategy, solidarity and weapons has them routed at Deptford, then slaughtered or dispersed.

There's a large, deserted market square and equally large, deserted granite church in the centre of St Keverne. Three old boys sit at a trestle table in a garage by the church, headphones in ears, moving wires from one metal box to another whilst mumbling. "All it takes is a few watts, and through these cables I can reach thousands of people all over the world", Ivan tells me. His finger gestures to a thin cable that leads from one large box up to the steeple. It's "white man's magic", one in which amateur radio enthusiasts can broadcast messages to thousands simultaneously, with the most minimal of wattage. As he explains one such device, his comrade begins shouting to someone in Skye.

The atmosphere is alive with countless signals, tune in if you wish. It's like the mysterious "numbers stations" Christy played as we drove through the Highlands, just empty series of synthetic numbers or polyphonic beeps, punctually broadcast by intelligence agencies to communicate with spies. A world bewitched, humans and machines communicating. The Poldhu club is more modest. "How's the weather there? Where are you?" He clears his throat, and shouts even louder into the speakerphone. "St Keverne, no... Lizard. The Lizard. Cornwall!"

I've lost track of time, and must manically pedal through the lung-bursting hills of Manaccan to catch the last ferry over the Helford River, thereby avoiding a very long cycle round. Phew! Evening's cooler climes are some relief, and as I ride into Falmouth Bay, the sun begins to set.

Falmouth is a large built-up port, a settlement the scale of Bridgwater, if not greater. The out-of-town supermarkets, apartment developments and car-showrooms stand in ugly contrast to Penwith and the Lizard. But there's pleasure in being around people again, and the old town centre is spirited and bohemian.

I pause at Discovery Quay, a large modern entertainment complex with Rick Stein restaurant and maritime museum. Though the luxury apartments and bogus timber maritime façades around "Events Square" are a little jarring, it's pleasant and a popular place with young families. Snacking on biscuits outside a Tesco Express, I get talking to Trevor about life in Falmouth. He fondly describes its large arts college, and the kinds of characters it brings. He gazes out wistfully at the jaunty boats of the harbour, and carries his five decades heavily. He talks of smuggling, and how once all of Britain's post passed first through Falmouth, the deepest natural harbour in Europe.

I push up Pendennis Point, following his tip, where a Tudor castle overlooks the town and bay from its bosky promontory. Scanning counter-clockwise, there's the verdigris of the Atlantic, the vast, modern warehouses of Falmouth docks, and a plethora of bobbing boats squaring up to a large harbour-town. Pulled by two boisterous Alsatians, Lee smiles as he explains life here. "It's a very friendly place... It's always fresh. New students, dockers... always new life in the town." He's come from the Midlands, and enjoys the liberalism and lack of pretentiousness here. His pub tips also prove sound.

Back in Falmouth centre, I put my feet up in the Chain Locker and listen to a local weird croon Cliff Richard to bemused onlookers. Barmaids talk of their lives, drunk students trade tales of blacking out like a competitive sport, and kebab-shop owners chuckle at the nocturnal shenanigans. People seem happy. "The poor man, he asked me what do I want, as if I knew?" A girl's offbeat statement answers a lingering question.

I find her camped out on the edge of Little Pendennis, another member of the bedouin of bohemia. As I clamber out of my nest, I notice her smiling, perched meditating several metres away. "Hello!" she says with a chuckle. Confused, a little self-conscious, I nervously issue a "hello!" back.

This ruined sea-battlement was totally deserted last night – I'd checked. I returned drunk, and indiscreetly pitched up at the water's edge, beneath a visitor car-park, Falmouth Bay around me. This morning it swarms with dog-walkers and bird-watchers.

Samantha's infectiously cheery, and invites me into the Sahara for a cuppa. It's a Parcelforce van now improbably housing a mattress and cooker unit. Tea boils up from one of the saucepans. She's about to start a crafts degree at the university, and has arranged with a farmer to pay £80 a month to stay on his land over winter, but in the meantime she's been exploring Falmouth's wild-parking spots.

She's not much older than me, but talks vividly of the last three years lived out on the road, exploring the Americas, sailing around Hawaii. She refused to travel by air, mostly hitchhiking. Her experiences were universally positive. "When you first cross into a country, you're unsure how it'll be." There's different etiquette, unwritten rules one must quickly learn, as well as the fortitude of standing for hours on a deserted dusky highway, thumb outstretched. "You've got to think that the person you're waiting for is about to turn up."

She hands me a jam-jar of green tea and a plate of rice cakes with peanut butter. How did she make it work? She cleaned houses, sold fruit on the beach, but often relied on people's generosity and friendliness. She stayed with an English millionaire, slept under bridges with bums in Denver, and befriended a Mexican gangster who turned out to be a nurse. The road was full of surprises. "I discovered an inner freedom and strength. I realised I could do anything I wanted, after that... like anything was possible."

"Freedom" is a word often used, rarely defined. Samantha comes closer than most when she describes freeing herself of material attachments and personal goals. She speaks of "getting rid of those objects and moving on", being driven by the pleasure of motion rather than reaching some aspirational terminus. Abandoning attachments to people "is hard", the arc of her smile diminishing. What matters, she rights herself, is "what's at hand, what's possible". Which means reckoning with the probability of an unsustainable society's inevitable collapse. "I think there's going to be turmoil, with people, and the environment." But, she adds, "before there's something new, there must be the death of the old".

Rejuvenated by her inspired outlook, I catch a ferry over the bay to St Mawes. The Roseland Peninsula east is mostly flat, hedgerowed and fertile, more like Devon or Somerset. Thatched roofs, fresh blackberries, tables bearing new potatoes and unsupervised honesty boxes. Through the villages of Veryan and Tregony I pedal, the headwind and W-hills wearing me out, til sometime later I reach St Austell.

It's a large and neatly arranged town, its dignified council low-rises caught beneath a swooping viaduct. The town centre has been half-heartedly "redeveloped". In the Seven Stars, a local studiously rolls up a cigarette and speaks of its "great highs and great lows", reeling out facts and dates with pace and precision. "Fifteen years ago, it was very closed to outsiders. Now there's a new shopping centre, the Eden Project... but there's pockets of unemployment, long-term, people that just don't want to work." I ask if he knows anyone who fits this description. No one, but he assures me he is correct.

Outside the local MP's office, shuttered, another woman complains about the incoherent new mall. China-clay production once brought trade and employment to the area until the 1960s. "There's not much life here now", she sighs. This is visible around St Austell's Bay, from the ruined and roofless auditorium of the Cornwall Coliseum on Carlyon Bay to the tightly cramped terraces of Par, with its dirty, dilapidated docks and warehouses. Yet clay-production still continues in some quantity, employing a fraction of the people it once did. And the Eden Project, burrowed in an old clay pit, is often quoted as one of the region's recent successes. So why don't some feel that?

Through a weird wealth wormhole that perhaps only England has got away with without provoking serious riots and mass robbery, I reach the quaint village and harbour of Fowey, a terrain of second homes, luxury yachts and Daphne du Maurier dross. OK, I admit, it is lovely. Over the briefest of bay-hops by ferry, I pedal along the rural coastline to Looe, a larger town also given over to tourism. Among its Cornish pasty and cream tea outlets are many memorial benches, guesthouses and a small still-active fishing harbour. I follow the road inland through the flatter hay-bale scapes of St Martin, No Man's Land and, after joining a busier A-road at Widegates, east over the River Seaton, through Hessenford, Sheviock and then Antony on the Rame Peninsula, a rural and undramatic terrain.

Daylight's curtains close sooner now with autumn's approach. The road ends at Torpoint, a warren of derelict boozers and shitstone terraces, surrounded by a large military base. Boredom seeps out of the broken paving slabs like municipal pesticide. I catch the final ferry of the day, pulled by chain-link over the Tamar and into Plymouth. This small naval city has much to commend it as it turns out, but its western edge, Devonport, is all over the place, mixing crass luxury apartment blocks with semi-derelict dock warehouses, and vast roads that seem to drain life rather than conduct it. The New Palace Theatre, a proud and gorgeous-looking bit of Victoriana, is all boarded up.

Confused by its layout, I head towards the train station, where I've kept Imke waiting. She often hosts couchsurfers with her husband Andrew and three teenage children. She sees it as vital for their upbringing, expanding their awareness of unfamiliar cultures. It's fitting for this old port city, where Francis Drake and the colonists of Canada, New Zealand, America and Bermuda first departed. They welcome me into their home, and over dinner, we discuss farming. The family has recently moved from Truro, and Andrew still works as a manager for a wealthy old couple's farm. He calls it a "way of life", and speaks like the veteran of a valiantly defeated platoon. "We used to go into the fields in the evenings and weekends, picking spuds." For him, dependence on seasonal labourers from Eastern Europe isn't simply down to low wages. "People just don't want to do hard work." Cannot, or will not?

Connected to such work is the *way of life* that Andrew, Rhonda, Gavin, Andy and others have been lamenting the loss of. A way of life that possessed a vast, specialist knowledge, passed on through family and community, now unskilled, demoralised and defanged, driven into the service sector, children following parents into working poverty. Across the country, as the City of London has prospered through financial trade, ostensibly at the developing world's expense, our own ways of life are collapsing, unable to compete in an unequal global market. It is more profitable to import new potatoes from Egypt than grow them in Cornwall; more profitable to mine in Chile or Indonesia than Penwith or Anglesey. But why should they compete? Why can we not give people jobs and protect our markets from slave-wage producers?

Property has taken the place of education or political reform as the prime means of social mobility. As men and women struggle to make ends meet in Camborne, St Austell, Bridgwater, Easton or Plymouth, the other population thrives, investing their riches into luxury second homes in Rock, Fowey and Salcombe. Peasants and gentry. This is an old country.

Plymouth's a strange beast. Little survives the efforts of Hermann Goering and Patrick Abercrombie. Drifting down James Street and Armada Way, I survey the scene: paternalistic Wrenaissance of the Edwardian city gallery, next to a jamboree of Blair-era glass cuboids and wacky curves of the university. There's the new Drake Circus mall, an airy temple of consumer somnambulance. Heading towards the sea, I'm surprised by the gallant concrete boulevards now around me, built in the post-WW2 reconstruction of the city. They're gridded yet prioritised for the pedestrian, teeming with citizens, not shoppers. It feels European, with little bits of Blighty creeping back in through its broken pavements, poundshops, mollycoddling street signs and the traffic sprawl surrounding it, an ill-fitting melange.

Though it claims to be the gateway to Cornwall, Plymouth looks more akin to a Yorkshire town, with its plethora of bakeries, discount shops and Olympic pool-like indoor market, roast beef and grease tea bubbling in formica caffs overlooking traders' tat. "Like every city", a baker tells me in Dewdney's. "It's got good and bad parts", she says, comfortable with its urban ailments, like the reassuring stroke of an old scar.

I wander around the monuments to Francis Drake and the naval dead at the Hoe, overlooking the sea. Feeling their insular vulnerability, the Europe-facing English have tried to dispel fear with an aggression of their own, launching wars from here against much of the world. Ray's ice cream van now guards the placid parkland and bay, untroubled by the spectacle of the Spanish Armada. He serves up apple crumble ice cream and tells me of the town's fishing and petrol reserves. "The world's not what it used to be", he sighs.

Age is like a passport, its privileges felt keenest when lost or near expiry. But is it just Plymouth that wears its age heavily? Beginning the world anew is a topic rarely posed here, an island burdened by centuries of inherited wealth and silly, harmful constitutional quirks. "The future is (y)ours", replies an optimistic graffito outside town, overlooking a polluted highway. Theoretically, it's possible, but imaginatively – or as we say today, *realistically*? The Mayflower also set off here in September 1620, its idealistic passengers fleeing religious persecution and monarchical government for a new life in America. They had given up on establishing a better society in England and sought somewhere new, but like all utopians, brought with them tyranny of another kind. Perhaps a new kind of voyage is needed, or something else entirely.

I keep the sea to my back as I cycle through the Plym valley, weaving through the pomona thickets of Yelverton, steepening as it approaches Dartmoor. It is a difficult climb, but the exertion is rewarded with an enormous tract of heathland, wild in many parts, populated with ponies, sheep, donkeys, and the occasional bison. Flinty tors glint in the distance. Pushing east towards Princetown, the road remains steep for some miles, but there's consolation in the epic scenery, deserted of trees, hedgerows and walls, an array of golds, russets and faded bottle-greens of wilted bracken, gorse and heather. Horses occupy the narrow road that crosses the fells, forcing drivers to divert around, onto the verge. Admire their pluck! The animals are still being grazed in common, without enclosure or walls, as was the case until only three centuries ago. Dartmoor does not acknowledge such time.

Princetown is one of its very few settlements. It is dominated by its prison, a gloomy granite garrison built by the prisoners of the Napoleonic Wars, some of whom later killed themselves in droves in this bleak, inhospitable place. In the 1540s, John Leland found "wilde morisch and forest ground", and three centuries on, Richard Brown still observed a "dreary mountainous-tract". It hasn't changed, though what for some is sheer desolation is to others, like myself, sublime.

In the village's visitor centre, a local woman says that the prison is one of the few employers here, and that most young people, like her son, move away for work. There's a military base at Okehampton, and the ludicrous Buckfast brewery and monastery stands nearby, a ready target for a future Scottish "War on Drugs", but is otherwise sparsely populated. Some visitors like to play hide and seek with watertight containers, she tells me, scattering letterboxes across the moorland. Others are drawn by its abundant ghost stories and general air of haunting. Dartmoor's reputedly troubled by a headless Yeth dog, inspiring Conan Doyle's *Hound of the Baskervilles*. Others report sights of pixies, or devils, or even ghostly hairy hands said to steer cars off-road between Princetown and Two Bridges. Or there's the tale of Childe, adrift here one night in a snowstorm, who in desperation disembowelled his trusty horse and slept inside its trunk. His remains were later discovered, frozen solid.

The landscape loses some of its drama after Postbridge and Moretonhampstead, til by Bridford those prehistoric tors are long behind me. As the sun sets, I chase down one hedgerowed lane after another, totally lost, til at last Colin's instruction bears fruit. I find this unlikely rebel beside a bridge, overlooking the gentle River Teign. "Welcome!" he says, smiling, and shakes my hand vigorously.

Colin's a difficult man to get hold of. He doesn't have an email address, mobile phone or even a fixed address. Yet for three decades he has single-handedly run the Exeter & Teign Valley railway. It is quite unlike anywhere I've ever been. We cross the bridge, and he shows me round the railway yard, crammed with 1950s-era carriages, brake vans, signal boxes and other rail ephemera.

A counter-history of British modernity could be written through the case of the trains. It'd feature John Betjeman, nationalisation, ticket stubs to train stations in cow fields, and maps, dozens of them, as romantic and hopeful as a teenage elopement. As W.G. Hoskins rightly remarks of their viaducts, tunnels and rewritings of urban centres, "[n]othing like their earthworks had been seen since the earlier Iron Age of pre-Roman times". Lines of communication, they stretched everywhere, and were reproduced across the globe. Publicly owned for a time, their privatisation has resulted in a colossal waste of public money and unnecessarily high ticket prices. Even the contemporary state of grumbling, and only grumbling, would be worthy of exhibit.

Colin insists that he's not nostalgic, and has little time for the steam railway enthusiasts one might compare him with. "Ask them what they think the future of the railways is", he states, with quiet conviction. "It's like history became trapped, and couldn't move." Instead of "raking over the past", his railways project seeks to restart time, a progressive vision of the future based on automated technological progress, ecologically sustainable and accessible to all. Hence his love of the railway, and his frustration at decades of sabotage by car-centred transport policy and the catastrophe of privatisation. He envisions the reopening of old railway lines, like this one through the Teign Valley, and a publicly owned and accountable railway, neither blighted by "parasitic" profiteers or a "care-home" of useless, lazy staff, as he recalls under British Rail.

Colin worked for British Rail for some time, collecting items and stowing them here, magpie-like. He now curates a small museum, and has a sympathetic neighbour transforming his inked missives into a vast, labyrinthine website. But best of all is another facet of Colin's operation, and the reason I first got in touch with him, thanks to a tip and telephone number from Kirsty in Luddenden Foot.

"Just you wait until you see it", he chuckles. "There's no TV!" But the 1950s Toad brake-van is fitted out with every amenity needed for a relaxing escape from the digital world. There's a cooker and a bed, an old Roberts radio, and a carefully curated bookshelf of rail and travel writing. Some concessions have been made to modernity: a fridge and a microwave for instance, but otherwise there is no shower, and the toilet is a chemical khazi in an old signal box, located with a signalman's torch. It costs £21 a night to stay in this extraordinary space – the price of a youth hostel bunk, and a fraction of a B&B – and later, Colin insists on not taking any money.

Initially he'd hoped to use the revenues from the Toad and adjacent Tadpole camping vans to fund the purchase of the remainder of the old Teign Valley line, once used as a diversion-line around the often-flooded Dawlish mainline. For much of the time he was fully booked. But like his railways, his modus operandi has become obsolete. Teign Rail's camping service will not be found on TripAdvisor or an online booking app. I doubt Colin's even heard of Facebook, and a description of Twitter would provoke riotous scoffing.

"When I opened this, I thought I was onto something, but perhaps it was just the tail-end of things." He traces a cultural shift towards accelerated consumption of things and ideas. "People don't realise that there's a world beyond the Internet. It's a lot deeper, and richer, and there's a lot more going on." Demoralised, he's planning to cease the camping service after my stay, making me its penultimate guest.

There is indeed something about his commitment to a socially progressive idea, and his meticulous care with words and concepts, that makes Colin an inspiring figure. Like Samantha, the druids, and their descendants, the cunning folk, Colin persists in dreaming and persists in his courage. "The world's changing", he says with sadness, as we stand at the foot of the Toad and the end of the line, gloaming setting, stars beginning to light. It will sadden me most if the world loses its capacity to dream like this. What to some is idealism is, for Colin, common sense yet to be implemented. "Things change when people start to talk to each other, positively. To the people around them about what could happen." The head shakes, but the heart understands. For as long as cunning folk retain this could, powerful things remain possible.

CHAPTER 11

Kill All the Gentlemen

"We're protected from their malice by their incompetence"
– Laurie.

I hear the tide rip a moment before it crashes down over my head, sea submerging me in icy verdigris. Surfacing again, I spit out the brine and clear my eyes, taking in the scene.

It's the latter half of September now, three and a half months since I left home. But today is the first day that's unseasonably warm enough for a dip in the sea. Rain's assailed me more days than not. Now the cool Atlantic tingles my nape as I splash towards the horizon, out far enough to turn round and regard the view of Burton Bradstock, a golden beach beneath secluded sandy cliffs, Jurassic in composition.

At some point yesterday as I left Colin and Christow behind, I crossed a border. Once it belonged to the ancient southwestern kingdom of Dumnonia. Yesterday it was unclear, but the medieval battlements of Exeter suggested a modern marker, separating untamed, cunning Devon and Cornwall from the golf clubs, rose bushes, Union Jacks, tax-effective investments and CCTV sets of Little England.

Were its frontier bastions in the Tudor twee of Exeter's cathedral quarter, with its adjacent British Town Centre dross malls, in place of the civic and social structures that might stir the feelings and desires of a people? Or the gated detached houses and paved-over driveways, surrounded by ornate palisades and warning notices, in its affluent, homogeneous suburbia? Or was it in the village of Swyre, later, where a pub landlady refused to give me tap water? "I'll have to charge you for it, I pay for it", she insisted. I'd never heard anything like it. Or perhaps in the nimby petitions of the South Devon and Dorset towns, like Sidmouth, Seaton, Axminster or Lyme Regis, where I ended up last night? No wind farms, no social housing, no benefits for the poor, no rubber rings for drowning refugees, no thank you, not in our name.

This was not the image of England and its radical commons I was seeking out, perhaps to reality's detriment. This was a mean and boring country, a classic Conservative country, with the kinds of settlements one sees in aspirational TV property shows like *Escape to the Country* or *Location, Location, Location*, often broadcast during the day as punishment to society's less economically productive members. This was the England whose tax-efficient investments have thrived out of the privatisation and deindustrialisation of the Midlands and North. It didn't care what the pinkos or plebs or woolly *Guardian*-reading liberals thought of it. The four-by-fours, neighbour disputes over boundary hedges, and CCTV security systems constitute a common sense of individual greed and selfishness, calling itself hard work and aspiration. It was a poisonous country, and compared to Scotland or the North, one I immediately felt uncomfortable in.

I camped behind a semi-disused chalet park at the edge of Lyme's old Cobb Harbour. In the Volunteers, I'd talked with Adrian, an ex-East Londoner living the good life out here after decades in the brewing game. At first we'd chuckled about the old haunts we both knew around the capital, til he slipped out something that stunned me.

"I rarely go back to London now. I was starting to feel... like a minority."

It pissed me off, and it stung me. What right had he to be the majority, on this mongrel island, settled by every people of the world for the last million years? Whose current infrastructure would've long collapsed were it not for these resilient, low-paid migrants, like my Irish and Jewish predecessors? But they've been subject to racism too, and immigration in many eras hasn't been popular. Liberal attitudes can take a generation to settle into orthodoxy.

Adrian's throwaway comment challenged many of my tentative discoveries. I'd been inspired by the generosity, irreverence, humour and goodwill I'd encountered on each corner of the island. I'd felt there might be something in it that could be administered as an antidote against the concrete and car-park brutalisation of the landscape, against the fattening of minds and bodies on cheap, mass-produced nonsense. But the prevalence of fear and anger was still there, and I figured that telling Adrian why he was wrong wouldn't help me understand why he thought that way. So I carried on questioning him, without judgement, as I knew that many others feel similarly "swamped" and endangered by boatloads of bogeymen.

We talked about it a while. I asked Adrian if there was a white working class experience, being sceptical myself, remembering the black and Asian working class people locked into the same low pay and bad housing. He was unsure. He spoke of out-of-control immigration, "people coming over for the benefits", but nothing was grounded on evidence, just an experience of feeling dislocated, a "minority". I was still unsure whether any kind of negative emotion like resentment, or fear, constituted a cultural identity. It seemed to stem from frustrated political beliefs around fair pay, the scarcity of provision of social housing and care, of being listened to and valued, that everyone should contribute to the common good to the best of their ability, and receive equal treatment in turn. "I don't miss London at all", he said.

I commiserated, not for what he said, but for the defeat in his voice. I have no doubt that were a distressed and dehydrated refugee to stagger into the boozer, having washed up in the Cobb, this friendly man would help them, clothe them, let them stay in his home a few nights. But like the retail parks and newspaper triangulation of debate, his misinformed fears had defeat built into them. His voice disserved his integrity and character. That felt indicative of something.

Here was Wessex, now largely made up of the wealthy or retired, whose brooding landscapes were once brought to life by Thomas Hardy as riven by rural poverty, superstition and sharply-drawn class and gender divisions. Now the young of Solentsea and Exonbury labour under zero hour contracts and five-figure student debts, living at home with mum, a future mortgaged to the plastic passions of the present. Even the children of the largely middle class population here struggle under current arrangements. Adrian, or the Swyre landlady, or the women of Heavitree I've spoken with, or the young people on Lyme Beach or working behind its bars, who talked of their university degrees and their tentative hopes, all have a similar point made in different ways.

But Hardy never took to the soapbox. There are no pages of *Tess of the d'Urbervilles* or *The Mayor of Casterbridge* that might be anthologised in a volume of English revolutionary thought. Hardy's concern was like William Cobbett's, that the rural ways of village life would become homogenised into a machinic urban labour-force, that "monster whose body had four million heads and eight million eyes", that Cobbett also saw in "the Wen and its villainous corruptions". He did not seek to reform what he found, to elevate the minds and manners of cloddish rural folk into some urban, middle class vision of utopian progress. Maybe that refusal to moralise, or remove the burden of responsibility for transforming the world from people themselves, was also indicative of something.

"Kill all the gentlemen" was the slogan of the Cornish rebels as they stormed Exeter in 1549, enraged by high taxes, the private enclosure of common land, the growing wealth of the gentry in an era of hardship, and the insensitive imposition of an alien, elite culture over their ways of worship. The Prayer

Book rebellion erupted out of Cornwall, a half-century after the Cornish Rebellion of An Gof and Flamank. Seven thousand Cornishmen brought war against the gentlemen, their prices, their fencing and enclosure of common land. Kett led his rebellion from Wymondham that same year; there'd be a similar uprising in Buckinghamshire and Oxfordshire. Despite immense courage, the Cornish were roundly defeated by a better-armed force of European mercenaries, and by traitors in their own camp. All of the rebels believed they were the *true commons*, acting in the interest of the king by challenging these rogue gentlemen, bad apples. But their leaders sought piecemeal reform, a deal with the king and the order of power. They didn't seek to bring war to London, but for challenging the establishment, London brought war to them. Whoever was not killed on the field was massacred off it.

And so I woke in Lyme, and spent the morning examining ammonites and pliosaurus bones, and wondered awhile at the species who'll one day embalm and display our broken tibia and jaws. And I wondered about contemporary dinosaurs, and whether foodbanks, privatised railway memorabilia, billionaires and coins of a hereditary monarchy might one day be exhibited like the slave's iron-bit, the burnt heretic or the feudal vassal. Reason prevails, though never soon enough. Americans in the garb of Georgian gentry willow along the promenade in wigs and frilly finery, heritage hallucinations of real England.

Burton Bradstock was revelatory, as was Swyre, then came Weymouth, a grubby Georgian seaside resort, where, behind its faded but still-pretty esplanade were rows of market lanes. My sister Lucy greets me outside Albion House, now a chain coffee shop. We range around the old harbour, where a fisherman struggles to keep hold of an errant crab, and a dark plaque notes where the Black Death beached onto the island. Pay tribute to the gods with a chip for the gulls, then fend off the rest as they peck round you. The harbour scene's irreverent and fun. From a cocktail bar we shift to the bustling Wetherspoon's, picking up clues for the days ahead.

But for once, release, like swimming in the sea. Not to have to think or snoop, but to be around a familiar face, debate old concerns, a brief taste of home. Then night, towards the stars that hang heavy over Chesil Beach, where in a caravan park opposite an abandoned military base, we pitch up tent.

Only nine miles wide and five miles long, it is no larger than the average London borough. Yet a disproportionate amount of assets and wealth are smuggled through the Bailiwick of Jersey, evading the tax controls of the UK and France. A few miles off the shores of Cherbourg, it has remained a possession of the British Crown for many centuries, and is protected by the UK but not a part of it.

As our ferry approaches St Helier, survey not a harbour or docks, nor the pastel-painted fishermen's terraces that charm Cornwall, but a Tetris game of luxury apartment high-rises. Investment portfolio pads, unadorned and unoccupied-looking, and beside them, a cinema-mall complex, and beyond that, a large and elegant Normandy town.

In the visitor office, questions about tax evasion are brushed off. "Financial services" or "tax-planning schemes" are preferred terms. Lucy hires a bike, and we set ourselves the goal of reaching the other side of the island along the coastal road. While she fills out the paperwork, Ann tells us about the island. "Lots of English people have moved to Jersey in recent years to work in finance. It's changed the island."

Beyond the sports cars and investment banks of St Helier, though, Jersey reveals itself in more natural and picturesque colours. We follow the southern coastal track round to St Aubin, a small harbour town dreamily gazing out to the Atlantic. A local catches our eye. John's a happy man and, like many, enjoys ineffectual grumbling. Local traffic systems in this case. He used to be a bar manager in a nearby hotel, but Jersey's tourism declined after changing holiday patterns and, he says, when the island relaunched itself as a financial centre. "The hotels, where are they? They've all closed down… Now it's finance, that's the thing." But like others witnessing a world spin faster than they can recognise, he attaches this to a cultural shift.

"People don't know what they want. They want money, so they go into those jobs, get big cars, buy places, send their kids to posh schools. Then they want something else." Golf club and elite gym membership, holiday homes, the discovery of their inner chi. He chuckles at the absurdity of it all, Democritus-like. "What can you do? I've given up caring!"

We follow a path through spindling spinneys, lofty and needling, cutting to Corbière on Jersey's western flank. Past ruined forts, castles and Nazi batteries, still trained on the rugged sea. We climb down into one gutted pillbox, its interior dark, damp and partially flooded, the air ripe with mould and piss. Vaguely anti-establishment graffiti inside: "Sort your lives out pigs", "МИЯDЭЯ", and the outline of a bearded face smoking a pipe. I hear a footstep behind me as I peer out into the sea. Someone's still lurking in this dank space. Spooked, I scramble.

We languorously ride along the vast golden dunes, before struggling again inland, among Jersey's flat, hedgerowed lanes, eventually tracking down a campsite in the fading light. Shattered, Lucy collapses into the tent, and I sneak off for a nightcap.

'Message in a Bottle' blares out of the jukebox at the Farmers, St Ouen. It's a friendly and rambunctious boozer, its English clientele trading complaints about their wives or making jokes about agricultural tools beyond my comprehension. Inebriated, I pedal back along the moonlit lanes, til a speeding car whooshes past, dazzling me off the road. My knee's badly cut by the asphalt, and the driver apologises. I laugh it off, but there's nothing to clean or cover it with back at the camp. It'll return to haunt me.

The sun is having wicked fun this morning, transforming the tomatoes and spuds that burst out the soil into an island-wide roast dinner. But Lucy's awoken unable to move her legs, exhausted by the previous day's exertions. She sorts a ride back to town, and I retake the road, completing this Jerriais circum-navigation. It's a beautiful little isle, perfect for cycling. I pedal through one green parish after another, each named after some saint like Ouen, Mary and John, each hamlet linked by tree-lined avenues. Potatoes lollop around tilled fields, marine-nosed, fed with seaweed that attracts the gulls. Farmers' trestle tables sell plump tomatoes and apples for a fraction of supermarket prices. Then Trinity, another old hamlet dominated by its parish church with a distinctive Jerriais stone steeple, and past the Durrell Park zoo, til I reach Jersey's eastern edge. There's Gorey, a small harbour village under the spell of Mont Orgueil, a gloomy granite garrison whose cuboid keep and battlements appear on the horizon like a fairy-tale nightmare. Then, completing the circle, I pedal back through Gronville and into bustling St Helier.

Lucy's among the memorial statues of Liberation bus station, back where we began. We dash to the ferry terminal for our next adventure. After a brief pause at St Peter Port, Guernsey, we board our next vessel. It's a smaller, cruder and more intimate boat, no room for a bike or baggage, which I instead hide behind a container in the port and hope for the best.

Conversation is unlike any familiar voyage. No birds, or dogs, or property prices, well, not quite. "As good as you'd imagine it", a young woman gushes mellifluously to a man, describing a sum-mer-long holiday in a private Caribbean resort. He describes in turn his friend's mansion on Grenada, bought by his family after selling shares in a supermarket chain.

The cool ocean sprays against the back of the boat. Sat beside me is the chief finance officer of a nameless international firm. His cheeks expand, his small teeth glimmering with delight as he describes his yachting trips to his various properties around the Mediterranean. I ask who the lonesome granite fortress belongs to, as we approach a tiny island. "That's the Barclays, on Brecqhou." The two reclusive brothers have bought up much of Sark, which we now approach, to the consternation of many Sarkees. Our man is keen to defend them. "They've done a lot of good for the island. It was very feudal. Women couldn't inherit property. They changed that." From another man, I hear more about what attracts people to this fiefdom. "There's no unemployment law here", or any kind of welfare. No local authority schools, no pensions or healthcare. One can leave school at 15. The only tax, much resented by locals, is a £250 "wealth tax", paid yearly. That makes Sark inviting to billionaires, difficult for residents and baffling to outsiders.

The Barclays attempted to buy the island's first democratic election in 2008 by flooding Sark with their preferred candidates. The Sarkees disliked their affairs being meddled in, and voted otherwise. As punishment the Barclays pulled investment out of their island businesses, plunging many into (temporary) redundancy. "It was like something out of…" but the young man's voice trails off. Because where else is like Sark?

We dock into the minuscule Creu harbour, where a dancing figure in a teddy costume greets those disembarking. There are no automobiles allowed except tractors. One pulls two wagons, filled with chairs, which everyone queues to board. The "toast rack" pulls us up a short steep hill, to a small settlement at the top called "the Village". There are no roads, only footpaths, and no streetlights, nor any other recognisably post-17th century amenities. It's not unlike The Prisoner, an ill-assorted toy-land with, of course, a major high street bank as its centre. Wooden signs point in all direction. And everyone seems to know each other…

At the top of the Village is the Bel-Air pub, a friendly little farmhouse of a boozer. Shots for £1.05, pints for £1.65 – both well under half the national rate, and directly subsidised by the

Barclays, a local later explains. Pleasantries are quickly dispensed with by a publication sitting on the bar.

"THE BRITISH CROWN DEPENDENCY OF SARK:
A LAWLESS ISLAND WHERE MEMBERS OF THE TOTALITARIAN ONE
RULING PARTY REGIME CAN COMMIT CRIMES WITH **IMPUNITY**
AND WITH THEIR UNELECTED LEADERS' APPROVAL,
JUST LIKE FASCIST GERMANY IN THE 1930S."

The *Sark Newsletter* trades in tirades against any islander vaguely critical of the Barclays. Each page assaults the intelligence of the reader. In an even stranger twist, the editor reports a recent bomb attack outside his office in the sleepy Village. Things are not what they seem.

With no streetlights, Sark's a hard place to navigate at night. A map suggests a pizzeria on the other side of the island, only a mile-long walk. But the narrow track cuts through a gnarled and knotted forest, and after half a mile of scrambling through the pitch-black trees, insects and birds wittering and whooping about us, Lucy insists we turn round. But the path's long-lost, and I realise we're moving round in circles til, by some serendipity, we find the track again, leading back into the Village. Unable to leave, we find its one restaurant still open, and the kitchen knocks up something off-menu to cater for two vegetarians.

Veins of lightning cut through the violet horizon. Loud rock music blares out from the Bel-Air. PJ's birthday party is in full swing, and every Sarkee seems to be here tonight, from catatonic adolescents to doddering old boys, drinking, dancing and cheering. "Is it always like this on Sark?" "Ah, you are a Sark virgin?" a Frenchman replies. "We are good, we like to party, this is us!" A pub-rock band takes the stage and rocks the place out. "Ride Sally ride!" shouts the portly frontman, "All I wanna do is ride around Sark!" Everyone's drunk on cheap spirits, and we're moving, dancing, laughing our heads off on this eccentric isle.

"This is one of the weirdest days I've ever had", Lucy repeats, as we feel our way back along the hedgerowed footpath to the field where we've camped, the distant storm thundering. I cannot disagree.

Sark is at war.

"They'd offer anyone money, good money, to buy their place", says Jill, still retaining a Lancs tang even after thirty years' separation. "And a lot of 'em took it. But there's some that won't sell no matter what." People like Jill and her family, who we talk to this morning in her cluttered farmhouse, are like those Highlands communities fighting for local power and self-rule over a dictatorship of distant wealth. But in their modesty and ease in tolerating suffering under maladministration, the Sarkees have no realistic means of changing their vulnerable situation. "I wish they'd just get together and bang their heads", the Barclays and their local critics, she adds.

Sarkees seem content to bask in their strange and harmless traditions. As Hardy would write of Ethelberta Petherwin, "like the British constitution, she owes her success in practice to her inconsistencies in principle". The island is still feudal, officially ruled by an unelected seigneur by inheritance (and now a corporate seigneur in practice), and until the 1970s women were disallowed from opening bank accounts. Only recently has a law been repealed that allowed men to freely cane their wives, so long as the birch was no thicker than their little finger. We wander through the village, and I chat to a young woman, about to leave for "the UK" again, Glasgow maybe, having been schooled elsewhere. GCSEs are completed online. Escape's on the cards.

Down by the jetty, we spot last night's pub-rockers. They're from Guernsey, and talk of the local patois, and complain of rapidly rising house prices as investors and tax-evaders buy into the island. "The young just can't get a foot in", says the frontman. "Everything's now built and sold on the open market. Nothing's built for the locals. They just can't afford to stay." "It's an expensive rock", the guitarist jokes.

They are not wrong, but these laments have been heard from Suffolk to Skye. Without the advantage of travel, many consider their problems to be local. And that's fair, as it accounts for what they've experienced. But my journey's lent the advantage of being able to recognise common struggles and links across the island. Property's commodification and its apparent scarcity, making it a form of currency and social mobility…

But hush, it's a lovely morning! The ferry approaches St Peter Port. In the distance to our left, notice the imposing garrison of Castle Cornet, its turrets metamorphosing imperceptibly into the craggy rocks. Ahead is a small 19th century French harbour town, with seabird steeples, pastel pigments and old terraces careering out into the country. The bicycle and bags are still there, but my cut knee has become infected, making movement painful. So instead we explore the old town on foot, finding the wistful townhouse of Victor Hugo, then strolling around the stalls of its old market, among butters, jams and Nazi-occupation newspapers. One old resident bemoans the disappearance of old Guernsey and its patois. "It was all tomato growing here when I arrived. Now… it's banking instead… More money", but, she adds, "something's being lost".

Another stallholder inquires incredulously about my burdened bike. I've been carrying five stone with me, Colin discovers, half my body weight in muesli and damp socks. Ray also complains about rising property prices and ferry rates. He feels caught between a rock and a hard place. "It's virtually impossible to leave the island!" But he and another stallholder become more heated about their own island elections. "It's becoming a dictatorship", she chips in. "People get ignored, they just do what they want." He complains of a huge government deficit after Guernsey stopped taxing resident banks when they threatened to leave the island. But their proposed solution is little different than the current settlement, and seems contradictory. "We need businessmen, people who will act in the wider interests of the island."

Enough times now, profit-driven and tax-avoiding individuals have proven themselves politically and morally unfit to act in the common interest. Yet if anyone occupies the invisible place of power I searched for in the Midlands and the North, it may well be these people, living without paying taxes in places like this. "How I hate and detest the common herd", says a man beside us jokingly, on the ferry back to "the UK" and its seemingly punitive taxes. But out here, people can make jokes like this and comfortably laugh at them. How does one initiate a reply?

I point out the Swanage Peninsula as it appears on our left, a haven of birds and boy scouts, and an older gentleman takes pleasure in describing it. He's currently overseeing the construction of a "super-house" on Guernsey for a young millionaire, who sought to avoid paying taxes whilst being able to work in nearby Bournemouth. It's only a thirty-eight-minute commute in his private jet, he tells us, oddly unmoved by his work or its implications. He only complains of local slowness, of difficulties obtaining permits and passes.

Time passes quicker on Poole. "I'm working all the time, always working", says a young port supervisor, gaunt and weary. But there's good surfing here, a view confirmed by a betting-shop worker up Poole's deserted high street. The town is built-up, a little bland, but not as faded or doomed in feeling as many other English seaside towns, and most of the high street has shops in business.

We're couchsurfing with Ricardo in Bournemouth. Lucy waits for a bus and I pedal down a dual carriageway, night now, knee in some pain. A conurbation of South East Dorset and Hampshire coastal towns has swollen up here, from Hamworthy, Upton and Broadstone in the west, to the larger town of Poole; south to wealthy Sandbanks, north to Bear Cross and Northbourne, its expansion arrested for now by the Stour. Bournemouth is at its centre, and dominates all; shifting east, through Boscombe and Southbourne along the coast, to the larger town of Christchurch, and further east to Barton-on-Sea and New Milton. It's a vast area, and one even more uncentred than the West Midlands towns. Perhaps it reflects travelling fatigue, but after the wilds of Cornwall and Wales, as I cycle around for an hour or two, I cannot distinguish one town from another, except that some border the beach, and others do not. Past corporate offices, chain supermarkets, tudorbethan semis, car forecourts, dual carriageways, fast-food drive-thrus and, as I reach Bournemouth centre, a racist brawl in the street. Oh Blighty!

Ricardo's a friendly Portuguese man who relishes his contradictions. A vegetarian who works in a fried-chicken grill, where I go to meet him in Southbourne, he's trained as an engineer but prefers to cook in care homes and restaurants. Despite living here some years, his friends are mostly migrant workers, many Polish, a language he's starting to master. He's become a little scathing of the island's pomposity and "insincere" mannerisms. "They're always taking the piss."

As we cook together in his bedsit, he gripes against the island's conservative palate. When he started at the care home, a six-weekly menu rotated an array of fried and processed slop. He developed a new menu, using fresh and healthy ingredients. Complaints came quick and fast. "How can people eat roast dinners all year round?" Pain and disbelief is evident in his voice. We all look at each other blankly.

It's a majestically hot late-summer afternoon. Lucy and I stroll down Bournemouth's long promenade, the vermilion sea glimmering around a long pier that children run under and around, the sandy beach filled with relaxing families.

Bournemouth's the first Victorian seaside resort I've encountered that's papered over the cracks, and seems even more luxurious and resplendent today than the halcyon days of the resort's early 19th century construction. There are prim gardens, vanity clock-towers and students lolling around, the affluent centre animated by them. "It's easy to get by here", a local woman tells us. It regularly returns Conservative MPs, and was the first town to install CCTV, and public beach huts. The day's warm and pleasant, conducive to just lazing around. But Lucy's train has her home in two hours. My route takes a week longer. We part ways, and it takes some determination to rejoin the lonely road.

More chain hotels, supermarkets and garages flank the A-road east, but I'm eventually out of their snares as I veer north, along a byway towards the New Forest. The lanes wind through freshly tilled cocoa-colour fields, green-fleck thickets and gold expanses of corn. *Pip pop* putter above me, clay pigeons volleyed and shot down. But green is the colour, every hue one can imagine, as shrubs, mosses, grasses, trees and bracken rule over every available surface. Forest becomes heathland at Hinchelsea and Wiverley moors, and drivers are forced to steer round bands of roaming horses and donkeys.

I stop for water and ice cream in the large village of Brockenhurst. Its red-brick Victorian terraces and timber gabling, alongside the proximity of woodlands and animals, imbues the place with a presiding tweeness. A young woman from the village tells me of her love of the animals here, and describes a distinct identity or "sureness" to the New Forest unlike anywhere else, removed but still near enough to Southampton. A place one can rove through and still become lost. I continue south through Boldre, reaching the old salting port of Lymington, where one more island merits investigation.

The ferry crossing to the Isle of Wight is quick, and soon the old harbour of Yarmouth comes into view. In the King's Head, Jenna concedes that small-island life can drive one mad, and exudes the charming despair of Dostoevsky's heroines. "It's a very small island... You can't just go down the street without people knowing you, or your mother and father." She's been driven back here after life away ("It can feel hard to escape"), but the comfort of the island's smallness is reassuring too. She speaks lovingly of Freshwater Bay, Tennyson Down and the Needles on Wight's wilder southwestern edge. She's interrupted by a heavily inebriated old boy, fixated on the topic of the Chelsea bun. As he wobbles around, I notice the sun setting, and move on.

I follow her words, heading through Totfield and along Freshwater Bay, where I drop the bike by the Albion Tavern and maunder along the pretty cliffs, gazing at the swell below. Jason dries himself off as I return, his surfboard stowed atop his car. "I came here for two weeks and here I am today", he beams. He points me to Blackgang Chine in the distance, a minuscule theme park situated precariously over a chalky promontory. The road ahead is "unspoilt... my favourite part of the island'\:. I follow the quiet road around Compton Bay, "bleak" as Jenna described. There are no villages or houses, and the flat heathland expands far into the horizon to my left, mirrored by the equally dark and unfathomable seas. The scene's rough but serene, lit scarlet in places by the bronze of the sun.

Chale. Darkness now sets around seven, and the hamlet's large pub entices me in. "It's so small here", says one local woman, as we sit round the bar. The tourist season is short – indeed, little asserts its existence – and further education must take place on the mainland. But though they're reluctant to concede it, she and her friend find comfort and cosiness in the little island. One makes peace with its faults, even if one feels one ought not to. Maybe it's not such a defeat after all. And later, as I pour a tin of veg curry over tortilla wraps on the edge of Chale's football pitch, and gaze down at the moonlit sea, I feel it too. Peace. Maybe this is enough.

England. A "vile antithesis of a nation", riven not by class but "social dis-ease", where everyone complains about the weather, finds rapture in tea and chocolate digestives, and has a hot-water bottle instead of a sex life. State-of-the-nation summaries by David Starkey, Kate Fox, Bill Bryson and Jeremy Paxman trade in such bollocks.

I'm sauntering around Blackgang Chine, surrounded by fibreglass pirates and dinosaurs. This is "the land of the imagination", and much of that is needed to enjoy this eccentric little theme park, the oldest in Britain. It may well be the inspiration for one national account that satires all these myths. Julian Barnes' *England, England* imagines a future Wight transformed into a heritage theme park, with its very own Big Ben, Stonehenge, royal fops, Tory MPs, yokel oiks and Samuel Johnsons. It sells back to the world old Blighty's "accumulation of time", and the world queues up to spend its shillings and farthings in abundance.

It is better than the real thing, of course, as for much of the last century writers have masked its urban and less affluent existence with cream tea and cricket club confabulations. Retail parks, dilapidated towns, bad food, endemic poverty and routine inequality, undereducated, overworked. This is England, and that is England, and it is nowhere, and everywhere else. Welcome to the land of the imagination.

Admire the morning vista of the hushed Channel instead then, as we stand by the Pepperpot, a grey stone lighthouse overlooking Blackgang. Tall and octagonal, it is an oddball medieval interpretation of a lunar rocket. The road disappears into the sea at Niton, recent victim of coastal erosion. Another veers inland where, standing beside an old village church, is a monument to Edward Edwards, the working class Londoner who helped establish the first public libraries in the mid-19th century. He died in dire poverty here, well-read but without a pension.

In Ventnor further east, I talk to various retired people who have made a final home on the island. One complains of isolation from mainland relatives, exacerbated by the hefty costs of ferries. She points out that schools are closing because there are not enough young people here now. Another sternly rebuffs the suggestion of building a bridge. "Oh no", he says, steadying his Labrador by St Boniface Downs, "that wouldn't work. It'd attract a criminal element over. They'd come and go as they please." What leads him to think so? He's just "sure", gifted with that faith many have in the truth of their own opinions. Then Shanklin, Sandown and Ryde gloop past into one coastal tract of bungalows. And as much as Blackgang or Tennyson Down, here is the real England, with its reassuringly similar and familiar suburban semis, supermarkets and fast-food joints. At the ferry terminal, I'm refused tap water a second time, this time on "health and safety" grounds, inexplicably. This is also England.

On the other side of the bay is Portsmouth, a somewhat jumbled-looking city. Watching it expand from the front of the ferry, clockwise one first sees the dull council high-rises of Gosport to the left, and beside them the vast harbour and functioning naval base, HMS Warrior's cannons trained towards the Continent. Then the remainder of a modern harbour, a grubby parade of small businesses and pubs behind that and, lastly, on the right, the Shanghai-alike Spinnaker tower gleaming white, overlooking a new mall.

Adam's in his late 30s and is held up by crutches, and asks passers-by for spare change. "You never know what's around the corner." He talks of a traumatic brain injury sustained at work as a roofer. He reports receiving no benefits, and seems abandoned by sclerotic social services. He was evicted from his council home for non-payment of rent after his parents died, and now uses the change to sleep in a B&B. "I'm starting to feel it", he says of the autumn, now tingling the air. Whatever the exact truth of his story, this is no good situation to be in.

I pause outside Charles Dickens' house on the perimeter of Portsmouth. It's a rare piece of preservation order surrounded by gaping roundabouts, supermarkets and closed-down shops. A young teenager begins to shout abuse at a rough-sleeper nearby, and then approaches me. Jordan proves to be oddly friendly, and tells me about Portsmouth as he swats greenflies, and points me west, to Southampton, and warns of the distance ahead.

These are edgelands, frontier spaces of people and places. There are more along the road to Southampton. Clusters of council estates, rusting brownfield sites, lank and broody, aware of their own abandonment. Through Cosham, Fareham, Titchfield, IBM science parks, retail parks, glooping again back into semi-detacheds and gated executive housing. It's a continuous conurbation of not quite anything, a Solent subtopia on soylent green.

The scene changes again over the Itchen Bridge and into Southampton. St Mary's is a curious melange of old gasometers and a football ground, Sikh temples and low-rise council estates. I ride through Northam and round to Southampton Common where, outside the Cowherds, Annie is waiting with her bicycle. "It's been a while since I used it!"

She's lived in Southampton for some time, my aunt, and takes me on a tour through the small city. First, threading through the students quartered around Bedford Place, the universities here now drawing in vast numbers of overseas students. Watts Park, with its memorials to the musicians of the Titanic and Southampton's volunteers in the Spanish Civil War. Then there's the classic and sober civic centre, oddly detached and "inaccessible", as she puts it, from the rest of the city.

Annie repeats a belief in the city's decline. This becomes clearer as we approach the centre, a crass confusion of malls and car-parks, each beside the other, from the concrete carbuncle of East Street or the Bargate, now awaiting demolition, or the poetically-titled "The Mall", or the newer West Quay nearby. "It has a strange effect on people. Many really dislike it." Protests against all manner of local and global injustices often begin or end here, more deeply wounded and aggrieved perhaps by this commercial occupying power, yet still attached to the dreams teased inside.

Further south along Oxford Street, past the grand old buildings that once housed transatlantic ocean-liners and hotels. The Southampton terminus station is now a casino, those White Star dreams long gone. The port has been partially "redeveloped" into a luxury yacht and apartment complex, Ocean Village. These are portfolio properties, investment opportunities, a stone's throw from the suffocated poverty of St Mary's and Sholing.

I ask Annie what it all means, feeling somewhat alienated by the terrain of the last week, not just Southampton but the whole South of England. I can't find any hooks in. It's the terrain I've come from, the apex of acquiescence and resentful defeat, a place of deferring responsibility. Now my terrain's been changed by the journey, by the courage of a few, and the stories of many. I don't want to return to the suburbs of the soul. But that's where I'm from, I know all its codes and rules, its secret signs. Survey the terrain: to the left, the downward glare, the allure of personal fitness, the tweets of indignation, the pleasure of publicly restricting one's appetites. To the right, the cynical impulses behind marriage and children, the shirts, shoes and tense facial expressions that keep a door open, the deference to Stephen Fry or Niall Ferguson, the desire to return to the 1950s, through hairstyles, clothing, baking, brewing and allotments. What's it all for, Annie? This mishmash assembly benefits no one. Even the rich are alienated, overworked and miserable in their overpriced apartments. Who wants any of this? But I keep these thoughts to myself, still unsure what they mean, as we look on at Ocean Village, where the steamers used to set off down the Itchen, out to the Continent.

Annie reflects. "Thatcher realised the poor don't vote." The memo's been handed down from one cabinet secretary to another. Southampton's circumstances are not unlike Portsmouth's, a working class city surrounded by wealthy Conservative-voting shires. The mess of malls and brash yuppiedromes reflect the encroaching power of that Hampshire wealth, turning So'ton into somewhere to shop in or profit from.

There's other stories too, like everywhere, greying the scene. We pedal through Shirley, a diverse area where independent stores still trade among familiar brands, for a time the city's alternative centre after the Luftwaffe razed much of the port. But Annie returns to this problem of poor town planning and a lack of civic coherence, a town too easily surrendered without a fight to corporate interests. As a final indictment, she talks of the vast Ikea warehouse by West Quay. In nowhere else but So'ton would an out-of-town store like this take up so much of the centre.

But I think of the pessimism on Guernsey, in Plymouth and Lyme, in most places actually, those grievances that link up an island story. Industries have, in many places, been sold off or allowed to collapse, and in their place, politicians and business magnates have issued the panacea of shopping. Malls, retail parks, supermarkets and chain hotels have been built all over the island, the only real architectural contribution of the late 20th and early 21st centuries, offering a familiar dream-world of brands in glassy atria and big sale barns. Some were built with good intentions, others merely opportunistically. They employ a few, and distract more, but this hallucination of economic activity is one most see through, though less often around.

Pessimism's the mood. Back in leafy Bassett, I eat with Annie, my uncle Tony and cousin Seth. Both Annie and Tony have worked in higher education and, like many, feel just as pessimistic about its recent shift to a marketised, customer-focused model, plagued by expensive and ineffectual management restructures. Tony recalls one departmental meeting.

"I'd drawn up a detailed plan, because a lot of things were inefficient. And this consultant sat there as we were talking, and started drawing boxes. Different responsibilities by different people. And I said, 'No, that won't work, things aren't hard-edged like that!'" He was ignored, and the solution invariably proposed by the consultant was more consultancy.

At a separate institution, Annie laughs in disbelief as she

recalls one manager justifying a cull of administrators in order to hire a big-name academic. "It's *Lean Production* now", she'd said, holding a business studies hardback like a potent talisman, its inane and oversimplified promises reflected in her zealous expression. The principles of the Japanese automobile industry are being applied to British higher education.

"Sometimes it's important to concentrate on rallying as many people as possible to support the lesser evil", Annie says, finally, tentatively extrapolating a hopeful strategy. Yes, there has to be something, for who wants all this? The slow decline of standards of life, work and thought in favour of pie charts, outputs and cheap entertainment. No one, surely. *No one* is the author of this settlement that we've postponed making a challenge to, in our depressed acquiescence. But the lesser evil cannot motivate change, only the greater good. Like the cruinneachadh north of the border, a collective movement that goes beyond the smallness of our lives. Trusting ourselves and others that an intelligent and versatile people like us islanders can surely produce a better world than this. Surely?

They do not like *wankers* or *bastards* here. Few have time for a *fuckface* or *twat*. And if you're an *arsehole* or a *dickhead*, forget it. Especially if you're on a bicycle.

A workman lays down the law as I enter Winchester. "You twat!" he shouts, by way of a greeting, in the manner of so many others since Dorset. I smile and wave, acknowledging his civic vigilance.

I'm on the edge of the affluent Home Counties, a largely agricultural expanse that surrounds London, spangled with wealthy commuter settlements. The city of Winchester is amongst these, but its history is more splendid. Explore its twee high street. Past the seven-figure townhouses billed in the estate agents, and the yummy-mummy clothing boutiques, there are some arresting medieval structures, like the 13th century Great Hall, with its recreation of King Arthur's Round Table, a medieval motif of equality. Or take Winchester Cathedral, a gargantuan fusion of gothic and Norman, mortal grandeur and divine submission. The city still bandies its connections to King Alfred, rebel Saxon who made here his capital as he waged war against the Danes. He translated works of philosophy and produced the first English law codes, stressing equality between rich and poor, and rebuilt London after three centuries of abandonment. As his statue overlooks the foot of the high street, I wonder what he'd make of the island scene.

An hour later, I'm flanked by the sloping grass expanses and golden corn wheels of the South Downs. It is a gentle hilly scape, nice certainly, though without the hunting birds, heather and roaming horses that make Dartmoor, Exmoor or the Peaks so wondrous. Perhaps it reflects traveller fatigue, but I fail to feel moved by the Downs in the way I'd anticipated; it appears instead like an unexceptional agricultural tract. I stop in Petersfield's old market square for a breather. I get directions in the town's library. "It's a really good place to bring up children", Kathryn says. "It's got everything you need."

She introduces me to David, an elderly fellow who recalls cattle being weighed for market in the town square. Its proximity to London has made it an expensive place to live, they agree, but as they list the local drama societies and community initiatives, it's clear that the commuters have more freely invested their energies into a community than one finds in the capital. House and travel prices equal London's affluent neighbourhoods, but there's something different here, a *pleasantness*, like that of Frome. I don't dislike it, far from it, I only note its contrast from much of everywhere else. But what's attaching me to the authenticity of that poverty? A habitual terrain of my own. If much of England were like Petersfield or Frome, or the quaint dormitory towns of Midhurst and Petworth east, that'd be *nice*. Not for the architecture of social composition, but the air of relaxedness and ease, the inverse of Newport or Sunderland. That is a material effect of being freer of stress. What one'd need is a minimum (and maximum) living wage, an abundance of cheap publicly owned housing, and a national investment bank reconstructing the roads, buildings and amenities of most settlements in a sensitive and imaginative manner. But here is the Daniel Defoe in me, planning the reform of the landscape, and the Don Quixote, confusing dreams for reality. Stop, and appraise what else is here.

The A-roads become increasingly clogged with traffic. Signs for London start to appear. *I could get there tonight...* but a little more of the island awaits. And so I pedal down into Horsham, a large settlement muddling both commuter belt and historic market town. It is surrounded by half-built homes, dominated by a bullish series of office blocks and a shopping precinct. At its heart is a network of narrow, pedestrianised market streets that web around the Carfax, and further along the Causeway are some quaint 17th century houses. I follow a lady's directions to the train station then peter off a side-road, spotting Ariel's head in an upstairs window. He calls down, then welcomes me in.

Ariel was my teacher at Goldsmiths, introducing me to the philosophers I now teach to bright and nervy teenagers, like myself once. He gave me the confidence to work hard in exploring my ideas and trust my analysis, so long as it was properly evidenced. "Always go back to the source", he'd say, as he does again today. Does the theory fit the evidence? If not, start again.

Like one of our old tutorials, we discuss my findings. He's struck by a "generational gap", the young worst affected by low pay, unaffordable housing and increasingly insecure working conditions. Yet he encourages a critical reflection on the project. "Who are you speaking to?" People often of similar age, willing or able to talk as I pass them by. It's true that there has been nothing systematic about my method, except the consistency of disorganisation. I've strived to be scrupulous with evidence and corroborating sources, but this is no impartial account, and the groups I feel most concerned for have been given more space. He thinks this is at the expense of working parents or professionals who I'd be less likely to bump into, a more "common" or at least representative category.

It's a reminder to not mistake one's perspective for an objective judgement. But it is clear that this is a wealthy island, inhabited and paid for by the poor. Though all ages are ensnared by poverty or the fear of it, the young have no free or easy-going education, no readily available social housing, no job for life, or job security at all, no pension to look forward to, nor any folk memory of victorious collective struggle. And actually, this impacts the middle classes too. Unless they have property to inherit or social connections, their social position is becoming subordinated to pay for a complacently wealthy older population that largely votes Conservative, and is rewarded accordingly.

Ariel's conversation bounds from book-burning to the perils of whistleblowing, and much in between. He traces his own life, from a modest Jewish household in Manchester to Oxford University, by way of a fee-paying grammar school that he was able to attend, in his final years, with the help of a local authority scholarship. Under the guise of improving social mobility, Blair's New Labour removed these scholarships. Even in one generation, Ariel's son will not have the same access to those resources he did. Increasingly, expensive private tuition and education early in life shapes one's destiny, and through this, social inequality will further widen.

"It's like we're moving back to the 1930s and 40s", Ariel reflects. An island ruled by an elite personally acquainted with each other, shrinking in size and expanding in power. George Osborne was in the year below at Oxford, and Ariel remembers the Bullingdon Club and the vast wealth required to be a part of their scene. A friend works for a prestigious private girls' school, regularly visited by MPs and business leaders. The girls are already being prepared for marriages and careers. Without an outlet even for the more ambitious and able elements of the working class, the UK may be facing a crisis of the "champagne model", he says, whereas once the very brightest at least could spill up to the top. The country stands at a crossroads though is unaware of it, having trudged backwards for some time.

Beside a window overlooking a quiet suburban backstreet, intricate ink-drawn maps of mysterious scenes. "Warning, this is a teenager's room!" Next to these, a bookshelf. A William Blake collection is prominent, perhaps recently perused. "If it were not for the Poetic or Prophetic Character, the Philosophic and Experimental would soon be at the Ratio of all things; and stand still, unable to do other than repeat the same dull round over again."

My knee has become painfully infected after its Jersey scrape. But I'm reaching the end of my circle, and against better judgement, press on early, parting ways with Ariel. I amble round Horsham, catching conversation. A middle-aged woman from the Midlands likes the town compared to the North, "overrun" as she sees it with Poles and other migrants of unspoken extraction. "You don't hear English being spoken. You feel like you don't know where you are."

Her disorientation about her identity leads to a conservative position, but like Adrian's, I don't read her comment as intentionally racist. It suggests instead the un-met need many have for a community and sense of pride in a collective identity, something that the English, "all middle class now" as they are told, have found no outlet for, unlike the Scots. But we have a whole history of revolutionary struggle, of fighting for the vote, or religious toleration, or against slavery. And so many don't know about it! Disorientation is instead the state of the commons, of not knowing where we are. And who speaks of *we*? In a vacuum, xenophobia festers.

In Horsham's labyrinthine-large museum, Becky speaks of another kind of fear. Communities disappearing, as individuals retreat into their own gadget-enabled worlds. Eventually "there'll be nothing left". She's an artist painting characters, and sketches my outline beside a crude animatronic prisoner in a cell. We discuss changing forms of punishment for a time until, in a way only psychologists understand, conversation turns to childhood and memory. "When I was young, me and my three younger brothers would take a picnic and go down to the river by the day. My youngest brother was two!" She doesn't say whether she allows her children the same liberties now.

South of Horsham, I'm back among the South Downs, and close to where P.B. Shelley grew up. "Ye are many – they are few" inspired the peaceful civil disobedience of Gandhi, but two centuries on, amidst this uncertain terrain, appeals for liberating our minds and heading unarmed to the streets are less relevant. Shelley's "Bees of England" need a ruder shaking and a sharper sting. But I take the quieter lanes through the gentle Sussex country, by Crabtree and Bolney, over the busy A23 to Ansty, bypassing the commuter town of Haywards Heath for Wivelsfield, Plumpton, and into the old town of a more troublesome English revolutionary, Thomas Paine.

Lewes is a market and county town beneath white chalk hills, and its construction still follows a long high street spanning over the Ouse, with a moderate-sized town surrounding it. There's a brewery and scattering of antiques shops at its foot, and as one proceeds up the ascending street, a monument to seventeen burnt Protestant "martyrs" appears, and the rump of an old castle behind it. I venture round a bookshop, where I find a copy of Paine's collected writings. A young bookseller from the town finds the place insufferably small, and talks of rowdy pubs and mercurial energies. Why? "It's on an energy line, a ley-line", words said only half in jest. "So there's something in the water?" "Yes, don't drink the Harveys!"

Tom Paine's not from here, but he made this fiery town his home, developing a hatred for the hereditary powers of the wealthy aristocracy and monarchy whilst working ineffectually as a local tobacconist and excise officer. In his spare time he'd attend the boozy Headstrong Club at the White Hart Hotel, which still stands today. I venture in for refreshment.

"What is that of England? Do not its own inhabitants say, it is a market where every man has his price, and where corruption is common traffic, at the expense of a deluded people?" The barman's unstirred by Paine's polemic. But he serves a good pint, and tells me about the pub's ghosts and the activities of the local bonfire societies. The Sussex villages take Bonfire Night very seriously, preparing costumes, explosives and effigies all year round. Lewes' festivities are best known of all. "Just mad", he chuckles. Spiderman, Shrek, Vladimir Putin and other colourful politicians are set alight. He stresses its historical aspect, commemorating the martyrs burnt alive by an unpopular Catholic queen. The festivities are a cathartic revenge. "Burn the Pope!" people shout.

It's early evening, and the traffic's backing up from Brighton. I weave past lines of frustrated estate- and eco-cars til I reach Falmer, site of the University of Sussex. The university is the most recent to be occupied by students, several times over 2013 – not so recent now, granted. They were protesting against the privatisation of its facilities and the low pay of staff. Though long associated with radicalism, the university's authorities were particularly draconian in clamping down on the occupation, with bailiffs and police used in April that year to evict them. Five students were suspended as a result, though that decision was overturned following public outcry. It was one of the few flashpoints in an otherwise orderly accession of a marketised higher education system.

Inside Bramber House, students shuffle along supermarket aisles or browse Facebook in the cafe. A couple don't remember it, or don't seem to know what I mean. Another, Becky, is studying business. But as I scan the student noticeboards,

I notice a Live Action Roleplay Society, at least four different Marxist groupuscules, and a meeting advertising "How can Palestine be free?" More familiarity with the genocide of Gaza than the foodbanks of Gateshead, Grimsby or Gosport. I wonder about this un-met desire for collective identity and power, to be a we, to be English in an affirmative and positive sense. Who wants this? Perhaps we're afraid to ask the question, unsure who to address it to.

One last bastion of dissent awaits. Brighton's a city long associated with youthful rebellion and dirty weekends, the pleasure-land of Londoners at leisure. It's been the only part of the island to return Green politicians at local and national level, and is still abub with youth subcultures, some decades old, reliving a now-tamed subversion around the Lanes. That's Entertainment, Paul Weller's doppelgängers shuffling coolly around the vintage parka stores. There's a cheery, seedy decay that hangs around the place. And look, no retail parks or shoddy malls! A busker croons Bob Dylan for the millionth time beneath the Anglo-Indian Royal Pavilion, to an audience of drunken vagrants. I scutter by the Palace Pier, admiring the flurry of gaudy twinkles, penny arcades and cheap kicks.

Brighton's also one of the few places I've visited before, so I skip the tour to huff up Albion Hill. My friends Erin and Neil live here, and we head out for curry and beer. Both work in film writing and research. Neil once ran a video shop in town, and though he thinks that Brighton's still retained much of its independent spirit, supermarkets are encroaching up St James Street.

But it's not the chain stores that worry him, but their passive acceptance, and that "peculiar nowhereness" of the moment Nathan described in Bristol. He despairs that the country's fight has gone, like that he recalls surrounding the miners in the 80s. Erin's explanation of why she fled exhausting PA jobs in the City offers one answer. "I'd get home, lie on the sofa, stare at the ceiling, and think 'What am I doing?' You just had to go into zombie mode, hold it down, but it was so tiring." The Bees of England are also known for their tragic indefatigability.

The chalk rock beneath the Downs terminates here. At Beachy Head, a little west of Brighton, it does so rudely and abruptly, its edge disappearing into the horizon as if forgotten by its maker, leaving behind a macabre ledge. Further east along the Sussex coast it fades into the Channel, like at the peeling Victoriana of Eastbourne and Hastings, the shells of burnt-out priers standing gracefully like the remains of prehistoric monsters. And there's Dungeness, where the rock disappears into the malarial marshes, and returns again in its desert-like shingle, expanding into every direction like a bad drug trip.

Figure the contributions of humankind. There are no standing stones or signs of ancient astronomy or divine connection. Brighton attempts to satisfy just the earthly pleasures. But unlike other European pleasure resorts, it is its faded boarding houses, beige curtains, bay windows and artex ceilings that exude a peculiarly indigenous sexuality, cheeky and disappointed. No red lights here. Rather lights off, a midnight fumble. "Is it in yet?" "Be quick darling, I've got work tomorrow."

Graham Greene, Patrick Hamilton, off for a jolly. Pink gin, rained off the promenade. Everyone complains about the town's useless Green politicians. "There's only a certain amount of times a day you can be outraged", says Laurie, in a retro clothier, as I try on dapper jackets I cannot afford. "People don't realise that crime's going down, that we've got a standard of life today that generations before could only dream of." But Londoners have priced out many into the surrounding towns, like Newhaven and Worthing, he complains, and even in England's paradise, rebellious angels grumble and conspire.

I leave Brighton and head east through Kemptown, a concrete contrast to green tea, gluten-free Hove. Shabby council terraces and ugly blocks bruise the horizon. The road curls over the Brighton

Marina, an idiotic retail park and complex of mock-maritime luxury housing beside it. It is flanked by Samaritans notices.

Saltdean and Newhaven trail after, places to either escape by ferry or burn waste in, as an old American and long-time resident bluntly puts it. "Not much is going on", he says beneath a series of massive billboards that shield the road from a derelict warehouse. I detour round East Dean to follow the cliff road, sloping up and down towards Beachy Head, where throngs of German high-schoolers roam up and down, cartwheeling downhill, pointing out the small crucifixes, memorial plaques and flowers of countless suicides.

A little on, Eastbourne: doyleys, cream-coloured steps, bay windows, paved-over driveways. Past harsh angles and Art Deco curves of 20th century retirement apartment blocks along the coast, their nascent modernism thwarted by the net curtains and colourful teddies gazing out from windowsills. A local mum speculates on the recent burning of the pier. "At first they said it was suspicious, now they're not saying anything... I'm not so sure."

The road to Bexhill is riddled with potholes. My wheel catches one and my pannier hooks snap clean off. Everything inside is broken, including my laptop. I tie the bag back on with bungee ropes, and sigh deeply, wondering what's left to give. My knee is in some pain, and the front brake still drags against the wheel unless I disengage it, something I've not yet been prepared to do on the busy roads. And now this. Egads, and so close to home. No... Not this close.

Bexhill's a drab assortment of nursing homes, dopamine-depleted, warfarin- and diazepam-scripted. But there is the De La Warr Pavilion, a fruity dabble in seaside Modernism, and worth a peak round. Further east are the peeling ex-guesthouses of St Leonard's, playing Morecambe to Brighton's Southport. Stunned by premature obsolescence, they still dream of day-tripping families holidaying along its deserted promenade and lovelorn beach huts.

Hastings is less glum, combining cheap and cheerful amusement arcades with an underwhelming theme park, and an old and intriguing town behind it. It makes a muddled trade of smugglers and the Battle of 1066, but there's more evidence of Robert Tressell's *Ragged Trousered Philanthropists*, a 1910 novel of working class tradesmen haplessly exploited by local businessmen, politicians and Christian preachers. The three become an amorphous, self-serving blob, like "the Thing" attacked by Cobbett in his *Rural Rides*, a century before Tressell. Like Orwell and Engels, Tressell saw little realistic hope of his working class bees ever shaking themselves loose of their fetters, and often tarred them all with the same dunce-brush, a massified misanthropy, confusing despair for ignorance, compromise for pragmatism, dupes of the "Great Money Trick". Though perhaps in my pained mood, I'm being too harsh even on his harshness.

The bar of the Albion Inn has staged an epic of Victorian-gothic despair. Nirvana blares loudly to locals on tottering bar-stools, each staring down at a half-empty glass, each in their own private psychodrama playing Mrs Haversham in the attic. What's it like here? The barman shrugs, and conversation's not forthcoming from any corner. I finish a half and leave the sullen scene.

There's a steep climb up to Fairlight, but once back down at Pett Level, the scenery becomes boundlessly flat. This is Romney Marsh, a vast expanse of wetland stretching over Sussex and Kent. "There's not much here", a young man in a Winchelsea supermarket confirms. Well, except sheep. Inland is marshland, once malarial, still humming with strange energies. But the coastline is pretty, where once seascape-seekers like Turner and Millais would travel to and work. Rye too is more picturesque, an old medieval port, though following the coastal road, Camber is little more than a string of caravan and holiday parks. The area's eerie and deserted. I pass a seemingly abandoned military firing range that ends at Lydd, a functional complex of early 20th century red-brick housing with virtually no amenities. Along the road I spy my first soul for some time, selling tomatoes at a stall. "People are the same everywhere, in my eyes", she says, flatly.

And then, Dungeness. The entire area seems to have been pounded with atomic bombs over the 20th century. Little seems alive in this vast flat expanse of shingle, lichen and bursts of glossy shrubs. Even their fronds seem plastic. Stagnant pools ferment by the edge of the thin road. It's now evening, and ahead are the distant lights of a nuclear-power station, and a series of isolated little dwellings to one side of it. There are countless birds however, like the oystercatchers flitting to my left and right, and the gulls, the only creatures who seem to know their way in this disorientating expanse.

There is no village here, just a scattering of timber shacks, caravans and occasional brick houses. This was once a fishing haven, and many fishermen still chance their luck, alone, by the tide. Many of the shacks are now occupied by artists, and one in particular has a feted garden, that of Prospect Cottage, once home to filmmaker Derek Jarman. Old machinery, rail track and exploded boats rust in the distance. There's a confusingly high number of lighthouses clustered. And one open pub, populated by a family grumbling over fish suppers, playing psychedelic rock. The barmaid likes the place but complains about some local levy proposed by the "incomer" artists that'll hit tourism. I drink up and head out.

There is a continual basso drone from the power station, which animates an otherwise desolate swathe of shingle. Bored and fatigued, I decide to ingest the last of my MDMA, but I underestimate its potency, and start coming up whilst ineffectually building my tent on the shingle. Weariness, dehydration, hunger and infection combine to quadruple its disorientating effect, and I soon regret my misjudgement.

It's a Damascene moment. I'm virtually blinded, or rather, I begin to see everything that is not there. Twinkling rubies all around me, floating over the sea and above the distant shacks. The lighthouse is dazzlingly white. And the beach is slowly populated with ten-foot-high figures that glide over the shingle, also radiant white, but dressed in a peculiar armour, like samurai warriors. I swish my hand through the stomach of one, confirming its nature as an apparition. I approach the edge of the sea, exhausted. There is a fisherman here, who is real. A friendly young Pole, he shows me his evening catch, mostly whitefish. I conceal my intoxication and wander back to my tent, but I've left my glasses by my bike, and now cannot find them.

And all around me, the shingle begins to zone out to infinity. I lie down on it, cool and gritty, rubbing the pebbles around my hands, feeling them grit against my sweating head as I frenetically grind my molars. No life here, nor sleep. I lift myself up as the dawn rises, having laid here some aeons, staring up at the blazing white jawbone godbone loveforsaken stars. In the distance I spot my half-built tent. Hail the contributions of humankind.

Driftwood, fishing boats, gutted hulls, ruins, rust, shrubs, and birds, the dazzling daylight, bands of bird-watchers. It's morning, and I've lost the capacity to articulate anything more than nouns in staccato, without grasping the adjectives, pronouns and verbs that link them together. "People come and say how barren it is", a friendly local woman tells me. I reassure her without citing my unusual experience that it is far from it.

Bungalow boxes, ready-meal boxes, recycle boxes, St George's flags, transit vans. Boxed in. Concrete sound mirrors, Martello towers, shingle, and shingle, and semi-detacheds, and supermarkets. Lydd-on-sea, Greatstone, New Romney, Dymchurch and Hythe, the modest semis encamped on the shores like an invasion of brick jellyfish.

Folkestone stands out, a struggling ex-port town. Its fortunes have sunk since the Channel Tunnel absorbed much of the Continental traffic that used to pass through here, as well as the same collapse of manufacturing that blights the Midlands and North.

Its arts triennial is on as I pass, and the old harbour is animated by temporary public artworks. Couples take turns prodding wooden forks into paper cones of chips, whilst others queue by the kiosks of the old Fish Market, gazing over the Channel. In one gallery, I spot a photograph of the Brandenburg Gate, Berlin, on a cold November back in 1989. A group of young adults are mostly standing on a graffitied wall. "I have seen the future", says one of their slogans, accusingly.

Some hours later, still sleep-cheated and weary, no longer registering the scenery, I reach Dover. It's a surprisingly small town, dominated by its ferry port. Everything about it announces a concern with entry, from its intimidating hilltop castle to its fortification-like white cliff walls. There's a faded promenade and offbeat array of boozers, angling shops, bookies and caffs. Two local women spot my laden bike and make inquiries. They are friendly, and insist on Dover's virtues, hand me a local map, and encourage me to stay a few days. I thank them, but I have an appointment to keep further up the coast, and will not be cheated of a bed, hot meal or shower!

Thinking of Slavo and Lucia waiting up the road gives me strength, these two strangers who've invited me into their home. I need that strength, especially after I make the mistake of following a cycle route instead of the road, as National Cycling Route 1 bizarrely goes out over the port by way of several steep staircases. The settlements become distinctly more middle class thereafter. Mud-spattered Volkswagen estates, genuinely Tudor-era farmhouses, streets with preservation-notice nooks and crannies. Past Walmer, Deal and into Sandwich, affluent old ports where people still proudly talk of the very first celery and elephant in Britain being brought here, a place where history is not wounding, but a comfort.

Thereafter the road becomes busier and harsher. I've also lost my bike light somewhere, making the sunset A-road dangerous to navigate. Nervously I keep to the hard shoulder, eventually reaching a great valley of chain store barns encircled by a huge car-park. Westwood. And soon after, Margate. Slavo's waiting outside the town's large, deserted railway station. He scans me from head to foot, and smiles sympathetically. "Don't worry, we'll sort you out."

I can hear a woman's voice calling somewhere ahead of me. My hands steady myself as I follow the tunnel, now plunging down a steep staircase, struggling to keep my balance.

Dark, grey and cavernous, at times I'm craning my head to fit under the curved tunnel walls. I can hear her clearer, closer. It seems that the light's playing tricks with the walls, which ripple and shimmer but, at the foot of the staircase, become made of something else entirely. "Look!" says Lucia, beaming. "Seashells!"

There are five million of them, arranged in all manner of esoteric symbols in this cramped basement grotto. Flowers, love-hearts and the tetractys, ten dots arranged in the shape of a triangle, a Pythagorean symbol of universal harmony. Workmen accidentally discovered it in 1835, but it has been here far longer. Its elaborate construction would've required at least one lifetime's dedicated construction. Marvel awhile at this unlikely temple to the majesty and mystery of the ocean.

I've slept well in my own Margate refuge. Slavo and Lucia welcomed me in last night, and over oolong tea and the last of our food supplies, some Kent tomatoes, a stick of bread and a jar of local honey, we traded trajectories. They spoke of earlier lives in Slovakia, and days spent roving its dense forests and mountains. For a long time we spoke of politics in "an era where wars never end", as Slavo put it, but I was most interested in their own story.

They were struggling to get by, raising a young daughter and working all hours they could get. Slavo's skill is wire-sculpture, his work exhibited internationally, and as we talk, he sculpts me some new pannier hooks using wire. But to pay the bills, he began as a farm labourer, and has now made it up to supervising a vegetable-washing machine in a supermarket factory. "When I came to England I couldn't speak much English."

"We were paid minimum wage picking apples." The hours were long, the sun cruel, and the work gruelling, carrying a fifteen-kilo full bag on his back all day. His co-workers were Polish, and rarely did the opportunity come to practice their English. Slavo didn't complain, but his circumstances are the other side of the coin to the "unholy mess" in food and farming Eden spoke of in Durham. Both are partly responsible yet unthanked for the low price of foods, exploited by supermarkets in different ways. Both bear the brunt of the media's disapprobation. Anti-European migrant feeling is already spiking, and likely to worsen.

Margate is a particularly washed-out resort, a haven for littoral mystics. Psychic evenings in tatty boozers, lady who claims to read all futures by the heart line and the finger of Saturn, or the bottom of a tea mug, or playing cards, or the moods of glass, the gestures of the insecure. Even the madcap violence of the Punch and Judy booth takes on revelatory power in this most unusual country, Kent, being the source of folk morals and mythology in *Riddley Walker*, a heady journey through post-apocalyptic Kent by Russell Hoban.

They call it the Isle of Thanet, but it has been connected to the mainland some centuries now, and the various settlements of Margate, Cliftonville, Broadstairs and Ramsgate, blurring into one. In Cliftonville, Slavo and Lucia point out a peculiarly melted house, a public artwork made from an abandoned building. Gaze out from the tatty promenade at the distant figures of a vast wind-farm, like some semi-submerged robot army attempting land invasion. That sky there, a murk of cobalt, gunmetal, jasmine and stewed lemons, has been seen a dozen times in the visions of J.M.W. Turner, who came to paint here, and later gave his works not to the market but the public. The town remembers him with a witless series of trapezoid blocks housing a gallery. But there are stranger wonders along the Thanet coast.

On our bikes, Ella bouncing and giggling in the child seat behind Slavo, we pedal along the promenade, past bricked-up booths and semi-demolished pleasure centres, staircases that begin halfway up a wall and end nowhere. "Dirty, poor-looking" is how Cobbett recalls Margate, and it remains true of the buildings and empty shelters. But secluded Botany Bay is beautiful, a secret white-sand cove where we stop and relax. The cliffs are scratched with etchings, ranging from the strange to mundane. *I am free*, *Jesus saves*, *Elvis*, *LC+KO97*, *Aaron@Luton*. As I sit on the sand, listening to distant laughter and the cries of the gulls, the surf sighing somewhere nearby, Ella dashes over and hands me a white shell for inspection. Marvel too at the child's unthinking act of generosity and wonder.

I follow the coast round to the ruined abbey of Reculver, still in awe of the sea. The ride is enjoyable, and the Kent landscapes are not what I'd expected. Sickly marshes, isolated strips of woodland, carpets of wildflowers and shingle deserts. Industry freely rusts. Less the "Garden of England" and more its grubby backyard, much has been allowed to rewild or go to seed. It is odd without contrivance, curt, blunt, a little blunted. A different country and a different kind of people. With the exception of small parts of Hampshire, Kent was the only region settled by the Jutes during the Anglo-Saxon migration, and was until the early Middle Ages a semi-autonomous region, one that never quite submitted to the Normans, with its own distinct dialect and culture. The mid-14th century *Ayenbite of Inwyt* (or in modern English, "again-bite of inner-wit") gives a sense of its peculiarly physical and lyrical qualities. "Amen" becomes "zuo by hit". So be it.

Through Herne Bay, Hawthorn, Hoath and then Sturry, where coal was discovered accidentally by cross-Channel railway prospectors back in Victorian times. It wasn't the branches of South Yorkshire or Durham that held out longest during the Miners' Strike either, but Kent, the last to return to work in 1985. Before Scargill it was Wat Tyler, John Ball, Jack Cade and Thomas Wyatt who led the people of Kent to attack the government and gentry of the 14th and 15th centuries. Rebellion's in its air. Kent, like Essex, subverts any easy North-South class distinction.

Its language and customs also carry more traces of the Continent than most places. Only twenty miles separate the White Cliffs from Calais, both visible to each other, and the Kent cinque ports of Sandwich and Dover were key trading posts with Europe. The Romans brought their legions through Richborough, and their Christianity through Canterbury. In more recent times, the Medway towns along the Thames were the sites of shipbuilding, naval bases and Dutch skirmishes, and the last decisive battle for the UK's sovereignty was fought in the air here in the early 1940s. A vastly underequipped RAF managed to defeat the Luftwaffe, as much through technological advantage like radar, as by the Luftwaffe's shift to bombarding cities over airfields, avenging British bombs over Berlin. The RAF was able to recuperate and recruit new pilots, coordinate forces with the exiled air squadrons of occupied Europe, and eventually re-secure the skies, thereby preventing the planned invasion of the island. It was Hitler's first defeat, as decisive as Stalingrad.

Kent doesn't seem to have forgotten its mixed relations with the Continent, but needs no monument to remind itself. It is has more in common with gruff Essex than the birdfeeder suburbs of Surrey, Sussex or Hampshire. Both are given definition by water and preoccupied with marshes. Both are pierced through with an aggressive Roman attempt at civilisation, be it Canterbury or Colchester, but the wider terrain's indifferent. No evidence of any religious idealism, nor enthusiasm for football. Houses resemble faces, affectless, aggressively ordinary.

Canterbury, a small city that stands in marked contrast to its surroundings. It remains defined by its bone-white cathedral, muddling Norman, Romanesque and gothic styles into the overlapping constructions of the expanding site. The shopping precinct around it attracts more pilgrims today. "Just pretend I said nothing", a man shouts to a woman beside him, obliquely. Another greets me using the Southern-English phrase for cyclist, that four letter word beginning with t. "People don't get it's another reality", recounts a drunk outside the Bishop Finger, a little more amiably but no less confusingly. I follow the tide, and wash up in a huge cathedral.

The awkwardness of how to display appropriate feelings like awe in these heritage zones is dispelled with the elaborate faffing of a photo. Handy thing, a camera. The cathedral's a vast gothic transmitter of fear and awe, crammed with gargoyles and grue-some details, from the demonic misery of Christ's effigy over the gatehouse to the diabolic monsters etched into St Gabriel's Chapel and the Norman Crypt. A candle marks the shrine to St Thomas a Becket, the courtier and archbishop murdered in the late 12th century. Locals claimed that rags dipped in his blood possessed power so holy they could cure leprosy and blindness. Littoral mystics... The myth soon attracted pilgrims from across the island, like those recorded in Chaucer's *Canterbury Tales*. When a reluctant St Augustine was dispatched by Pope Greg-ory to "the ends of the world" fifteen hundred years ago to con-vert the local heathens, his operation was only half-successful. Strange powers still emanate from the marshes, clothing even gloomy Canterbury in Kent's off-tone colours.

Sunlight's fading. I ride out west along busy roads, reaching Faversham, a pleasant market and brewing town, with a number of timber-framed houses on Abbey Street catching my eye. Then along Watling Street, where pilgrims once shuffled along from London, trading tales of their own. Sittingbourne is an aggressively doltish sprawl of suburban semis, light-industrial warehouses, car forecourts and supermarkets. Drivers slow down to shout abuse through passenger windows. Perhaps there's a swastika on the back of my helmet. On a whim, I decide to press north instead of west, riding off the mainland and into the swampy Isle of Sheppey.

In the distance, night now, a concrete flyover's lined with pin-head golden flares. Power stations and oil refineries spill their guts out into the Thames estuary. The main settlements are the port of Sheerness ahead, the village of Minster, and the Saaf Laandener's caravan retreat of Leysdown on the eastern edge. The island was for a time occupied by the Dutch, who spent a few days here in 1667 and then burnt everything down. Today it is otherwise populated with sheep, scorpions and a number of prisons. Beneath the deserted highway, bass blares from a boombox, a one-man raver alone in the swamps.

Too dark to ride and, without a front light, I tape my phone onto the front of my bike and illuminate the highway with my welcome screen. Eventually I reach the rustlands of Blue Town and into Sheerness. It's a Saturday night and the Albion Inn is heaving with mods and rudeboys, all in their sixties. Reggae bounces out in the street. "We all knew each other on the island... I was a biker but I loved ska, Trojan", says one man, as I join a line of heavily refreshed gentlemen at the bar. "You and your dad were very close", two geezers confide candidly of repressed emotions, whilst overdolled daughters and wives look on over empty tumblers, bored. "You loved and hated each other but you needed each other." The bloke goes quiet, as does the bar. "The best fella to teach you how to drive a lorry: that was my father."

Sheerness is a small and sour town, one that'd fit easily into the North Lincolnshire and South Wales coast, and has an abundance of takeaways and boozers, net-curtained, quid shots offered on fluorescent labels, Carlsberg the most exotic tipple available. Everyone is drunk. A woman hails me like a rickshaw and asks me to take her wasted husband home. One more pint first.

In the Napier, courting rituals are salty. One man proposes a threesome with his friend's wife, present. His wife interjects and proposes instead a foursome. Disputes over orifical logistics lead to impatient rowing. "You could'n even av a wansome!" Her flopping hand gestures fail to distract his attention from another woman who enters the boozer. "Ere Kel, can I cam inta the toilet wiv ya?"

I can make no more sense of this terrain and its structures of feeling. In the town's pizza takeaway, James waits with his girl-friend. They talk of financial struggles, "not much in the way of work", aimless inertia, in-betweenness, the disappointments of one's mid-twenties, often discovered alone. They talk of dreams, "cos you've gotta av dreams", getting out, getting on, getting beyond all this. And they laugh at my story, and I do too. But it's my last night for real, and I celebrate with a takeaway pizza which, after all the pints of beer, my current account can just about accommodate. "Good luck mate", he calls out to me, as I pass them later, the only bits of life and colour against the peb-bledash terraces. "You too", I reply.

Full up and sleepy, I lie my head down among rushes and reeds of Barton's Point Park, on the outskirts of Sheerness. My last night on the road is just like the first, illegally camped in a public park just off the Thames estuary. In the distance, drunk teenag-ers laugh and scream. I'm safely away from them, and the rain, and everything of a life I once knew and considered the world.

It was going to happen eventually. Returning home? No, some-thing even more inevitable. And cruel. Everyone had warned me of it, joked "how many times?" I'd even brought a spare one all round the island in anticipation. In Rainham, the repetitive rubbery *flip-plip-plip* and careering steering provides confirma-tion. Puncture!

With Google as my guide, I eventually manage to replace the back wheel and fit the new inner tube. My efforts are clumsy and protracted, but the pleasure's profound, a microcosmic experi-ence of my unlikely success circumnavigating the island. Nearly home.

I left Sheerness a couple hours earlier, filled with fried eggs, bread and mushrooms, and a gallon of milky tea. American pop music videos blared out to a packed, indifferent caff. Oblivious of its Turkish proprietors, punters inside debated immigration with a depressingly familiar sense of fear. One older man told a younger woman that he feared "civil war", a term she'd never heard of before. But reciting almost note-perfect the business-friendly stance of the right-wing press, the fella corrected himself. "Anyone who wants a better life, fine, so long as you work for it." What counts as work, or contributing, is never made clear.

Symptoms of political frustration, and of tribal affiliation, like Adrian, or the lady of Horsham. But no one speaks of common sense or gentlemen. They've never known power, or found out who has it. Like the dispossessed of any land, they hate most those they judge below them, those they're most familiar with. And I know they deserved better, that they are disserved by the words that spill from their mouths. They desire communal identity and belonging, and with that pride, alongside a reasonable standard of living, a sense of purpose and hope. The empowerment of the commons, and common sense.

Perhaps I had been naïve in expecting to find rebellion and optimism on every corner. But I know now that their grievances are common, and felt all round the island. But whereas Scotland, Wales and to a lesser extent the North have absorbed these grievances into a collective regional identity, the people of Essex, the Midlands, Kent, Devon and elsewhere lack this. They don't even see themselves as English, and even the St George's flags I've often seen in houses or on forearms seems uncertainly stated. The students lecture them on Israel and financial capitalism, the middle classes lecture them on their bad diet and unruly children. What can I tell this man and woman? Reader, you may have hoped for a speech. But no, I was tired, and just wanted to go home.

Drifting out, I reassess the town in daylight. There was once a little seaside resort to the east of its naval docks, but both have been closed-up since the 60s. Despite appearances, its dock still receives cars and veg from the rest of the world. Foraging the modest shingle beach, one notices countless pieces of small plastic between the pebbles. I go to skim one into the sea, but a dog-walker warns me not to, as there's a sunken WW2 ship filled with unexploded ordinance just off the coast.

Back into town, past faded bingo halls, fish and chips, imperial raj tandooris, doner kebabs and, just outside the cramped Victorian terraces of the town, a McDonald's drive-thru and a hypermarket. Then derelict steelworks, empty roads, concrete flyovers and, from the window of a passing car, a snippet of Tupac, take these broken wings, the common harking back to angel motifs, also seen in tattoos, suggestive of emotional breakdown and resilience.

And with all its melancholic yearning, I realise that Sheerness stands in for everywhere else. This is where the island's at. In its internal and external architecture, in its overlapping time zones. It's a poor place, like most settlements on the island, and not an easy one to live in, but there's a kind of community clustered here, a blunt but friendly one. No one I've met could recall the name of the local MP. Politics happens elsewhere.

Veering off the Sheppey Way, a wee by-lane cuts through narrow hedgerowed lanes, the air humming with manure and skittering dragonflies. This is orchard country, where juicy red apples fall from the trees. Help yourself. They're more delicious than anything I can remember.

Wheel repaired a little later, I discover that Rainham is in fact a border-zone of a vast conurbation of Medway towns. It begins here and blends into the suburban terraces of Gillingham and its depressed town centre that, like the deindustrialised zones north and west of London, has been given nothing to recover with since the closure of the vast Chatham Dockyard in 1984. It stews west into Chatham, the naval docks reconstructed as a cobbled, Georgian heritage piece, some feat indeed, and a more bustling centre. Even the Pentagon shopping mall, ugly by any objective measure, has a certain charm about it, an open-air museum of

1970s consumer optimism. Like in Sheerness, time seems to have snagged, delayed by two decades. A Kentish counterculture of punk, poetry and art flourished here in the 80s, Billy Childish's Medway Delta. Best of all is The Claim from nearby Cliffe, with their songs of disappointed yearning. Like much else of Kent, they are little-known. West, the Medway soup gloops into Rochester, a prissy cathedral town that pinches its nose at its surrounds. The cathedral is sober but meditative, and outside a crooner entertains a beer garden. Come fly with me...

The Medway towns possess many of the virtues and vices of their unusual county. Unlike any other part of the island, Kent has no poet, past or present, who has offered any deep account of the landscape, and no writer aside from Russell Hoban has come remotely close to tackling its brooding, chthonic energies. Kent should be understood as a country, with a culture and history as distinctive as Cornwall, Yorkshire or Sark. Left to rust in the nearby Thames, the U-475 Black Widow submarine symbolises a broader incongruity. An old Soviet attack vessel built in 1967, it was decommissioned and bought up by an entrepreneur, and later abandoned by the Strood. Get a dinghy and sail out to it. Breaking in is easy, as writer Bradley Garrett has proven. The entire world is oblivious of it.

I keep the water just over my right shoulder as I pass the gargantuan refineries and docks of the Isle of Grain. The Medway towns ooze into the wider wen of London, a place one enters with no announcement. Ugly Northfleet and Greenhithe, and a little later Gravesend. Large suburban villas square up to a bevy of dingy offies and takeaways. Behind a crap shopping precinct is a statue of Pocahontas, an indigenous American princess kidnapped by English colonists, who later died here. Close by, a middle-aged woman talks of the area in the past tense. "They all used to work in the river, but now that's gone." She points me west, to Bluewater and Ebbsfleet, the "new town". I spot my first London bus heading towards the Bluewater mallopolis. Home?

It's become clichéd to begin a tirade against modern British life with the Bluewater mall. I see less pain here than Meadowhall, but Ebbsfleet is more indicative of the island's future. Like the mall, it is being built in a deindustrialised quarry, a new "garden city" proposed. Vast swathes of public money are being passed into the private sector to create this. The result is not a civic town centre, good libraries or schools, but more retail parks, a leisure complex and ugly, monotonous, boxed housing. There is nothing here, except this.

"Cyclist's got big legs!" two scallywags shout in Stone. Cheeky, inexplicable banter, the London I know. Like crossing into Scotland so many moons ago, I raise a fist to the air with the panache of a fallen Z-list celebrity. Home!

Dartford, the M25 perimeter town with its struggling suburban villas and town centre, another vast and more bustling shopping complex further west at Bexleyheath, giving away to the more random and run-down storefronts of Welling. And then up Shooters Hill, the priapic palisade of Canary Wharf and the bank skyscrapers of the Isle of Dogs coming into sight, and down into Blackheath.

> When Adam delved and Eve span, who was then the gentleman?
> From the beginning all men by nature were created alike, and our
> bondage or servitude came in by the unjust oppression of
> naughty men.

Blackheath, that green expanse of South London where so many rebellions come to end. Wat Tyler, Jack Cade, Michael An Gof, together again. John Ball preached against the gentlemen here during the Peasant's Revolt, dreaming of an equal and free commons, unhindered from the rule of private property and those who defend it.

Naughty men still plague the island. Today's fence enclosures are of the public sphere, in the privatisation of healthcare and utilities, transport and education, policing and government. The gentry cuts wages, increases rents, and tears up contractual rights and safety regulations as expensive luxuries. Their godly defenders in government and the media justify it as the distant, divine laws of the market. Most are indebted by mortgages, student loans, credit cards, payday loans, their future wages sold to financial lenders. Welfare is being dismantled, and many forced into low-paid underemployment or hunger and dependence on relatives. Inherited wealth, in the form of property, is the one means of social mobility.

This is England, in the second decade of the 21st century. I'm implicated here too, for my mum and dad both own their homes. I can't claim to be among the dispossessed. But like Eden said, I've seen and heard of an unholy mess developing, and it worries me.

Think of those that rallied behind Tyler and Ball, Cade, An Gof and Kett, Cromwell and Lilburne, King Ludd and Captain Swing, Rebecca, the Chartists, the early Labour Party, the Suffragettes, the striking miners or the austerity protests and riots of more recent memory. They were not merely of one class or identity: labourers were joined by yeomen, sympathetic gentry and dissenting clergy, motivated by a common demand for a settlement that was equal and fair, benefitting all. Popular movements demanding equal rights for all, the right to live without state intrusion or harassment, or the right to work, or vote, or the right to freedom of thought and speech, to live peaceably as one wishes, the right to a better quality of life equal to one's parents.

These are the rights of the commons, the collective grouping of all those who live and work on the island, as well as the resources they use. Commons connotes stewardship over the land and built environment, the seas, fields, woodland, the atmosphere. Equal and one, the historical commons harked back to earlier traditions, as much as embracing a fairer and happier future. There could be no lords or kings alongside the commons, for they sought the abolition of inequality, and that meant no private wealth beyond what was immediately needed to provide for a modest life. They demanded a return of power to public institutions, best placed to disinterestedly administer the common good. Yet today that desire's been sullied. There is a House of Commons, beside the monarch and Lords, today filled with upper class gentry, lawyers and other naughty men, and a minority, perhaps, who mean and do well.

Some commons created a mythic prehistory of natural equality, but so be it. Imagining utopia has a long history here, from Albion to Cockaigne, Communism to "Jerusalem on England's green and pleasant land". Even the name "commons" is a myth, albeit an operative one, a declaration. The commons has no fixed attachment to nation (the island has been site of many countries), but still emanates from the local identities that bind people. There could be a Kent commons, a London commons and a Cornish commons, an English commons, an island commons. But even these aren't fixed, and much remains unknown, and therefore possible.

The fences in the distance are vertical, not horizontal. It'd take some match to burn down the bank speculation, aristocratic political takeover, rotten voting systems, the black currency of property ownership, the rule of inherited wealth, and pontifical power of the headlines. But fences will not fall down themselves. Hatred of the establishment has never been higher, and no movement has absorbed that discontent.

One can still dream of an island with a political and economic settlement apt for its temper, egalitarian and irreverent, generous yet pessimistic, overwhelmingly fair. One can still dream of a return to common sense, of equality and democracy, public power. In this long night for political progressives, here is my refuge, in dreaming and storytelling. I'm not sure if it's been worth it, but it has brought me happiness. So be it.

Back into the smoggy Blackheath traffic. West, Deptford Bridge, a Berlin-alike bombsite of municipal housing blocks. I indulge in a cheeky ride the wrong way up the High Street, past familiar butchers, bakers and poundshops, then rejoin the A2, the city's gastrointestinal tract, into New Cross. Places like Peckham, Battersea, the Elephant & Castle and Stratford are all still obviously deprived areas where large injections of capital are being made at specific points in the built environment. These add to their topsy-turvy inequality, where those on low incomes can only afford to remain if they're housing association tenants and sufficiently employed or disabled enough to avoid the benefits cap, and a larger remainder who pay exorbitant rents to live in cramped house-shares, usually in Victorian terraces. Stories to be told another time.

I park the bike opposite Goldsmiths library. A group of young people with expensively educated accents pass me. "It's so ghetto", they laugh, and I admire their pluck for braving it down here amongst our slums. I stroll around, past a hipster coffee shop and an Irish boozer, a Turkish kebab shop and an Afro-Caribbean hair salon, the local Venue club, the old town hall, the Iceland in the distance where a V2 rocket once landed, killing 168 local shoppers. Deptford Town Hall on the other side, its galleon weathervane and clock-tower that shows the correct time twice daily, and the oriel window beneath, held up by elaborately carved mermen. It now belongs to the university, like much else here, which dominates the scene with a line of tall cuboids behind it.

Goldsmiths, a university oddly disconnected from its surrounding communities. The idea to undertake this journey stole on me here, whilst at a critical theory conference. Academic verbiage about the crises of capitalism, papers regurgitating staid analyses with faddish theorists. None of it made sense of my life, or the people I knew, or the communities I'd worked in. Losing the will to live, I sneaked off to the library and, fingers browsing the spines, picked out George Orwell's *Road to Wigan Pier*, a book I'd never read before. I sat down and devoured it in one sitting, over some hours. It filled me with many questions about the present that couldn't be answered by books.

And now I'm back here, outside the Marquis of Granby. "London's where it's at" says a young man, slapping my hand, when I tell this stranger of my accomplishment. I disagree but he doesn't get me, and why would he? Inside, among dark walls decked out with images of Donegal, I enjoy my final pint of the road. Conversations witter among middle-aged Irishmen and cockneys, each freely talking balls, handing out snouts and racing tips. "I've got the skills to pay the bills... Come on Carl, they were big fuckers!"

Nearly home. I see cyclists on the roads, for the first time in months. They pedal through red lights and between pedestrians, with a lack of self-restraint characteristic of the modern city. Then the last mile through Peckham, past non-European food stores and chicken shops, Georgian townhouses and designer libraries. The Woolworths, gone, the cheap multiplex cinema, the car-park that's now also a hipster bar, the full-moon nights in the Kentish Drovers. An area always accommodating to migrants, reflected in the nail parlours, butchers and tenuous churches of Rye Lane, and the delicatessens, artisan bakeries and bourgeois bars of Bellenden Road. I push on, past the post-war housing estates along Camberwell Church Street, and then Camberwell Green.

Home, where every building and alley is haunted by ghosts. The hospital where I was born, the school I attended, the registry office where relatives married, all my years living here, pissing about there, vomiting drunk in some corner aged seventeen. Past the swimming baths, and the pubs, the McDonald's and the restaurants where we celebrated too many birthdays. Small memories of a life. Down Camberwell New Road, more takeaways, pubs, supermarkets, familiar landmarks. Home. Then Vassall Road, the red gothic bell-tower of St John the Divine ahead, trilling bucolically over a terrain of Victorian townhouses and early-1970s council housing, much now in the process of demolition to build luxury apartments. Oh London!

I turn into my estate, its houses named after old Labour politicians, mainly occupied today by Latin American and West African families. Dumped furniture peopling an otherwise deserted place, the same as I remember, except the scattering of autumn's russet leaves in the gutters. I press the buzzer and hear Sarah's voice. I pull the cycle up the concrete staircase. As I wheel it into the store cupboard from where I'd taken it four and a bit months earlier, locking the door behind, I feel immense relief. Even roads come to an end. *Home*.

Epilogue

So, the *truth* of the island. Perhaps the final days' breakdowns and breakthroughs leave you no clearer, or you've skipped to the end for the obligatory revelation about the *genius loci* or the great in Great Britain. In which case, brace yourself for that most characteristic of island emotions: disappointment.

For there has been no island story here but many, selected, examined and rolled up into one. Some are the consequence of random encounters, others are curated from a near-infinite array of historical and literary sources. In telling many, they have also told one, the terrain of my journey and its perspective.

There are many ways of capturing a place's story. Architectural impressions in a Moleskine pad, a flâneur's side-eyed disapproval of the lumpenproles, or clichés about biscuits and tea. Or even staying at home, collating obscure TV shows and bands as tenuous metaphors for the state of the nation. One could go around talking to the public, telling them what they should think. Instead, I listened to people.

Perhaps I could've been more methodical in deciding who I spoke to and stayed with, and where I went. Perhaps I should've gone to Oxford or Slough. But I didn't want to! And wanderlust swung it. The great majority of conversations in this book, and cut out of it, were with random strangers who I approached in the street. Had they been elsewhere that hour, I would not have their story, but someone else's. I was consistent in my disorganisation.

Means made the method. The bung I set out with soon disappeared in beer, bike repairs and a bunk when it rained. My shabby setup built sympathy and rapport wherever I went, and it wasn't necessary to remove my bags off the bike when I locked it, where I locked it at all. But there are few who'd set out to sleep in public parks or on strangers' sofas, or cycle several thousand miles without waterproofs or a decent ride. It exposed me to a more primitive existence. It catapulted me to the generosity of others. I do not regret it, though the schadenfreude is undeniable. It also indicates that such a journey can be repeated. The vast sums that the lycra-clad few spend need not deter the rest of us.

The mind is a terrain formed by its accents and aptitudes. My London voice and youthful appearance shaped how people related to me. Curiosity of a mutual sort was involved. I asked people about their lives and stories, and they in turn asked me about mine, and how I'd managed to get to where we stood. I'm glad to have made so many laugh in disbelief all around Britain. A fair trade! But if one is still sceptical of the courage, generosity, pessimism, political nous and strangeness of our fellow islanders, I suggest you get on your bike, and ask, and listen, and observe. With grace and gratitude, kindness and humour. It will be reciprocated.

Now, my background in philosophy and charity work plays out in the search for intellectual answers to social problems, something I tried to keep in check. But I couldn't help observing that in almost every town I encountered, people were financially struggling. Beneath a veneer of getting-by, many worked several jobs to keep afloat, often in the service sector because of no demand for their degrees or industrial skills. I noted the rapid emergence of foodbanks, and the common acquiescence in an unfair fate.

Young adults are worst affected by the "peculiar nowhereness" of the moment, to take Nathan's phrase again. No more free university education, or jobs for life, or affordable housing, or liveable welfare provision, or likely prospect of retirement. This is a failure of stewardship, as some older people spoke of on my journey. "A terrible world we've left", said Father Michael. Of course, there is poverty among the elderly and the middle-aged. Misery is politically correct, after all. There is little worse than struggling to provide comfort for one's children, and many parents I met worked long hours to this end, without the opportunity to retrain or take a new direction.

Yet young people should be free and capable enough to dream about making the world a better place, to learn what love feels like, or to discover that making mistakes is alright. They should be free to be, not merely do. Instead there is this pressure to become robotic, to work harder and faster and earn more money, or else land on the scrap heap.

The reasons for this poverty and prevailing aura of defeat are complex, but preventable. The method throughout the book has been like Paul's in Monkseaton, showing not telling, enabling the reader to make up their own mind. But to placate any lingering desires for resolution, I'll present one political solution. It will take all but three paragraphs. The more cynical can skip those if they wish.

Difficulties paying rents or mortgages could be assuaged by a major construction programme of publicly owned, not-for-profit homes. Or better still, by nationalising private property altogether and placing it in democratic community ownership. The unequal distribution of employment could be reduced by a legal restriction on maximum working hours to thirty per week. A genuine minimum and maximum living wage implemented. Who will pay for it? The fifth wealthiest country in the world can afford to give all its people an elementary quality of life free from hunger, cold or distress. Share out the tax burden to wealthy individuals and corporations, nationalise the banks and tighten regulations to prevent capital flight, tax evasion and offshore ownership. Proceeds could be distributed through a universal basic income to all those not in employment. Likewise, public ownership could reduce high utility bills and transport costs, and improve the quality of health and social care.

Education and training could be free public resources, producing a far more highly skilled (and with that, satisfied) workforce, with investment in automation to replace as much unskilled work as feasible, with the aim of developing an island economy fit for the 21st century. The collapse of ways of life like fishing, mining and farming could be minimised by establishing tariffs that protect local producers from slave-wage producers or better-resourced competitors overseas. A national investment bank could fund the (re)construction of heavy industries and manufacturing, as well as interest-free loans to cooperatives to purchase equipment. The secession of the island from some international trade and reliance on imports could lead to a renaissance in local production and labour, with controls ensuring responsible ecological stewardship. Fewer out-of-town retail parks selling cheap TVs and trainers from South Asian sweatshops, more people in dignified and real jobs, working with their minds and hands.

The sheer contempt for politicians across the island suggests getting rid of them altogether. Decisions made instead by local assemblies and worker co-operatives could bring communities together, value everyone's input equally, foster a sense of personal and collective responsibility, with a longer-term interest in success. A confederation of regionally autonomous assemblies could be formed from these. Broader issues could be debated in an island assembly of independent citizens, partly selected through sortition (or lottery of eligible candidates, used in ancient Athens and modern jury service), partly through election by proportional representation, with an upper elected assembly composed of experts. All vetted to ensure they have a modicum of public-spirited ethics, with measures ensuring equal demographic representation. An independent senate could meet regularly to review the civil laws, and the UK's one constitutional virtue, its independent judiciary, would remain. Issues could be voted on directly by individual members at community assemblies, with voting compulsory to ensure as wide a social representation as possible.

Dreams, the dreams of an island. Perhaps I confuse Blighty for revolutionary Russia or France. But this island has seen many revolutions before, some forgotten, some absorbed into tradition. The uprisings against Roman imperialism to the rights of the commons, the Reformation against a corrupt church that thrived on the fear and ignorance of its members. Or parliamentary sovereignty, republicanism, or industrial capitalism, or the abolition of slavery. Or the emergence of trade unions and a language of "workers rights", indeed "human rights". Or a universal, free education system and the abolition of child labour. Or the right for all men and women to vote, the establishment of pensions and welfare, and a national health service. Or sexual liberation, and the enshrining of equality in law. Even community landownership at the moment.

An impressive list of rebellions that began as minority voices were lambasted as madness, immorality or idealistic impossibility, yet persisted through dreaming and courage. In most cases, they have become part of the much greater quality of life we enjoy today. If anything, this era stands out by its lack of chutzpah. But this sense of inertia and in-betweenness suggests the accruement of desiring energies around a block. Gathering force yet unable to release, time is slowing into one interminable moment before the extraordinary happens, what few considered possible, even moments before...

There is no fixity to the island's history, and the stability of its parliament, monarchy and Anglican traditions is a Victorian fantasy. There have been countless nations, languages, peoples and belief-systems on this distant isle, making it a home. Their motives differed, but success was founded on their ability to cooperate with each other. Even the simplest political demands have given coherence to much greater desires, like free university education, or regional autonomy. If independence means a rejection of greedy and dishonest Westminster politicians and their war against the poor, then it is hard to see which regions beyond southern England might vote to remain part of the UK.

But politics can make one a little too hopeful, and one can become addicted to the highs of hope, instead of appraising what surrounds. It can make one desire some figure or party to alleviate the responsibility to think and act for oneself and for others, with wisdom and compassion. The vote is too small a price to pay for societal change. Some will come to feel they've been sold a pup by the nationalist parties.

I may be guiltier instead of confusing Blighty with a place where *things happen*. Disappointment *is* the island, in its mercurial weather and in its irreverent humour, in its despair at underachievement in any international competition you care to mention, be it sports, politics, Eurovision or war, despite its geographical obscurity. It's the prevailing feeling I encountered in others, dismayed at the lack of movement around them, and in me, disappointed that in most places there was little unrest. Disappointment is the sadness that follows the failure of one's hopes to manifest. Hope is a form of fantasy. Disappointment is also the sadness that says *this is it, because we were wrong*. It's a mistaken judgement, but makes sense of the landscape, mentally and physically, of these retail parks and brutalist blocks, the corporate phalli and supermarkets, and the boring advertisements on every street and screen. No one wants this, but this is it.

Yet everywhere sparks, sparks of something. In the humour, and escapism, and creative obsessions, in the welcome of a stranger not yet a friend. I found generosity and courage everywhere. Our story is all of us, doing what we want done, thinking what we want thought, living and acting as a collective endeavour. It is we, the people of an island; we, the island.

References

Introduction

"*reasoning with some...*": Cobbett in the *Political Register*, 1822, quoted in
   Rural Rides, ed. Ian Dyck (London: Penguin, 2001), p. xxii.

"*Map of... Empire*": Jorge Luis Borges, 'On Exactitude in Science', *The
   Aleph and Other Stories*, trans. Andrew Hurley (New York: Penguin,
   2004), p. 181.

"*fell beside...*"; "*Laboriouse...*": In *Leland's Itinerary in England and Wales.
   Volume One*, ed. Lucy Toulmin Smith (London: Centaur, 1964), pp.
   xxxvii, xli.

Chapter 1. Prehistories

"*colonized... landscaping*": Laura Oldfield Ford, 'Olympic drift: making
   way for the games', *Granta: the magazine of new writing's blog*, 08
   August 2012. Cf. *Savage Messiah* (London; New York: Verso, 2011).

"*scam... scams*": Iain Sinclair, 'Fence wars', in *Ghost Milk: calling time on
   the grand project* (London: Hamish Hamilton, 2011), location 902
   (Kindle version).

"*Brixton in... Scourie*": Muir, *Scottish Journey*, quoted in Murray Watson,
   Being English in Scotland (Edinburgh: Edinburgh University Press,
   2003), p. 107.

"*landscape itself... possess*": W.G. Hoskins, *The Making of the English
   Landscape* (Toller Fratrum: Little Toller, 2013), p. 14.

"*Don't you find shopping...*": *Play for Today*, 'Abigail's Party', BBC, 1977.

"*I feel like my soul...*": *Peep Show*, 'Handy Man', Channel 4, 2007.

"*all men should be free...*": from the *Anonimalle Chronicle*, reproduced in
   R.B. Dobson, *The Peasants' Revolt of 1381* (London; Basingstoke:
   Macmillan, 1983). Summary drawn from parts 1-4 of Dobson's work.

"*supply a place...*": H. Rider Haggard, *Regeneration* (Rockville: Wildside, 2000), p. 196.

"*strange decay...*": Daniel Defoe, *A Tour through the Whole Island of Great Britain* (Harmondsworth: Penguin, 1979), p. 55.

"*vital... monstrous*": H.G. Wells, 'The War of the Worlds', in *The Time Machine and the War of the Worlds* (North Charleston: Createspace, 2013), p. 79.

"*Elemental change...*"; "*emblem of...*": Jonathan Meades, *The Joy of Essex* (BBC, 2013).

"*Courage shall... faileth*": *The Battle of Maldon*, in *The First Poems in English*, ed. trans. Michael Alexander (London: Penguin, 2008), p. 104.

Boudica and Anglesey: see Graham Webster, *Boudica: the British Revolt against Rome AD60* (Abingdon: Routledge, 1999), chs. 4-5.

"*[M]ost of England...*": Hoskins, *Making of the English Landscape*, p. 274.

"*Half a century ago...*": Arthur Young, quoted in Hoskins, *Making of*, p. 176.

"*hand-made world*": Eric Gill, quoted in Hoskins, *Making of*, p. 79.

Doggerland: the findings of the Ancient Human Occupation of Britain project are summarised in Rob Dinnis and Chris Stringer, *Britain: One Million Years of the Human Story* (London: National History Museum, 2013).

"*quietly proliferating... life*": Sebald, *The Rings of Saturn*, trans. Michael Hulse (London: Vintage, 2002), p. 255.

"*the disappearance...*"; "*erosion*": Fisher, *Ghosts of My Life: Writings on Depression, Hauntology and Lost Futures* (Alresford: Zero, 2014), p. 13.

"*There is no antidote...*": Browne, *Religio Medici and Urne-Buriall*, ed. Stephen Greenblatt and Ramie Targoff (New York: New York Review of Books, 2012), p. 134.

"*[N]o lord of no manor...*": 'Kett's demands being in rebellion (1549)', in *Tudor Rebellions*. Revised 5th Edition, ed. Anthony Fletcher and Diarmaid MacCulloch (Harlow: Pearson, 2008), p. 157; cf. Edward Vallance, *A Radical History of Britain*, (London: Little, Brown, 2009), ch. 4.

"They are really…": Nelson, *The Dispatches and Letters of Vice Admiral Lord Viscount Nelson: Volume I*, ed. Nicholas Harris Nicolas (New York: Cambridge University Press, 2011), pp. 295-97, 10 December 1792.

"wines, spices…": John Ball in the chronicles of Froissart, in Dobson, *The Peasants' Revolt of 1381*, p. 371 (translation updated).

Captain Swing: see E.J. Hobsbawm and George Rudé, *Captain Swing* (London: Lawrence & Wishart, 1970).

"family… dog": Orwell, 'The Lion and the Unicorn', in *Why I Write* (London: Penguin, 2004), pp. 30, 33.

Chapter 2. Made in England

"To neither condemn…": Spinoza, 'Political Treatise', in *Opera. Volume II*, ed. Carl Hermann Bruder (Leipzig: Tauchnitz, 1843), 1.4, p. 52 (my loose translation).

"And at… life": John Clare, 'The Cottager', in *The Poems of John Clare. Volume One*, ed. J.W. Tibble (London: J.M. Dent, 1935), p. 384.

Cognitive dissonance: see Leon Festinger and James M. Carlsmith, 'Cognitive consequences for forced compliance', *Journal of Abnormal and Social Psychology*, 58 (1959), pp. 203-10.

"You could… audience": Dammers, interviewed in Alexis Petrides, 'Ska for the madding crowd', *The Guardian*, 8 March 2002.

"It is more easy…": Burke, 'Thoughts on the cause of the present discontents', in *Select works of Edmund Burke: Volume 1* (Indianapolis: Liberty Fund, 1999), p. 75.

"the exercise of…": Lilburne et al., 'An agreement of the free people of England [1649]', in *The English Levellers*, ed. Andrew Sharp (Cambridge: Cambridge University Press, 2002), p. 169.

"Foolery, sir…": Shakespeare, 'Twelfth Night', in *The Complete Works* (Oxford: Oxford University Press, 1998), Act 3, Scene 1, p. 703.

"proletarian hell": Hanley, *Estates: An Intimate History* (London: Granta, 2007), p. 44.

"went from… hoped": Meek, *Private Island: Why Britain Now Belongs to Someone Else* (New York; London: Verso, 2014), Introduction, location 23 (Kindle version).

"*There… inn*": Johnson, in James Boswell, *Boswell's Life of Johnson* (London: Oxford University Press, 1965), p. 697.

"*We're all middle class*": there is no reliable original source for this. See 'Corrections and Clarifications', *The Guardian*, 05 August 2012.

Iberdrola…: see Meek, *Private Island*, chs. 3-4.

"*Two fucking…*": Combo, *This is England*, dir. Shane Meadows (2006).

"*like sheep… cars*": Sillitoe, *Saturday Night and Sunday Morning* (New York: Vintage, 2010), p. 221.

King Ludd: see Vallance, *A Radical History of Britain*, ch. 12.

"*savage… pilgrimage*": letter to John Middleton Murray, 2 February 1923, in *The Letters of D.H. Lawrence. Volume IV 1921-24*, ed. Warren Roberts, James T. Boulton and Elizabeth Mansfield (Cambridge: Cambridge University Press, 1987), p. 375.

"*[i]t's time… sake*": letter to Charles Wilson, 28 December 1928, in *The Letters of D.H. Lawrence. Volume VII November 1928 – February 1930*, ed. Keith Sagar and James T. Boulton (Cambridge: Cambridge University Press, 1993), p. 99.

Chapter 3. The People's Republic

"*waste and…*": Defoe, *A Tour through the Whole Island*, p. 476.

"*that tree of which…*": *The Poetic Edda*, trans. Carolyne Larrington (Oxford: Oxford University Press, 2014), p. 32.

Kinder Trespass: see Stephen G. Jones, *Sports, Politics and the Working Class: Organised Labour and Sports in Interwar Britain* (Manchester: University of Manchester Press, 1992), pp. 142-44.

"*Life is like…*": Einstein, writing to his depressed son, quoted in Walter Isaacson, *Einstein: His Life and Universe* (London: Simon & Schuster, 2008), p. 367.

"*more than half…*": Flann O'Brien, *The Third Policeman* (London: Picador, 1974), p. 75.

Hillsborough: special thanks to Matt Bolton for sharing his unpublished research on the events surrounding Hillsborough.

"*ideological belief in…*": Lawson quoted in Meek, *Private Island*, Introduction, loc. 15 (Kindle version).

"*the enemy within*": on the Miners' Strike, see Seumas Milne, *The Enemy Within: the Secret War Against the Miners* (London; New York: Verso, 2014).

"*They might find…*": Stan Barstow, *A Kind of Loving* (Cardigan: Parthian, 2010), p. 344.

"*This changing of focus…*": Nan Shepherd, *The Living Mountain* (Edinburgh: Canongate, 2011), p. 11.

"*six hundred trawlers*": on Grimsby's recent history, see James Meek, 'Why are you still here?', *London Review of Books*, vol. 37, no. 8, 23 April 2015.

"*Cheap suits…*": Philip Larkin, 'Here', in *The Whitsun Weddings* (London: Faber & Faber, 1977), p. 9.

Chapter 4. Seek Bewilderment

"There is always…": Anne Brontë, The Tenant of Wildfell Hall, ed. Herbert Rosengarten (Oxford: Clarendon Press, 1992), p. 202.

"How then… handspike": Herman Melville, Moby Dick (London: Penguin, 1994), p. 508.

"space age…": Owen Hatherley, A New Kind of Bleak: Journeys Through Urban Britain (London; New York: Verso, 2012), p. 49.

"air biscuit", etc.: see Viz, Profanisaurus: Hail Sweary (London: Dennis Publishing, 2013), and the regularly updated list at www.viz.co.uk.

"man hands…": Larkin, 'This be the verse', in High Windows (London: Faber and Faber, 1974), p. 30.

"man appears…": Bede, A History of the English Church and People, trans. Leo Sherley-Price, rev. R.E. Latham (Harmondsworth: Penguin, 1968), p. 127.

Columba and Aidan: see Bede, A History of the English Church, pp. 144-169.

"It is easier…"; "No hope…"; "Words!": Basil Bunting, Briggflatts (London: Fulcrum, 1967), pp. 14-16.

"*Sell your cleverness…*": Rumi, *Masnavi i Ma'navi*, trans. abridged. E.H. Whinfield (Ames: Omphaloskepsis, 2001), Book IV, p. 278.

"*we became sensible…*": Playfair, quoted in Michael Welland, *Sand:*

The Never-ending Story (Berkeley: University of California Press, 2009), p. 213.

"*new forms…*": Woolf, 'Hours in a Library', in *Collected Essays. Volume II*, ed. Leonard Woolf (London: Hogarth Press, 1967), p. 39.

Chapter 5. Freedom is Best

One-Nation island: for a useful corrective to the common English-centric understanding of British history, see Norman Davies, *The Isles: a History* (London: Papermac, 2000); and Chris Bambery, *A People's History of Scotland* (London; New York: Verso, 2014).

"*Freedom is best…*": Wallace. I can find no reliable original source for this statement. It is quoted in David R. Ross, *On the Trail of William Wallace* (Glasgow: Bell & Bain, 2001), p. 29.

"*[o]ne may see…*": reproduced in Nathaniel Wanley, *The Wonders of the Little World; Or, a General History of Man… Volume 2* (London: W.J. and J. Richardson, 1806), p. 456.

"*We, the most…*": Tacitus, in *The Agricola and the Germania*, trans. H. Mattingly, rev. S.A. Handford (London: Penguin, 1970), p. 80.

"*island of Britain…*": Gildas, *The Ruin of Britain and Other Works*, ed. trans. Michael Winterbottom (London: Phillimore, 1978), p. 16.

"*possess their women…*": Cassius Dio, *Roman History. Volume IX*, trans. Earnest Cary (Bury St Edmunds: Loeb, 2001), p. 263.

"*I dare do all…*": Shakespeare, *The Tragedy of Macbeth* (New York: Oxford University Press, 1998), Act 1, Scene 7, p. 78.

"*It's up to brave…*": Miguel Cervantes, *Don Quixote*, trans. John Rutherford (London: Penguin, 2003), p. 934.

Culloden: see Bambery, *People's History of Scotland*, ch. 4.

On the Clearances, I have drawn on David Craig, *On the Crofters' Trail: In Search of the Clearance Highlanders* (London: Jonathan Cape, 1993).

Chapter 6. Cruinneachadh

"*The sea is…*": John Kemp, *Observations on the islands of Shetland, and their inhabitants* (Edinburgh: Charles Stewart, 1801).

"*[s]uch a set…*": William Young, quoted in Eric Richards, *The Leviathan of*

Wealth: the Sutherland Fortune in the Industrial Revolution (Abingdon: Routledge, 2007), p. 180.

"haunted... wolves": William Camden, 'Strath-Navern', *Britannia*, trans. Philemon Holland (1610), digitised at www.philological.bham.ac.uk/cambrit/scoteng.html.

"More remote... God": Morton quoted in Nicholas Crane, *Great British Journeys* (London: Weidenfeld & Nicolson, 2007), p. 243.

"desolation itself"; *"[T]hey wandered..."*; etc.: Pennant, *A Tour in Scotland, and voyage to the Hebrides, 1772* (London: Benjamin White, 1776), pp. 329, 365-66, 424.

"Only two topics...": Yeats, quoted in Brian Arkins, *The Thought of W.B. Yeats* (Bern: Peter Lang, 2010), p. 49.

February 1883: on the Crofters Party and context, see H.J. Hanham, 'The Problem of Highland Discontent, 1880-1885', *Transactions of the Royal Historical Society*, 19 (Dec. 1969), pp. 21-69.

Goidelic... Brythonic: see James Fife's helpful 'Introduction', in *The Celtic Languages*, ed. Martin J. Ball (Abingdon; New York: Routledge, 2005), pp. 3-25.

Eigg: see Alastair McIntosh, *Soil and Soul: People versus Corporate Power* (London: Aurum, 2004), chs. 13-17.

Chapter 7. Stravaig

"There's man...": Samuel Beckett, *Waiting for Godot* (London: Faber and Faber, 1977), Act 1, p. 11.

"From his study...": exhibited at the lighthouse. Cf. Peter Hill, *Stargazing: Memoirs of a Young Lighthouse Keeper* (Edinburgh: Canongate, 2003).

Columba and...: on the history of Iona, see Rosemary Power, *The Story of Iona* (Norwich: Canterbury Press, 2013).

Statutes of Iona: see John L. Roberts, *Clan, King and Covenant: History of the Highland Clans from the Civil War to the Glencoe Massacre* (Edinburgh: University of Edinburgh Press, 2000), pp. 14-16.

John Maclean...: on Maclean and Scotland's modern radical history, see Bambery, *People's History of Scotland*, chs. 9-14.

"A city under siege...": in *London*, dir. Patrick Keiller (1994).

"*Down with class rule...*": Hardie and Henderson, quoted in Cyril Pearce, *Comrades in Conscience: The Story of an English Community's Opposition to the Great War* (London: Francis Boutle, 2001), p. 62.

"*Macdonagh and...*": Yeats, *Selected Poems*, ed. Timothy Webb (London: Penguin, 2000), p. 121.

Chapter 8. Among Ghosts

"*Whatever is...*"; "*A time for...*": Ecclesiastes 3: 15; 8; 1, *Holy Bible. New International Version*.

"*I wandered...*": William Wordsworth, 'I wandered lonely as a cloud', *The Major Works*, ed. Stephen Gill (New York: Oxford University Press, 2000), p. 303.

Magnus Mills: see *All Quiet on the Orient Express* (London: Flamingo, 1999).

"*The loveliest spot...*": Wordsworth, 'Farewell, thou little Nook of mountain ground', *The Major Works*, p. 278.

"*Electronical and mechanical...*": Kenneth Lindley, *Seaside Architecture* (London: Hugh Evelyn, 1973), p. 143.

"*White bread...*": Orwell, *The Road to Wigan Pier* (London: Penguin, 1989), p. 88.

"*England is...*": Orwell, 'England your England', *Inside the Whale and Other Essays* (Harmondsworth: Penguin, 1964), p. 77.

"*lost generation...*": Greenwood quoted in Pamela Fox, *Class Fictions: Shame and Resistance in the British Working-Class Novel, 1890-1945* (Durham: Duke University Press, 1994), p. 185.

"*slum*": on urbanisation, see Hoskins, *Making of the English Landscape*, pp. 205-08.

"*Heavy physical work...*": Orwell, *Nineteen Eighty-Four* (London: Heinemann, 1982), p. 55.

"*I was sorry...*": Lowry quoted in Shelley Rohde, *A Private View of F.S. Lowry* (London: Collins, 1979), p. 245.

Surveying... Albert Square: special thanks to John Fitzgerald for emailing a choice itinerary.

"What a fuck up…": Hook, *The Hacienda: How Not to Run a Club* (London: Simon & Schuster, 2009), p. xi.

"these dreadful feelings…": Greenwood, *Love on the Dole* (London: Vintage, 1993), p. 84.

"of His signs…": *The Qur'an*, Saheeh International Translation, ed. A.B. al-Mehri (Birmingham: Maktabah, 2011), Surah 30:21.

"Many thanks…": Pliny, *Natural History. Volume II*, trans. John Bostock and H.T. Riley (London: Henry G. Bohn, 1840), p. 331.

"The last and…": Friedrich Engels, *The Origin of the Family, Private Property and the State* (London: Penguin, 2010), p. 200.

"machines…"; *"silent vegetation"*: Engels, *The Condition of the Working Class in England*, ed. David McLellan (New York: Oxford University Press, 1999), p. 17.

"The working class…": Thompson, *The Making of the English Working Class* (New York: Vintage, 1966), p. 9.

"even among fierce flames…": the quote is actually from Wu Ch'eng-en, *Monkey*, trans. Arthur Waley (London: Penguin, 1961), ch. 2, p. 23.

Todmorden's Incredible Edible: for a critical perspective, see Steve Hanson, *Small Towns, Austere Times* (Alresford: Zero, 2014).

Blacklisting: readers are directed to Dave Smith and Phil Chamberlain, *Blacklisted: the Secret War between Big Business and Union Activists* (Oxford: New Internationalist, 2015).

"concentration of hopelessness": quoted in Alan Travis, 'Thatcher government toyed with evacuating Liverpool after 1981 riots', *The Guardian*, 30 December 2011.

"They say that memories…": *Boys from the Blackstuff*, 'George's Last Ride', BBC2, 1982.

"Realize that…": Thucydides, *The Peloponnesian War*, trans. Martin Hammond (New York: Oxford University Press, 2009), p. 95.

"Faced with…": Confucius, *The Analects*, trans. D.C. Lau (London: Penguin, 1979), Book II, 24, p. 66.

"The collapse…": Taaffe and Mulhearn, *Liverpool: a City that Dared to Fight* (London: Fortress, 1988), p. 11.

Chapter 9. Annwn

"Ready to be...": Browne, *Urne-Buriall*, p. 139.

Owain Glyndwr: see Elissa R. Henken, *Owain Glyndwr in Welsh Tradition* (Ithaca: Cornell University Press, 1996).

"vasty deep": Shakespeare, 'Henry the Fourth', *Complete Works*, Part 1, Act 3, Scene 1, p. 468.

See Simon's online encyclopaedia of languages, www.omniglot.com; also Janet Davies, *The Welsh Language: A History* (Cardiff: University of Wales Press, 2014), ch. 11.

"hands raised"; *"[A]mongst..."*: Tacitus, *The Annals*, trans. J.C. Yardley (New York: Oxford University Press, 2008), p. 318.

"All things Begin..."; *"You have..."*: William Blake, 'Jerusalem', *Poems and Prophecies* (London: Everyman's Library, 1991), p. 218.

"The moisture...": Cheyne, *The English Malady (1733)*, ed. Roy Porter (Hove; New York: Routledge, 1991), p. xxx.

"extreme moistness...": Tacitus, *Agricola*, p. 63.

"Amor fati": Nietzsche, 'Ecce Homo', in *The Anti-Christ, Ecce Homo, Twilight of the Idols and Other Writings*, ed. Aaron Ridley and Judith Norman, trans. Judith Norman (Cambridge: University Press, 2006), p. 99.

"sloeblack...": Thomas, *Under Milk Wood* (London: J.M. Dent, 1961), p. 1.

"Only mystery...": Lorca, quoted in *A Companion to Federico Garcia Lorca*, ed. Federico Bonaddio (Woodbridge: Tamesis, 2007), p. 19.

Annwn: features prominently in 'The Four Branches of the Mabinogi', *The Mabinogion,* trans. Gwyn Jones and Thomas Jones (London: J.M. Dent, 1975), chs. 1-4.

"a cliff-perched...": Thomas, 'Quite Early One Morning', in *On the Air with Dylan Thomas. The Broadcasts*, ed. Ralph Maud (New York: New Directions, 1991), p. 14.

"observing...": Thomas, 'Dear Tommy, please, from far, sciatic Kingsley', in *The Collected Poems. The New Centenary Edition*, ed. John Goodby (London: Weidenfeld & Nicolson, 2014), p. 163.

"Let thy seed...": Genesis 24:60, *Holy Bible. King James Version*.

Rioting Rebeccas: see David J.V. Jones, *Rebecca's Children: a Study of Rural*

Society, Crime, and Protest (Oxford: Oxford University Press, 1989).

Luckless Colonel Tate: see Hywel M. Davies, 'Terror, treason and tourism: the French in Pembrokeshire 1797', in *"Footsteps of Liberty and Revolt": Essays on Wales and the French Revolution*, ed. Mary-Ann Constantine and Dafydd Johnston (Cardiff: University of Wales Press, 2013), pp. 247-70.

"ugly lovely town": Thomas, 'Reminiscences of Childhood', *On the Air*, p. 3.

Dic Penderyn: on the radical history of the Valleys, see Hatherley, *A New Kind of Bleak*, pp. 236-39.

"Life lies...": Manic Street Preachers, 'Motorcycle Emptiness' (Columbia, 1992).

"We have been..."; Bevan, quoted in David Kynaston, *Austerity Britain 1945-51* (London: Bloomsbury, 2008), p. 64.

"This is...": Bevan, quoted in Nicklaus Thomas-Symonds, *Nye: The Political Life of Aneurin Bevan* (London: I.B. Tauris, 2015), p. 72.

"West Wales": see Bernard Deacon, *Cornwall: a Concise History* (Cardiff: University of Wales press, 2007), ch. 1.

"United Kingdom is...": Keiller, 'Port Statistics', *The View from the Train: Cities & Other Landscapes* (London; New York: Verso, 2013), p. 49.

"picturesque"; *"kept constantly..."*: Gilpin, *Observations on the River Wye* (London: R. Blamire, 1789), pp. 47, 1.

Chapter 10. Cunning Folk

"war of all..."; *"nasty..."*; *"The greatest..."*: Hobbes, *Leviathan*, ed. Edwin Curley (Indianapolis: Hackett, 1994), pp. 50, 76-77.

Avebury... Stonehenge: on their history, see Francis Pryor, *Britain BC: Life in Britain and Ireland before the Romans* (London: HarperCollins, 2004), particularly chapters 8-9; and Mike Parker Pearson and the Stonehenge Riverside Project, *Stonehenge: Exploring the Greatest Stone Age Mystery* (London: Simon & Schuster, 2012).

"playsome whimsies...": Hume, 'The Natural History of Religion', in *Essays and Treatises on Philosophical Subjects*, ed. Lorne Falkenstein and Neil McArthur (Ontario: Broadview, 2013), p. 504.

"legalised... murder": Richard van Emden with Harry Patch, *The Last*

Fighting Tommy (London: Bloomsbury, 2009), p. 189.

"*I have done…*": Constable, quoted in John E. Thornes, *John Constable's Skies: A Fusion of Art and Science* (Birmingham: University of Birmingham Press, 1999), pp. 56-7.

"*green and pleasant land*": Blake, Preface to 'Milton', in *Poems and Prophecies*, p. 120. *Joseph of Arimathea*: on Glastonbury's mythologised history, see William of Malmesbury, *The Early History of Glastonbury*, trans. John Scott (Woodbridge: Boydell, 1981), pp. 43-47.

Hinkley Point: see Meek, *Private Island*, ch. 4, loc. 131-2 (Kindle version); Alex Barker, 'Brussels backs Hinkley Point C as cost forecasts soar', *Financial Times*, 08 October 2014.

"*painted ocean*": Samuel Coleridge, 'The Rime of the Ancient Mariner', in *The Complete Poetical Works. Volume I*, ed. Ernest Hartley Coleridge (London: Oxford University Press, 1968), p. 191.

"*Window and wall…*": Hawker, 'Morwenna statio', *Cornish Ballads and Other Poems* (Oxford; London: James Parker, 1869), p. 67.

"*hillock hides…*"; "*tinned minds*": Betjeman, 'Sunday Afternoon Service in St Enodoc Church, Cornwall' and 'Slough', in *Collected Poems* (London: John Murray, 2006), pp. 20, 113.

"*Promised Land…*": letter to S.S. Koteliansky, 25 February 1916, in *The Letters of D.H. Lawrence: Volume II 1913-16*, ed. George J. Zytaruk and James T. Boulton (Cambridge: Cambridge University Press, 2002), p. 554.

"*Re dheffo…*": one of several translations of the Lord's Prayer in Cornish (see www.penzancecatholicchurch.org/prayers/cornish.htm).

Tin Islands: see William Page, *The Victoria History of the County of Cornwall. Part 5* (London: St Catherine Press, 1924), pp. 16-18.

William of Worcester: see William H.P. Greswell, *Dumnonia and the Valley of the Parret* (Taunton: Barnicott and Pearce, 1922), p. 35.

21-thousand pieces: 'Orbital Debris FAQs', NASA Orbital Debris Program Office (http://orbitaldebris.jsc.nasa.gov/faqs.html).

Prayer Book Rebellion: see 'The Demands of the Western Rebels (1549)', reproduced in *Tudor Rebellions*, ed. Fletcher and MacCulloch, pp. 151-53; Julian Cornwall, *Revolt of the Peasantry 1549* (London: Kegan & Paul, 1977), chs. 1-4.

"wilde morisch...": Leland, in *Leland's Itinerary. Vol. I*, p. 219.

"dreary...": Brown, *Domestic Architecture* (London: George Virtue, 1841), p. 118.

"[n]othing like...": Hoskins, *Making of the English Landscape*, p. 231.

Chapter 11. Kill All the Gentlemen

"white working class experience": a useful counterpoint to this debate is Michael Collins, *The Likes of Us: A Biography of the White Working Class* (London: Granta, 2005).

"monster whose body...": Hardy, quoted in Raymond Williams, *The Country and the City* (New York: Oxford University Press, 1975), p. 216.

"the Wen...": Cobbett, *Rural Rides*, p. 452.

"Kill all the gentlemen": quoted in Steven G. Ellis and Christopher Maginn, *The Making of the British Isles: The State of Britain and Ireland 1450-1660* (Abingdon: Routledge, 2013), p. 133.

"like the British...": Hardy, *The Hand of Ethelberta* (London: Macmillan, 1971), p. 77.

"vile antithesis...": Starkey, 'The Death of England', *The Times*, 20 April 1966; *'social dis-ease'*: Fox, *Watching the English: The Hidden Rules of English Behaviour* (London: Hodder & Stoughton, 2005), p. 401; *chocolate digestive*: Bryson, 'Notes from a Small Island', *The Complete Notes* (London: Black Swan, 2009), p. 71; *hot-water bottle*: Jeremy Paxman, *The English: A Portrait of a People* (London: Michael Joseph, 1998). p. 1.

"accumulation of time": Barnes, *England, England* (London: Vintage, 2008), p. 39.

"Edgelands": a poetic extrapolation of this phenomena can be found in Paul Farley and Michael Symmons Roberts, *Edgelands: Journeys into England's True Wildernesses* (London: Vintage, 2012); see also Richard Mabey, *The Unofficial Countryside* (Toller Fratrum: Little Toller, 2010).

Southampton: see also Owen Hatherley, *A Guide to the New Ruins of Great Britain* (London: New York: Verso, 2010), ch. 1.

King Alfred: I draw from the biased contemporary source by Asser, in *Alfred the Great: Asser's* Life of King Alfred *and Other Contemporary Sources*, trans. Simon Keynes and Michael Lapidge (London: Penguin, 2004), pp. 109-10.

"If it were not…": Blake, 'There is no natural religion', *Poems and Prophecies*, p. 5.

"Ye are many…"; *"bees of England"*: Percy Bysshe Shelley, 'The Mask of Anarchy'; 'Men of England: A Song', in *The Major Works*, ed. Zachary Leader and Michael O'Neill (New York: Oxford University Press, 2003), pp. 411, 422.

"What is that…": Paine, 'Rights of Man (1791)', *Rights of Man, Common Sense and Other Political Writings*, ed. Mark Philp (New York: Oxford University Press, 2008), p. 165.

"muda": e.g. Michael A. Lewis, 'Lean production and sustainable competitive advantage', *International Journal of Operations & Production Management*, Vol. 20.8 (2000), pp. 959-78.

"Great Money Trick": Tressell, *The Ragged Trousered Philanthropists* (London: Flamingo, 1993), pp. 210-14.

"Dirty, poor-looking": Cobbett, *Rural Rides*, p. 161.

"zuo by hit": familiar to readers of Joyce's *Ulysses*, quoted in Seth Lerer, *Inventing English: A Portable History of the Language* (New York: Columbia University Press, 2007), p. 97.

"the ends…": Pope Gregory's phrase, in *Morals on the Book of Job*, trans. anon. (London: J.G.F. and J. Rivington; Oxford: John Henry Parker, 1844), Vol. III, Bk. XXVII, 21.

U-475 Black Widow: see Bradley L. Garrett, *Explore Everything* (London; New York: Verso, 2014), pp. 38-40.

"When Adam delved…": John Ball, in the translated Walsingham Chronicle, quoted in Pamela M. King, *Medieval Literature, 1300-1500* (Edinburgh: University of Edinburgh Press, 2011), p. 74.

Acknowledgements

This journey would not have been possible without those people who shared it with me, and who feature in these pages. I warmly thank everyone who offered me a bed or bought me a pint of beer, who talked to me on a street corner or in a supermarket, guiding the way. Thanks also to those who helped me make connections across the island, and everyone who supported me online at www.searchingforalbion.com. Listing many hundreds of people would be both tiresome for the reader and impossible for the writer, who often forgot to ask names. I thank them all, and hope I have been honest and fair in my depiction of those inspiring conversations.

I also thank the University of Roehampton for providing the means that made the journey possible. Tariq Goddard and the team at Repeater, for their commitment to intellectually uncompromising and necessary writing. To my partner Sarah, for her love and trust. And to my Dad most of all, who taught me how to ride a bike and to love words, without which none of this would be possible.

Repeater Books

is dedicated to the creation of a new reality. The landscape of twenty-first-century arts and letters is faded and inert, riven by fashionable cynicism, egotistical self-reference and a nostalgia for the recent past. Repeater intends to add its voice to those movements that wish to enter history and assert control over its currents, gathering together scattered and isolated voices with those who have already called for an escape from Capitalist Realism. Our desire is to publish in every sphere and genre, combining vigorous dissent and a pragmatic willingness to succeed where messianic abstraction and quiescent co-option have stalled: abstention is not an option: we are alive and we don't agree.